THE NEW AVENGERS

BREAKOUT

KT-451-116

THE NEW AVENGERS

BREAKOUT

WRITER: **BRIAN MICHAEL BENDIS**

PENCILER: **DAVID FINCH**

INKER: **DANNY MIKI**

WITH **MARK MORALES, ALLEN MARTINEZ & VICTOR OLAZABA**

COLORIST: **FRANK D'ARMATA**

LETTERERS: **RICHARD STARKINGS &**

COMICRAFT'S ALBERT DESCHESNE

ASSISTANT EDITORS: **NICOLE WILEY,**
MOLLY LAZER & STEPHANIE MOORE
ASSOCIATE EDITOR: **ANDY SCHMIDT**
EDITOR: **TOM BREVOORT**

COLLECTION EDITOR: **JENNIFER GRÜNWALD**
SENIOR EDITOR, SPECIAL PROJECTS: **JEFF YOUNGQUIST**
DIRECTOR OF SALES: **DAVID GABRIEL**
BOOK DESIGNER: **JEOF VITA**
CREATIVE DIRECTOR: **TOM MARVELLI**

EDITOR IN CHIEF: **JOE QUESADA**
PUBLISHER: **DAN BUCKLEY**

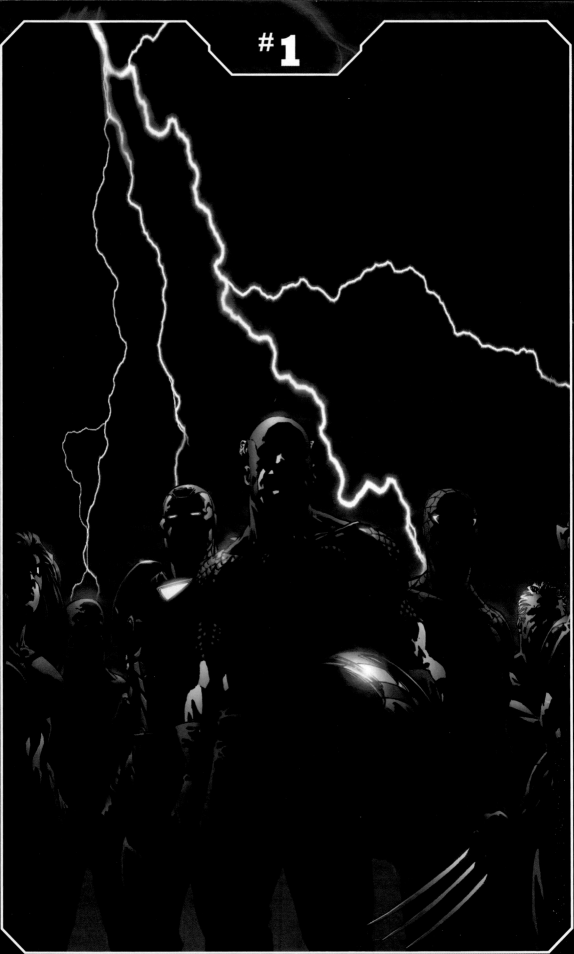

It was the worst day in Avengers history.

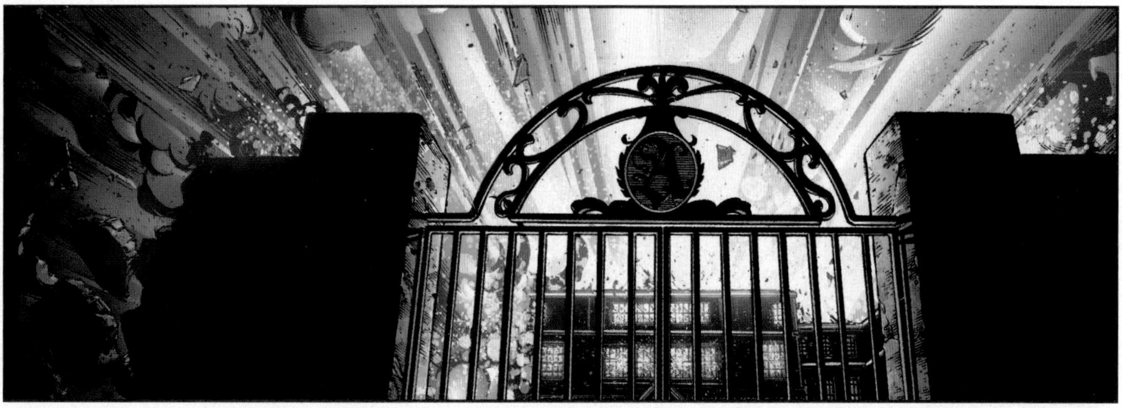

The Scarlet Witch suffered a total nervous breakdown after losing control of her reality-altering powers.

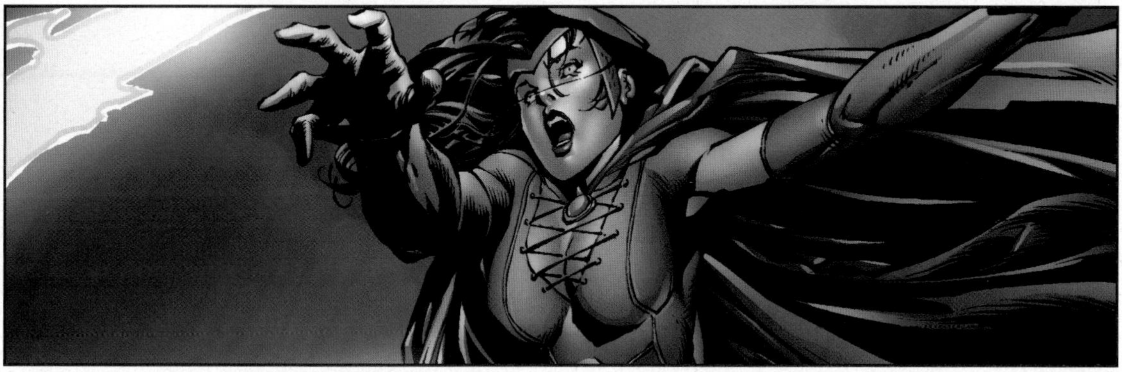

In the chaos created around the breakdown,
beloved Avengers Hawkeye, Ant-Man and the Vision lost their lives.

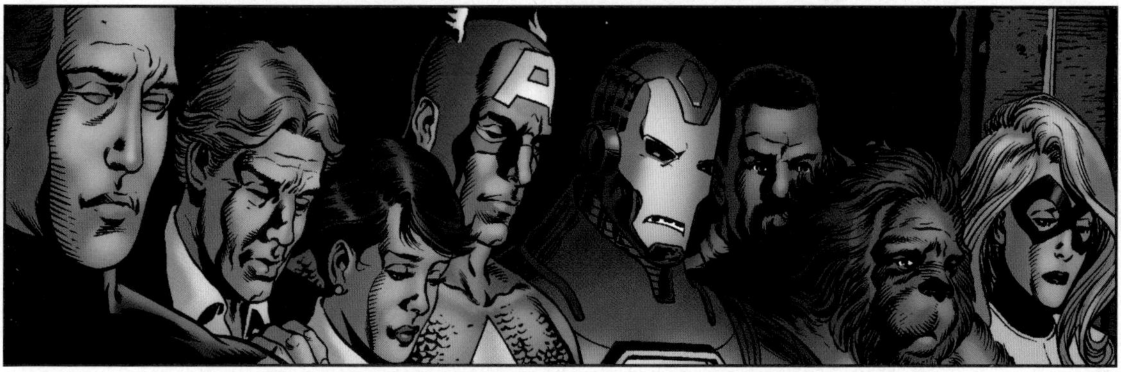

Many of the other Avengers were hurt, both emotionally and physically.
Without funding to keep going, the rest of the team quietly disbanded.

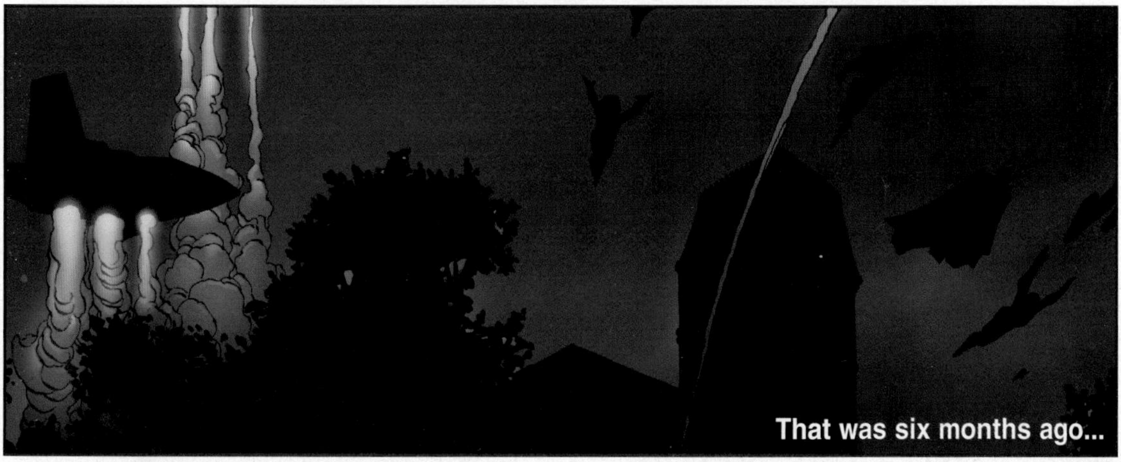
That was six months ago...

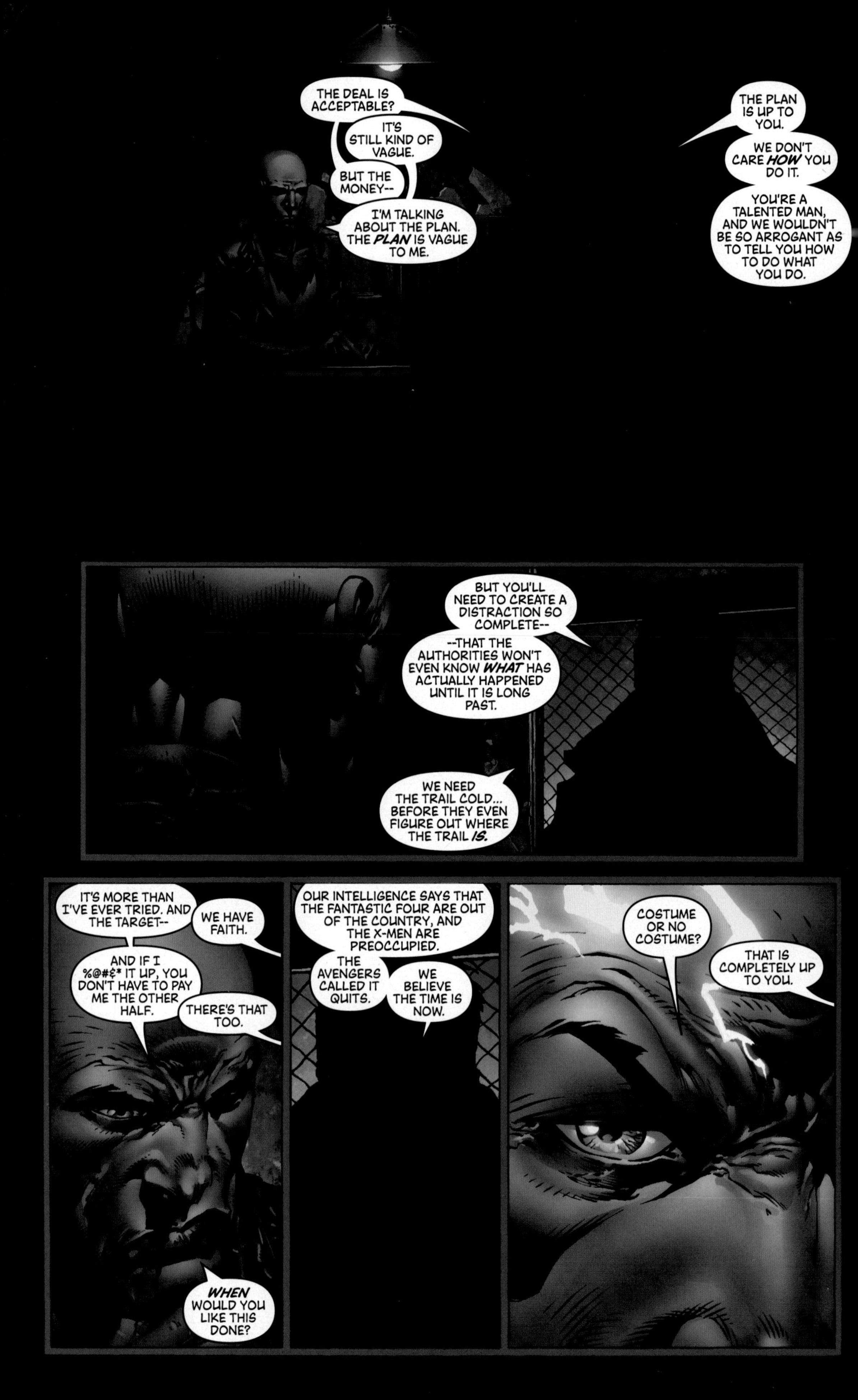
THE DEAL IS ACCEPTABLE?
IT'S STILL KIND OF VAGUE.
BUT THE MONEY--
I'M TALKING ABOUT THE PLAN. THE PLAN IS VAGUE TO ME.
THE PLAN IS UP TO YOU.
WE DON'T CARE HOW YOU DO IT.
YOU'RE A TALENTED MAN, AND WE WOULDN'T BE SO ARROGANT AS TO TELL YOU HOW TO DO WHAT YOU DO.
BUT YOU'LL NEED TO CREATE A DISTRACTION SO COMPLETE--
--THAT THE AUTHORITIES WON'T EVEN KNOW WHAT HAS ACTUALLY HAPPENED UNTIL IT IS LONG PAST.
WE NEED THE TRAIL COLD... BEFORE THEY EVEN FIGURE OUT WHERE THE TRAIL IS.
IT'S MORE THAN I'VE EVER TRIED. AND THE TARGET--
WE HAVE FAITH.
AND IF I %@#&* IT UP, YOU DON'T HAVE TO PAY ME THE OTHER HALF.
THERE'S THAT TOO.
WHEN WOULD YOU LIKE THIS DONE?
OUR INTELLIGENCE SAYS THAT THE FANTASTIC FOUR ARE OUT OF THE COUNTRY, AND THE X-MEN ARE PREOCCUPIED.
THE AVENGERS CALLED IT QUITS.
WE BELIEVE THE TIME IS NOW.
COSTUME OR NO COSTUME?
THAT IS COMPLETELY UP TO YOU.

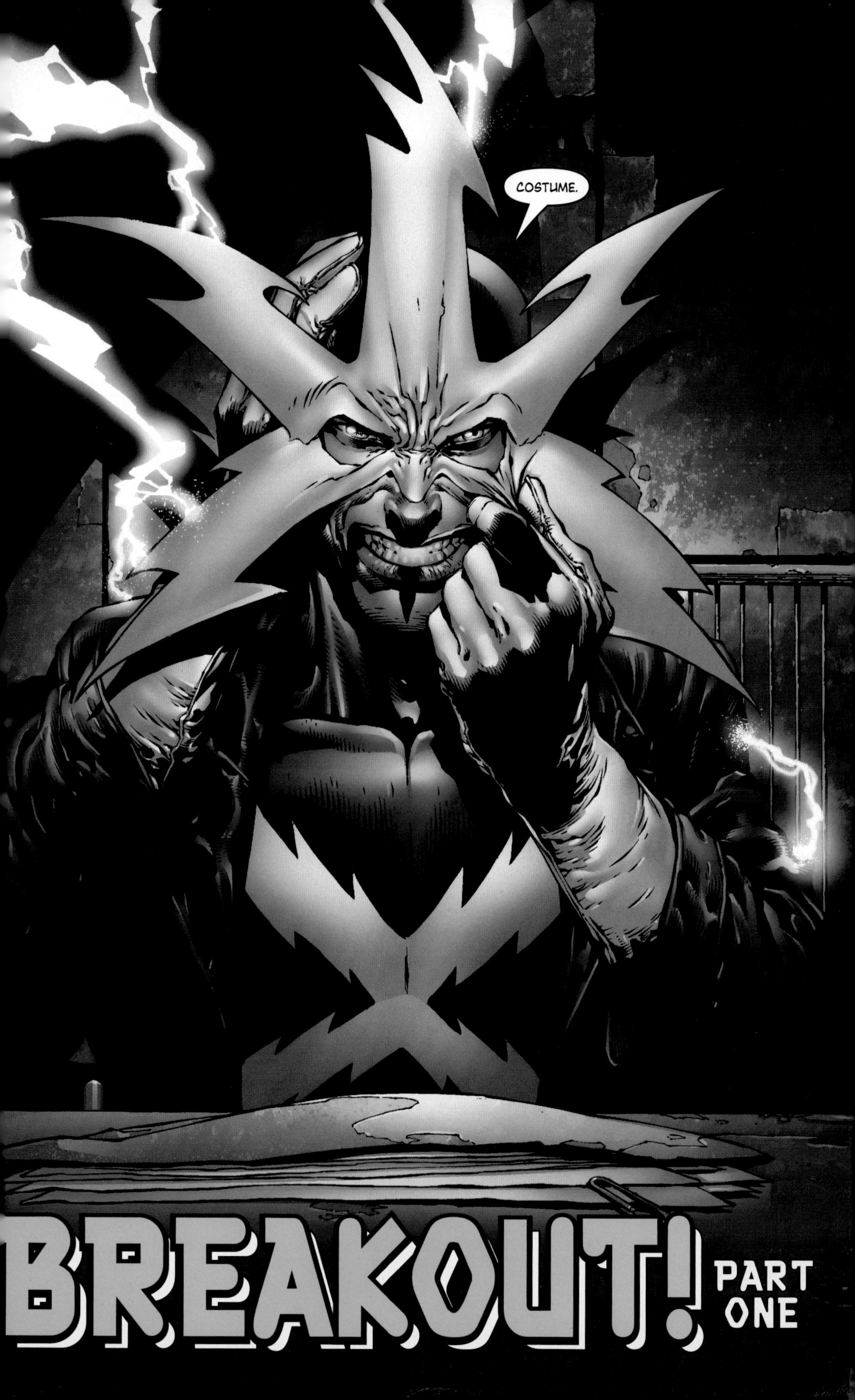
COSTUME.
BREAKOUT! PART ONE

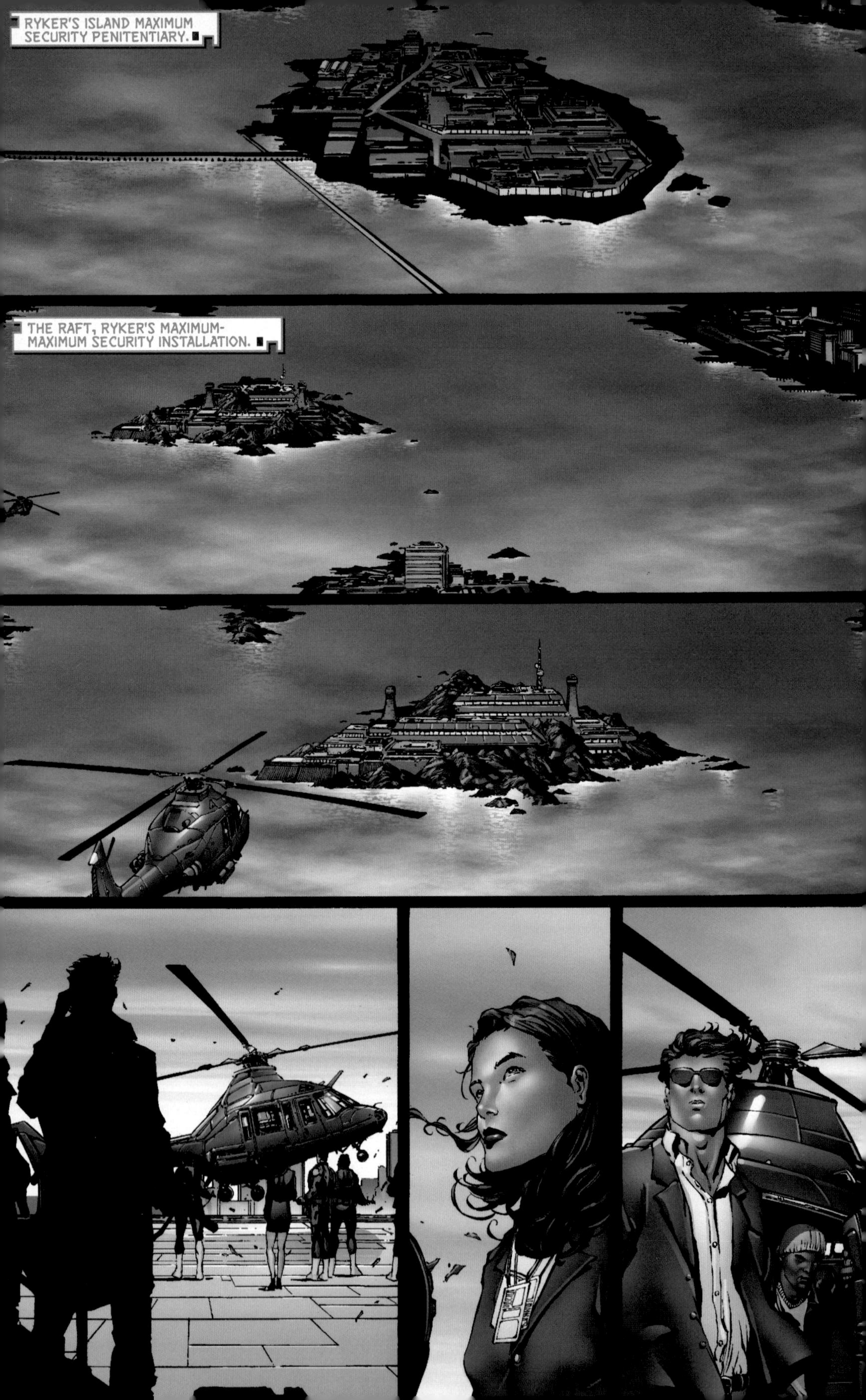
RYKER'S ISLAND MAXIMUM SECURITY PENITENTIARY.
THE RAFT, RYKER'S MAXIMUM-MAXIMUM SECURITY INSTALLATION.

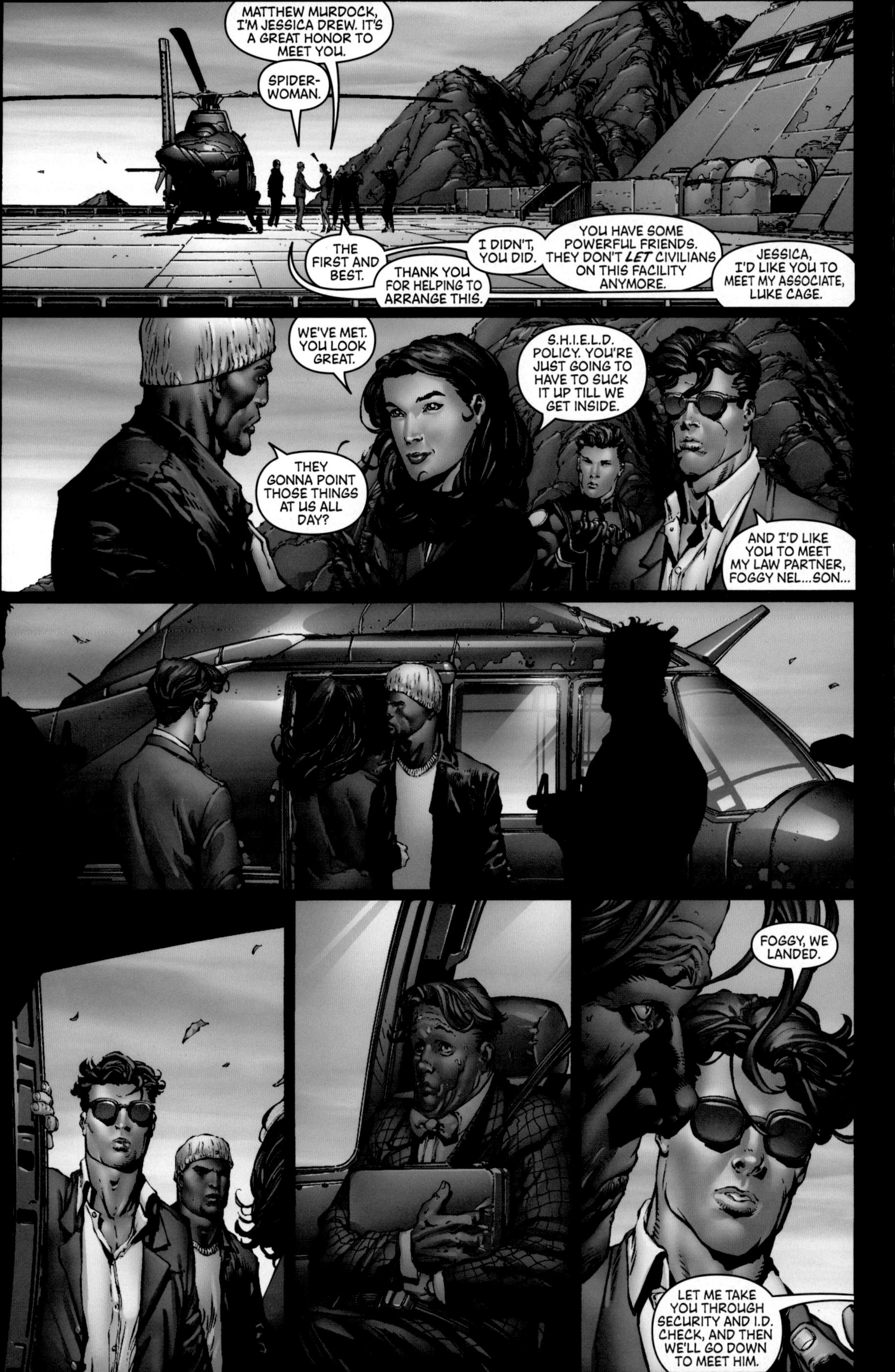
MATTHEW MURDOCK, I'M JESSICA DREW. IT'S A GREAT HONOR TO MEET YOU.
SPIDER-WOMAN.
THE FIRST AND BEST.
THANK YOU FOR HELPING TO ARRANGE THIS.
I DIDN'T, YOU DID.
YOU HAVE SOME POWERFUL FRIENDS. THEY DON'T LET CIVILIANS ON THIS FACILITY ANYMORE.
JESSICA, I'D LIKE YOU TO MEET MY ASSOCIATE, LUKE CAGE.
WE'VE MET. YOU LOOK GREAT.
THEY GONNA POINT THOSE THINGS AT US ALL DAY?
S.H.I.E.L.D. POLICY. YOU'RE JUST GOING TO HAVE TO SUCK IT UP TILL WE GET INSIDE.
AND I'D LIKE YOU TO MEET MY LAW PARTNER, FOGGY NEL...SON...
FOGGY, WE LANDED.
LET ME TAKE YOU THROUGH SECURITY AND I.D. CHECK, AND THEN WE'LL GO DOWN TO MEET HIM.

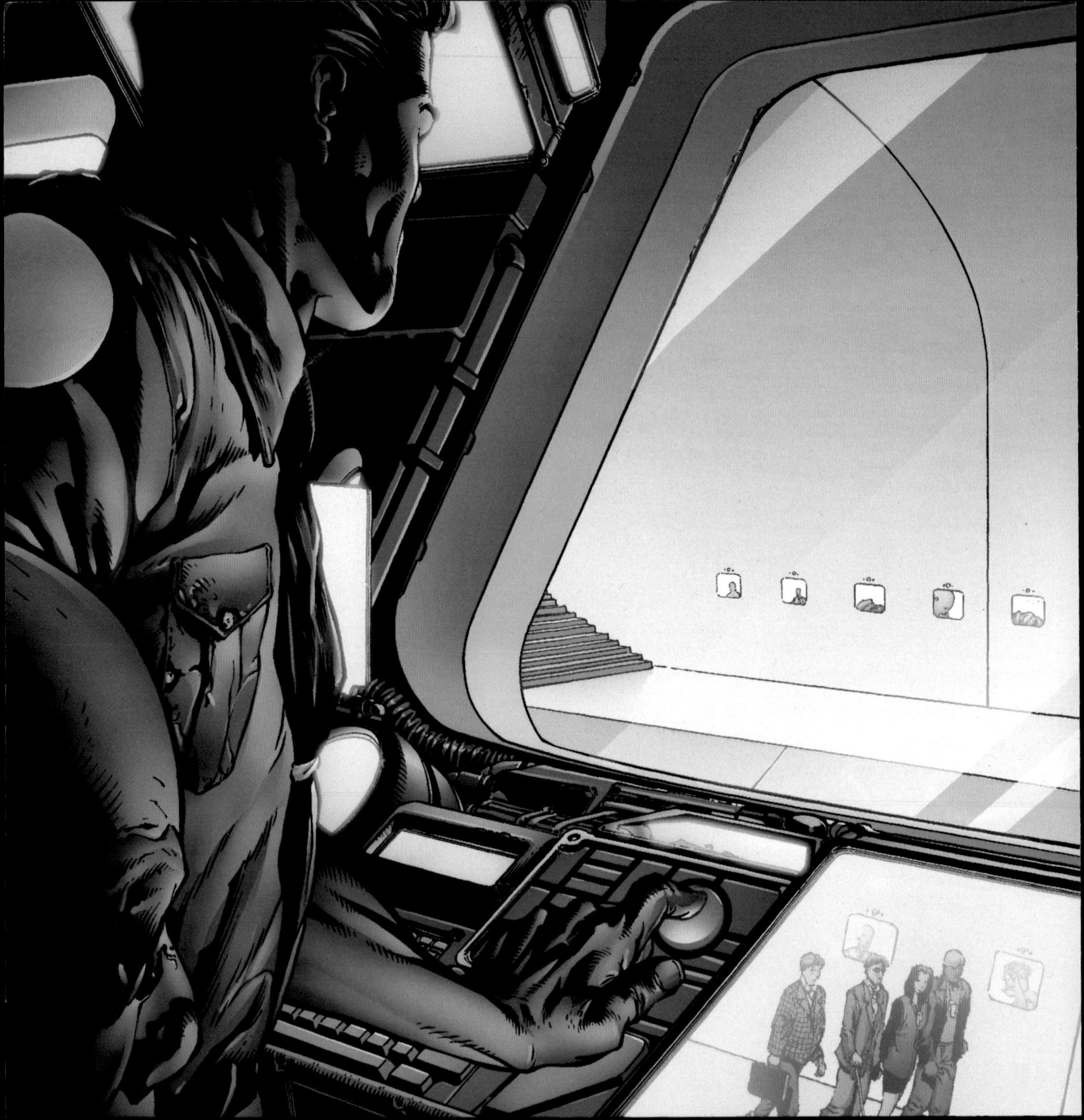

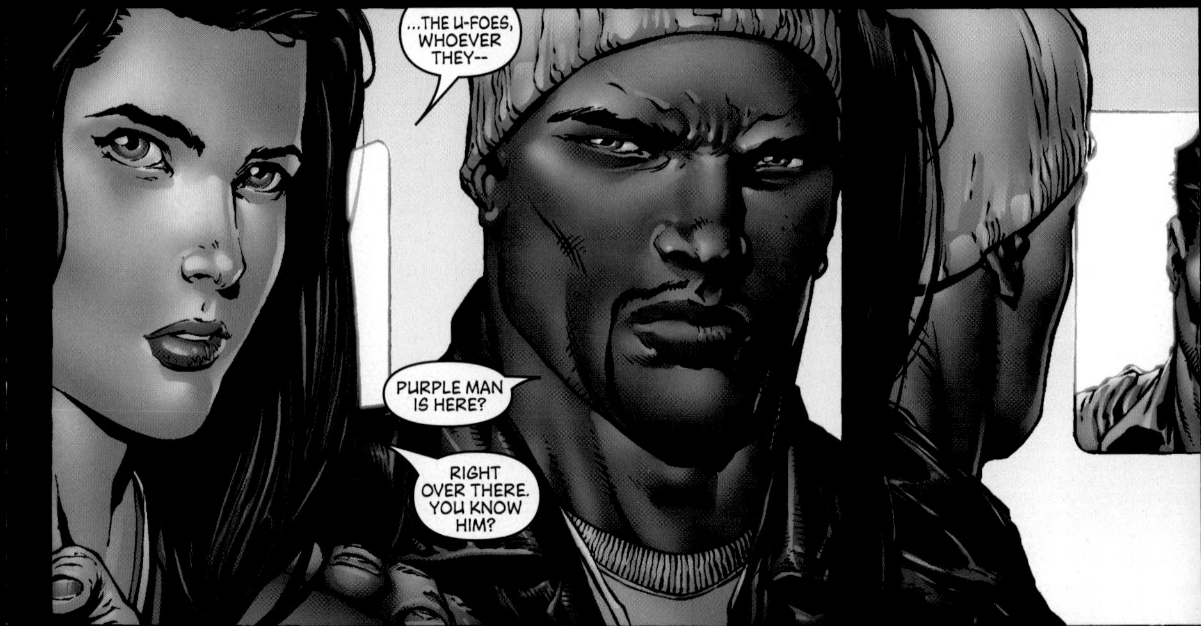
...THE U-FOES, WHOEVER THEY--
PURPLE MAN IS HERE?
RIGHT OVER THERE. YOU KNOW HIM?

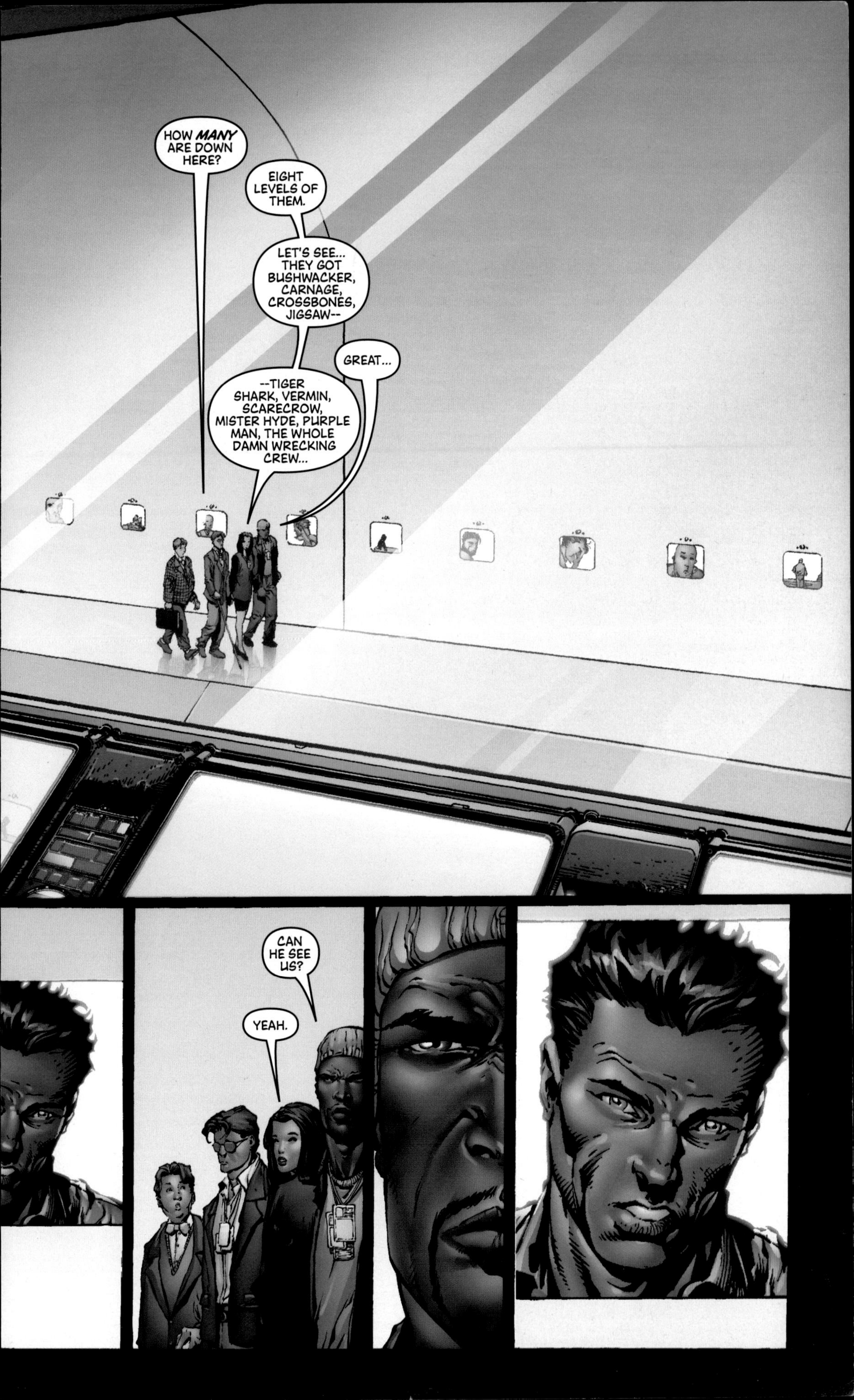
HOW MANY ARE DOWN HERE?
EIGHT LEVELS OF THEM.
LET'S SEE... THEY GOT BUSHWACKER, CARNAGE, CROSSBONES, JIGSAW--
--TIGER SHARK, VERMIN, SCARECROW, MISTER HYDE, PURPLE MAN, THE WHOLE DAMN WRECKING CREW...
GREAT...
CAN HE SEE US?
YEAH.

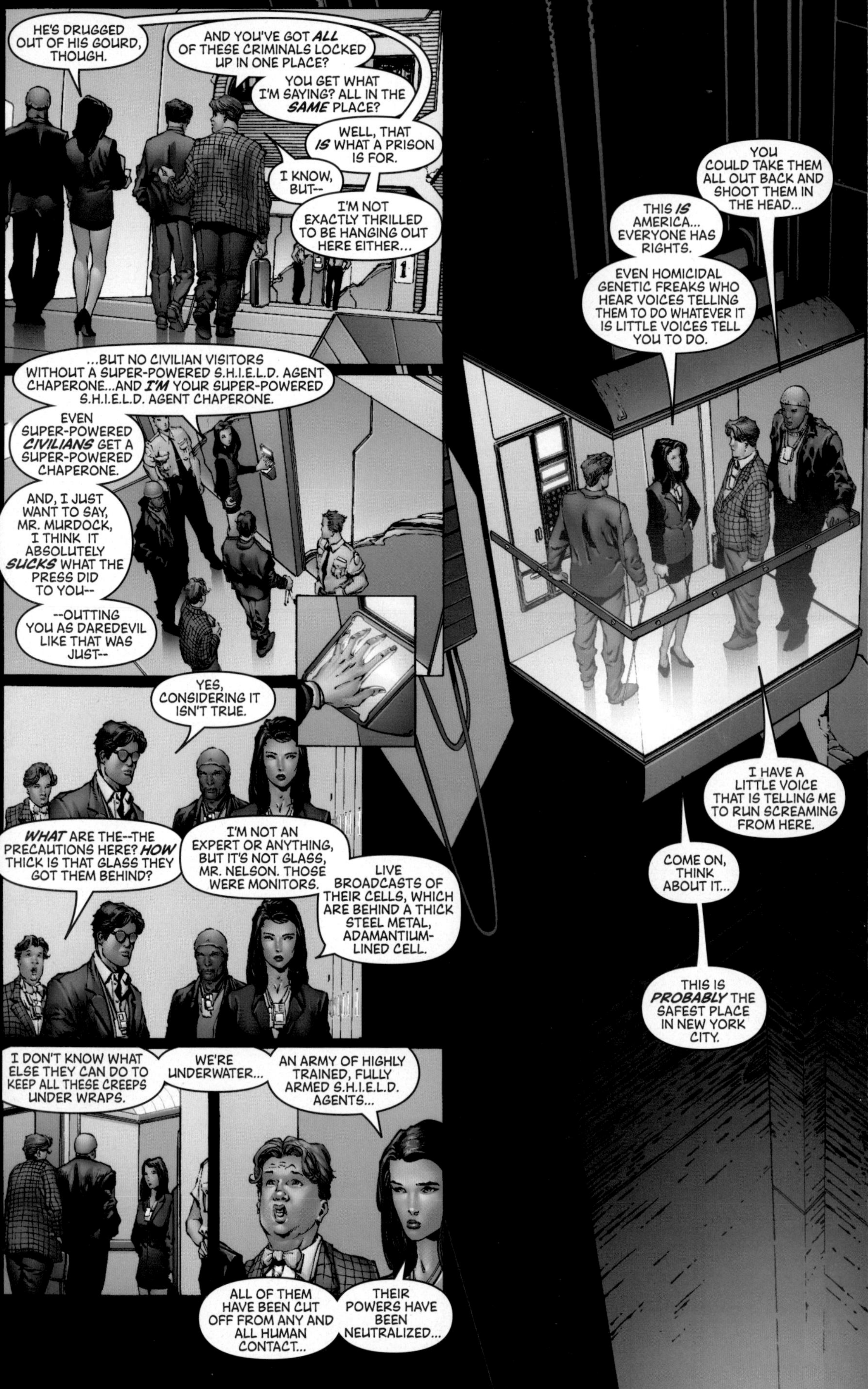

HE'S DRUGGED OUT OF HIS GOURD, THOUGH.
AND YOU'VE GOT *ALL* OF THESE CRIMINALS LOCKED UP IN ONE PLACE?
YOU GET WHAT I'M SAYING? ALL IN THE *SAME* PLACE?
WELL, THAT *IS* WHAT A PRISON IS FOR.
I KNOW, BUT--
I'M NOT EXACTLY THRILLED TO BE HANGING OUT HERE EITHER...
1
...BUT NO CIVILIAN VISITORS WITHOUT A SUPER-POWERED S.H.I.E.L.D. AGENT CHAPERONE...AND *I'M* YOUR SUPER-POWERED S.H.I.E.L.D. AGENT CHAPERONE.
EVEN SUPER-POWERED *CIVILIANS* GET A SUPER-POWERED CHAPERONE.
AND, I JUST WANT TO SAY, MR. MURDOCK, I THINK IT ABSOLUTELY *SUCKS* WHAT THE PRESS DID TO YOU--
--OUTTING YOU AS DAREDEVIL LIKE THAT WAS JUST--
YES, CONSIDERING IT ISN'T TRUE.
WHAT ARE THE--THE PRECAUTIONS HERE? *HOW* THICK IS THAT GLASS THEY GOT THEM BEHIND?
I'M NOT AN EXPERT OR ANYTHING, BUT IT'S NOT GLASS, MR. NELSON. THOSE WERE MONITORS.
LIVE BROADCASTS OF THEIR CELLS, WHICH ARE BEHIND A THICK STEEL METAL, ADAMANTIUM-LINED CELL.
I DON'T KNOW WHAT ELSE THEY CAN DO TO KEEP ALL THESE CREEPS UNDER WRAPS.
WE'RE UNDERWATER...
AN ARMY OF HIGHLY TRAINED, FULLY ARMED S.H.I.E.L.D. AGENTS...
ALL OF THEM HAVE BEEN CUT OFF FROM ANY AND ALL HUMAN CONTACT...
THEIR POWERS HAVE BEEN NEUTRALIZED...
YOU COULD TAKE THEM ALL OUT BACK AND SHOOT THEM IN THE HEAD...
THIS *IS* AMERICA... EVERYONE HAS RIGHTS.
EVEN HOMICIDAL GENETIC FREAKS WHO HEAR VOICES TELLING THEM TO DO WHATEVER IT IS LITTLE VOICES TELL YOU TO DO.
I HAVE A LITTLE VOICE THAT IS TELLING ME TO RUN SCREAMING FROM HERE.
COME ON, THINK ABOUT IT...
THIS IS *PROBABLY* THE SAFEST PLACE IN NEW YORK CITY.

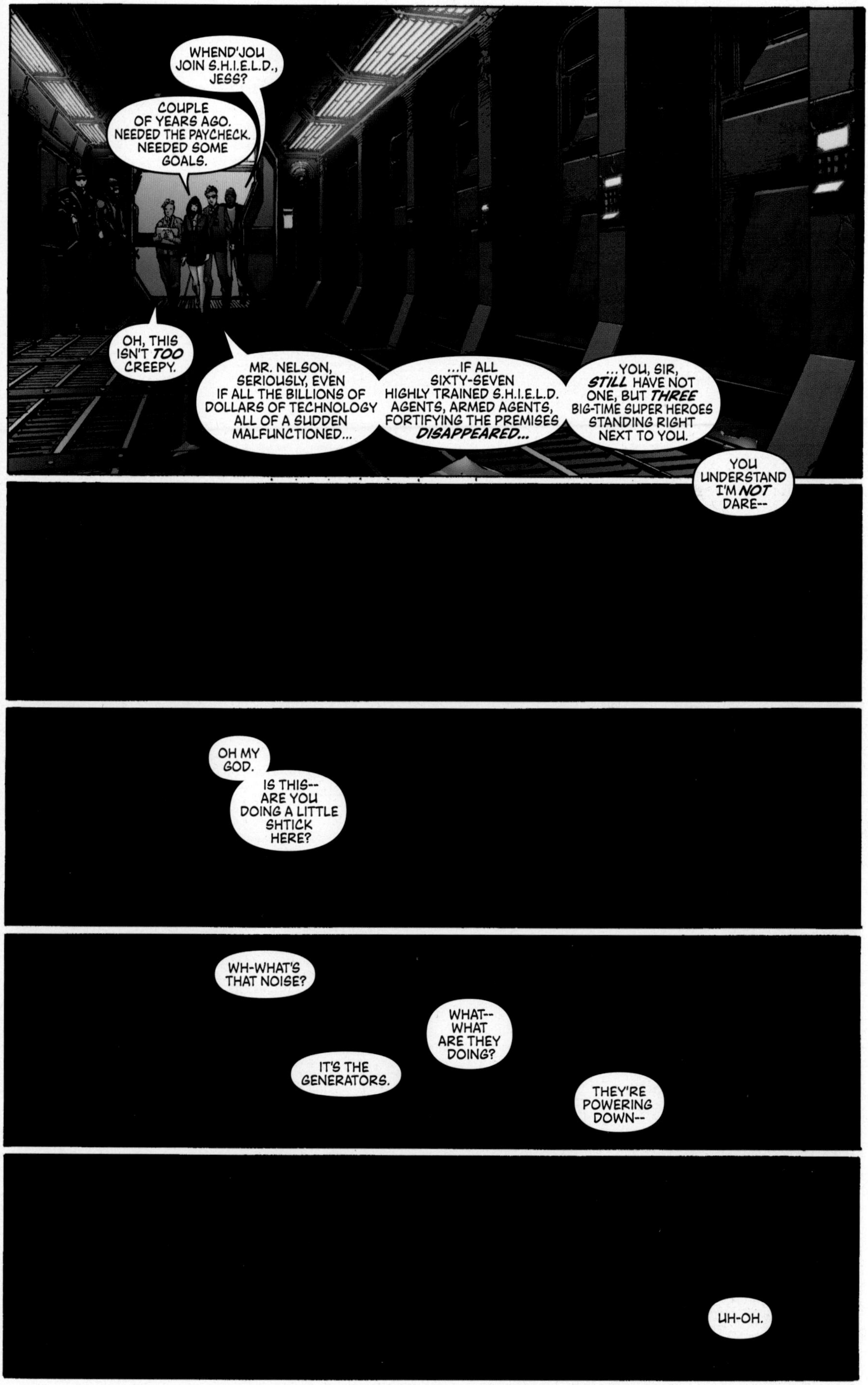
WHEND'JOU JOIN S.H.I.E.L.D., JESS?
COUPLE OF YEARS AGO. NEEDED THE PAYCHECK. NEEDED SOME GOALS.
OH, THIS ISN'T *TOO* CREEPY.
MR. NELSON, SERIOUSLY, EVEN IF ALL THE BILLIONS OF DOLLARS OF TECHNOLOGY ALL OF A SUDDEN MALFUNCTIONED...
...IF ALL SIXTY-SEVEN HIGHLY TRAINED S.H.I.E.L.D. AGENTS, ARMED AGENTS, FORTIFYING THE PREMISES *DISAPPEARED...*
...YOU, SIR, *STILL* HAVE NOT ONE, BUT *THREE* BIG-TIME SUPER HEROES STANDING RIGHT NEXT TO YOU.
YOU UNDERSTAND I'M *NOT* DARE--
OH MY GOD.
IS THIS-- ARE YOU DOING A LITTLE SHTICK HERE?
WH-WHAT'S THAT NOISE?
WHAT-- WHAT ARE THEY DOING?
IT'S THE GENERATORS.
THEY'RE POWERING DOWN--
UH-OH.

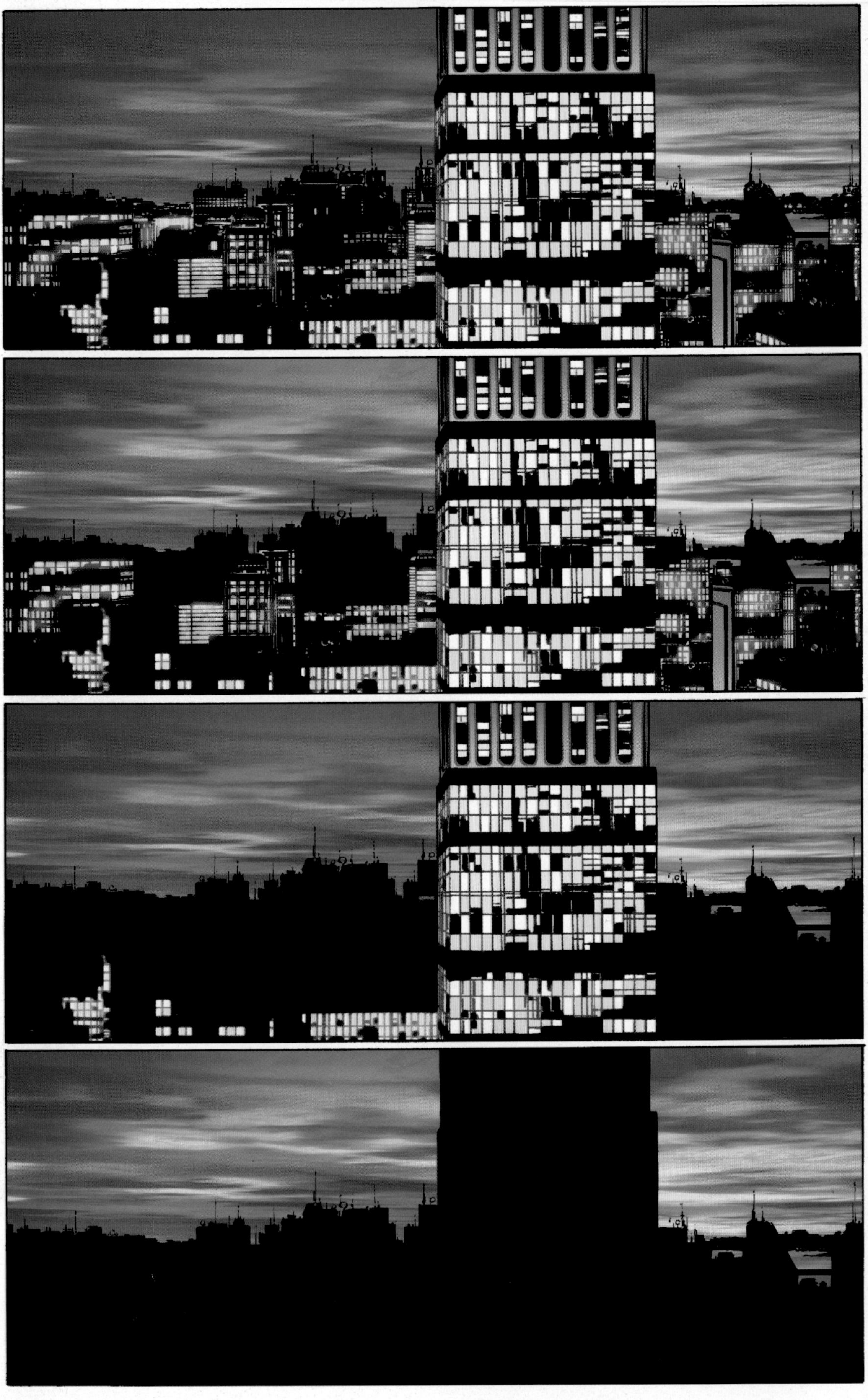

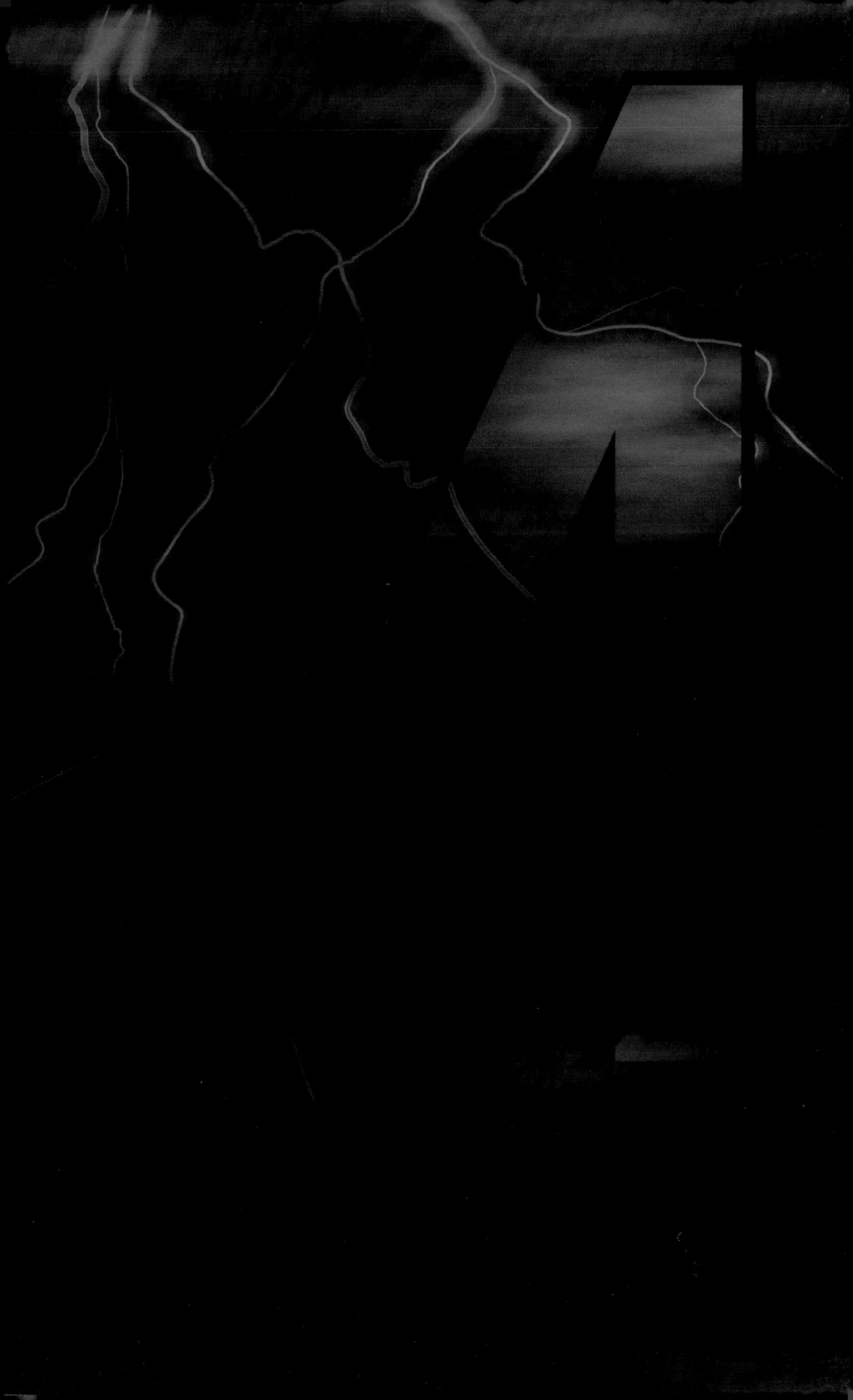

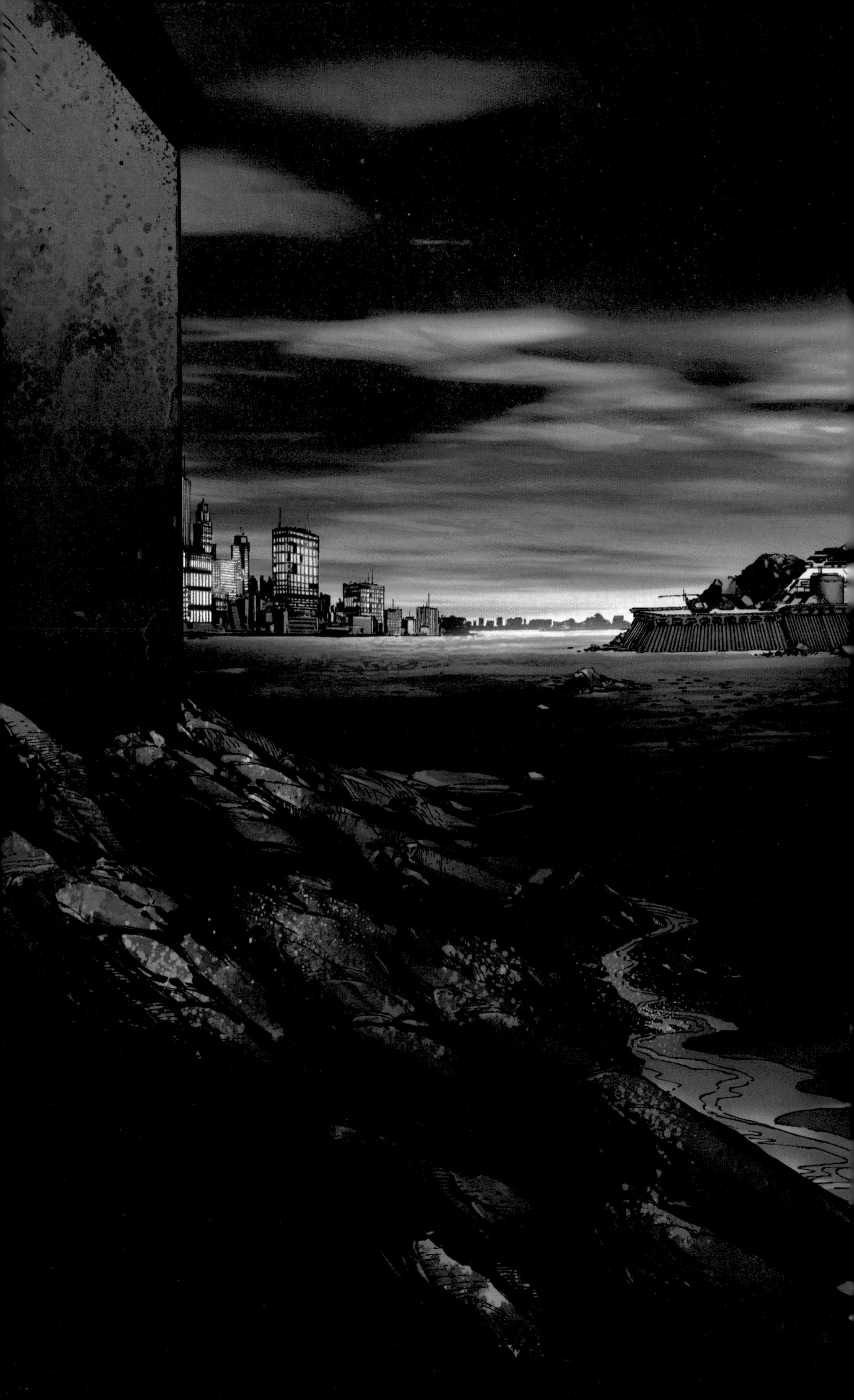

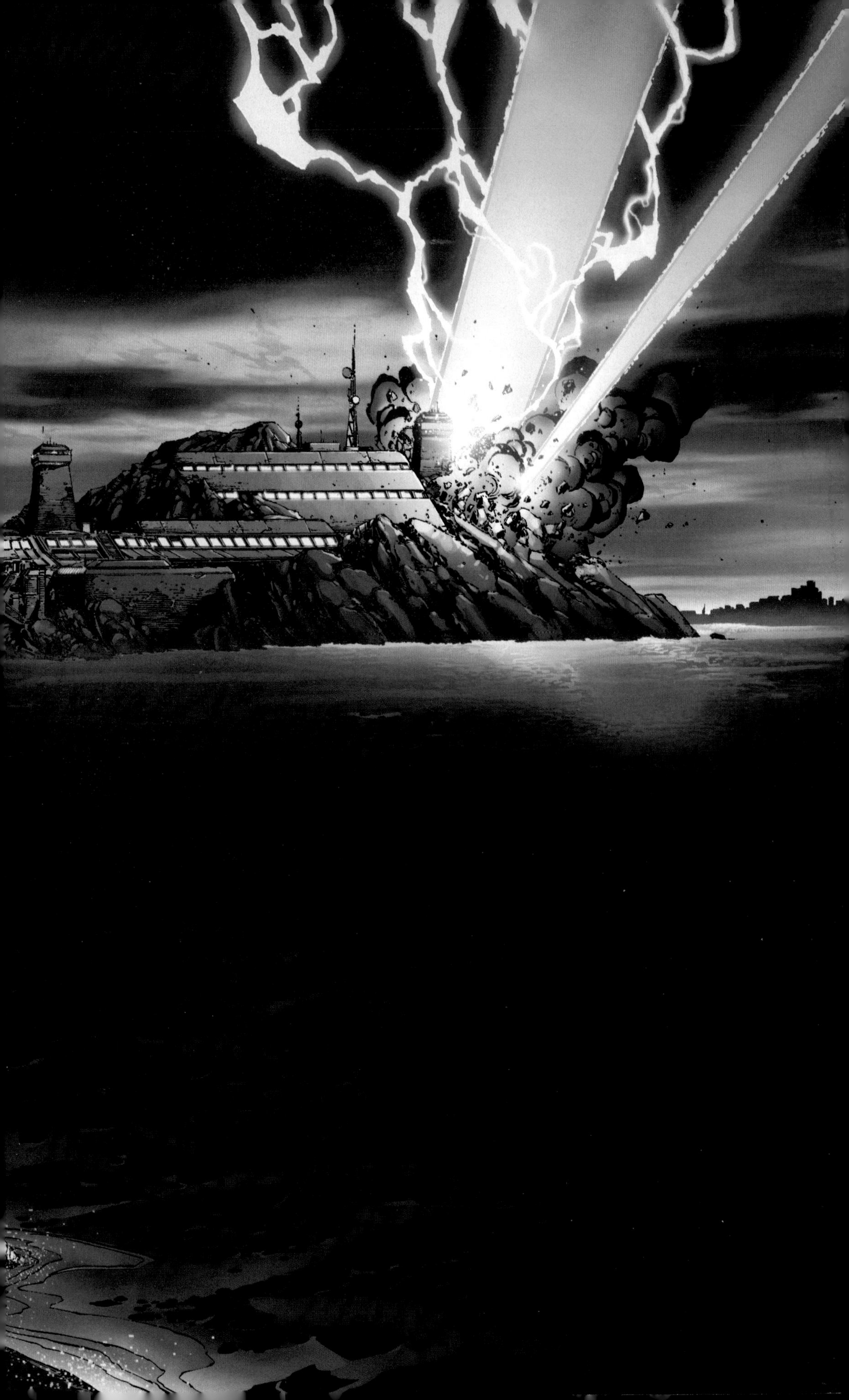

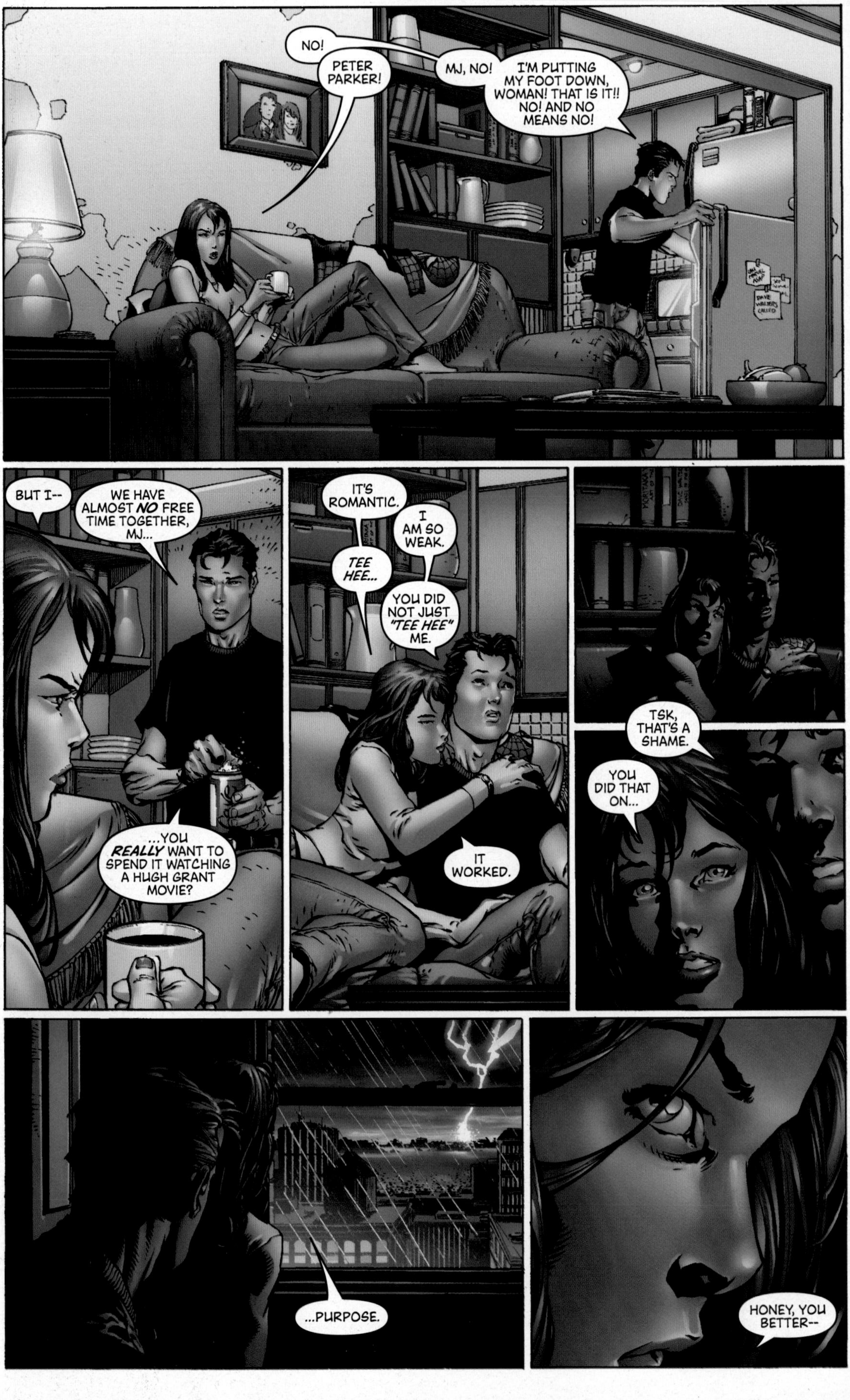
NO!
PETER PARKER!
MJ, NO!
I'M PUTTING MY FOOT DOWN, WOMAN! THAT IS IT!! NO! AND NO MEANS NO!
BUT I--
WE HAVE ALMOST NO FREE TIME TOGETHER, MJ...
...YOU REALLY WANT TO SPEND IT WATCHING A HUGH GRANT MOVIE?
IT'S ROMANTIC.
I AM SO WEAK.
TEE HEE...
YOU DID NOT JUST "TEE HEE" ME.
IT WORKED.
TSK, THAT'S A SHAME.
YOU DID THAT ON...
...PURPOSE.
HONEY, YOU BETTER--

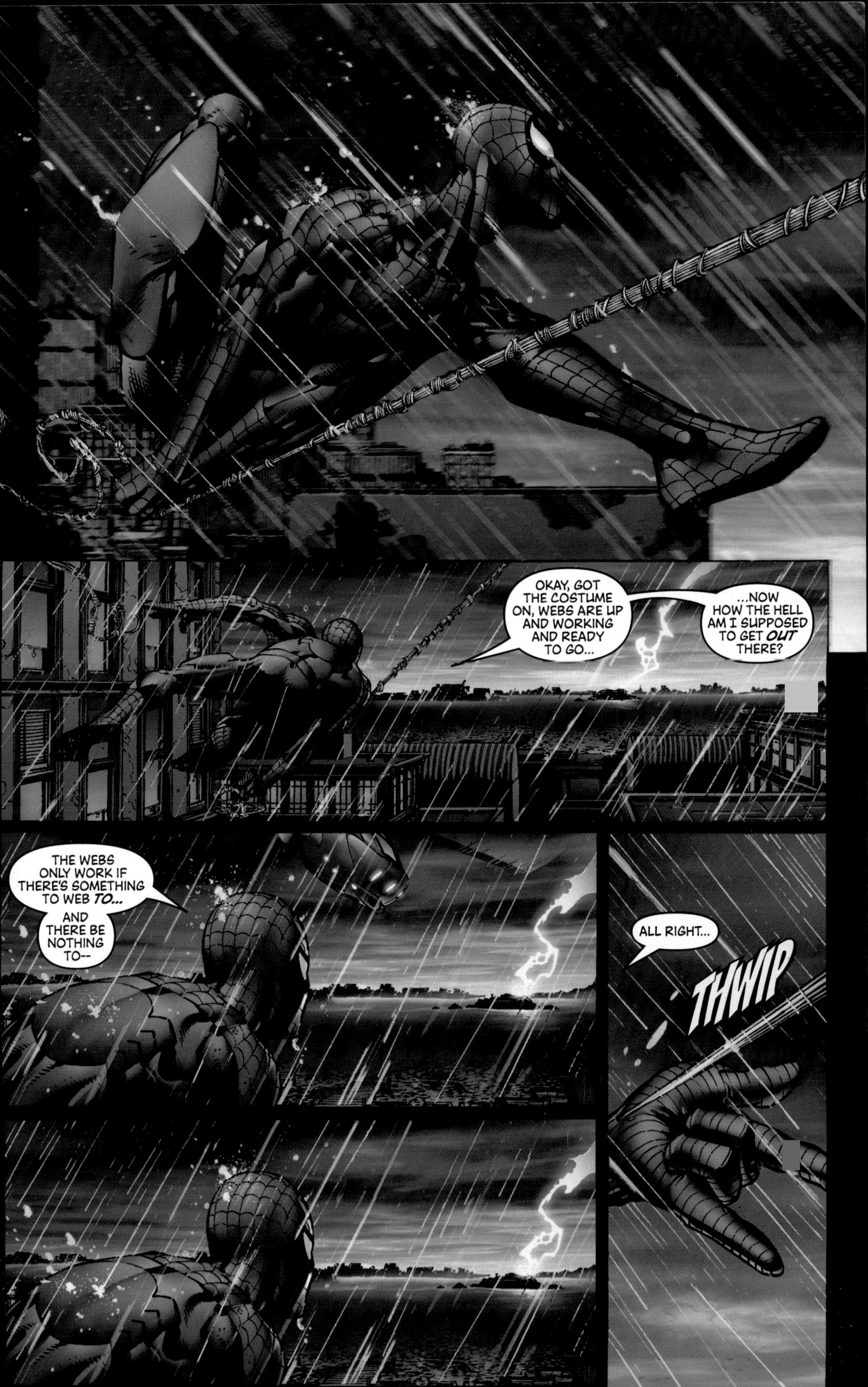
OKAY, GOT THE COSTUME ON, WEBS ARE UP AND WORKING AND READY TO GO...
...NOW HOW THE HELL AM I SUPPOSED TO GET OUT THERE?
THE WEBS ONLY WORK IF THERE'S SOMETHING TO WEB TO...
AND THERE BE NOTHING TO--
ALL RIGHT...
THWIP

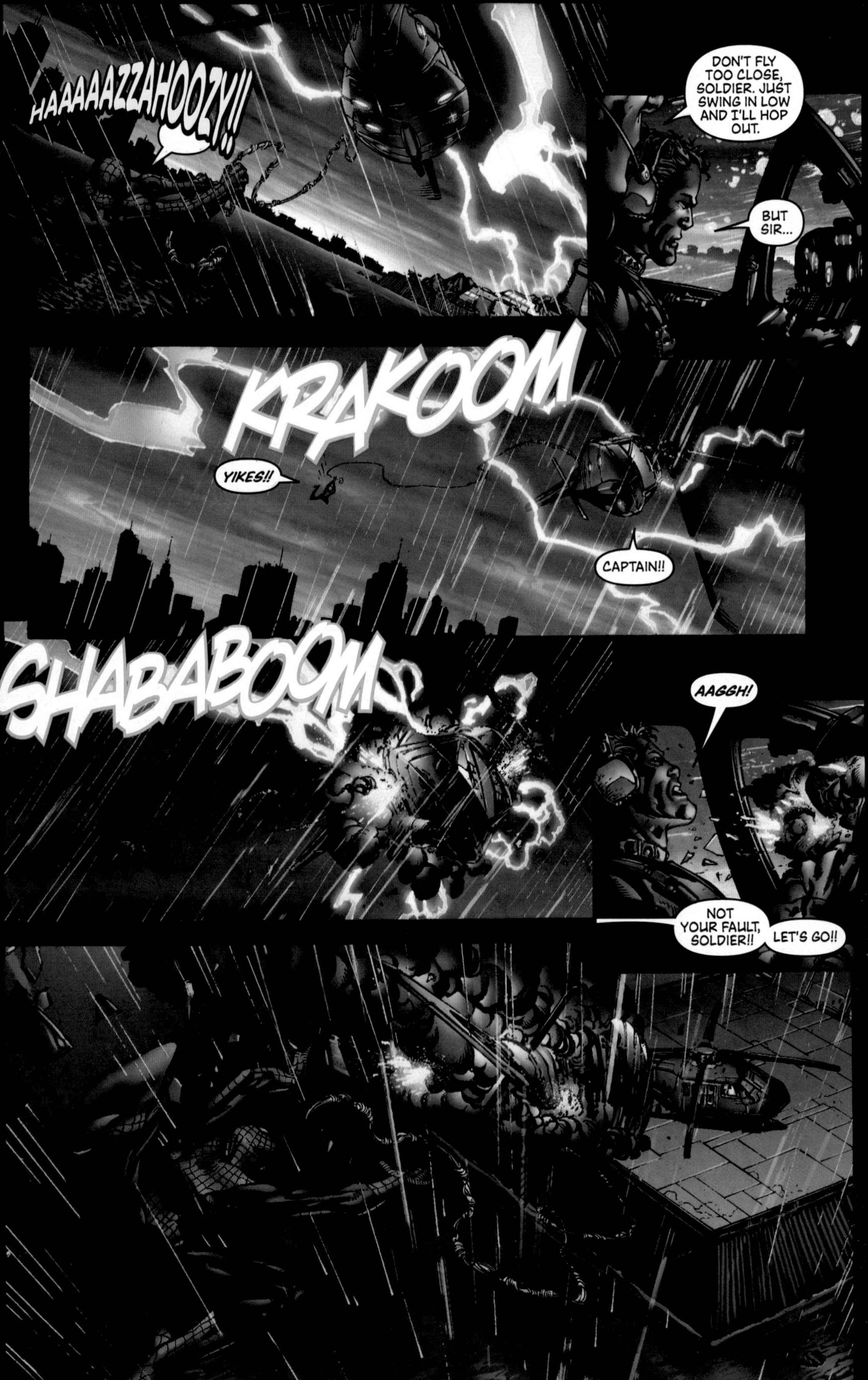
HAAAAAZZAHOOZY!!
DON'T FLY TOO CLOSE, SOLDIER. JUST SWING IN LOW AND I'LL HOP OUT.
BUT SIR...
KRAKOOM
YIKES!!
CAPTAIN!!
SHABABOOM
AAGGH!
NOT YOUR FAULT, SOLDIER!!
LET'S GO!!

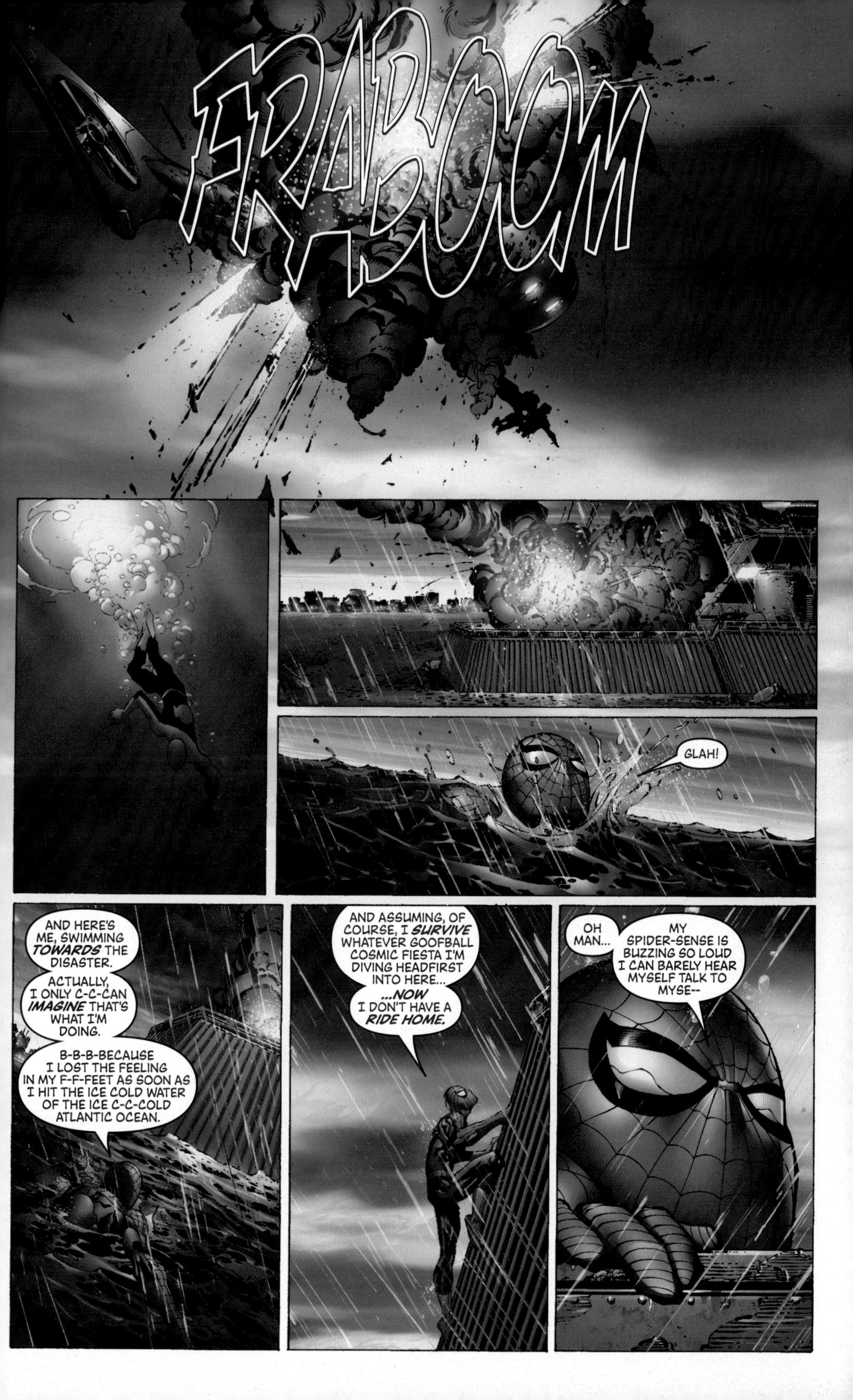
FRABOOM
GLAH!
AND HERE'S ME, SWIMMING TOWARDS THE DISASTER.
ACTUALLY, I ONLY C-C-CAN IMAGINE THAT'S WHAT I'M DOING.
B-B-B-BECAUSE I LOST THE FEELING IN MY F-F-FEET AS SOON AS I HIT THE ICE COLD WATER OF THE ICE C-C-COLD ATLANTIC OCEAN.
AND ASSUMING, OF COURSE, I SURVIVE WHATEVER GOOFBALL COSMIC FIESTA I'M DIVING HEADFIRST INTO HERE...
...NOW I DON'T HAVE A RIDE HOME.
OH MAN...
MY SPIDER-SENSE IS BUZZING SO LOUD I CAN BARELY HEAR MYSELF TALK TO MYSE--

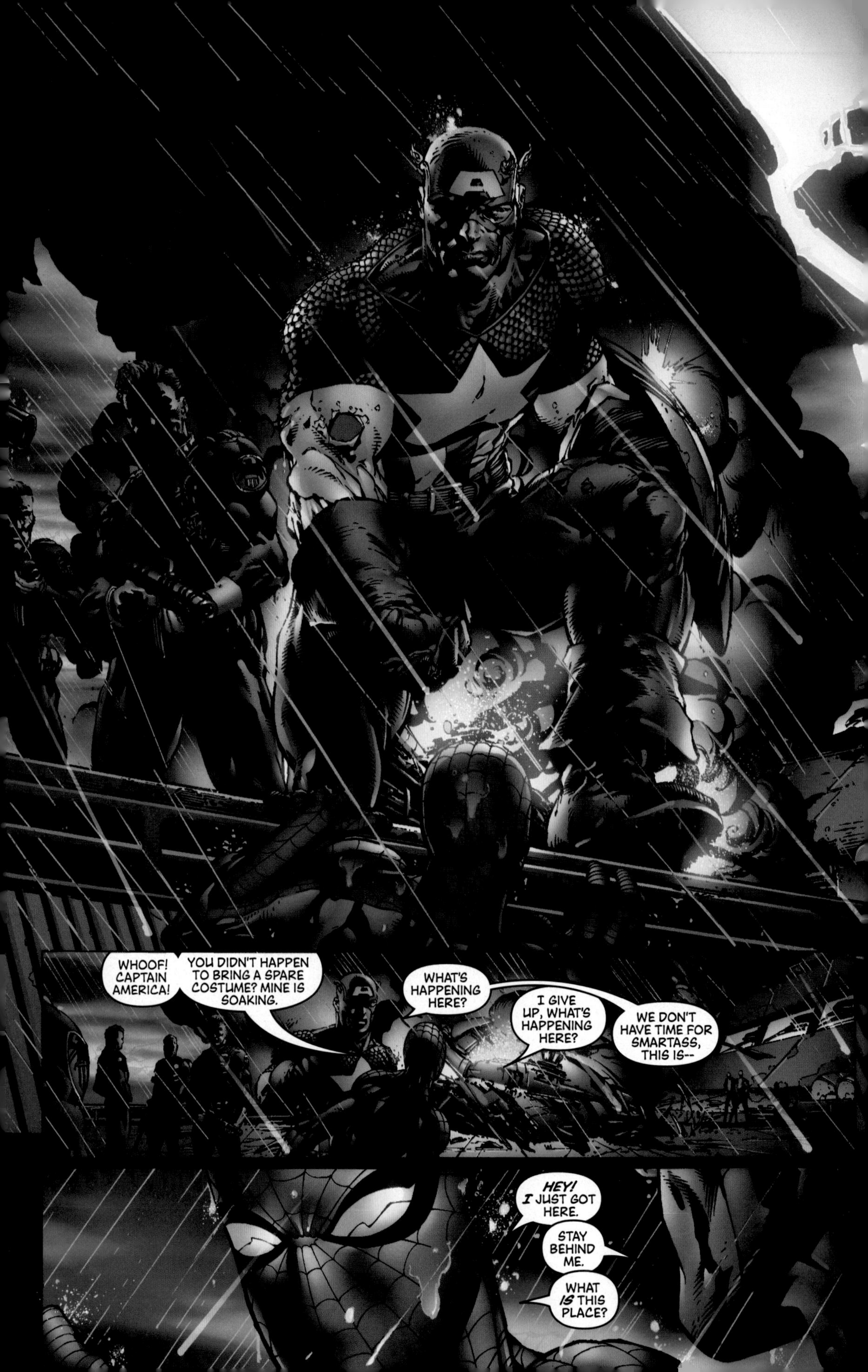
WHOOF! CAPTAIN AMERICA!
YOU DIDN'T HAPPEN TO BRING A SPARE COSTUME? MINE IS SOAKING.
WHAT'S HAPPENING HERE?
I GIVE UP, WHAT'S HAPPENING HERE?
WE DON'T HAVE TIME FOR SMARTASS, THIS IS--
HEY! I JUST GOT HERE.
STAY BEHIND ME.
WHAT IS THIS PLACE?

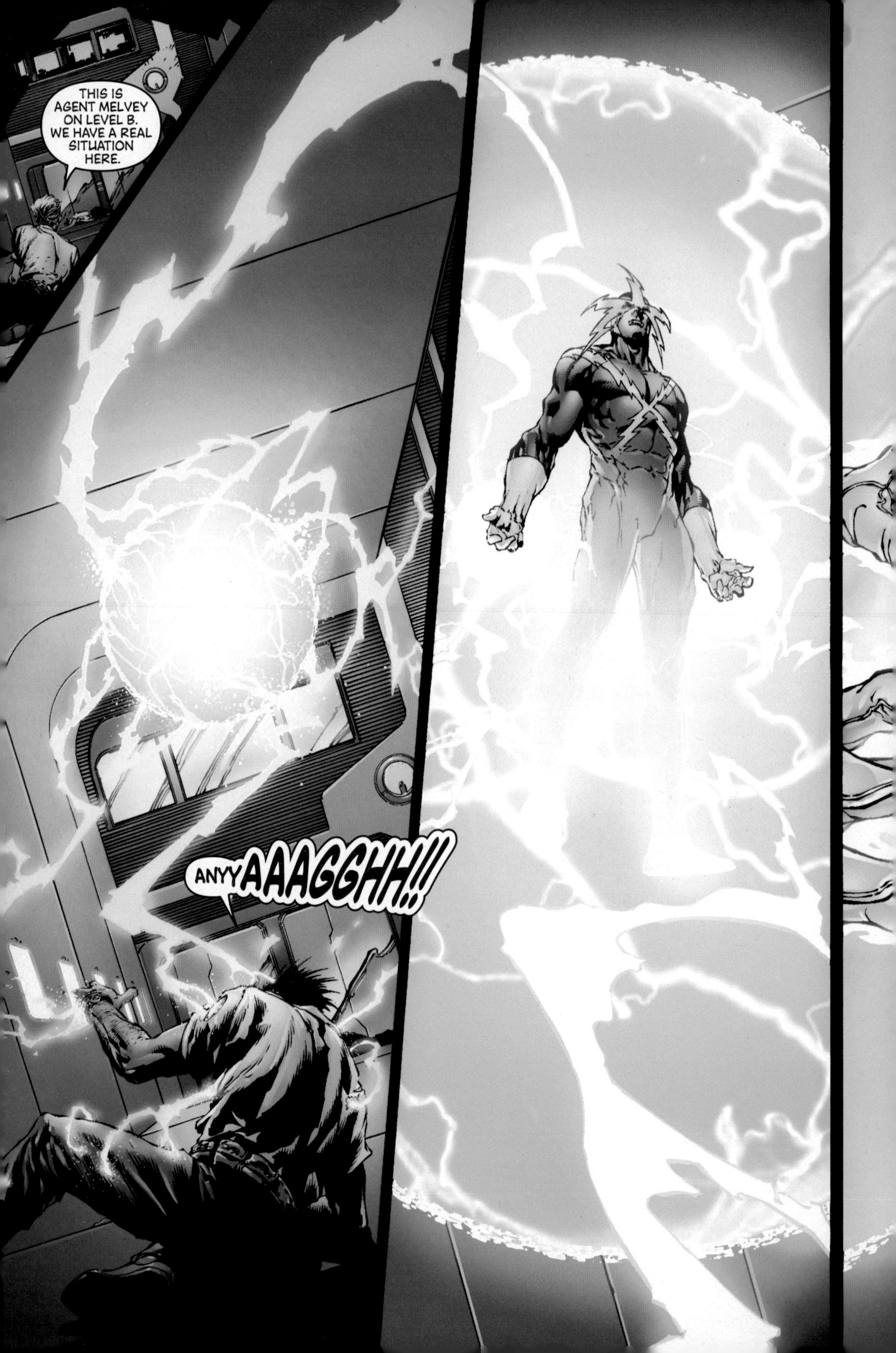
THIS IS AGENT MELVEY ON LEVEL B. WE HAVE A REAL SITUATION HERE.
ANYYAAAGGHH!!

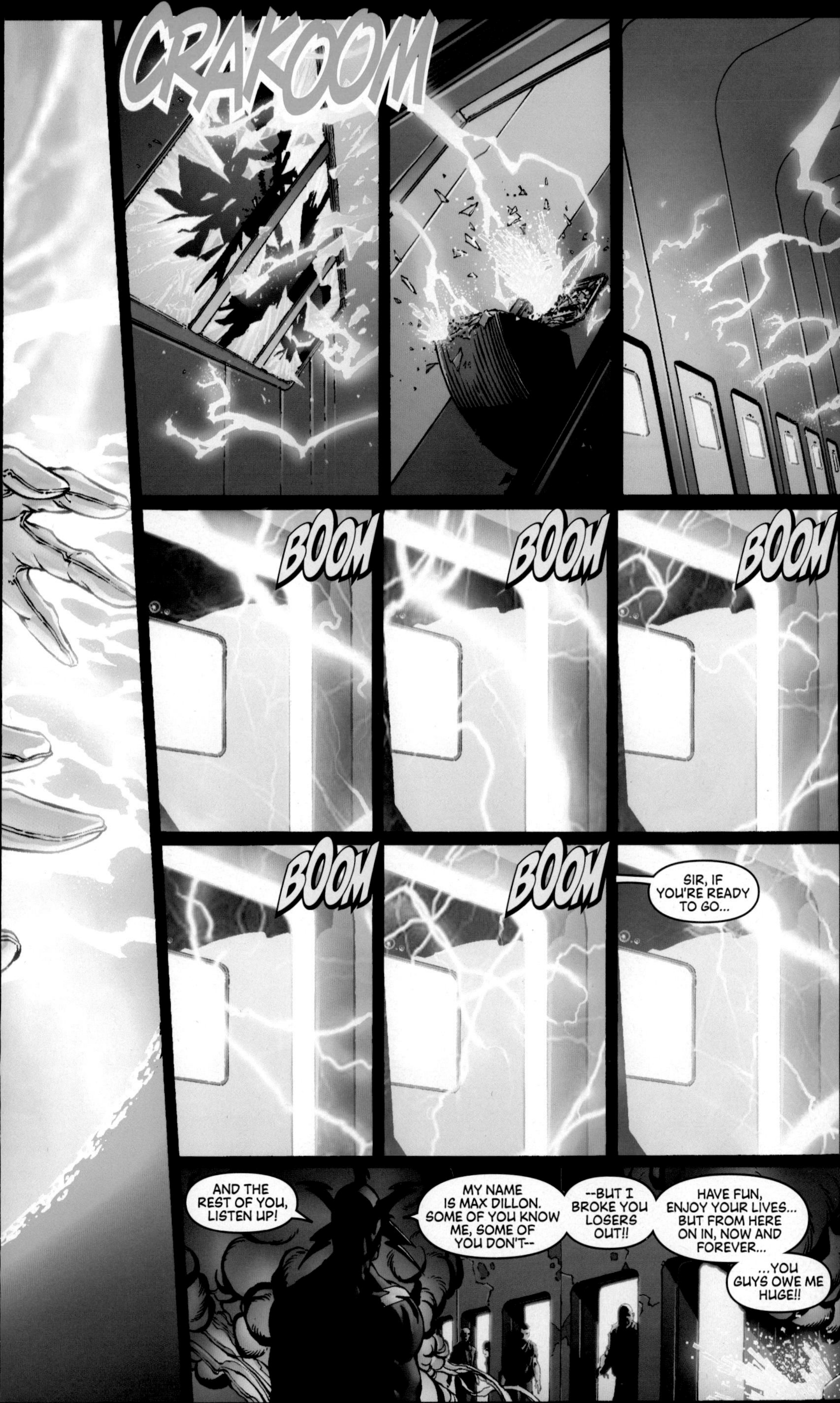
CRAKOOM
BOOM
BOOM
BOOM
BOOM
BOOM
SIR, IF YOU'RE READY TO GO...
AND THE REST OF YOU, LISTEN UP!
MY NAME IS MAX DILLON. SOME OF YOU KNOW ME, SOME OF YOU DON'T--
--BUT I BROKE YOU LOSERS OUT!!
HAVE FUN, ENJOY YOUR LIVES... BUT FROM HERE ON IN, NOW AND FOREVER...
...YOU GUYS OWE ME HUGE!!

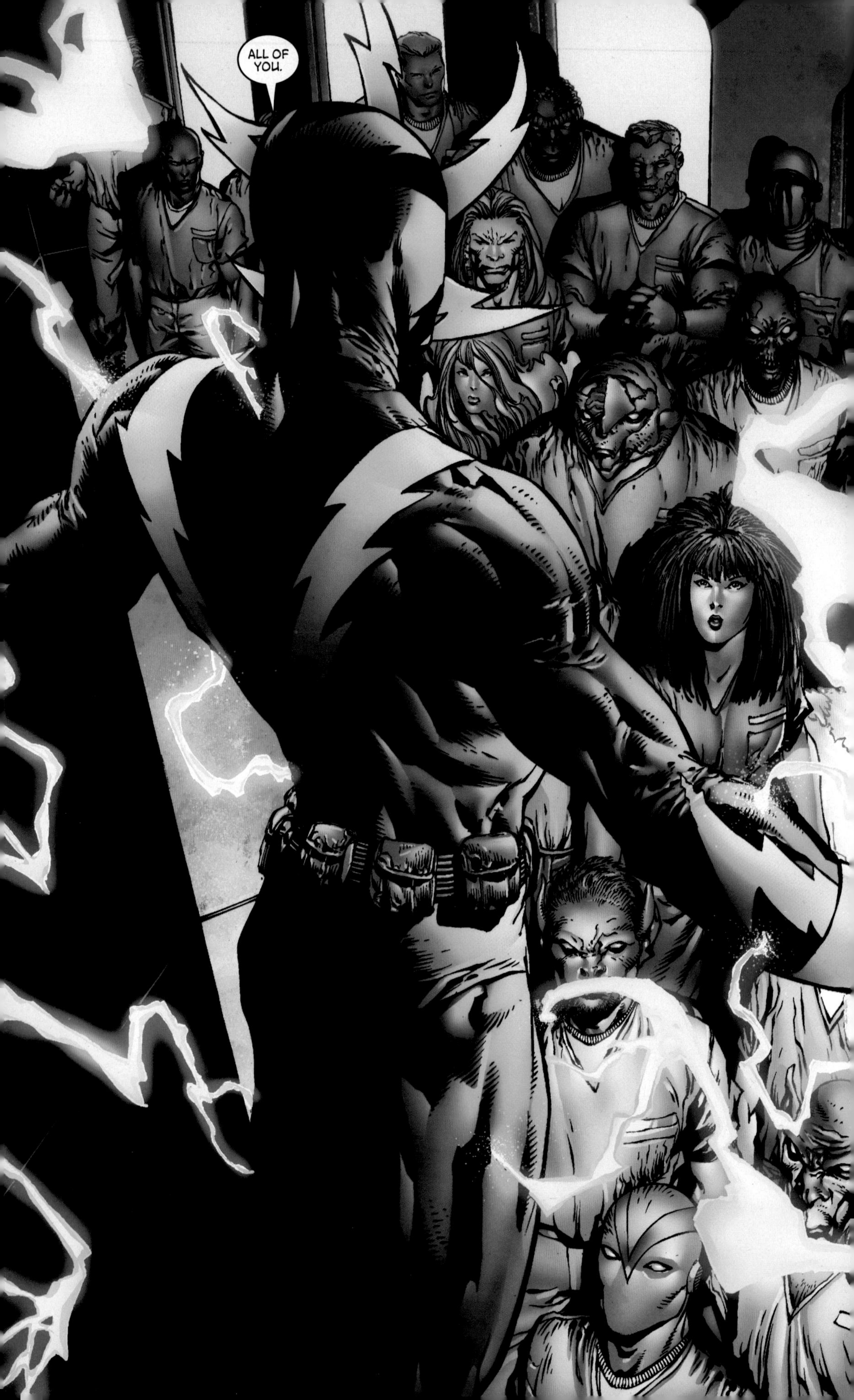
ALL OF YOU.

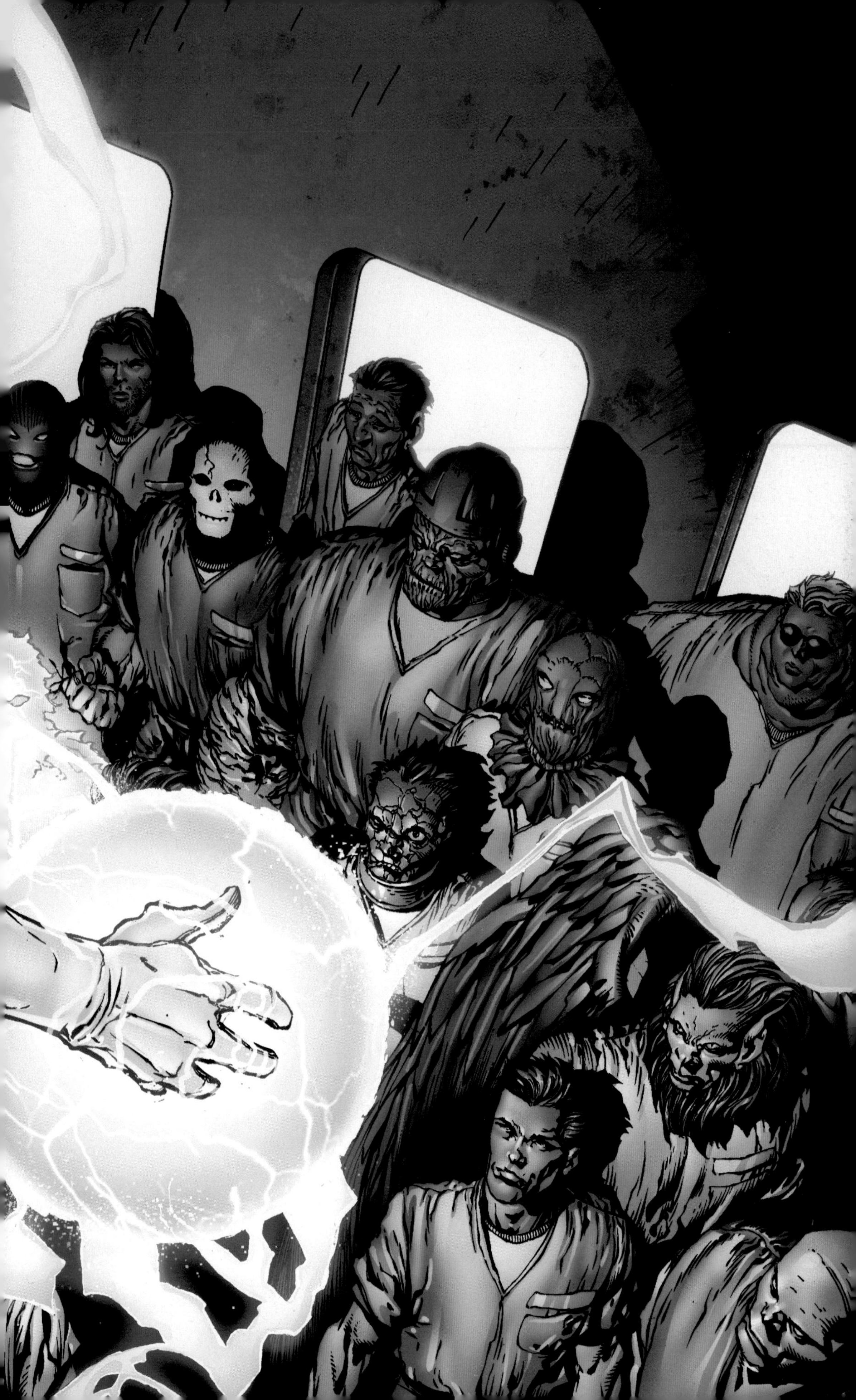

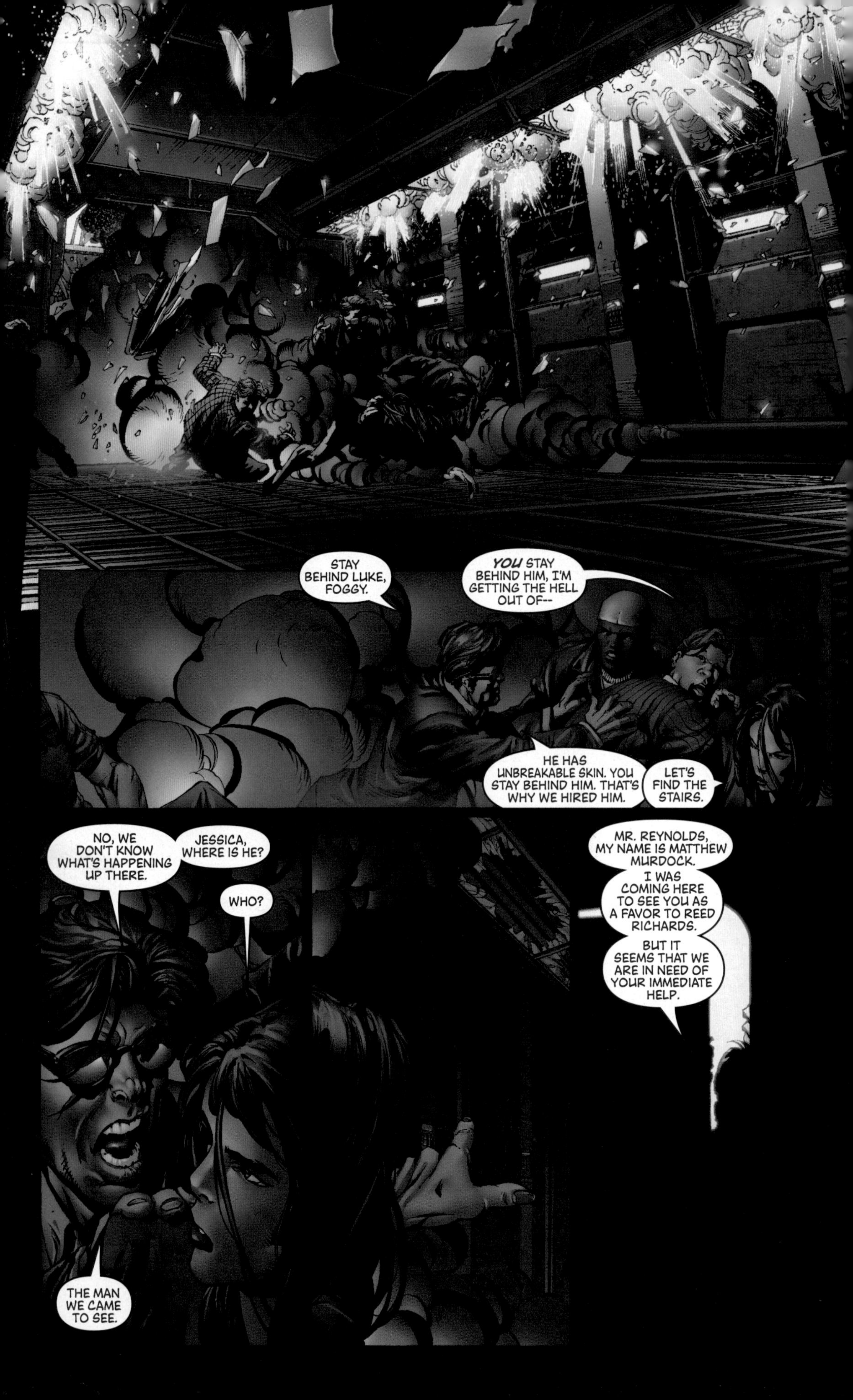
STAY BEHIND LUKE, FOGGY.
YOU STAY BEHIND HIM, I'M GETTING THE HELL OUT OF--
HE HAS UNBREAKABLE SKIN. YOU STAY BEHIND HIM. THAT'S WHY WE HIRED HIM.
LET'S FIND THE STAIRS.
JESSICA, WHERE IS HE?
NO, WE DON'T KNOW WHAT'S HAPPENING UP THERE.
WHO?
THE MAN WE CAME TO SEE.
MR. REYNOLDS, MY NAME IS MATTHEW MURDOCK.
I WAS COMING HERE TO SEE YOU AS A FAVOR TO REED RICHARDS.
BUT IT SEEMS THAT WE ARE IN NEED OF YOUR IMMEDIATE HELP.

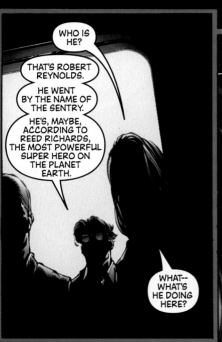

WHO IS HE?

THAT'S ROBERT REYNOLDS.

HE WENT BY THE NAME OF THE SENTRY.

HE'S, MAYBE, ACCORDING TO REED RICHARDS, THE MOST POWERFUL SUPER HERO ON THE PLANET EARTH.

WHAT-- WHAT'S HE DOING HERE?

HE KILLED HIS WIFE.

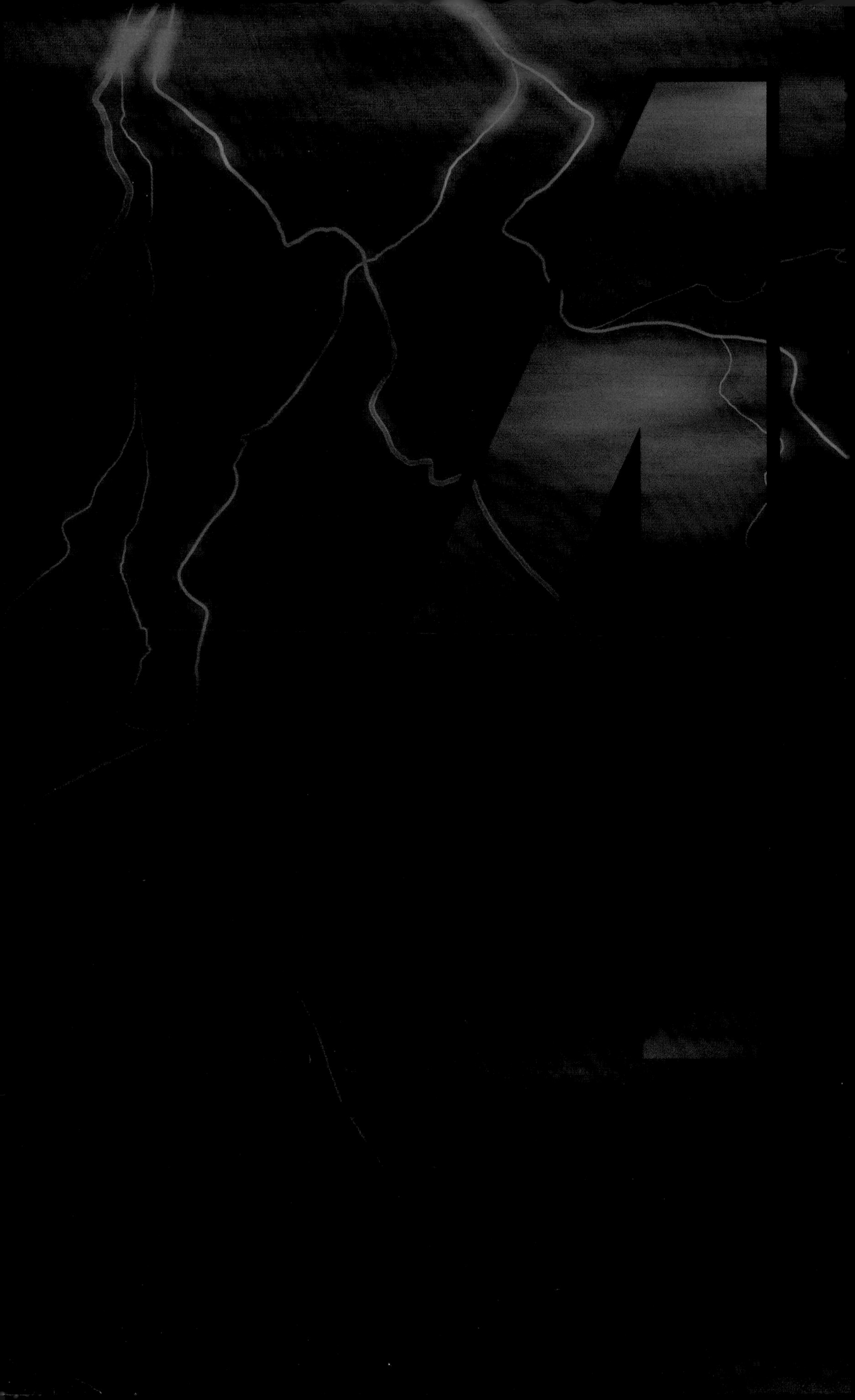

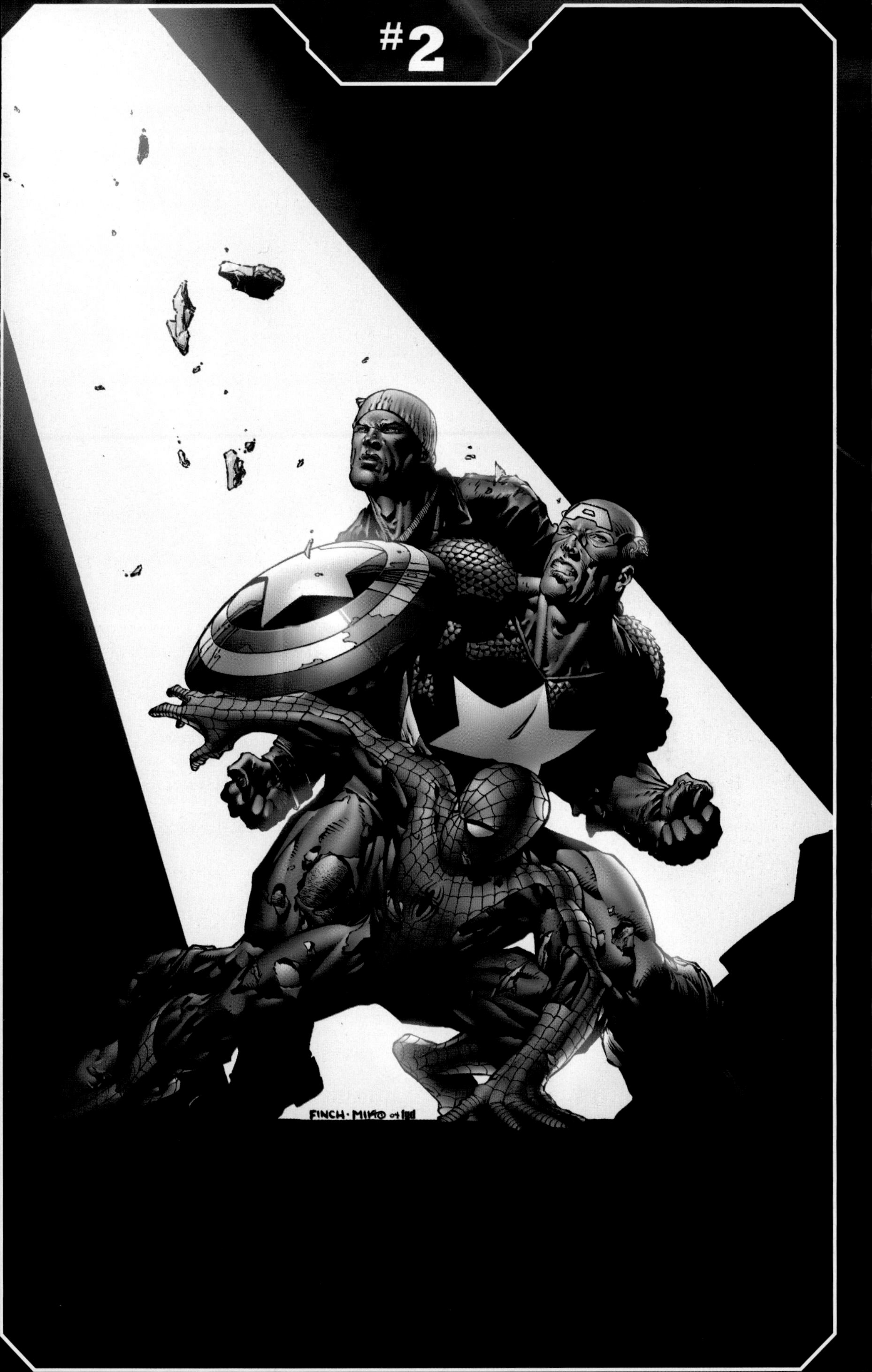
#2

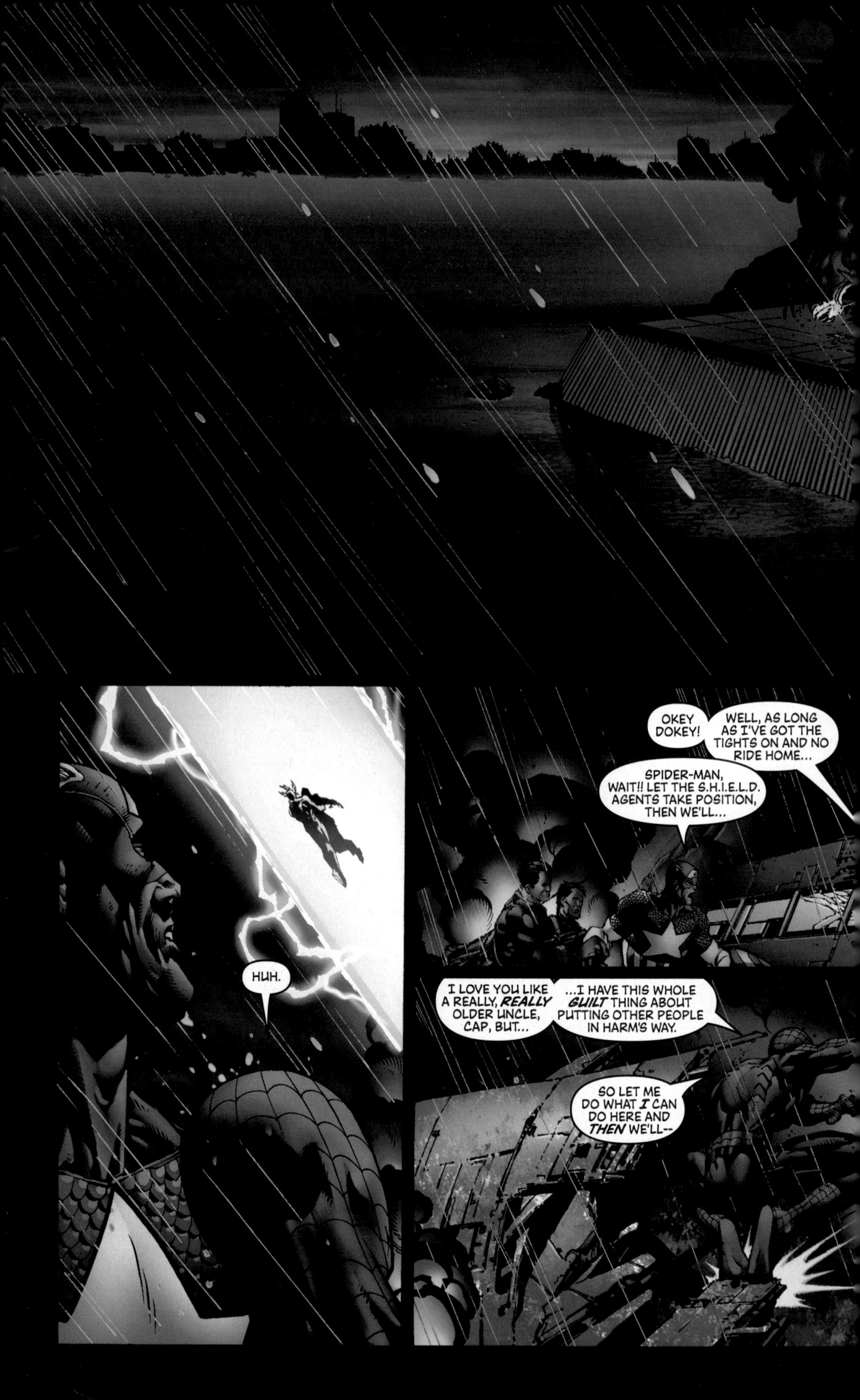
HUH.
OKEY DOKEY!
WELL, AS LONG AS I'VE GOT THE TIGHTS ON AND NO RIDE HOME...
SPIDER-MAN, WAIT!! LET THE S.H.I.E.L.D. AGENTS TAKE POSITION, THEN WE'LL...
I LOVE YOU LIKE A REALLY, ***REALLY*** OLDER UNCLE, CAP, BUT...
...I HAVE THIS WHOLE ***GUILT*** THING ABOUT PUTTING OTHER PEOPLE IN HARM'S WAY.
SO LET ME DO WHAT ***I*** CAN DO HERE AND ***THEN*** WE'LL--

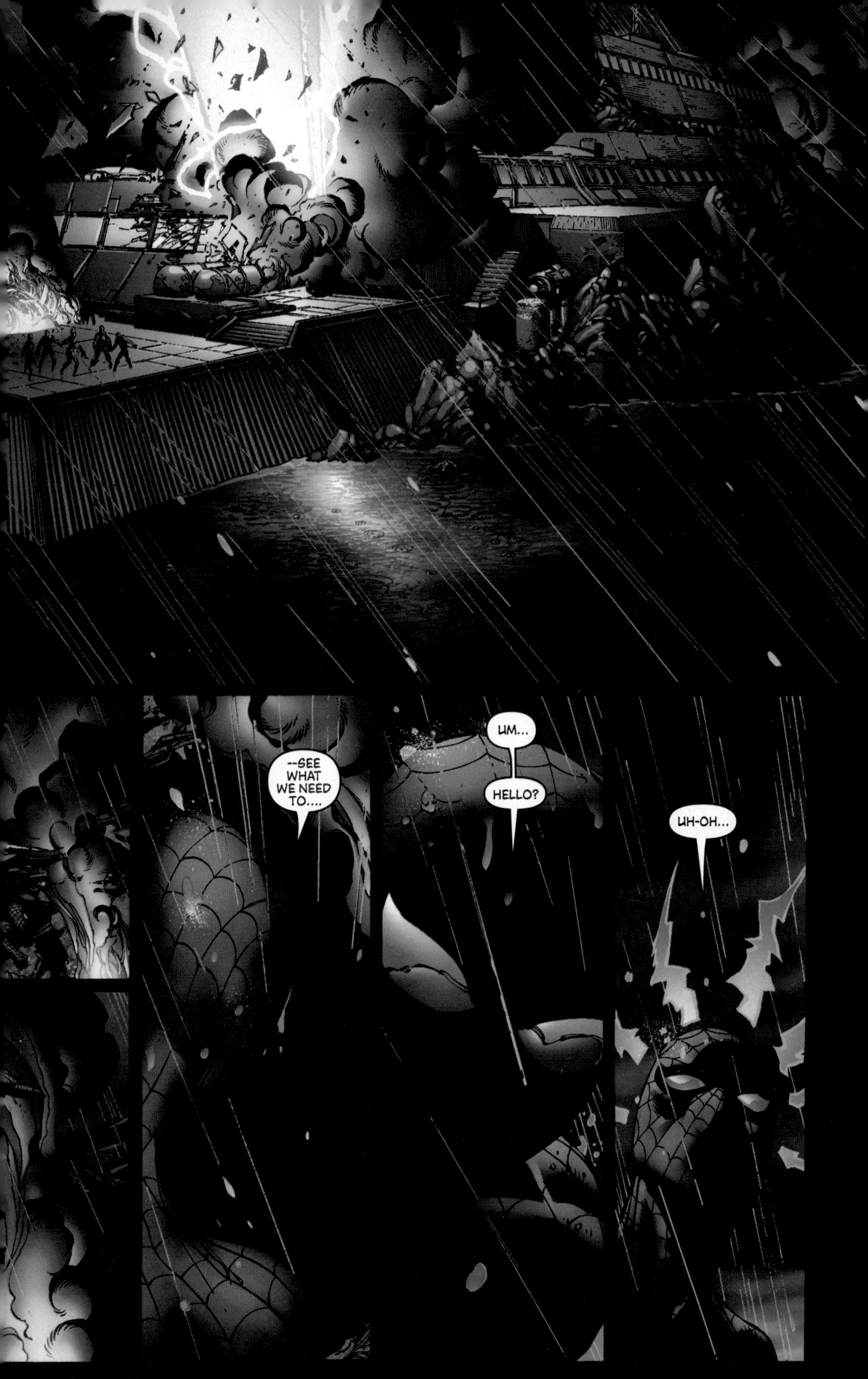
--SEE WHAT WE NEED TO....
UM...
HELLO?
UH-OH...

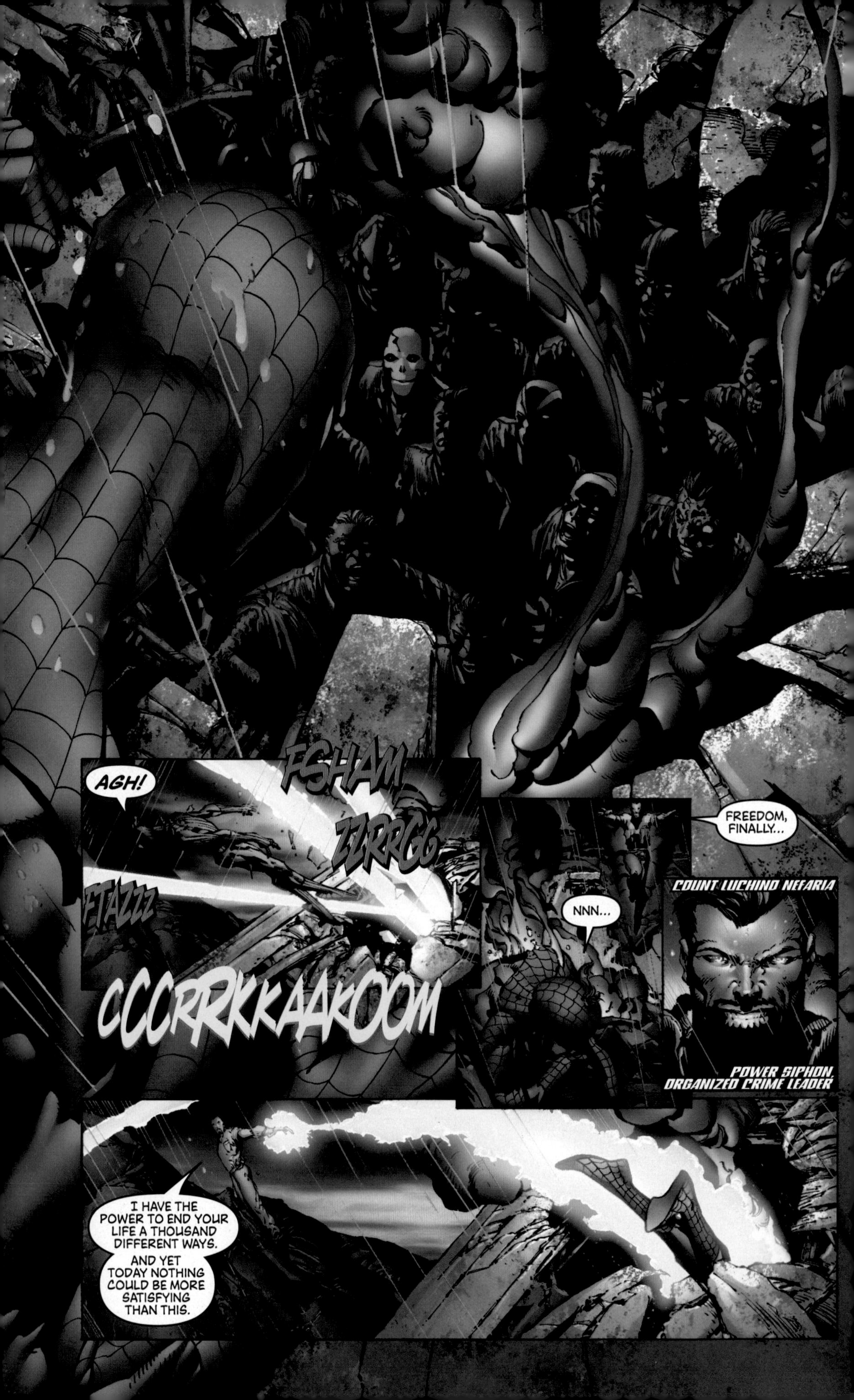
AGH!
FSHAM
ZZRRGG
FTAZZZ
CCCRRKKAAKOOM
FREEDOM, FINALLY...
NNN...
COUNT LUCHINO NEFARIA
POWER SIPHON, ORGANIZED CRIME LEADER
I HAVE THE POWER TO END YOUR LIFE A THOUSAND DIFFERENT WAYS.
AND YET TODAY NOTHING COULD BE MORE SATISFYING THAN THIS.

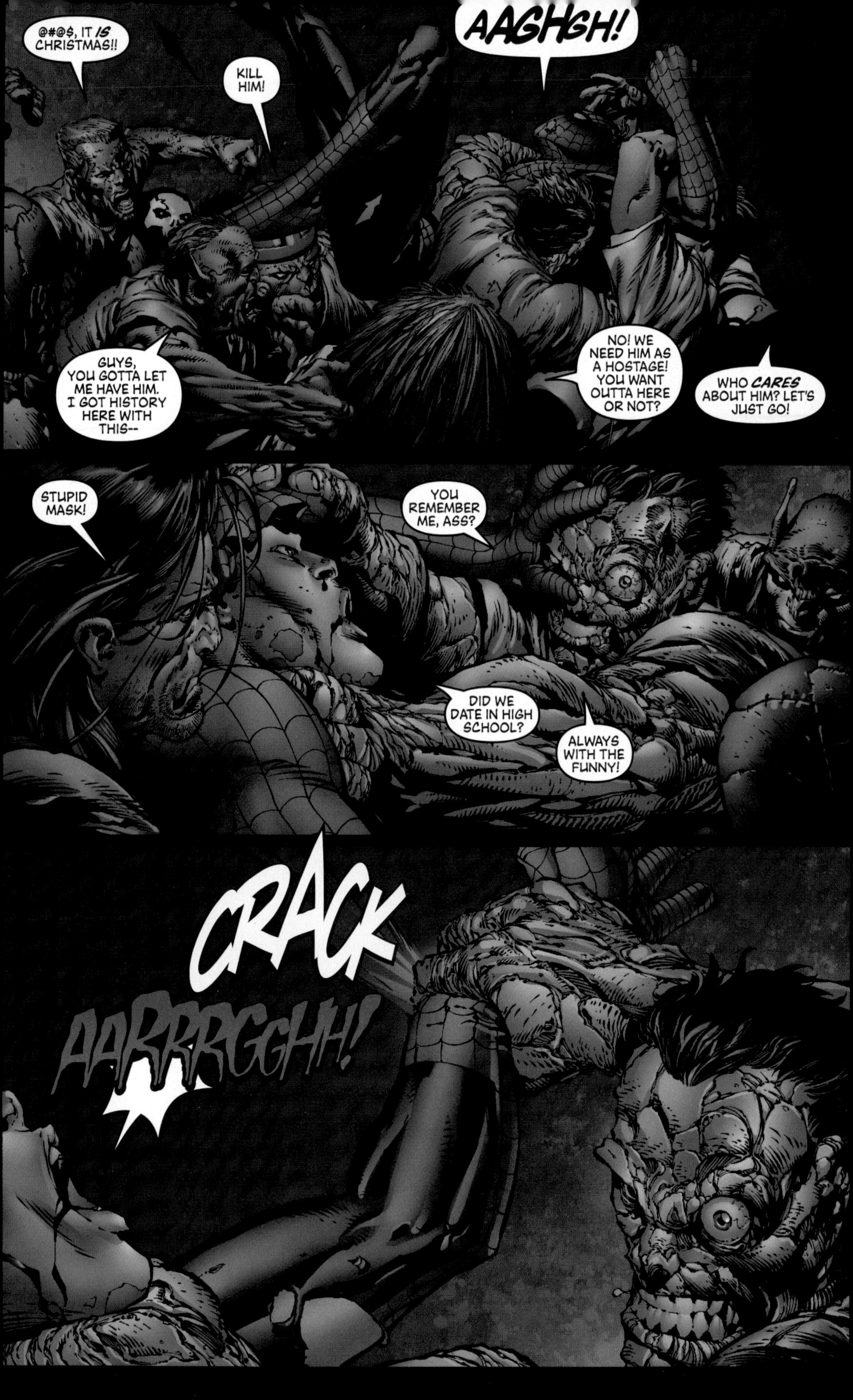

@#@$, IT IS CHRISTMAS!!
KILL HIM!
AAGHGH!
GUYS, YOU GOTTA LET ME HAVE HIM. I GOT HISTORY HERE WITH THIS--
NO! WE NEED HIM AS A HOSTAGE! YOU WANT OUTTA HERE OR NOT?
WHO CARES ABOUT HIM? LET'S JUST GO!
STUPID MASK!
YOU REMEMBER ME, ASS?
DID WE DATE IN HIGH SCHOOL?
ALWAYS WITH THE FUNNY!
CRACK
AARRRGGHH!

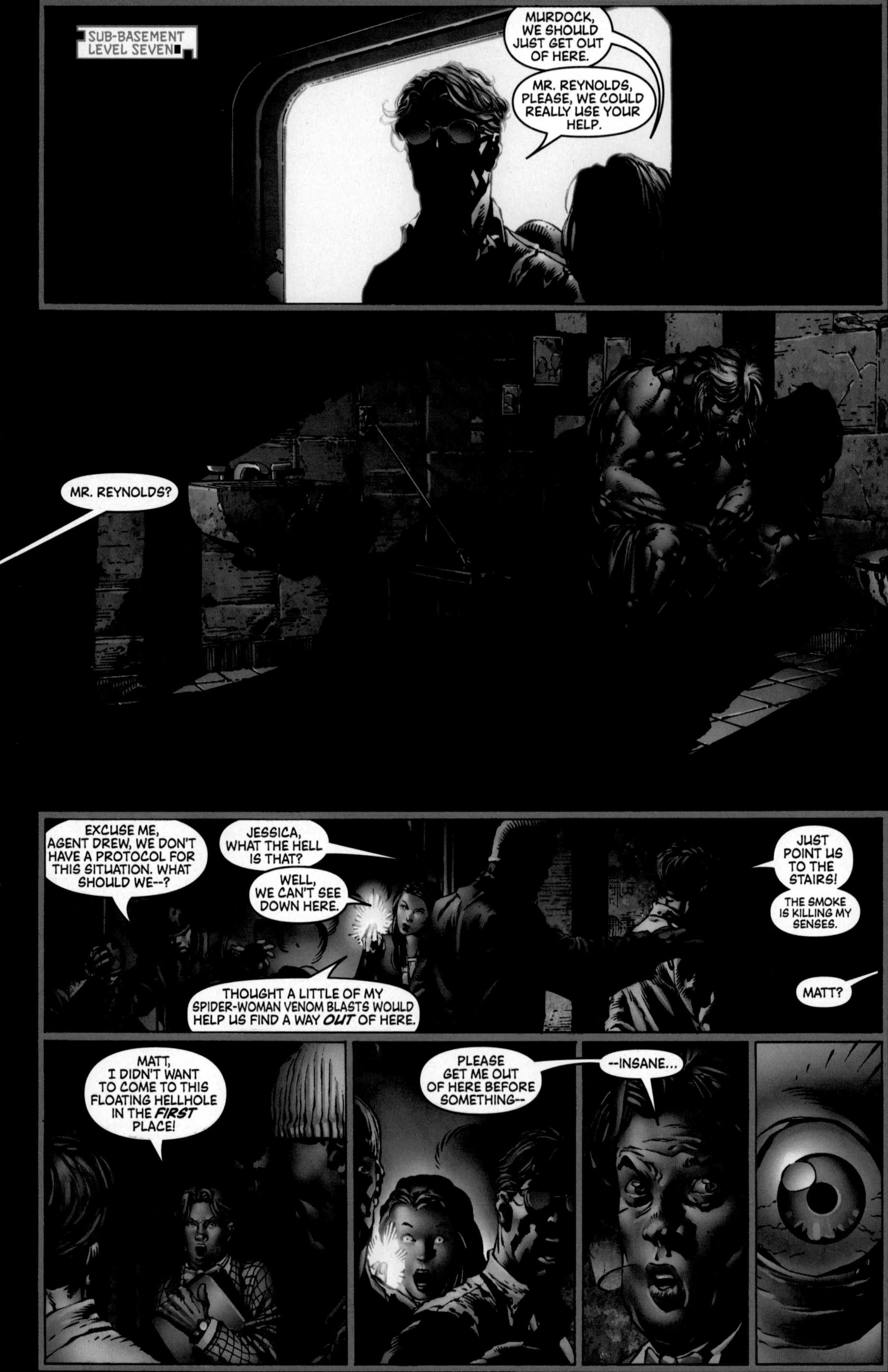
SUB-BASEMENT LEVEL SEVEN
MURDOCK, WE SHOULD JUST GET OUT OF HERE.
MR. REYNOLDS, PLEASE, WE COULD REALLY USE YOUR HELP.
MR. REYNOLDS?
EXCUSE ME, AGENT DREW, WE DON'T HAVE A PROTOCOL FOR THIS SITUATION. WHAT SHOULD WE--?
JESSICA, WHAT THE HELL IS THAT?
WELL, WE CAN'T SEE DOWN HERE.
THOUGHT A LITTLE OF MY SPIDER-WOMAN VENOM BLASTS WOULD HELP US FIND A WAY OUT OF HERE.
JUST POINT US TO THE STAIRS!
THE SMOKE IS KILLING MY SENSES.
MATT?
MATT, I DIDN'T WANT TO COME TO THIS FLOATING HELLHOLE IN THE FIRST PLACE!
PLEASE GET ME OUT OF HERE BEFORE SOMETHING--
--INSANE...

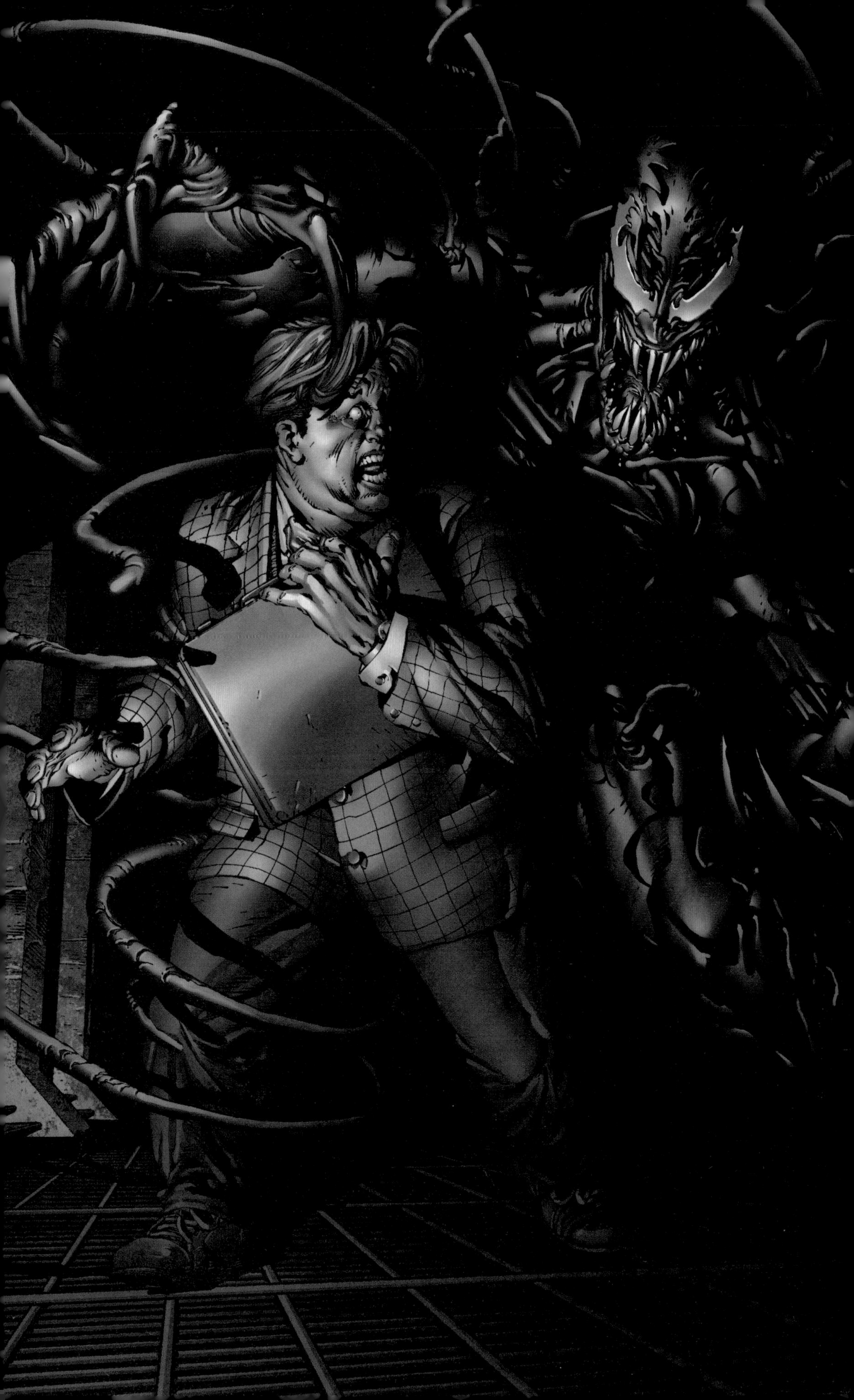

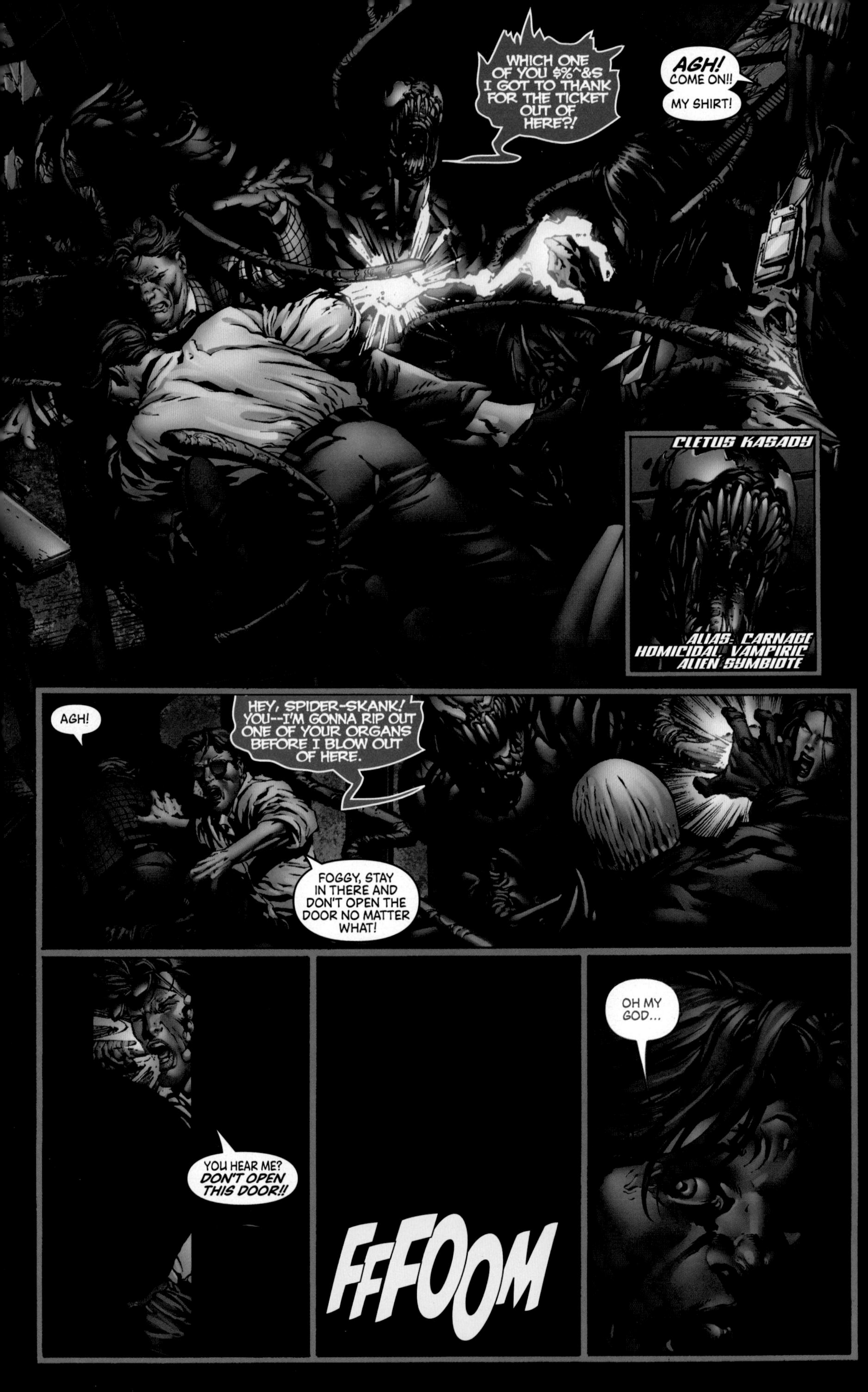
WHICH ONE OF YOU $%^&S I GOT TO THANK FOR THE TICKET OUT OF HERE?!
AGH! COME ON!!
MY SHIRT!
CLETUS KASADY
ALIAS: CARNAGE
HOMICIDAL VAMPIRIC ALIEN SYMBIOTE
AGH!
HEY, SPIDER-SKANK! YOU--I'M GONNA RIP OUT ONE OF YOUR ORGANS BEFORE I BLOW OUT OF HERE.
FOGGY, STAY IN THERE AND DON'T OPEN THE DOOR NO MATTER WHAT!
YOU HEAR ME? DON'T OPEN THIS DOOR!!
FFFOOM
OH MY GOD...

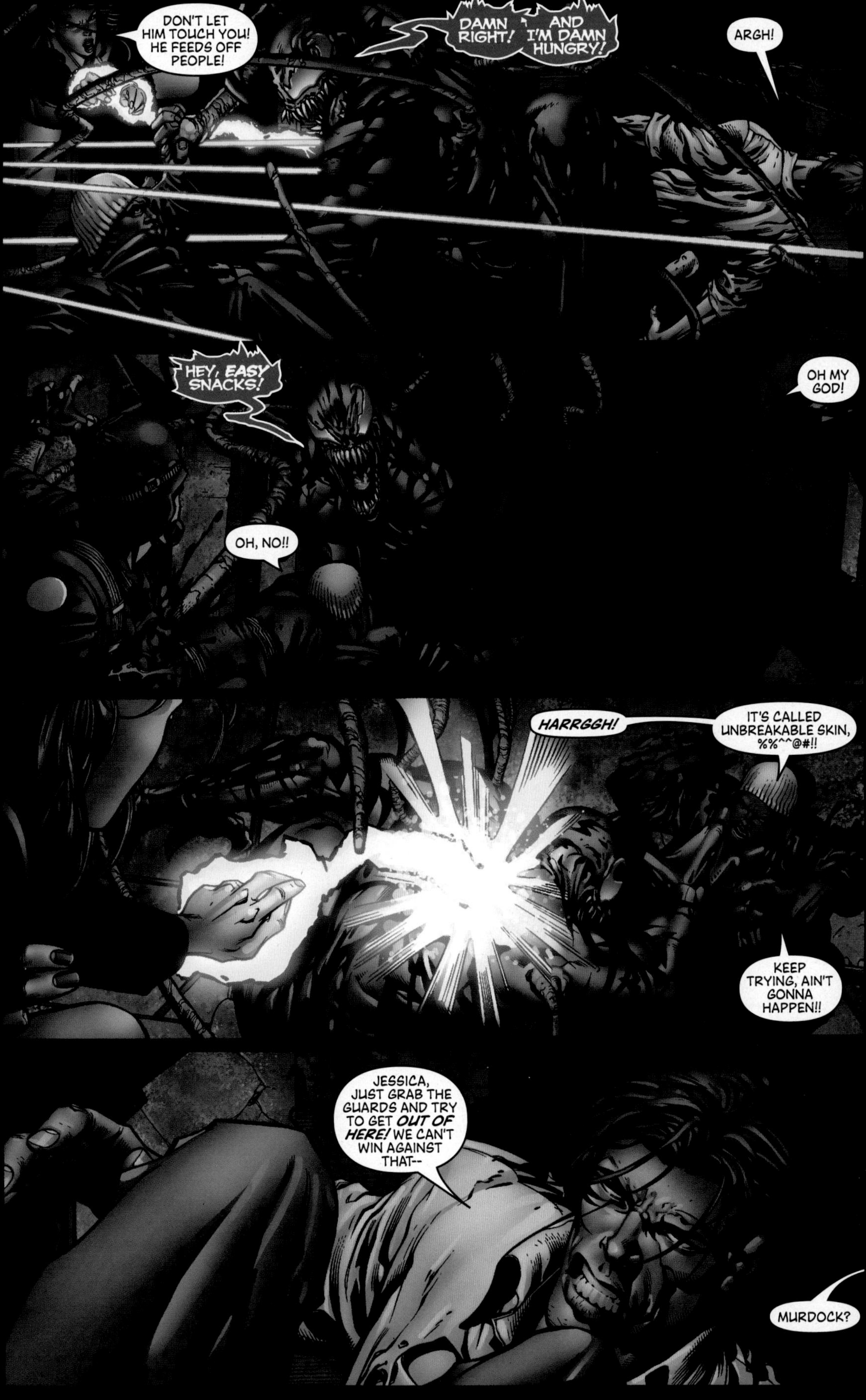
DON'T LET HIM TOUCH YOU! HE FEEDS OFF PEOPLE!
DAMN RIGHT!
AND I'M DAMN HUNGRY!
ARGH!
HEY, EASY SNACKS!
OH MY GOD!
OH, NO!!
HARRGGH!
IT'S CALLED UNBREAKABLE SKIN, %%^^@#!!
KEEP TRYING, AIN'T GONNA HAPPEN!!
JESSICA, JUST GRAB THE GUARDS AND TRY TO GET OUT OF HERE! WE CAN'T WIN AGAINST THAT--
MURDOCK?

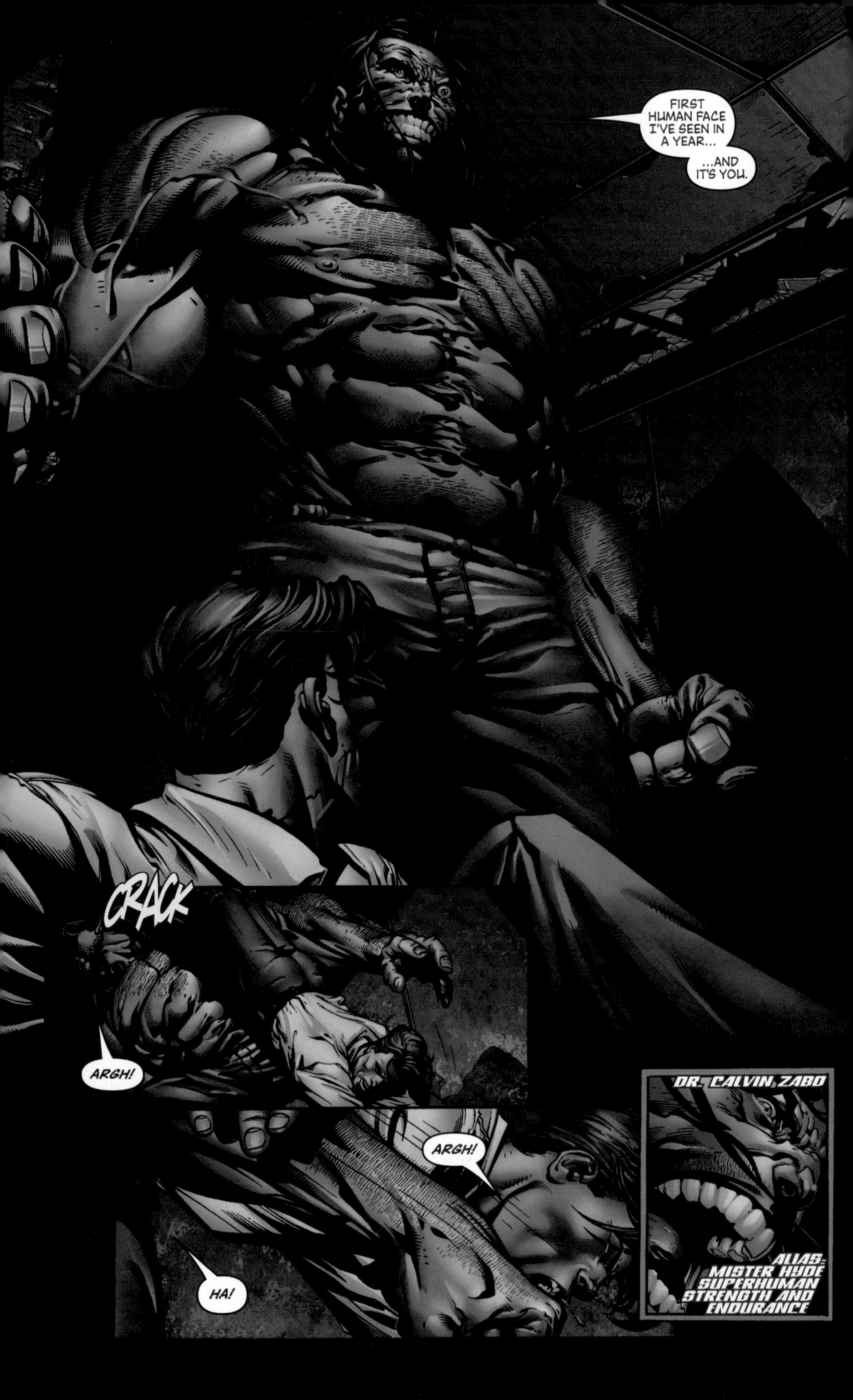
FIRST HUMAN FACE I'VE SEEN IN A YEAR...
...AND IT'S YOU.
CRACK
ARGH!
DR. CALVIN ZABO
ALIAS- MISTER HYDE SUPERHUMAN STRENGTH AND ENDURANCE
ARGH!
HA!

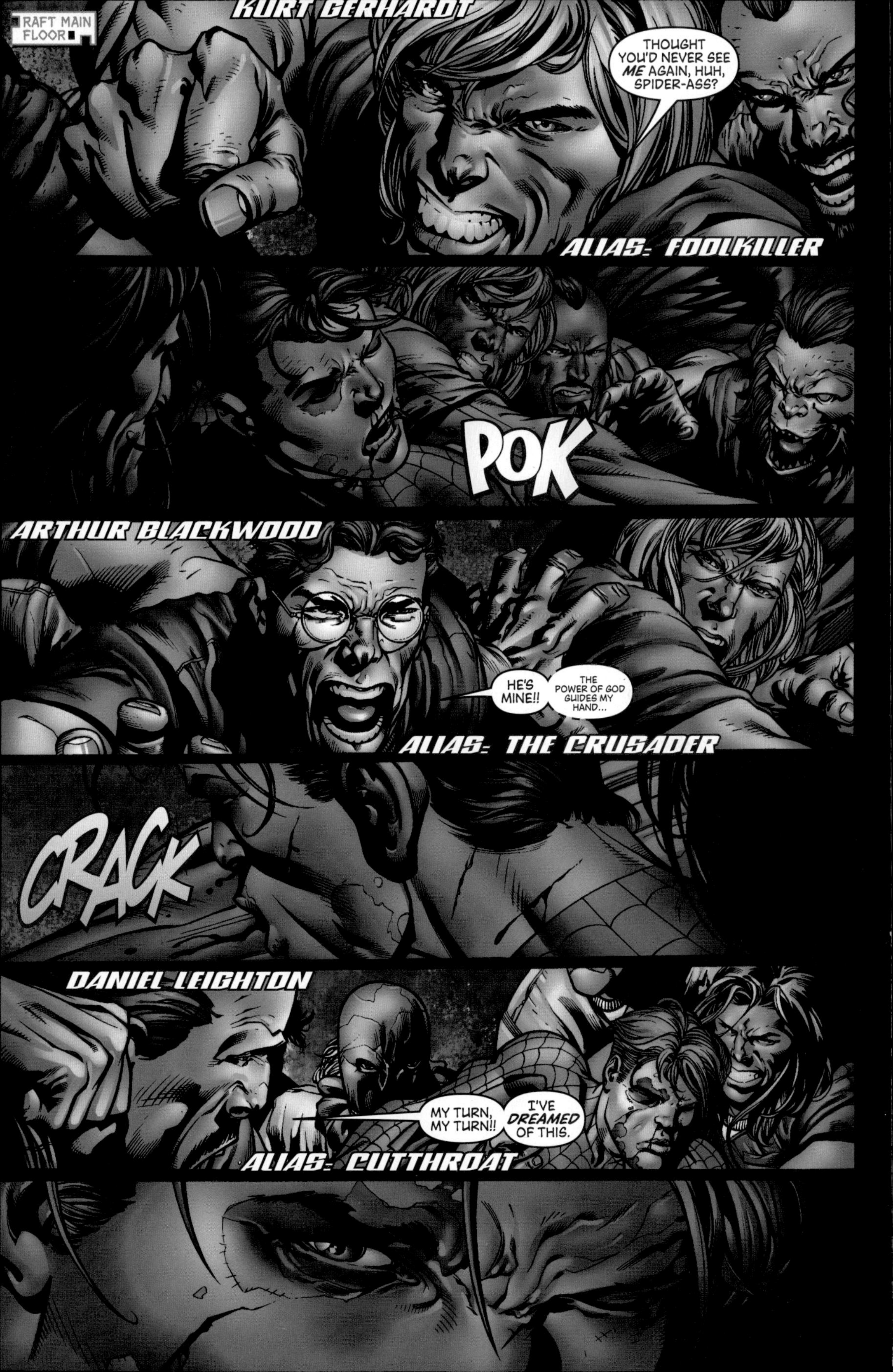
KURT GERHARDT
RAFT MAIN FLOOR
THOUGHT YOU'D NEVER SEE ME AGAIN, HUH, SPIDER-ASS?
ALIAS: FOOLKILLER
POK
ARTHUR BLACKWOOD
HE'S MINE!!
THE POWER OF GOD GUIDES MY HAND...
ALIAS: THE CRUSADER
CRACK
DANIEL LEIGHTON
MY TURN, MY TURN!!
I'VE DREAMED OF THIS.
ALIAS: CUTTHROAT

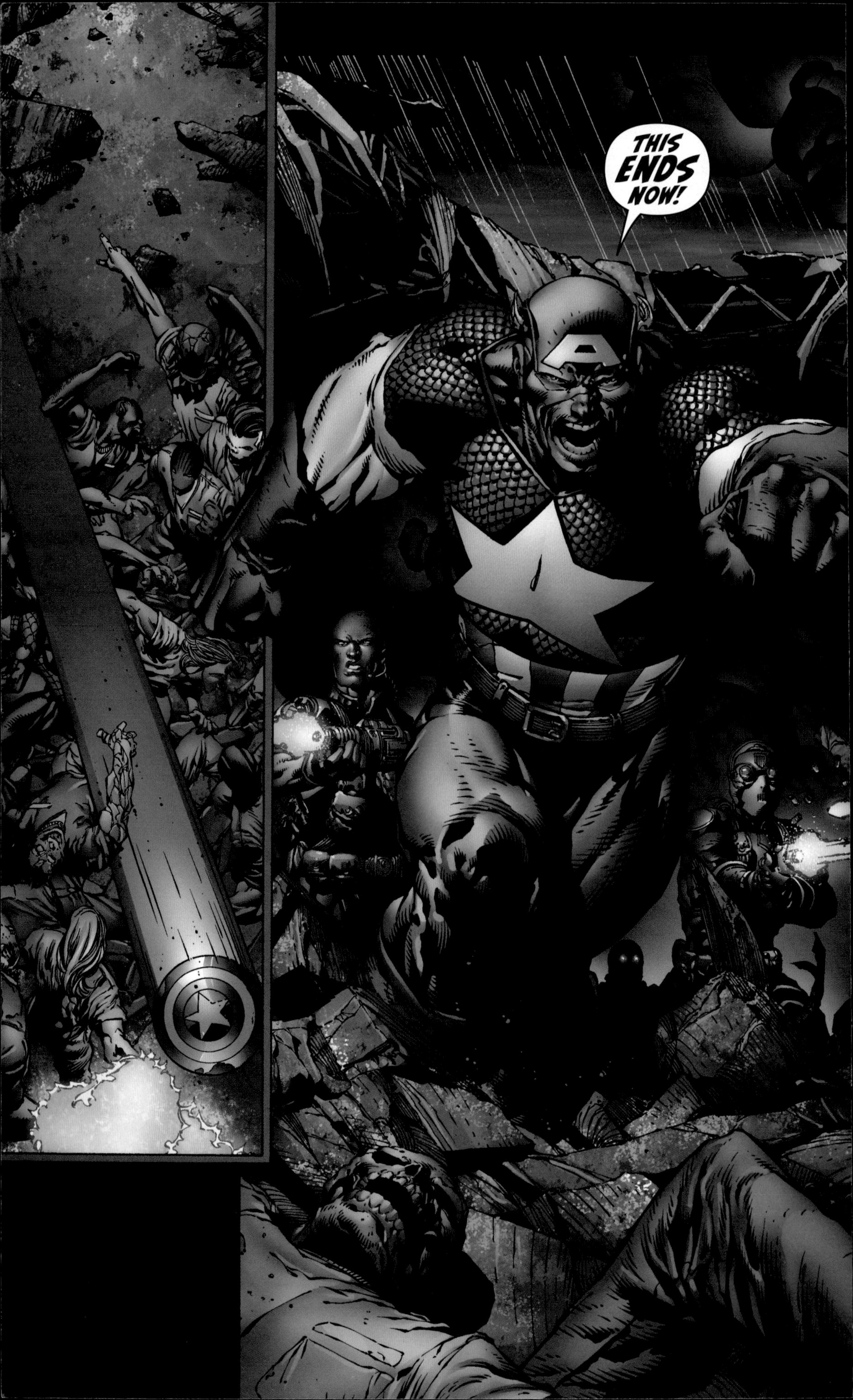
THIS ENDS NOW!

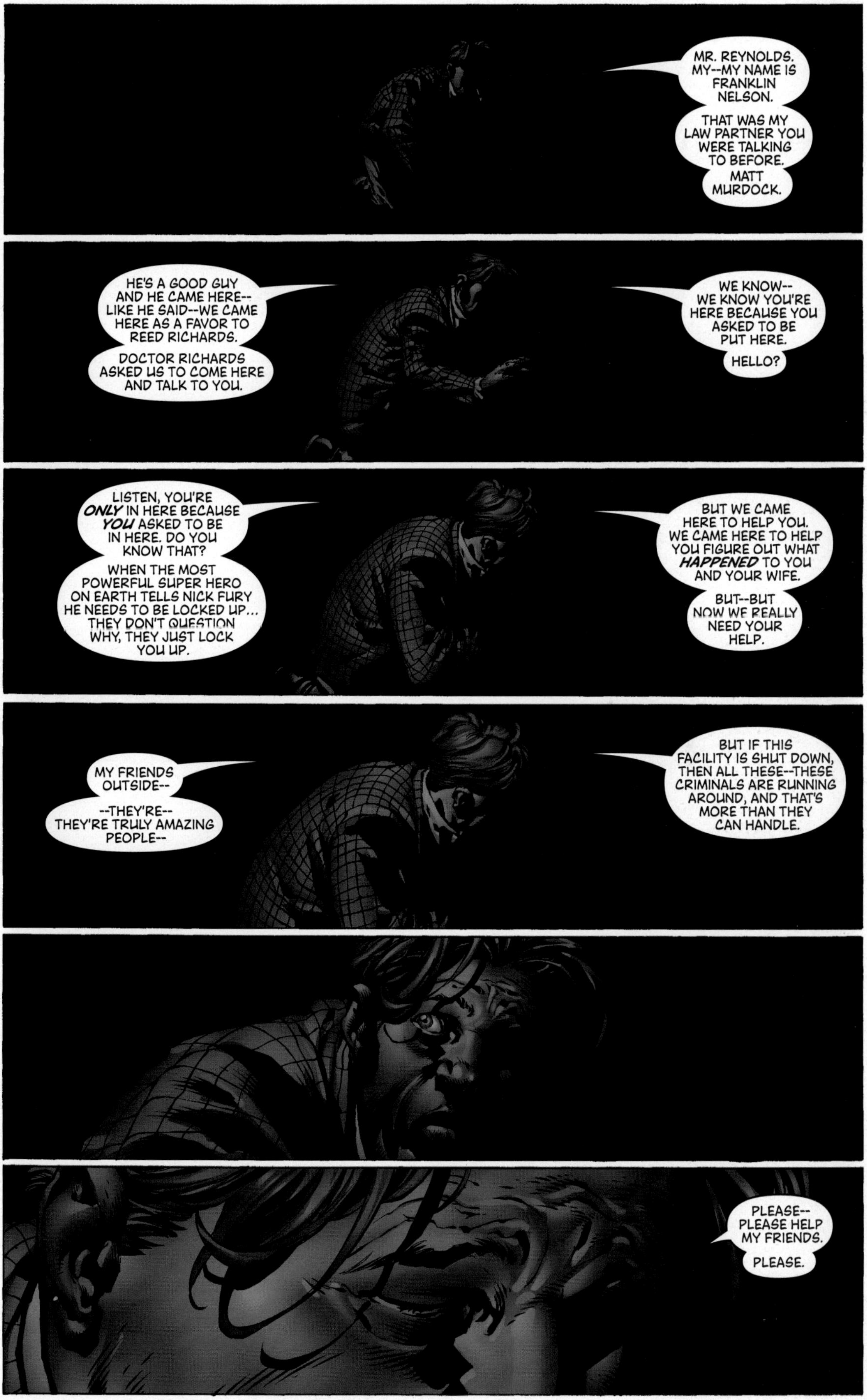

MR. REYNOLDS. MY--MY NAME IS FRANKLIN NELSON.
THAT WAS MY LAW PARTNER YOU WERE TALKING TO BEFORE. MATT MURDOCK.
HE'S A GOOD GUY AND HE CAME HERE--LIKE HE SAID--WE CAME HERE AS A FAVOR TO REED RICHARDS.
DOCTOR RICHARDS ASKED US TO COME HERE AND TALK TO YOU.
WE KNOW--WE KNOW YOU'RE HERE BECAUSE YOU ASKED TO BE PUT HERE.
HELLO?
LISTEN, YOU'RE *ONLY* IN HERE BECAUSE *YOU* ASKED TO BE IN HERE. DO YOU KNOW THAT?
WHEN THE MOST POWERFUL SUPER HERO ON EARTH TELLS NICK FURY HE NEEDS TO BE LOCKED UP... THEY DON'T QUESTION WHY, THEY JUST LOCK YOU UP.
BUT WE CAME HERE TO HELP YOU. WE CAME HERE TO HELP YOU FIGURE OUT WHAT *HAPPENED* TO YOU AND YOUR WIFE.
BUT--BUT NOW WE REALLY NEED YOUR HELP.
MY FRIENDS OUTSIDE--
--THEY'RE--THEY'RE TRULY AMAZING PEOPLE--
BUT IF THIS FACILITY IS SHUT DOWN, THEN ALL THESE--THESE CRIMINALS ARE RUNNING AROUND, AND THAT'S MORE THAN THEY CAN HANDLE.
PLEASE--PLEASE HELP MY FRIENDS.
PLEASE.

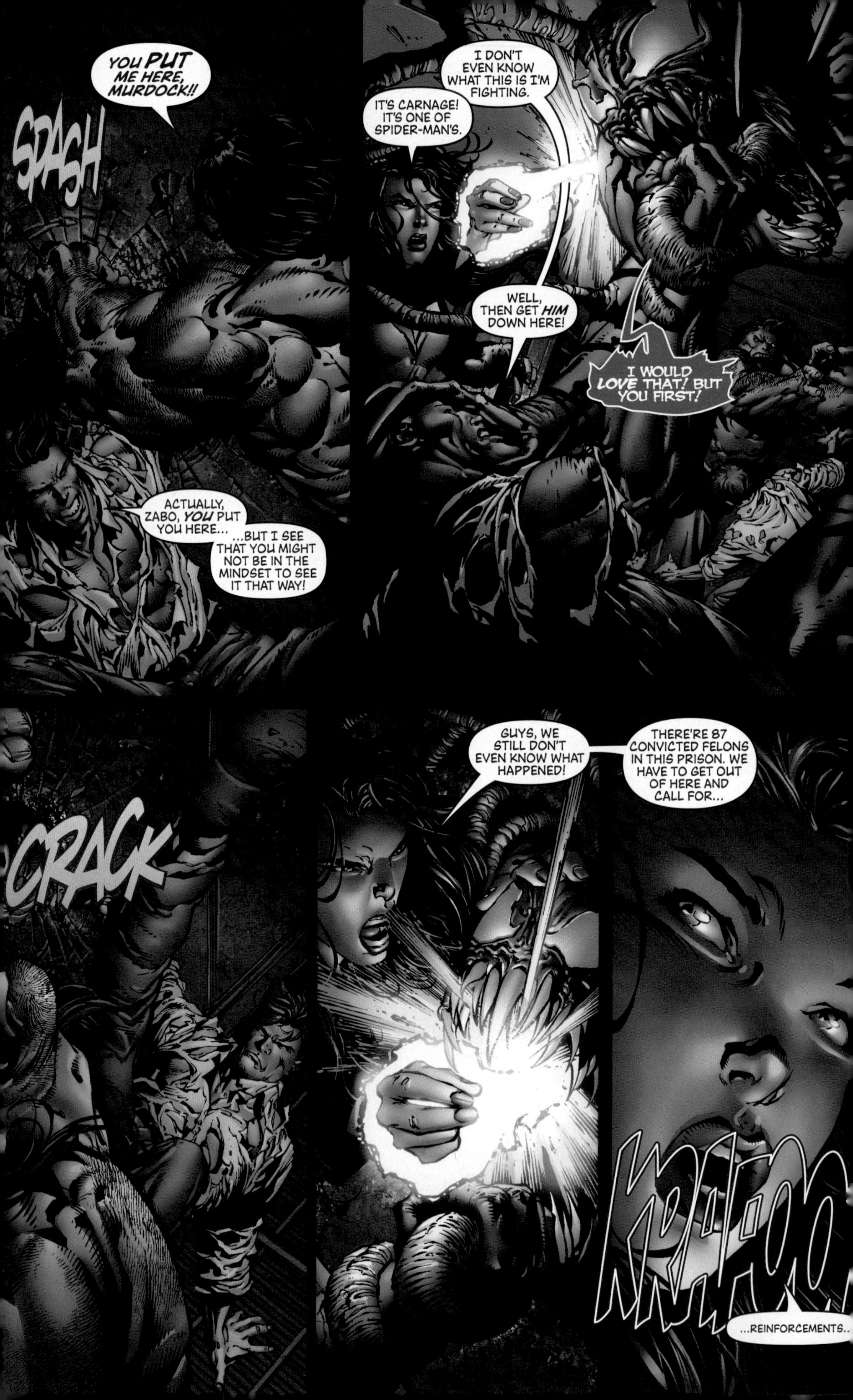
YOU PUT ME HERE, MURDOCK!!
SPASH
ACTUALLY, ZABO, YOU PUT YOU HERE...
...BUT I SEE THAT YOU MIGHT NOT BE IN THE MINDSET TO SEE IT THAT WAY!
I DON'T EVEN KNOW WHAT THIS IS I'M FIGHTING.
IT'S CARNAGE! IT'S ONE OF SPIDER-MAN'S.
WELL, THEN GET HIM DOWN HERE!
I WOULD LOVE THAT! BUT YOU FIRST!
CRACK
GUYS, WE STILL DON'T EVEN KNOW WHAT HAPPENED!
THERE'RE 87 CONVICTED FELONS IN THIS PRISON. WE HAVE TO GET OUT OF HERE AND CALL FOR...
...REINFORCEMENTS...

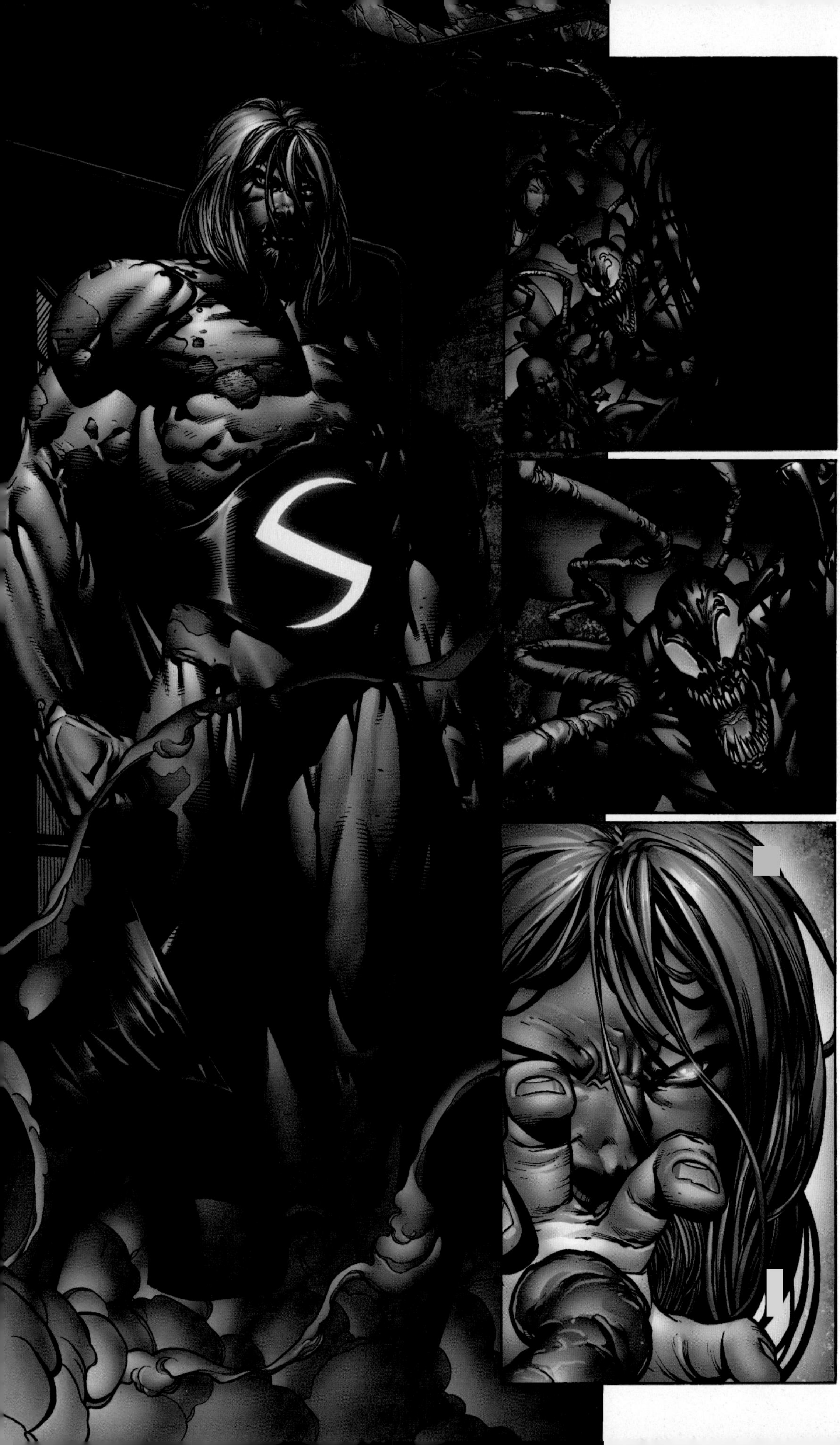

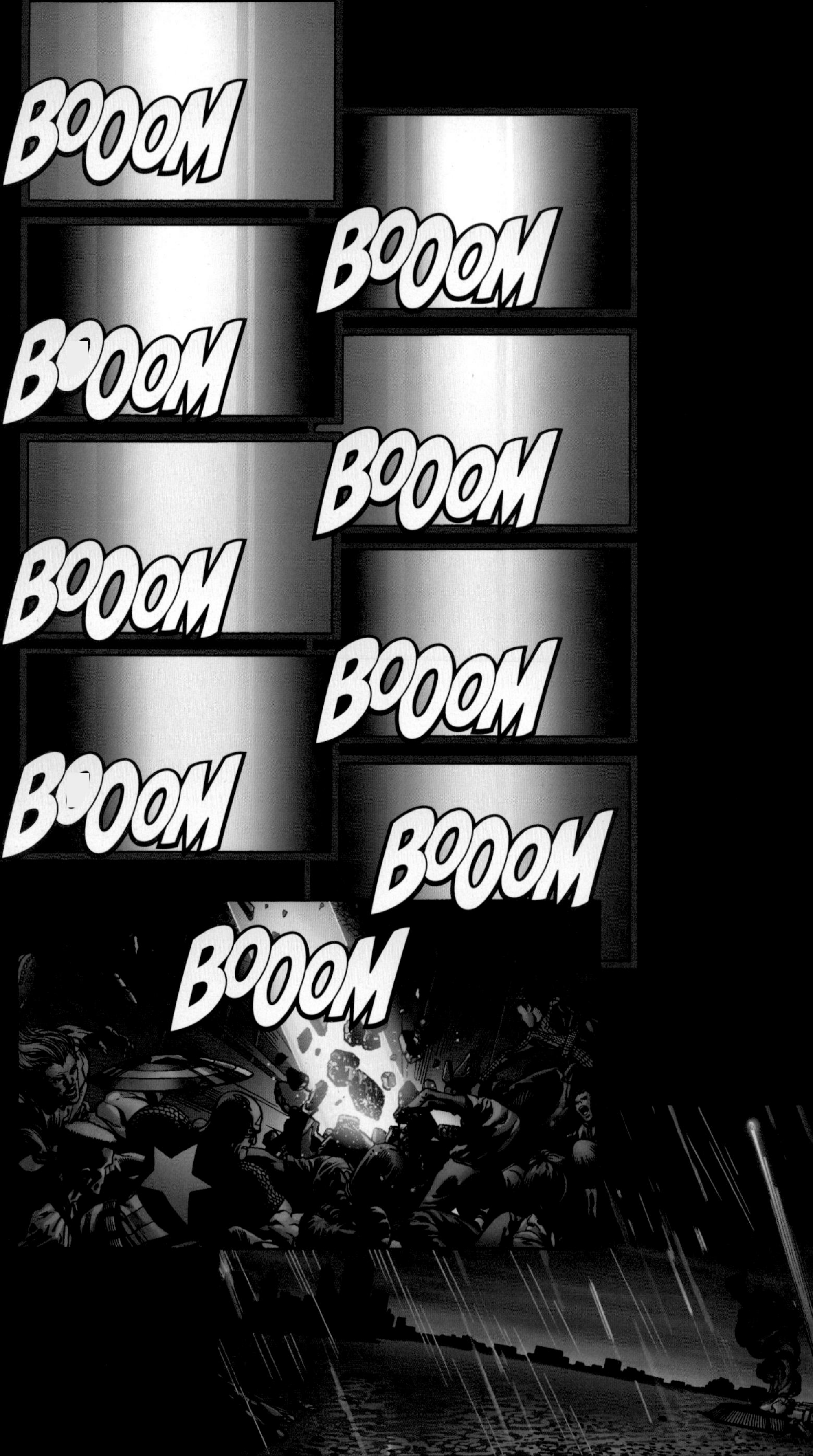

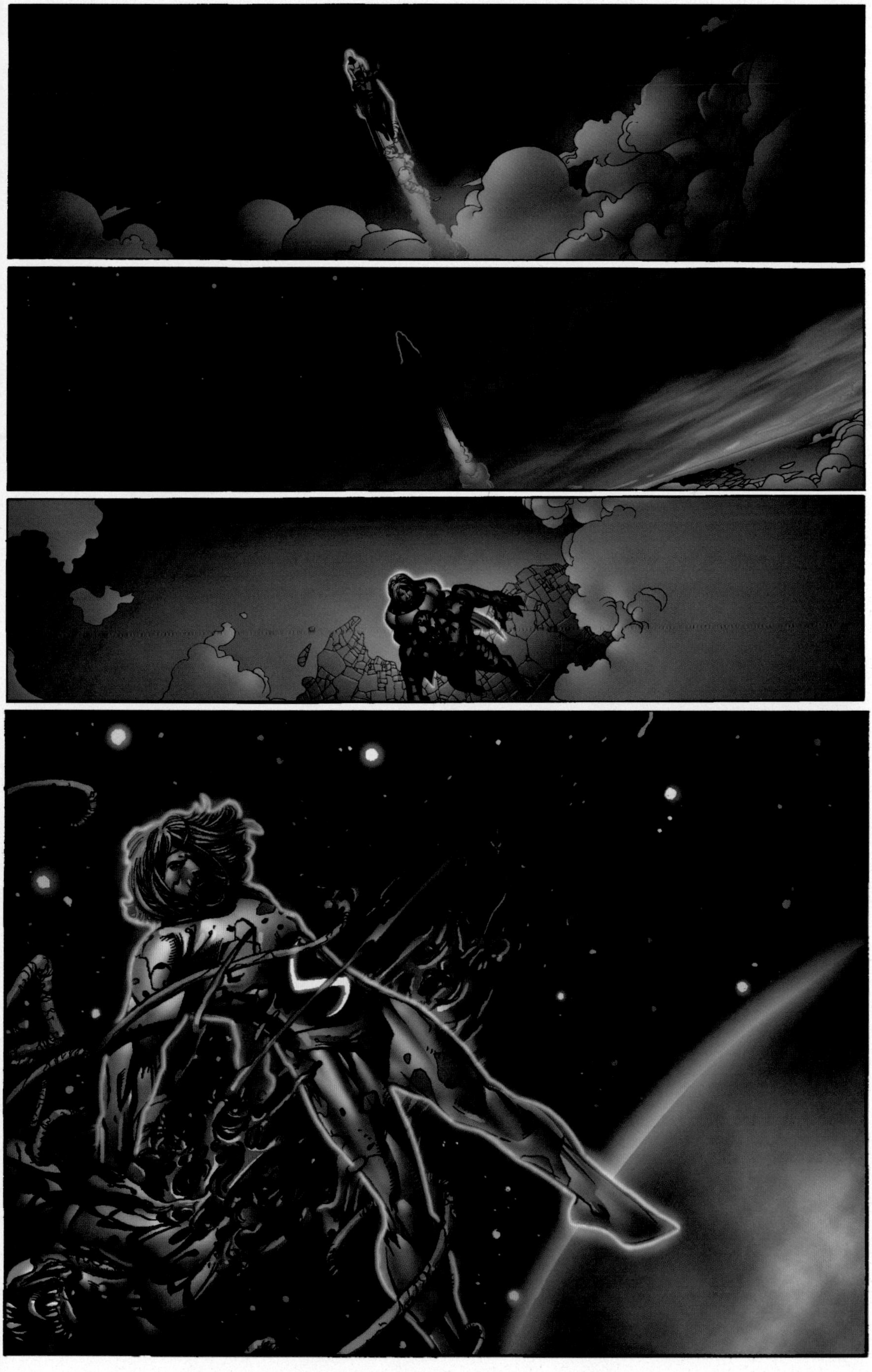

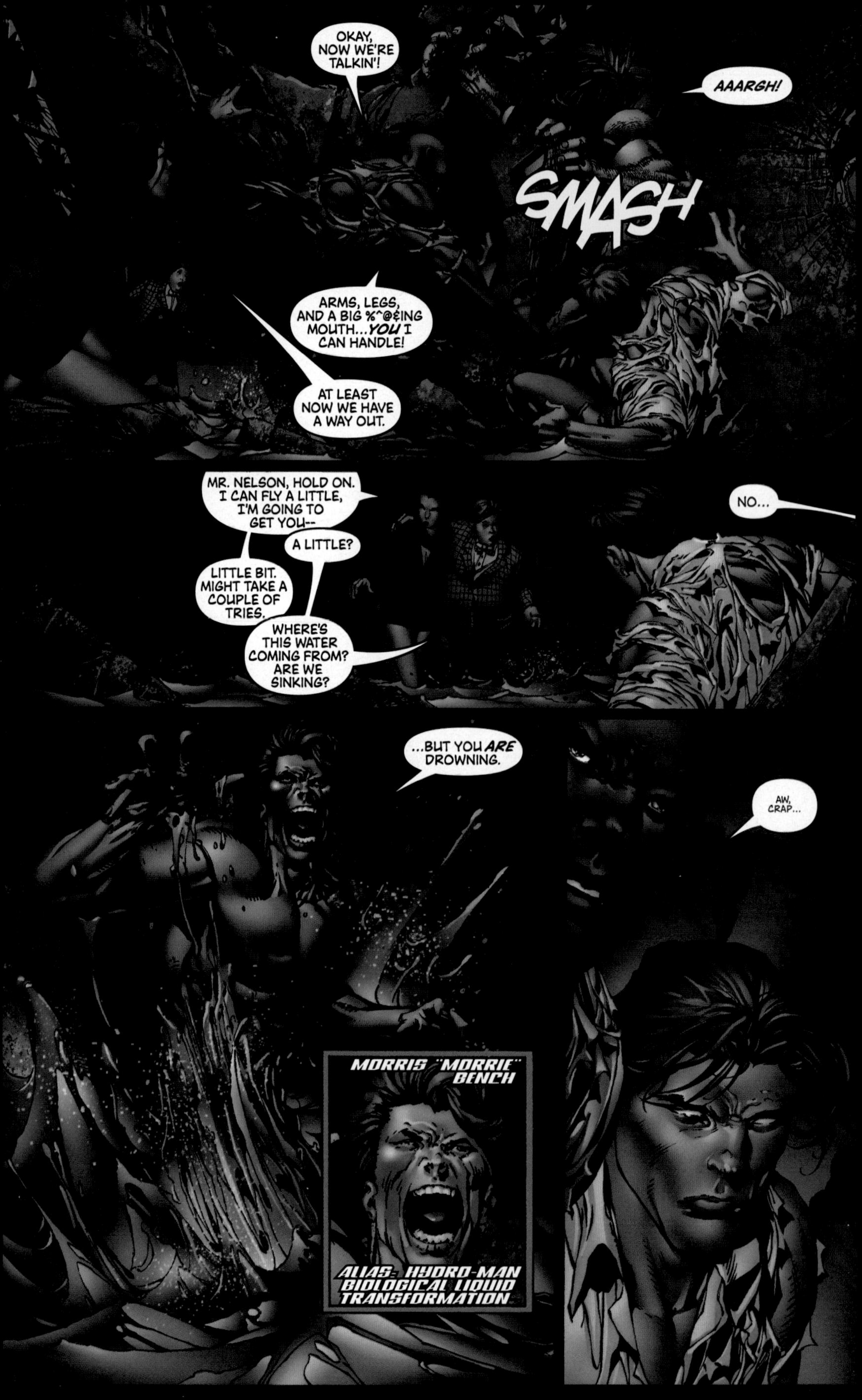
OKAY, NOW WE'RE TALKIN'!
AAARGH!
SMASH
ARMS, LEGS, AND A BIG %^@&ING MOUTH...YOU I CAN HANDLE!
AT LEAST NOW WE HAVE A WAY OUT.
MR. NELSON, HOLD ON. I CAN FLY A LITTLE, I'M GOING TO GET YOU--
A LITTLE?
LITTLE BIT. MIGHT TAKE A COUPLE OF TRIES.
WHERE'S THIS WATER COMING FROM? ARE WE SINKING?
NO...
...BUT YOU ARE DROWNING.
AW, CRAP...
MORRIS "MORRIE" BENCH
ALIAS: HYDRO-MAN
BIOLOGICAL LIQUID TRANSFORMATION

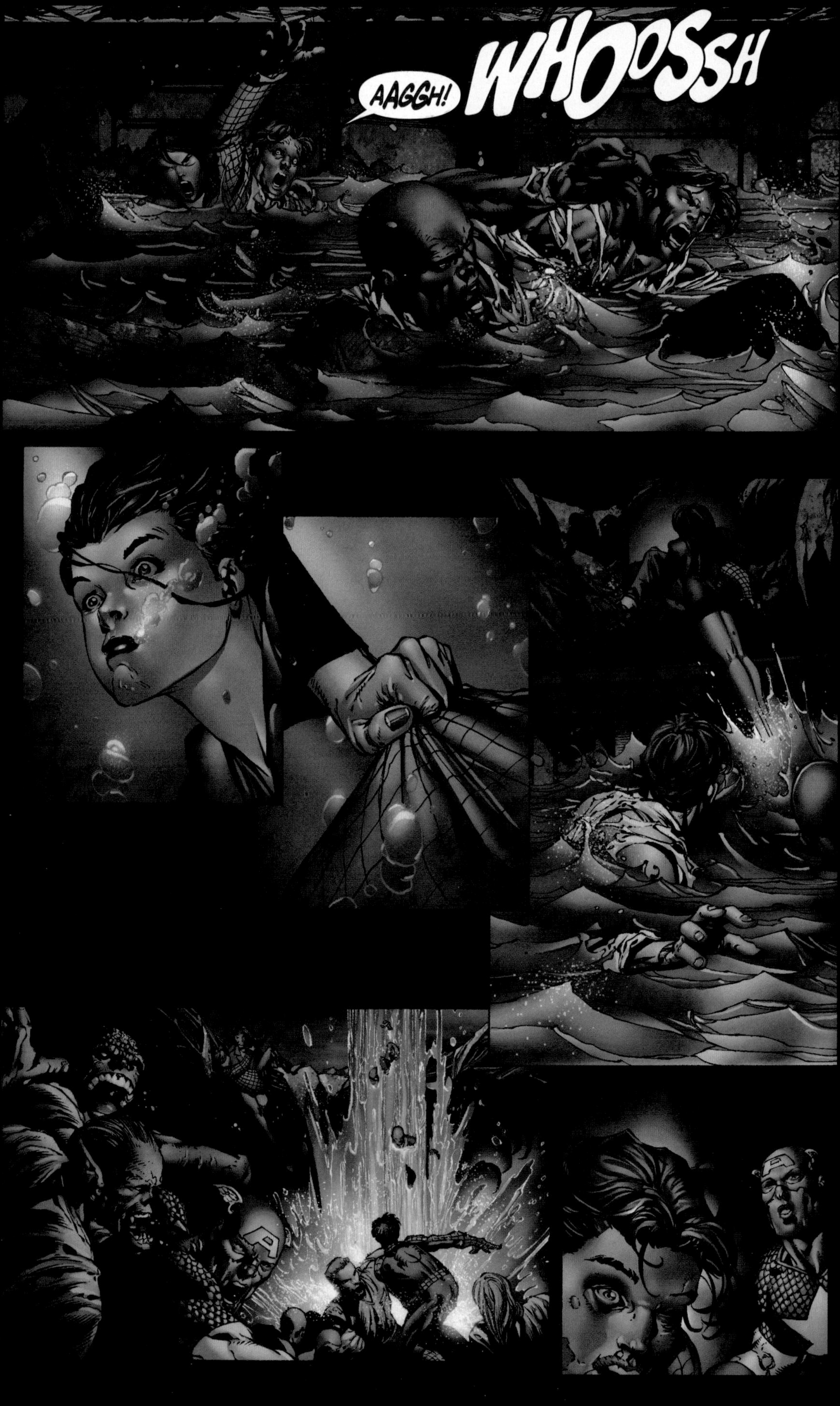
AAGGH!
WHOOSSH

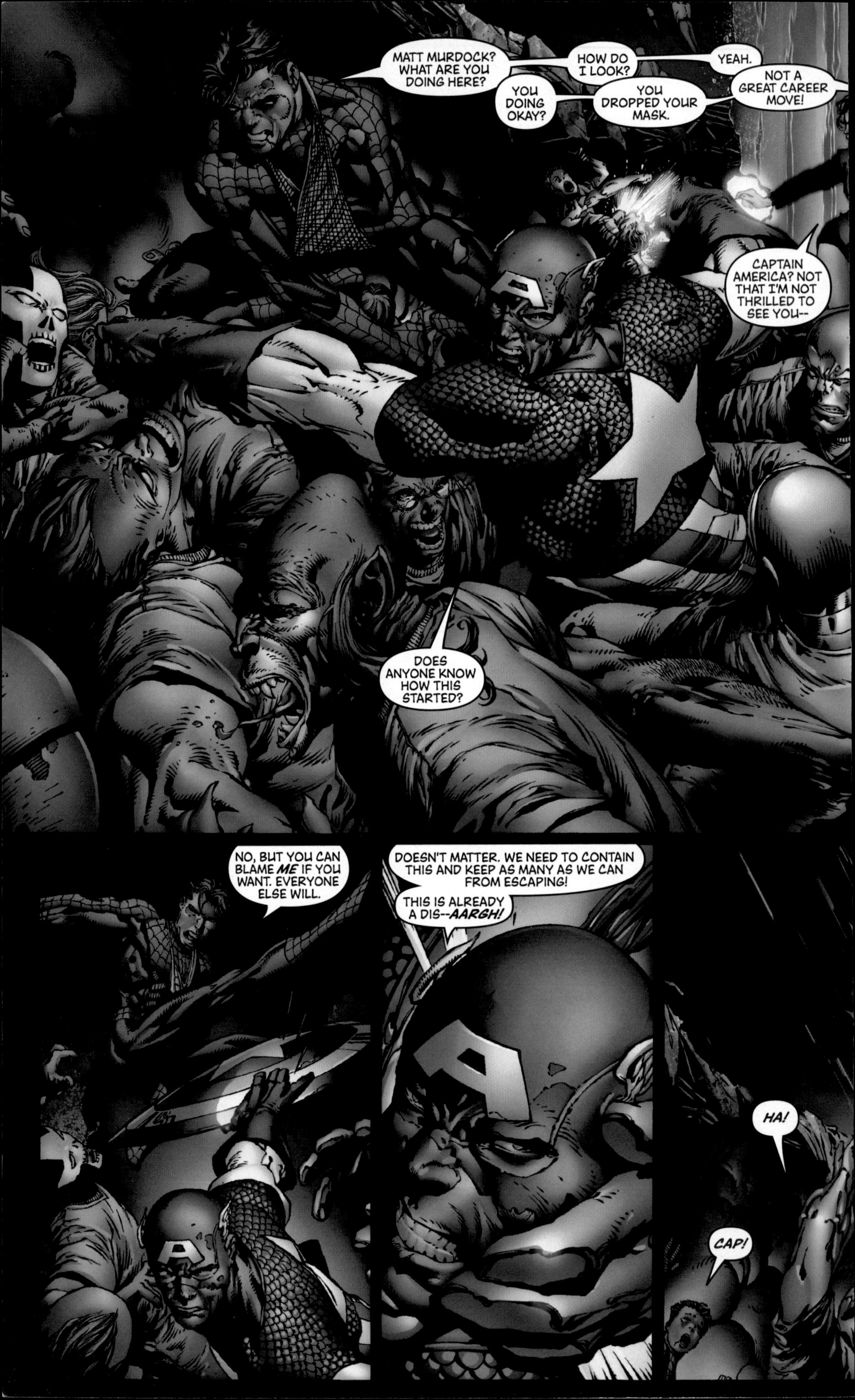
MATT MURDOCK? WHAT ARE YOU DOING HERE?
HOW DO I LOOK?
YEAH.
YOU DOING OKAY?
YOU DROPPED YOUR MASK.
NOT A GREAT CAREER MOVE!
CAPTAIN AMERICA? NOT THAT I'M NOT THRILLED TO SEE YOU--
DOES ANYONE KNOW HOW THIS STARTED?
NO, BUT YOU CAN BLAME *ME* IF YOU WANT. EVERYONE ELSE WILL.
DOESN'T MATTER. WE NEED TO CONTAIN THIS AND KEEP AS MANY AS WE CAN FROM ESCAPING!
THIS IS ALREADY A DIS--*AARGH!*
HA!
CAP!

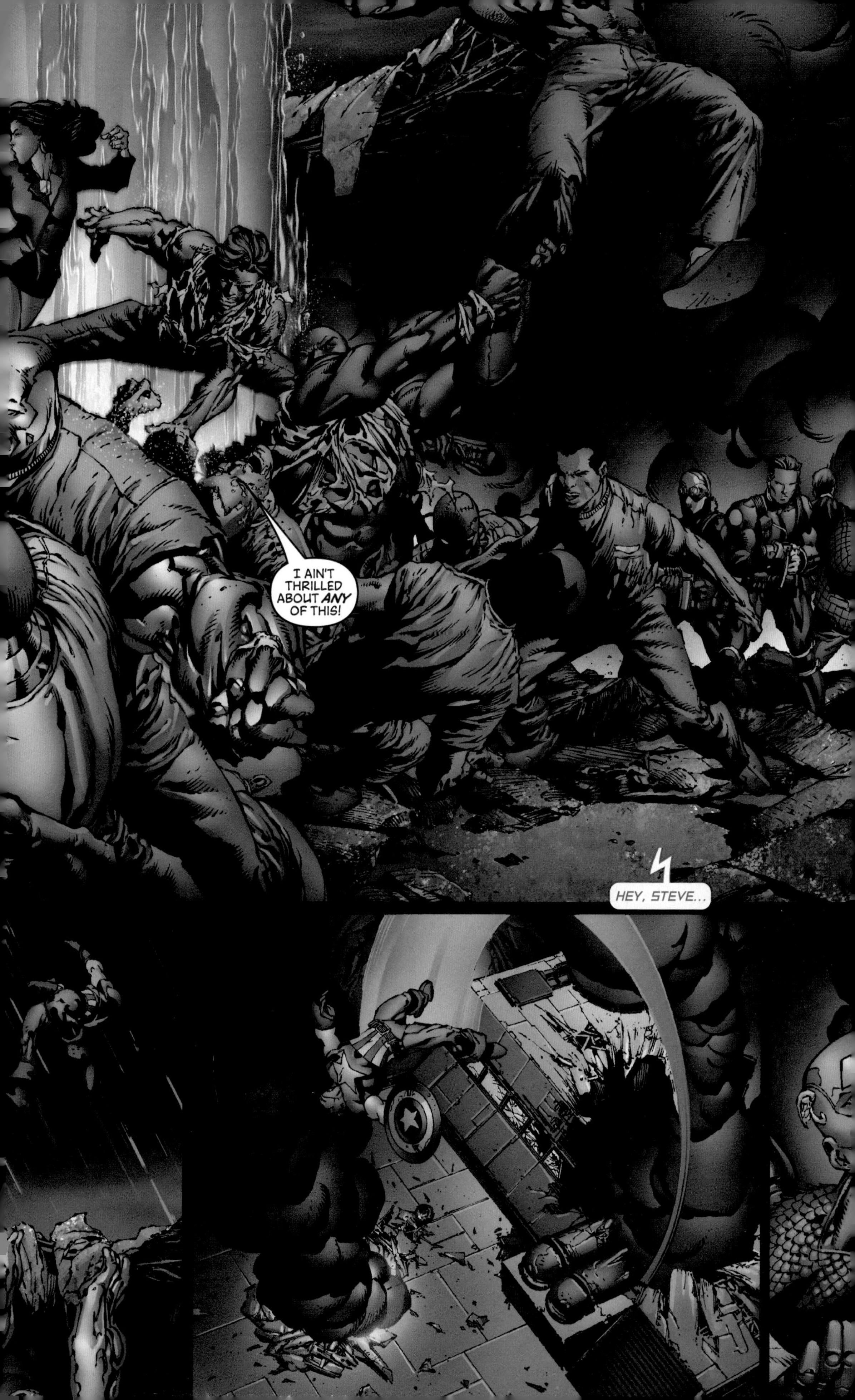
I AIN'T THRILLED ABOUT ANY OF THIS!
HEY, STEVE...

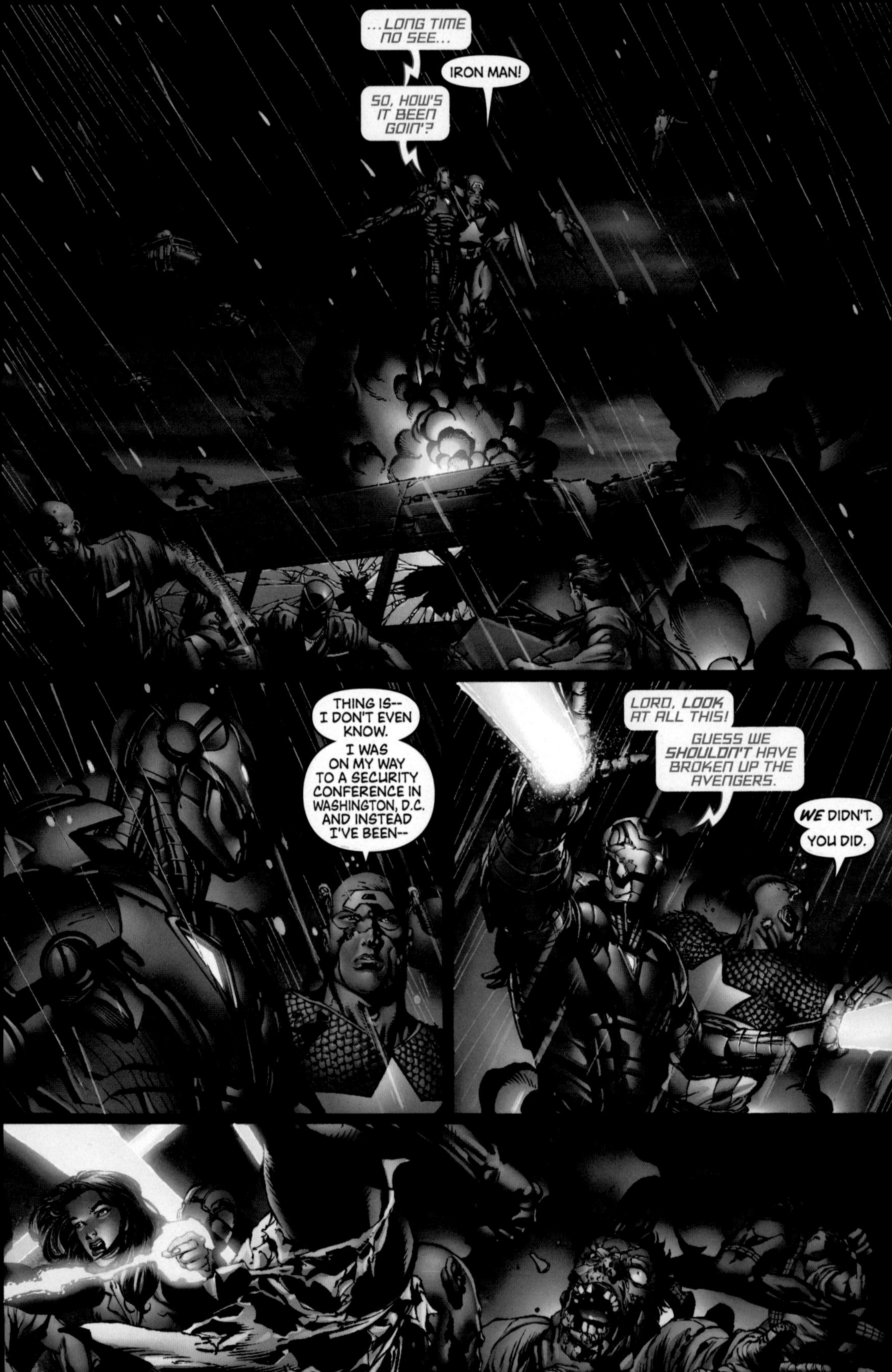
...LONG TIME NO SEE...
IRON MAN!
SO, HOW'S IT BEEN GOIN'?
THING IS-- I DON'T EVEN KNOW.
I WAS ON MY WAY TO A SECURITY CONFERENCE IN WASHINGTON, D.C. AND INSTEAD I'VE BEEN--
LORD, LOOK AT ALL THIS!
GUESS WE SHOULDN'T HAVE BROKEN UP THE AVENGERS.
WE DIDN'T.
YOU DID.
LUKE CAGE...

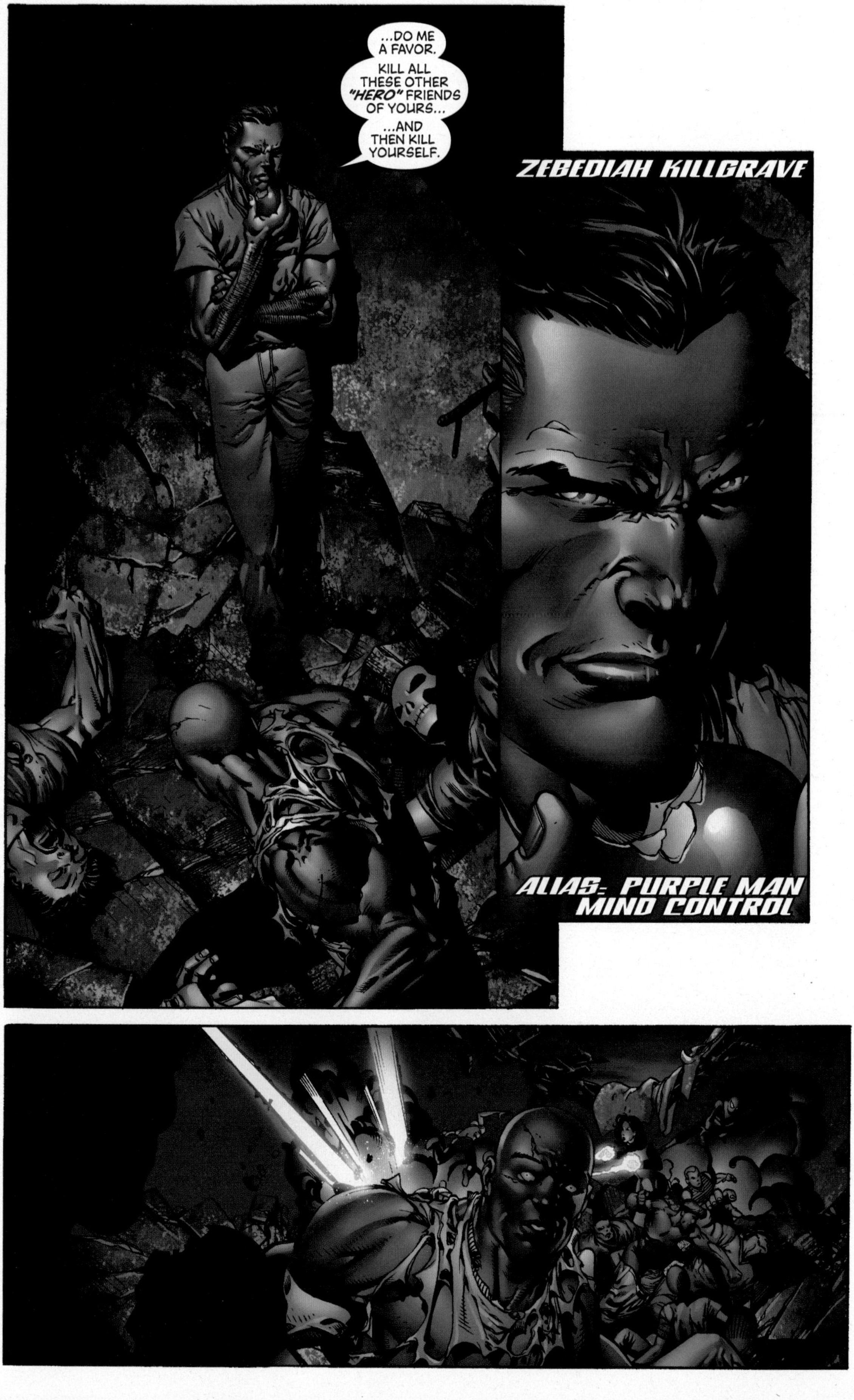
...DO ME A FAVOR.
KILL ALL THESE OTHER "HERO" FRIENDS OF YOURS...
...AND THEN KILL YOURSELF.
ZEBEDIAH KILLGRAVE
ALIAS: PURPLE MAN
MIND CONTROL

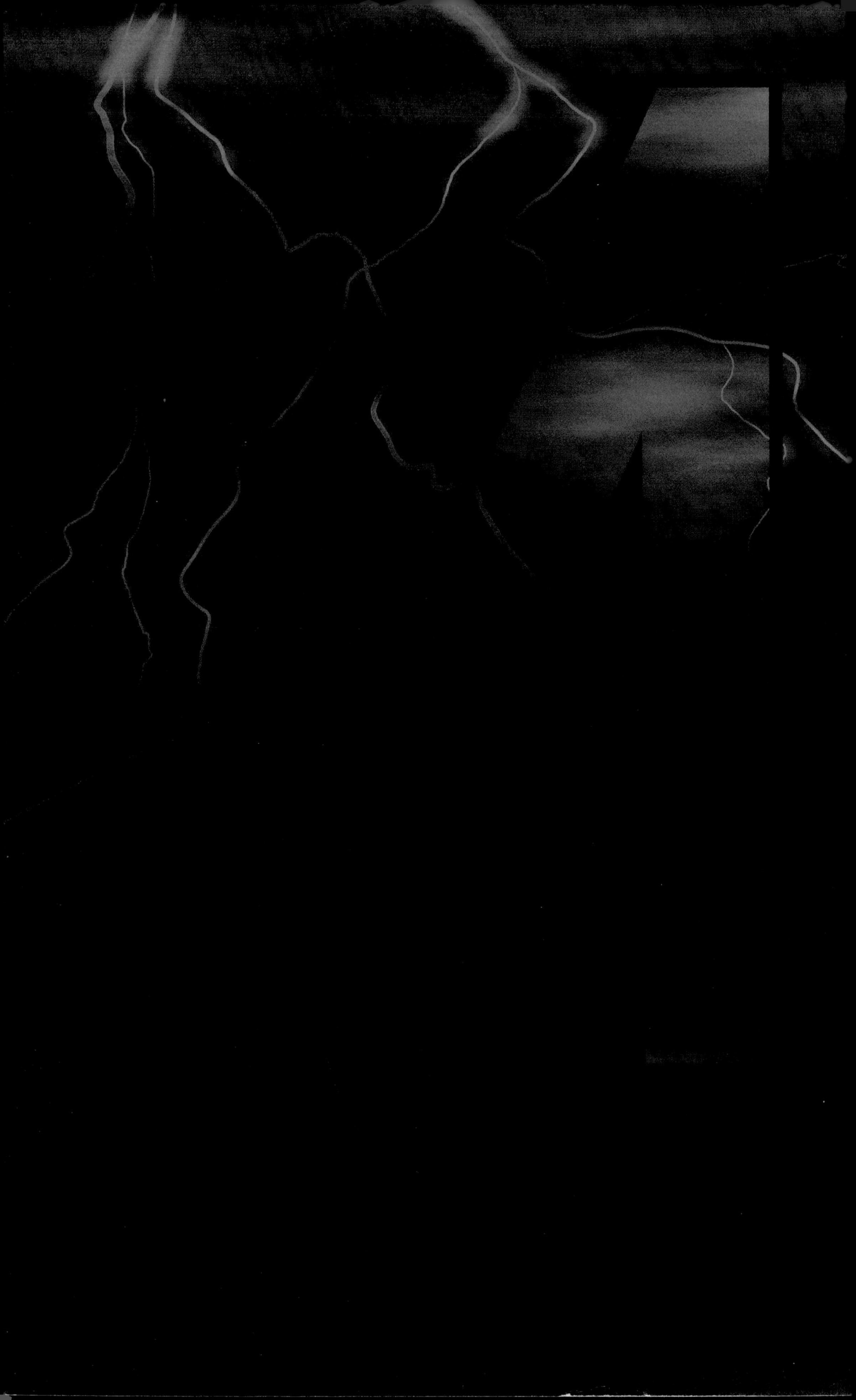

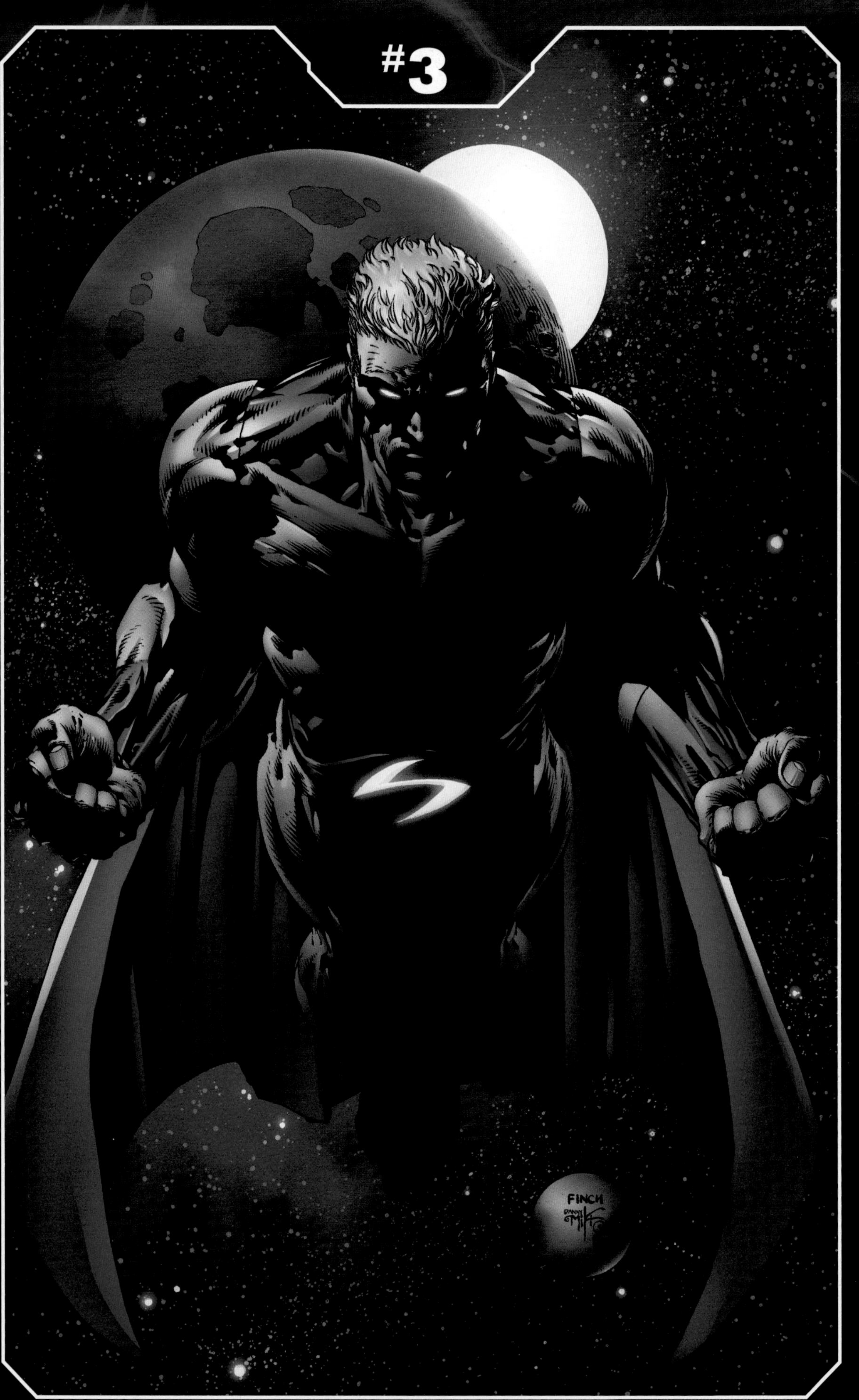
#3
FINCH

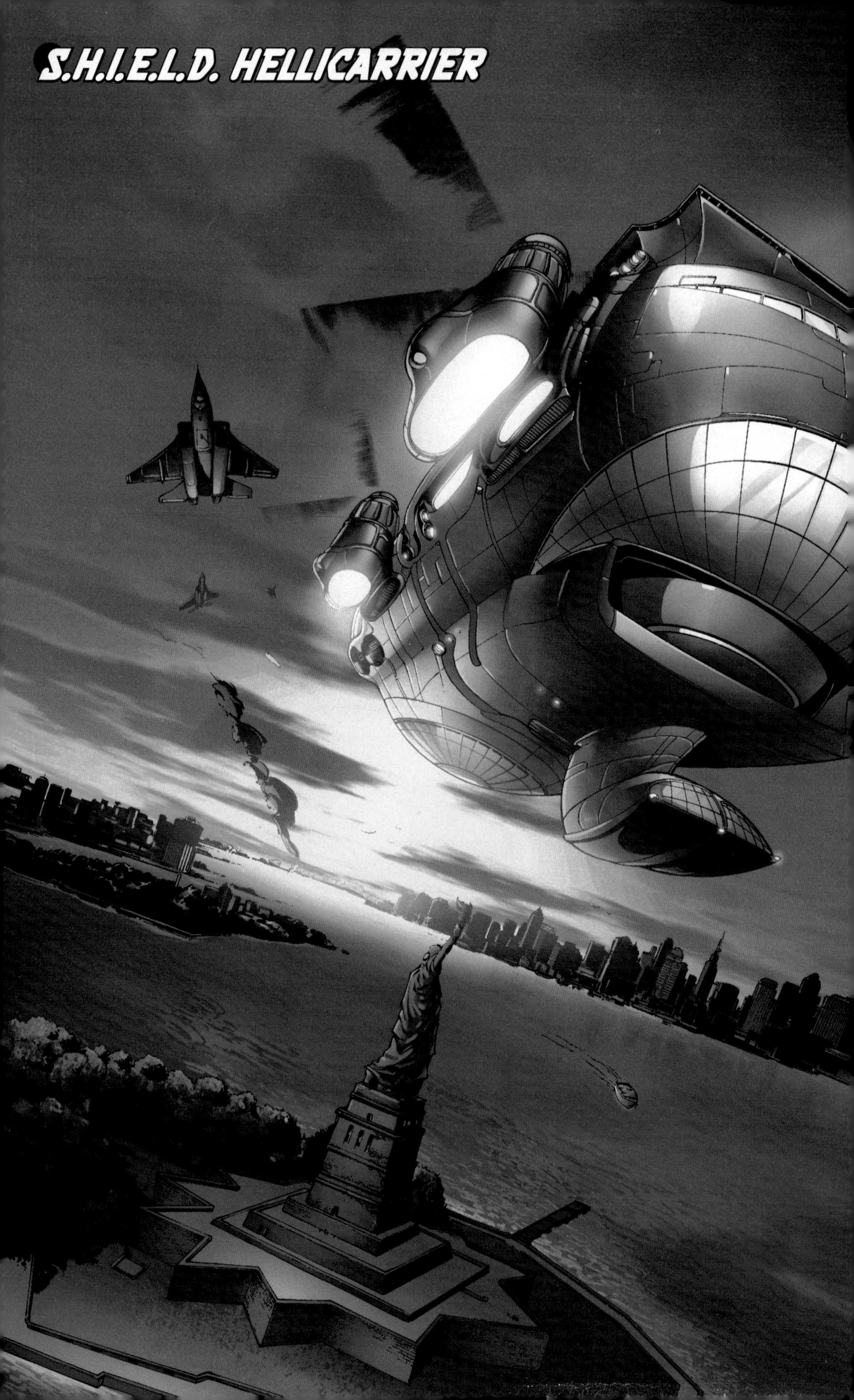
S.H.I.E.L.D. HELLICARRIER

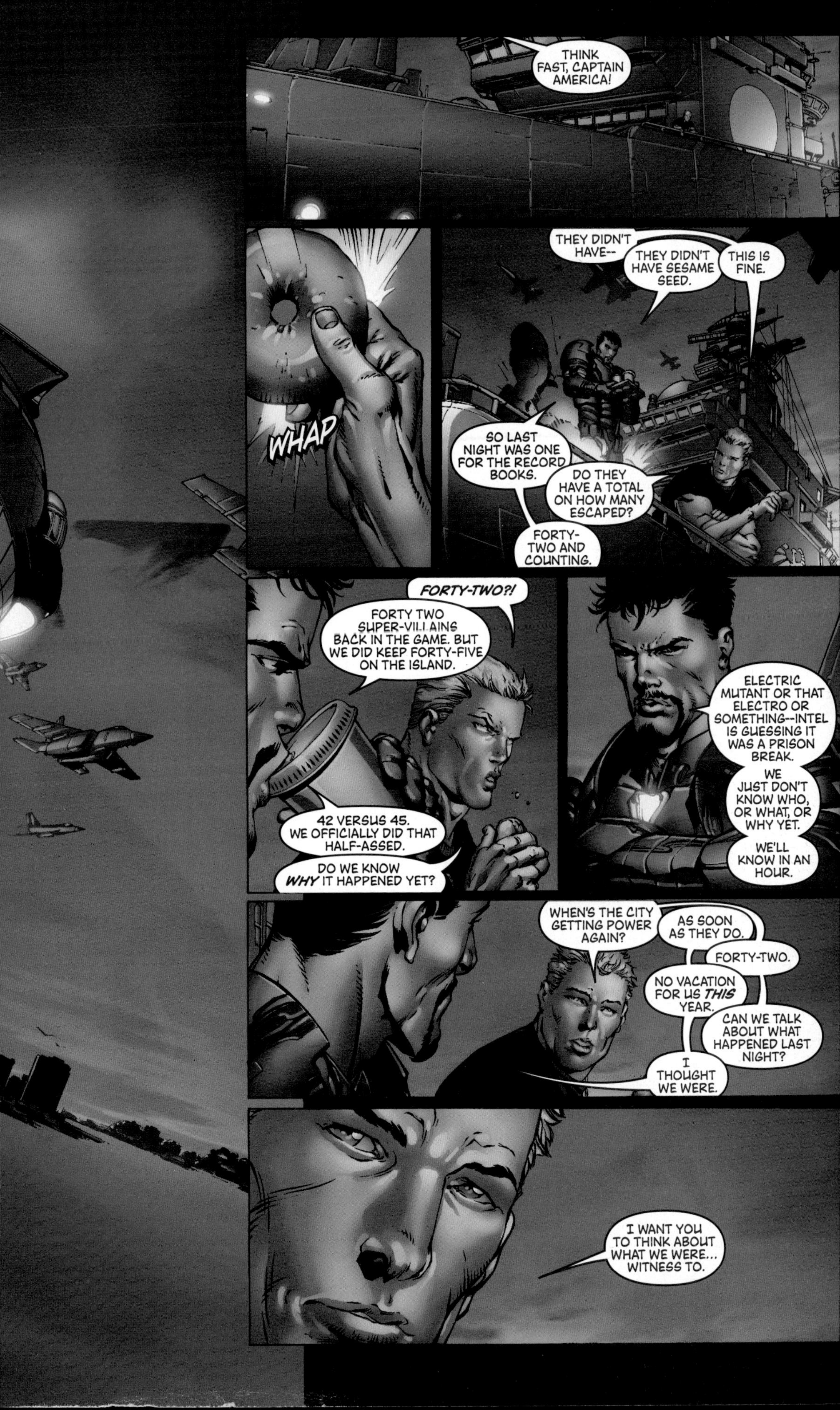

THINK FAST, CAPTAIN AMERICA!
WHAP
THEY DIDN'T HAVE--
THEY DIDN'T HAVE SESAME SEED.
THIS IS FINE.
SO LAST NIGHT WAS ONE FOR THE RECORD BOOKS.
DO THEY HAVE A TOTAL ON HOW MANY ESCAPED?
FORTY-TWO AND COUNTING.
FORTY-TWO?!
FORTY TWO SUPER-VILLAINS BACK IN THE GAME. BUT WE DID KEEP FORTY-FIVE ON THE ISLAND.
42 VERSUS 45. WE OFFICIALLY DID THAT HALF-ASSED.
DO WE KNOW WHY IT HAPPENED YET?
ELECTRIC MUTANT OR THAT ELECTRO OR SOMETHING--INTEL IS GUESSING IT WAS A PRISON BREAK.
WE JUST DON'T KNOW WHO, OR WHAT, OR WHY YET.
WE'LL KNOW IN AN HOUR.
WHEN'S THE CITY GETTING POWER AGAIN?
AS SOON AS THEY DO.
FORTY-TWO.
NO VACATION FOR US THIS YEAR.
CAN WE TALK ABOUT WHAT HAPPENED LAST NIGHT?
I THOUGHT WE WERE.
I WANT YOU TO THINK ABOUT WHAT WE WERE... WITNESS TO.

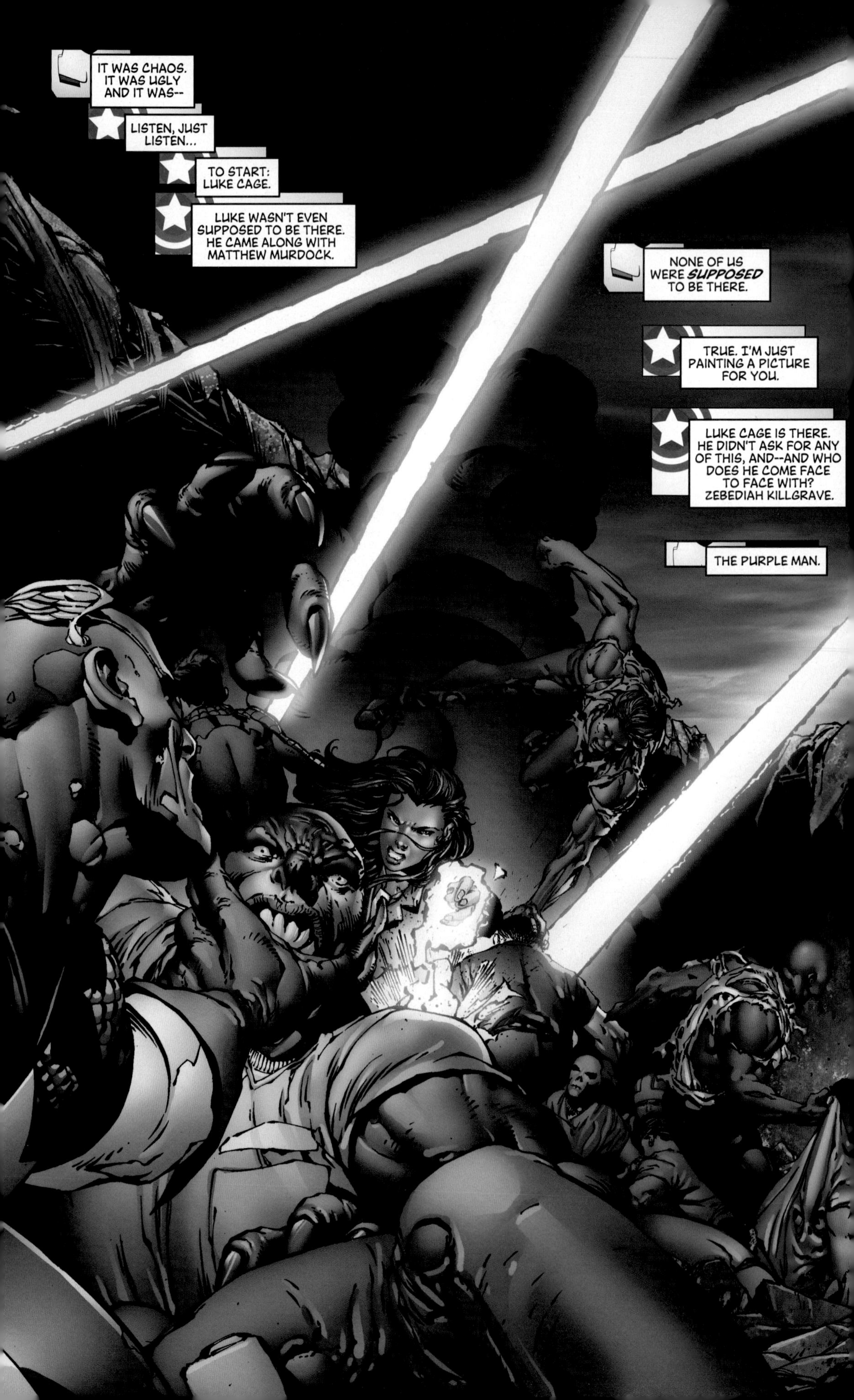
IT WAS CHAOS. IT WAS UGLY AND IT WAS--
LISTEN, JUST LISTEN...
TO START: LUKE CAGE.
LUKE WASN'T EVEN SUPPOSED TO BE THERE. HE CAME ALONG WITH MATTHEW MURDOCK.
NONE OF US WERE *SUPPOSED* TO BE THERE.
TRUE. I'M JUST PAINTING A PICTURE FOR YOU.
LUKE CAGE IS THERE. HE DIDN'T ASK FOR ANY OF THIS, AND--AND WHO DOES HE COME FACE TO FACE WITH? ZEBEDIAH KILLGRAVE.
THE PURPLE MAN.

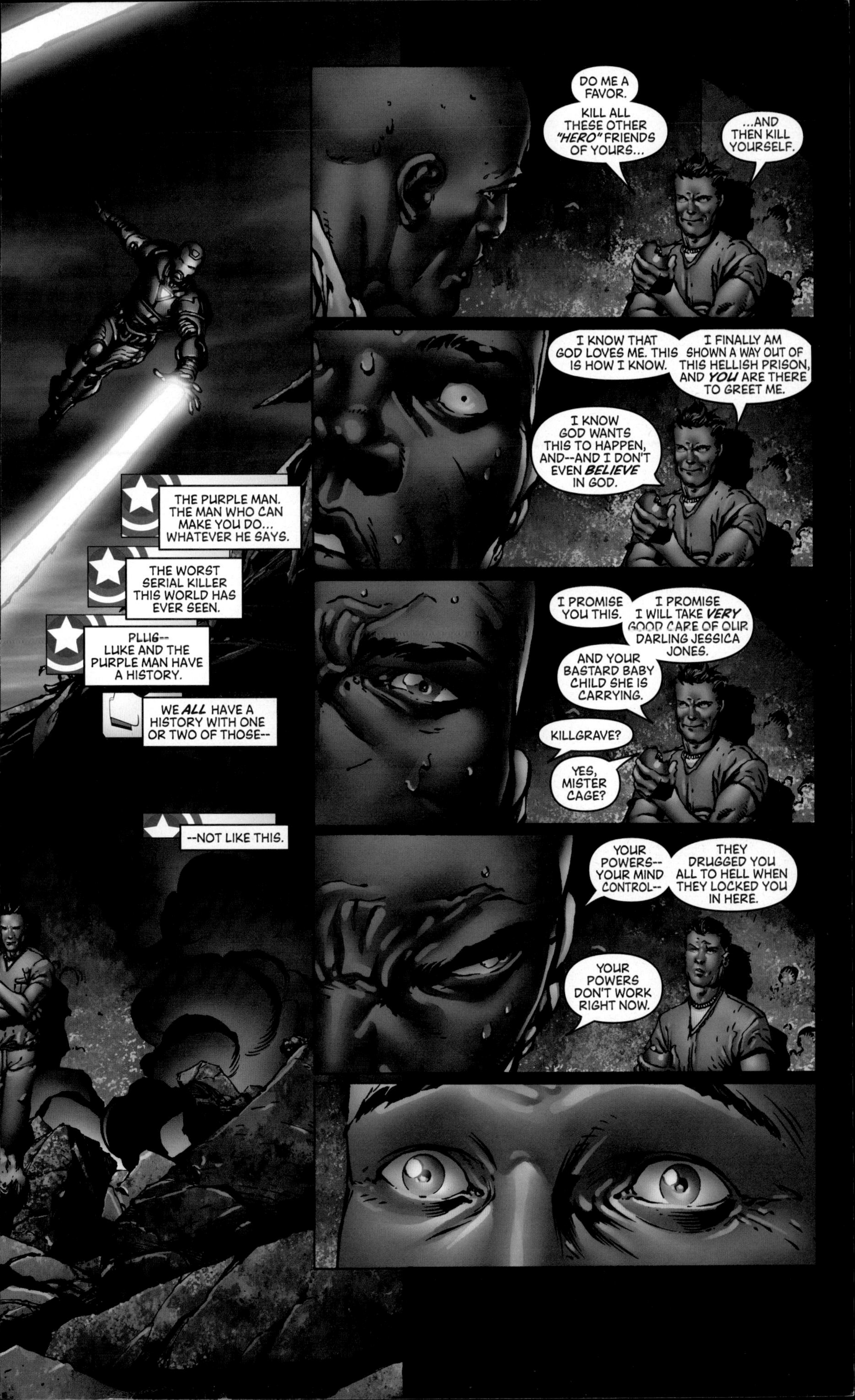
DO ME A FAVOR.
KILL ALL THESE OTHER "HERO" FRIENDS OF YOURS...
...AND THEN KILL YOURSELF.
I KNOW THAT GOD LOVES ME. THIS IS HOW I KNOW.
I FINALLY AM SHOWN A WAY OUT OF THIS HELLISH PRISON, AND YOU ARE THERE TO GREET ME.
I KNOW GOD WANTS THIS TO HAPPEN, AND--AND I DON'T EVEN BELIEVE IN GOD.
THE PURPLE MAN. THE MAN WHO CAN MAKE YOU DO... WHATEVER HE SAYS.
THE WORST SERIAL KILLER THIS WORLD HAS EVER SEEN.
PLUG-- LUKE AND THE PURPLE MAN HAVE A HISTORY.
WE ALL HAVE A HISTORY WITH ONE OR TWO OF THOSE--
I PROMISE YOU THIS.
I PROMISE I WILL TAKE VERY GOOD CARE OF OUR DARLING JESSICA JONES.
AND YOUR BASTARD BABY CHILD SHE IS CARRYING.
KILLGRAVE?
YES, MISTER CAGE?
--NOT LIKE THIS.
YOUR POWERS-- YOUR MIND CONTROL--
THEY DRUGGED YOU ALL TO HELL WHEN THEY LOCKED YOU IN HERE.
YOUR POWERS DON'T WORK RIGHT NOW.

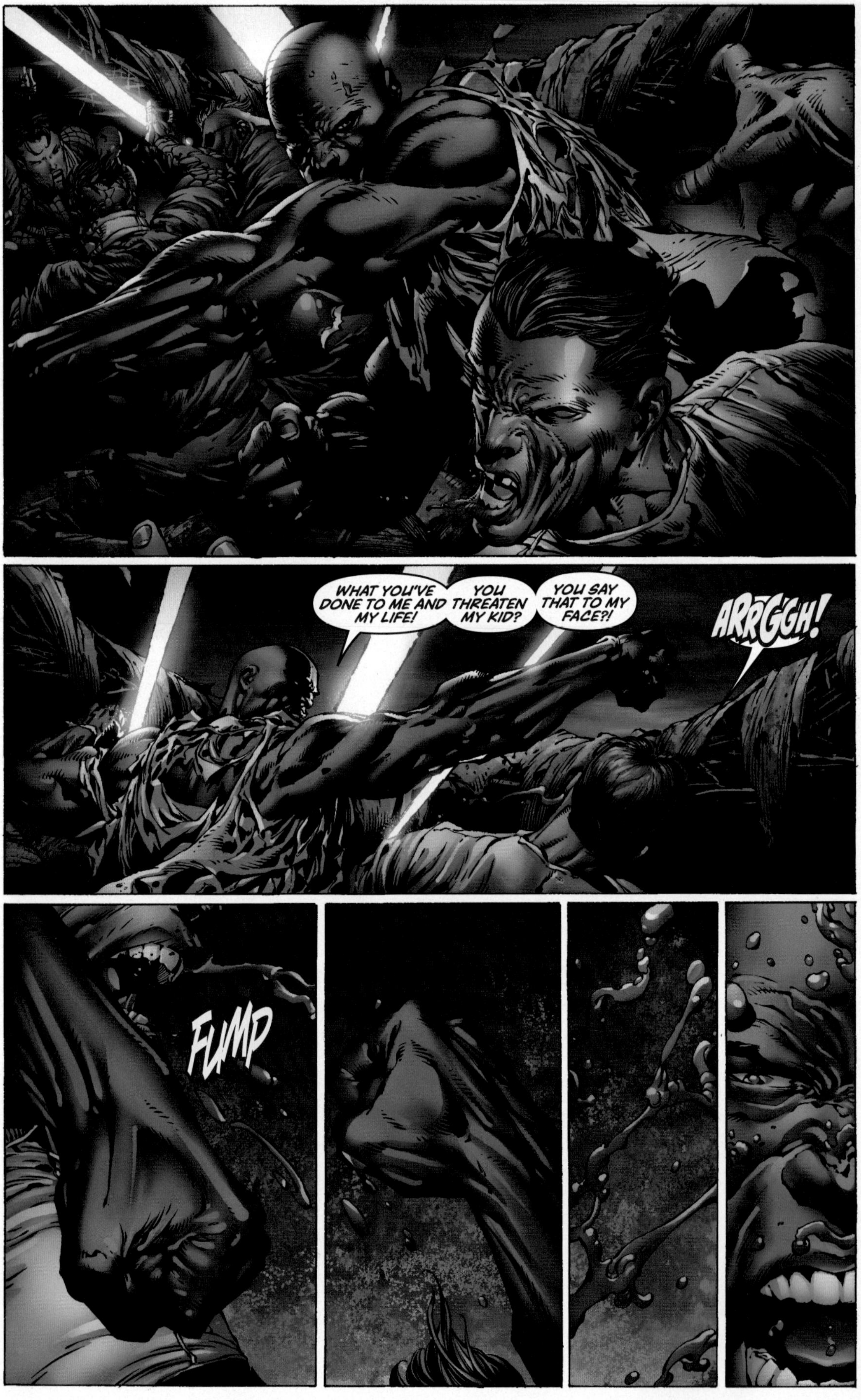
WHAT YOU'VE DONE TO ME AND MY LIFE!
YOU THREATEN MY KID?
YOU SAY THAT TO MY FACE?!
ARRGGH!
FUMP

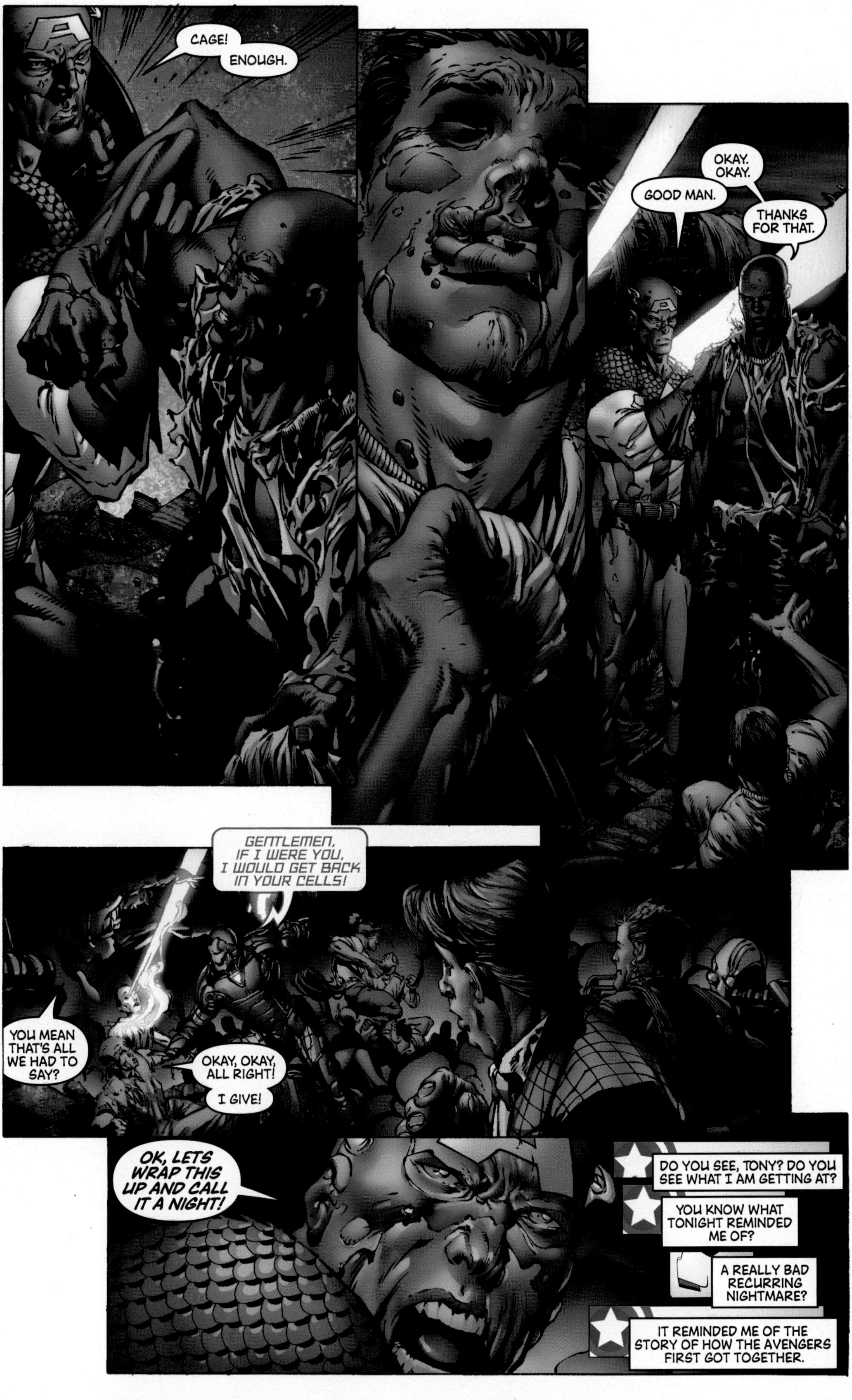
CAGE!
ENOUGH.
OKAY. OKAY.
GOOD MAN.
THANKS FOR THAT.
GENTLEMEN, IF I WERE YOU, I WOULD GET BACK IN YOUR CELLS!
YOU MEAN THAT'S ALL WE HAD TO SAY?
OKAY, OKAY, ALL RIGHT!
I GIVE!
OK, LETS WRAP THIS UP AND CALL IT A NIGHT!
DO YOU SEE, TONY? DO YOU SEE WHAT I AM GETTING AT?
YOU KNOW WHAT TONIGHT REMINDED ME OF?
A REALLY BAD RECURRING NIGHTMARE?
IT REMINDED ME OF THE STORY OF HOW THE AVENGERS FIRST GOT TOGETHER.

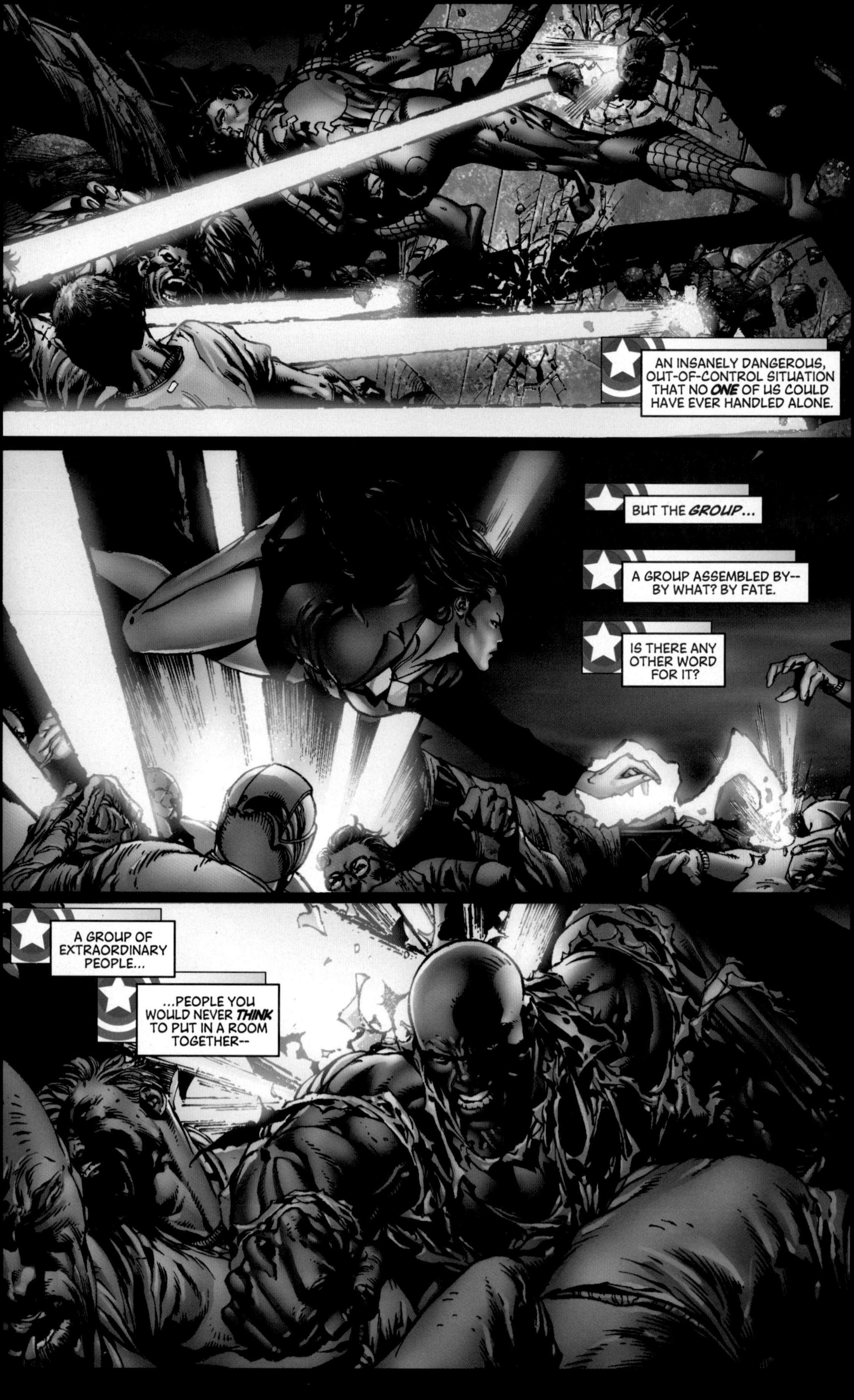
AN INSANELY DANGEROUS, OUT-OF-CONTROL SITUATION THAT NO ONE OF US COULD HAVE EVER HANDLED ALONE.
BUT THE GROUP...
A GROUP ASSEMBLED BY-- BY WHAT? BY FATE.
IS THERE ANY OTHER WORD FOR IT?
A GROUP OF EXTRAORDINARY PEOPLE...
...PEOPLE YOU WOULD NEVER THINK TO PUT IN A ROOM TOGETHER--

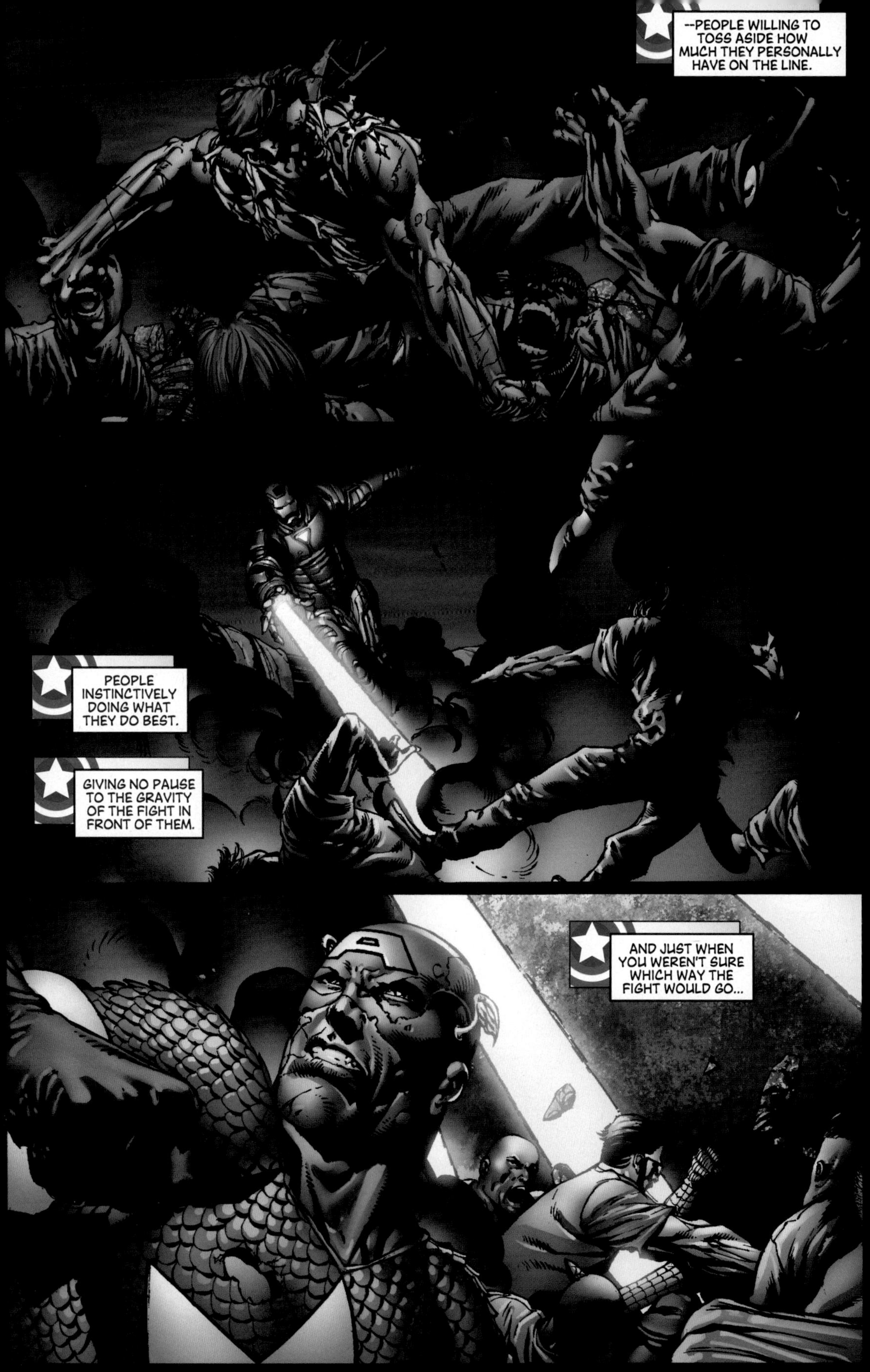
--PEOPLE WILLING TO TOSS ASIDE HOW MUCH THEY PERSONALLY HAVE ON THE LINE.
PEOPLE INSTINCTIVELY DOING WHAT THEY DO BEST.
GIVING NO PAUSE TO THE GRAVITY OF THE FIGHT IN FRONT OF THEM.
AND JUST WHEN YOU WEREN'T SURE WHICH WAY THE FIGHT WOULD GO...

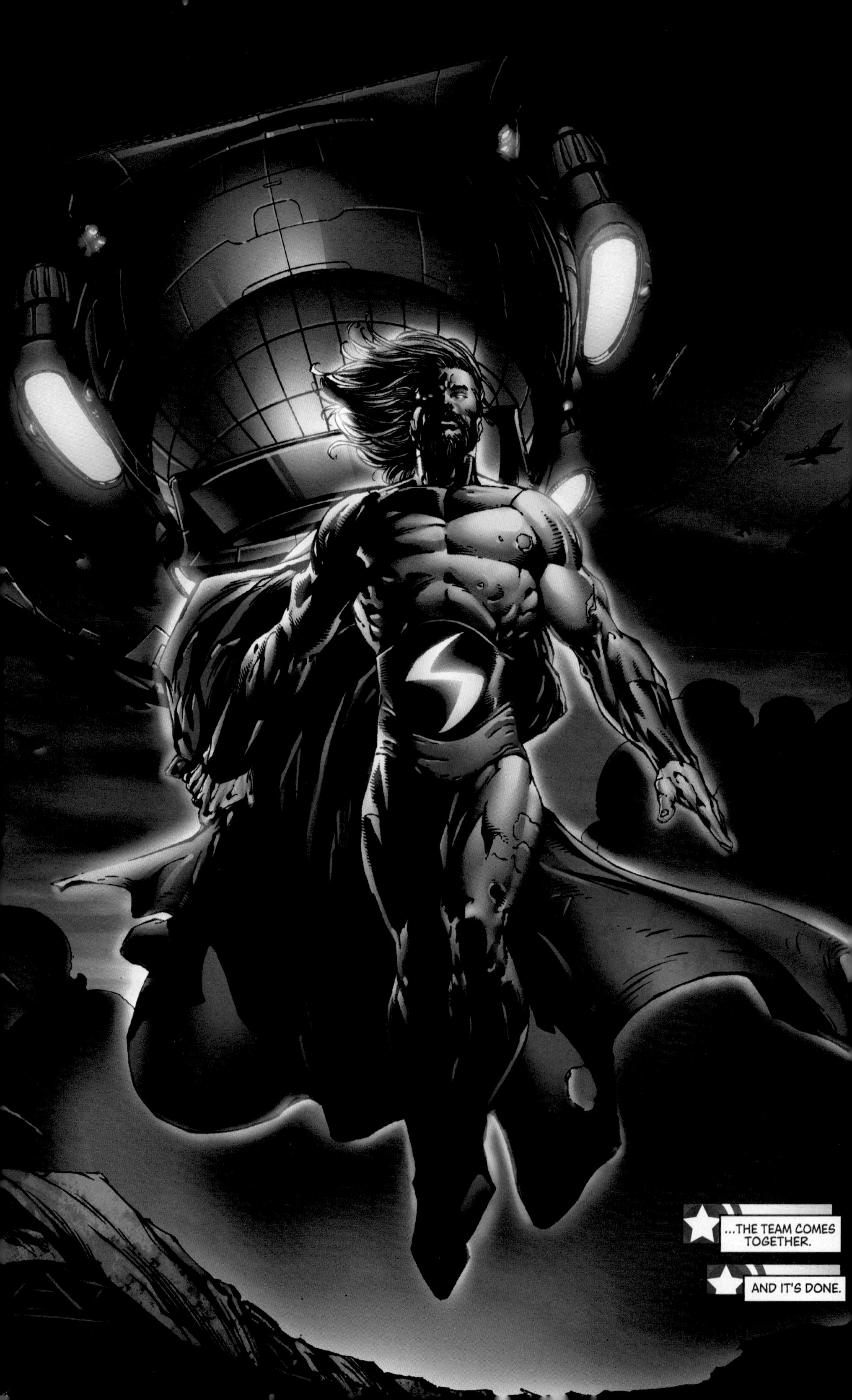
...THE TEAM COMES TOGETHER.
AND IT'S DONE.

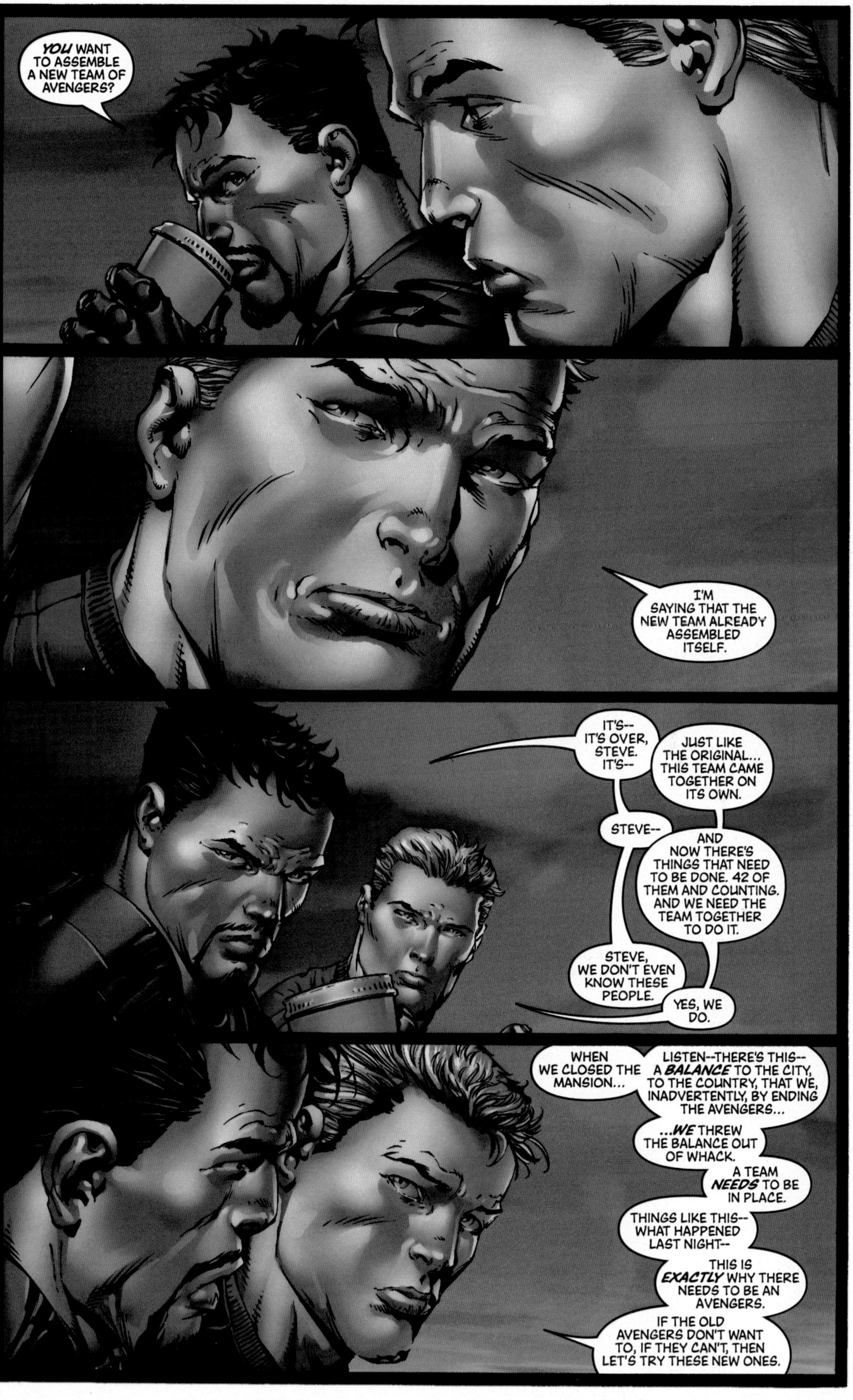
YOU WANT TO ASSEMBLE A NEW TEAM OF AVENGERS?
I'M SAYING THAT THE NEW TEAM ALREADY ASSEMBLED ITSELF.
IT'S-- IT'S OVER, STEVE. IT'S--
JUST LIKE THE ORIGINAL... THIS TEAM CAME TOGETHER ON ITS OWN.
STEVE--
AND NOW THERE'S THINGS THAT NEED TO BE DONE. 42 OF THEM AND COUNTING. AND WE NEED THE TEAM TOGETHER TO DO IT.
STEVE, WE DON'T EVEN KNOW THESE PEOPLE.
YES, WE DO.
WHEN WE CLOSED THE MANSION...
LISTEN--THERE'S THIS-- A BALANCE TO THE CITY, TO THE COUNTRY, THAT WE, INADVERTENTLY, BY ENDING THE AVENGERS...
...WE THREW THE BALANCE OUT OF WHACK.
A TEAM NEEDS TO BE IN PLACE.
THINGS LIKE THIS-- WHAT HAPPENED LAST NIGHT--
THIS IS EXACTLY WHY THERE NEEDS TO BE AN AVENGERS.
IF THE OLD AVENGERS DON'T WANT TO, IF THEY CAN'T, THEN LET'S TRY THESE NEW ONES.

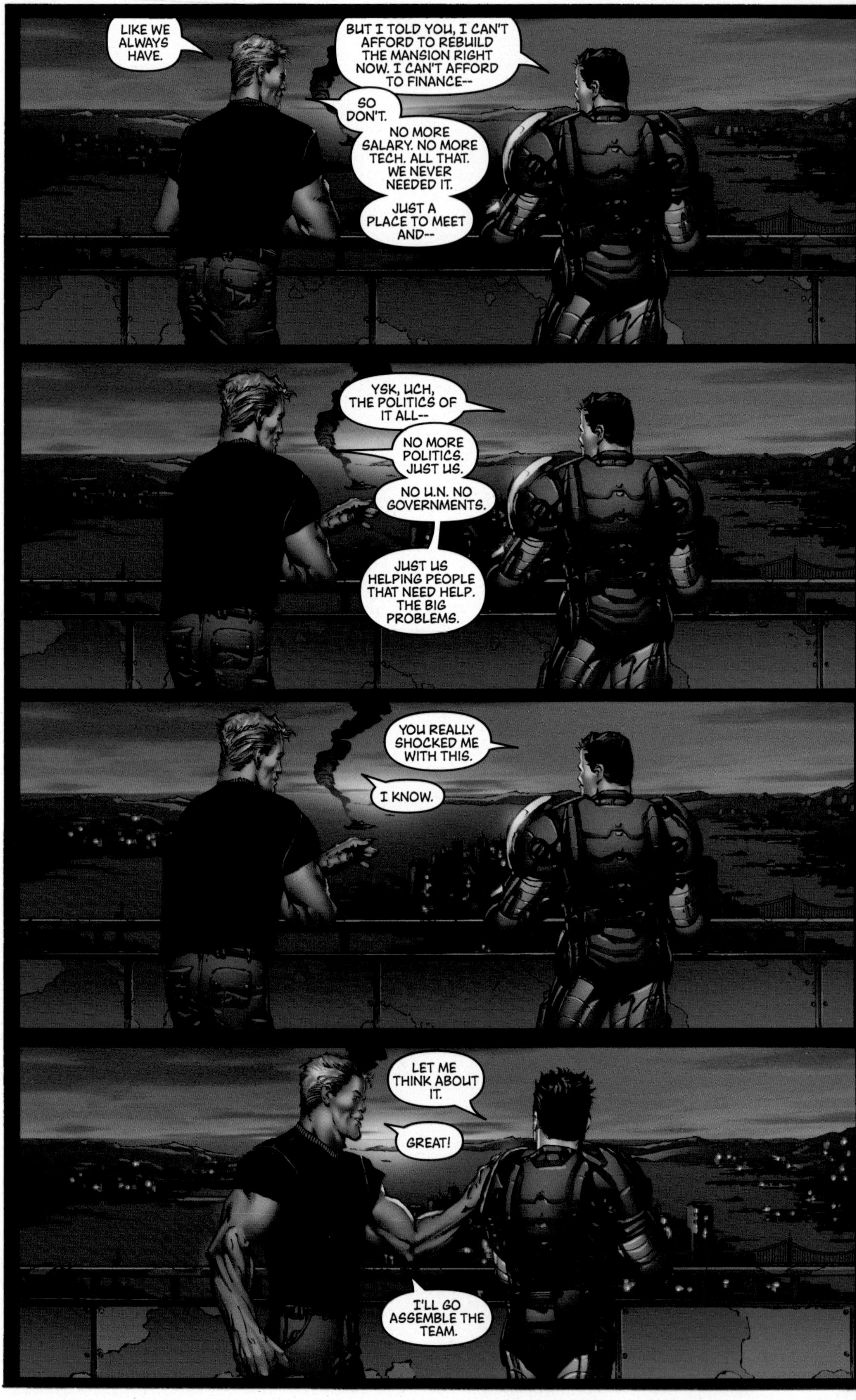
LIKE WE ALWAYS HAVE.
BUT I TOLD YOU, I CAN'T AFFORD TO REBUILD THE MANSION RIGHT NOW. I CAN'T AFFORD TO FINANCE--
SO DON'T.
NO MORE SALARY. NO MORE TECH. ALL THAT. WE NEVER NEEDED IT.
JUST A PLACE TO MEET AND--
YSK, UCH, THE POLITICS OF IT ALL--
NO MORE POLITICS. JUST US.
NO U.N. NO GOVERNMENTS.
JUST US HELPING PEOPLE THAT NEED HELP. THE BIG PROBLEMS.
YOU REALLY SHOCKED ME WITH THIS.
I KNOW.
LET ME THINK ABOUT IT.
GREAT!
I'LL GO ASSEMBLE THE TEAM.

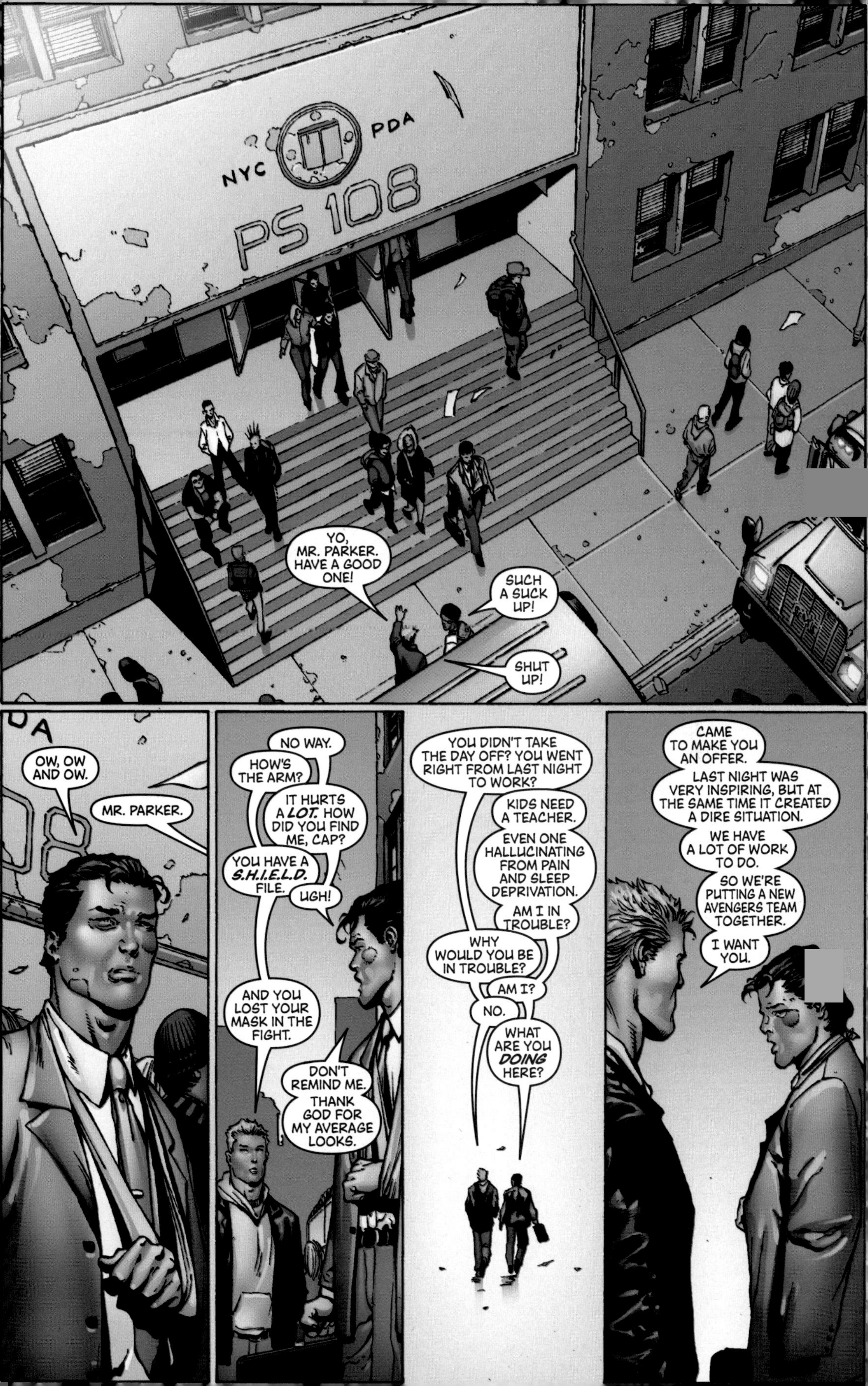
NYC
PDA
PS 108
YO, MR. PARKER. HAVE A GOOD ONE!
SUCH A SUCK UP!
SHUT UP!
OW, OW AND OW.
MR. PARKER.
NO WAY.
HOW'S THE ARM?
IT HURTS A ***LOT.*** HOW DID YOU FIND ME, CAP?
YOU HAVE A ***S.H.I.E.L.D.*** FILE.
UGH!
AND YOU LOST YOUR MASK IN THE FIGHT.
DON'T REMIND ME.
THANK GOD FOR MY AVERAGE LOOKS.
YOU DIDN'T TAKE THE DAY OFF? YOU WENT RIGHT FROM LAST NIGHT TO WORK?
KIDS NEED A TEACHER.
EVEN ONE HALLUCINATING FROM PAIN AND SLEEP DEPRIVATION.
AM I IN TROUBLE?
WHY WOULD YOU BE IN TROUBLE?
AM I?
NO.
WHAT ARE YOU ***DOING*** HERE?
CAME TO MAKE YOU AN OFFER.
LAST NIGHT WAS VERY INSPIRING, BUT AT THE SAME TIME IT CREATED A DIRE SITUATION.
WE HAVE A LOT OF WORK TO DO.
SO WE'RE PUTTING A NEW AVENGERS TEAM TOGETHER.
I WANT YOU.

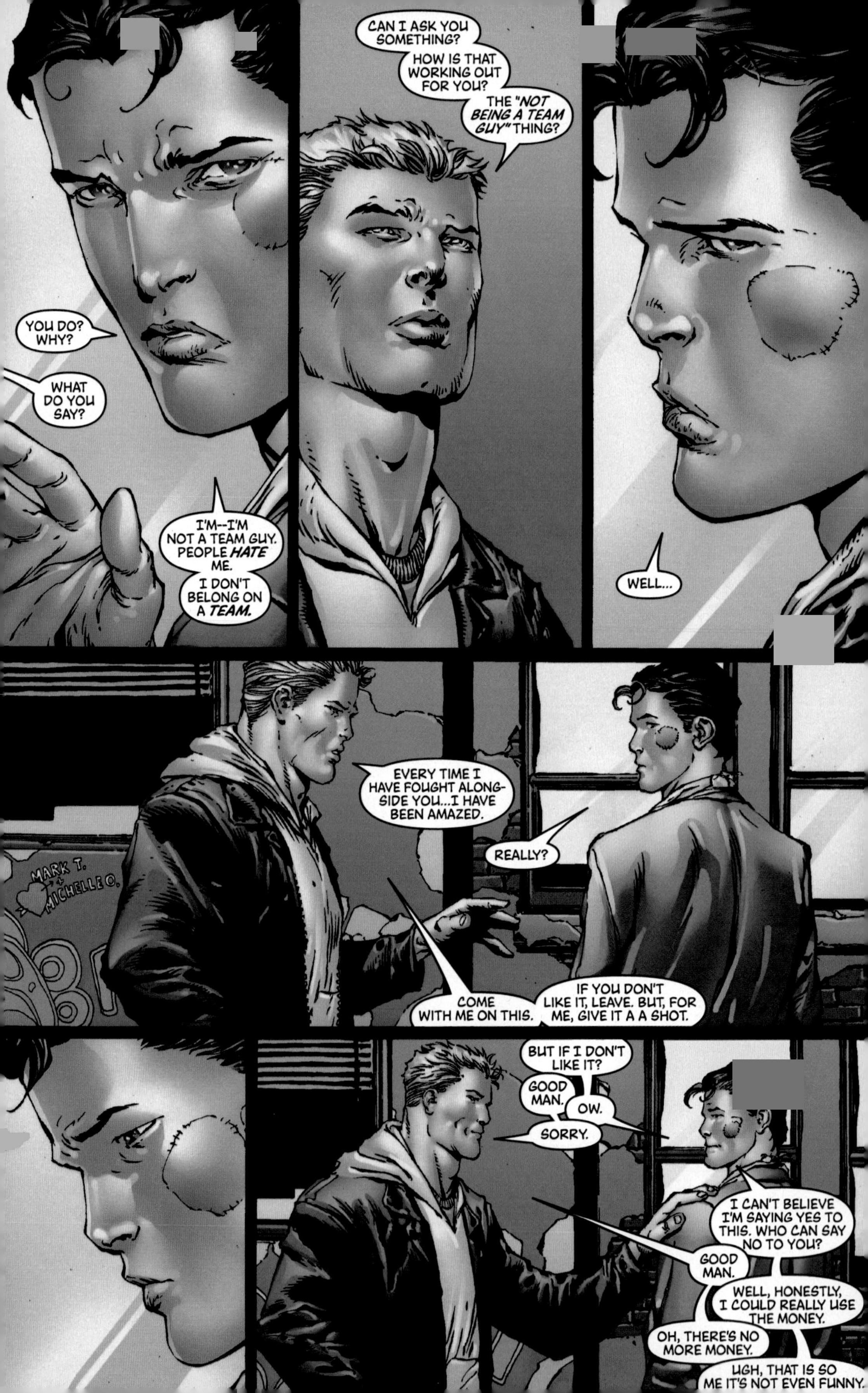
YOU DO? WHY?
WHAT DO YOU SAY?
I'M--I'M NOT A TEAM GUY. PEOPLE *HATE* ME.
I DON'T BELONG ON A *TEAM.*
CAN I ASK YOU SOMETHING?
HOW IS THAT WORKING OUT FOR YOU?
THE *"NOT BEING A TEAM GUY"* THING?
WELL...
EVERY TIME I HAVE FOUGHT ALONG-SIDE YOU...I HAVE BEEN AMAZED.
REALLY?
MARK T. + MICHELLE O.
COME WITH ME ON THIS.
IF YOU DON'T LIKE IT, LEAVE. BUT, FOR ME, GIVE IT A A SHOT.
BUT IF I DON'T LIKE IT?
GOOD MAN.
OW.
SORRY.
I CAN'T BELIEVE I'M SAYING YES TO THIS. WHO CAN SAY NO TO YOU?
GOOD MAN.
WELL, HONESTLY, I COULD REALLY USE THE MONEY.
OH, THERE'S NO MORE MONEY.
UGH, THAT IS SO ME IT'S NOT EVEN FUNNY.

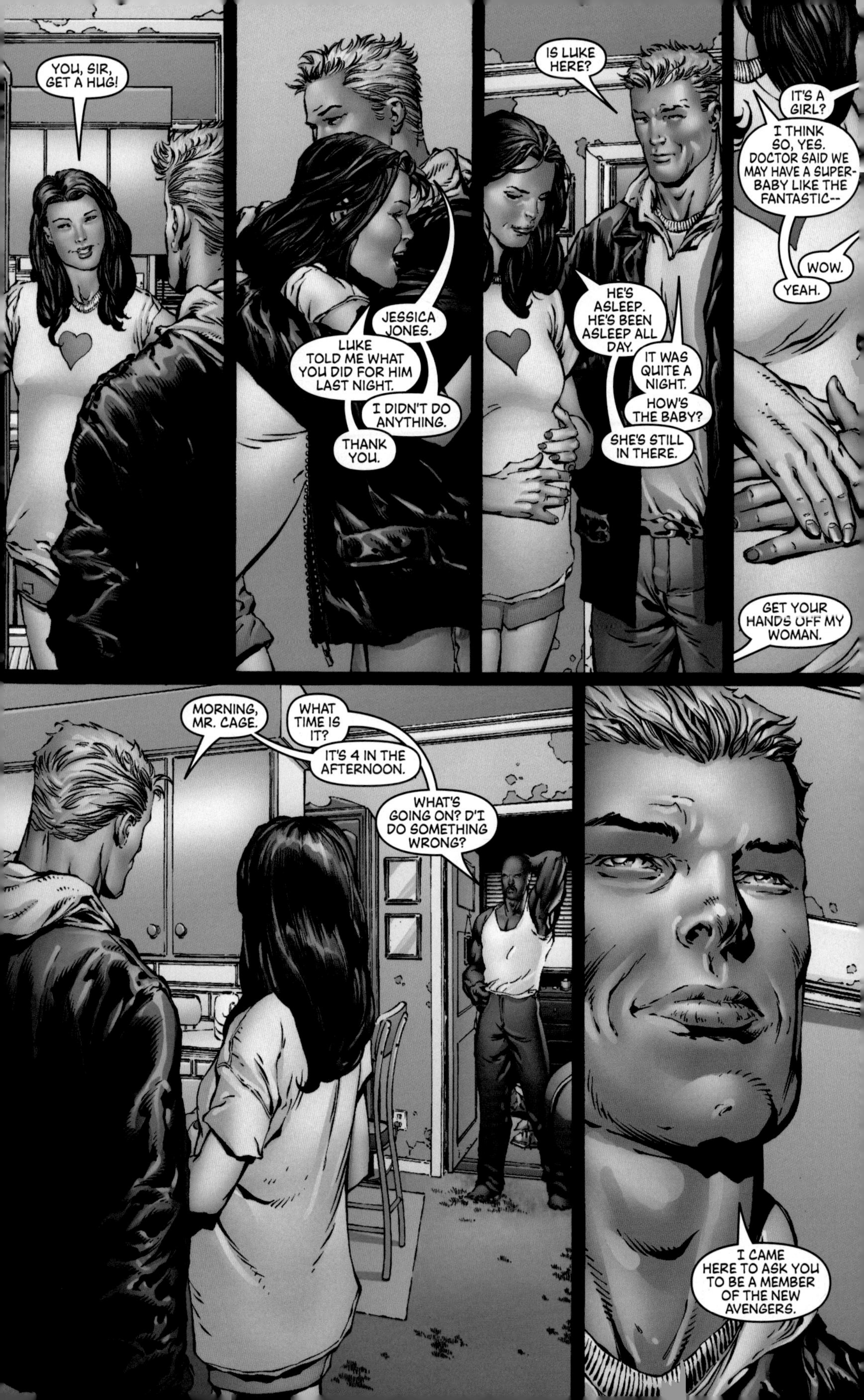
YOU, SIR, GET A HUG!
JESSICA JONES.
LUKE TOLD ME WHAT YOU DID FOR HIM LAST NIGHT.
I DIDN'T DO ANYTHING.
THANK YOU.
IS LUKE HERE?
HE'S ASLEEP. HE'S BEEN ASLEEP ALL DAY.
IT WAS QUITE A NIGHT.
HOW'S THE BABY?
SHE'S STILL IN THERE.
IT'S A GIRL?
I THINK SO, YES. DOCTOR SAID WE MAY HAVE A SUPER-BABY LIKE THE FANTASTIC--
WOW.
YEAH.
GET YOUR HANDS OFF MY WOMAN.
MORNING, MR. CAGE.
WHAT TIME IS IT?
IT'S 4 IN THE AFTERNOON.
WHAT'S GOING ON? D'I DO SOMETHING WRONG?
I CAME HERE TO ASK YOU TO BE A MEMBER OF THE NEW AVENGERS.

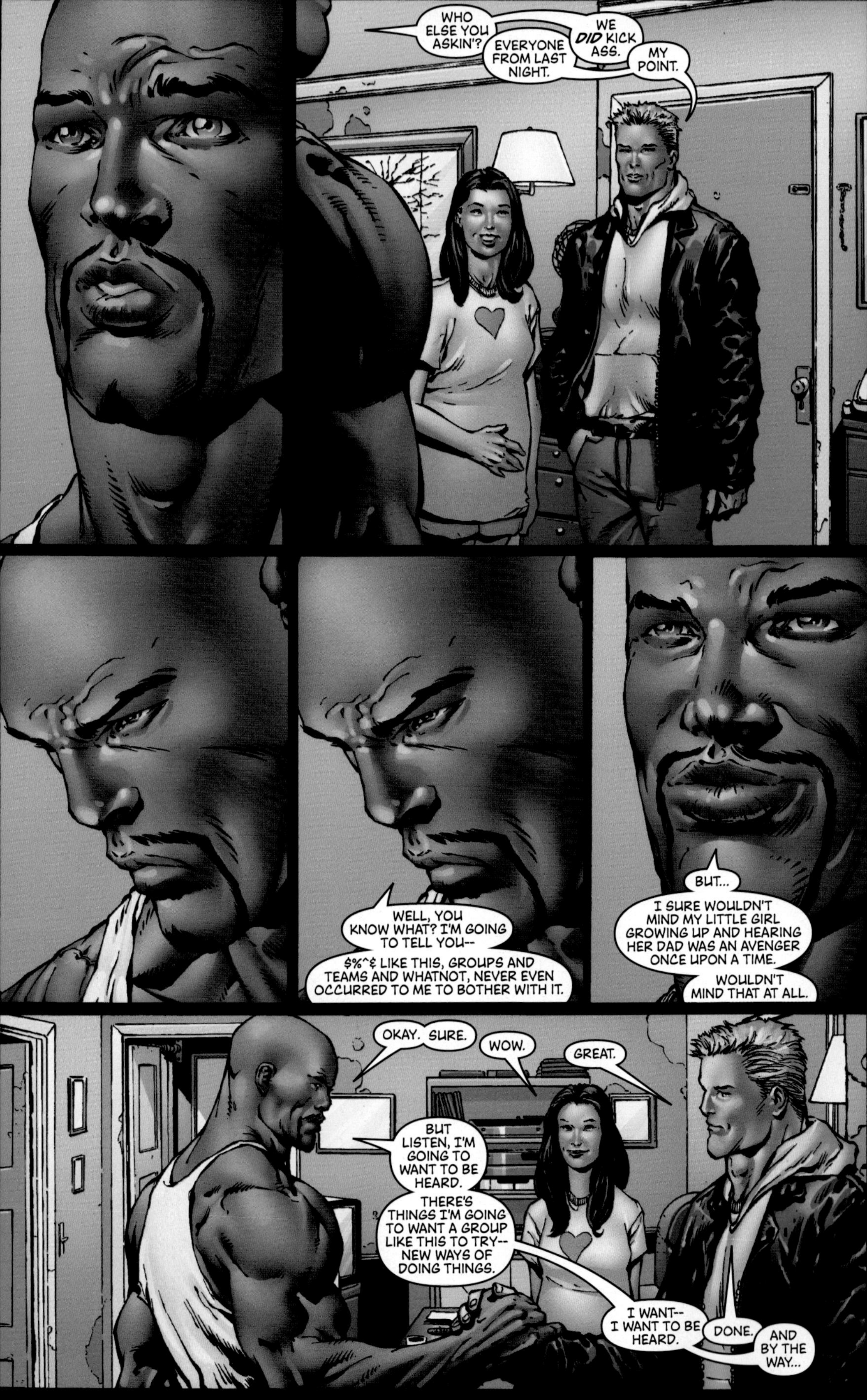
WHO ELSE YOU ASKIN'?
EVERYONE FROM LAST NIGHT.
WE DID KICK ASS.
MY POINT.
WELL, YOU KNOW WHAT? I'M GOING TO TELL YOU--
$%^& LIKE THIS, GROUPS AND TEAMS AND WHATNOT, NEVER EVEN OCCURRED TO ME TO BOTHER WITH IT.
BUT...
I SURE WOULDN'T MIND MY LITTLE GIRL GROWING UP AND HEARING HER DAD WAS AN AVENGER ONCE UPON A TIME.
WOULDN'T MIND THAT AT ALL.
OKAY. SURE.
WOW.
GREAT.
BUT LISTEN, I'M GOING TO WANT TO BE HEARD.
THERE'S THINGS I'M GOING TO WANT A GROUP LIKE THIS TO TRY-- NEW WAYS OF DOING THINGS.
I WANT-- I WANT TO BE HEARD.
DONE.
AND BY THE WAY...

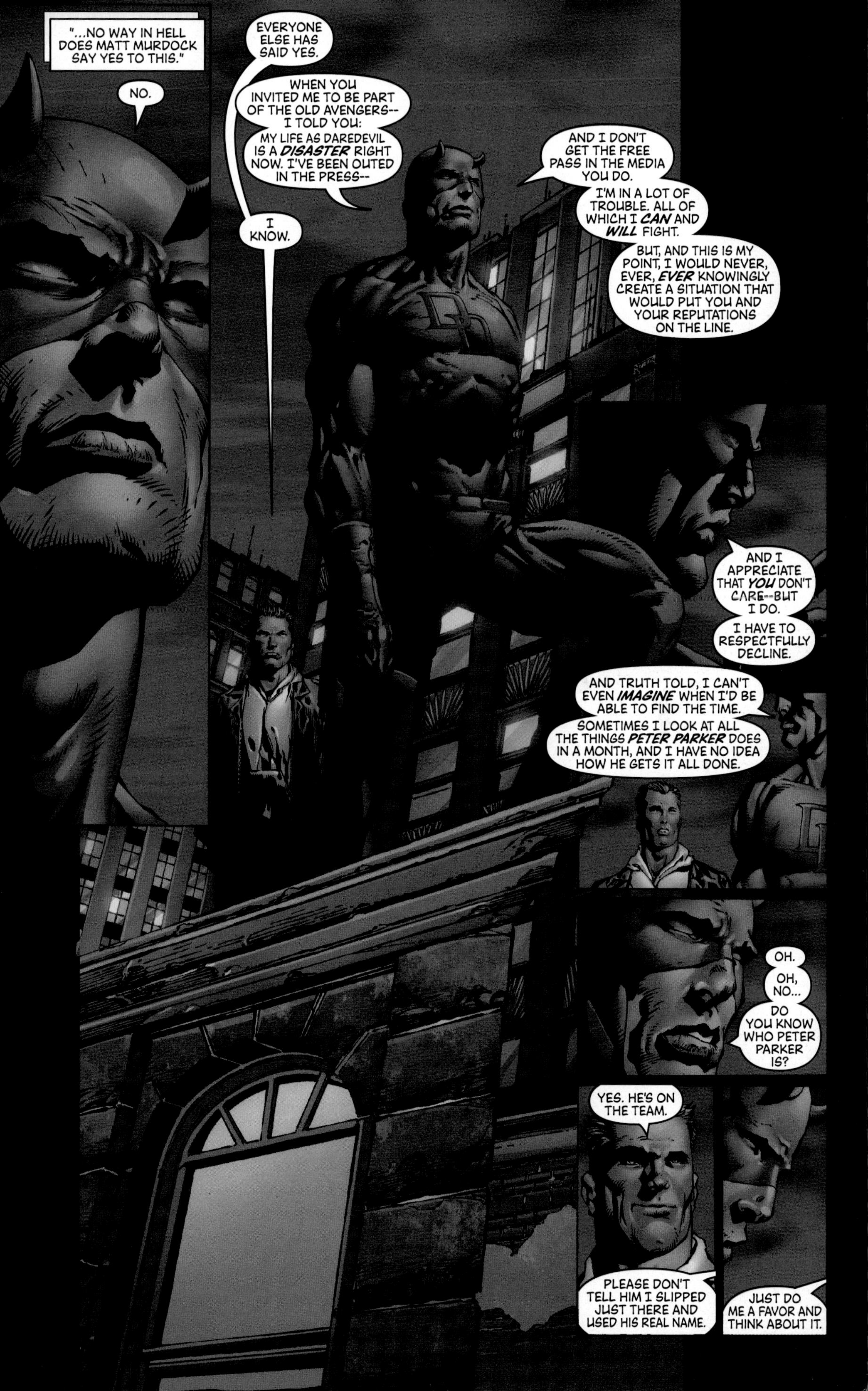
"...NO WAY IN HELL DOES MATT MURDOCK SAY YES TO THIS."
NO.
EVERYONE ELSE HAS SAID YES.
WHEN YOU INVITED ME TO BE PART OF THE OLD AVENGERS-- I TOLD YOU:
MY LIFE AS DAREDEVIL IS A DISASTER RIGHT NOW. I'VE BEEN OUTED IN THE PRESS--
I KNOW.
AND I DON'T GET THE FREE PASS IN THE MEDIA YOU DO.
I'M IN A LOT OF TROUBLE. ALL OF WHICH I CAN AND WILL FIGHT.
BUT, AND THIS IS MY POINT, I WOULD NEVER, EVER, EVER KNOWINGLY CREATE A SITUATION THAT WOULD PUT YOU AND YOUR REPUTATIONS ON THE LINE.
AND I APPRECIATE THAT YOU DON'T CARE--BUT I DO.
I HAVE TO RESPECTFULLY DECLINE.
AND TRUTH TOLD, I CAN'T EVEN IMAGINE WHEN I'D BE ABLE TO FIND THE TIME.
SOMETIMES I LOOK AT ALL THE THINGS PETER PARKER DOES IN A MONTH, AND I HAVE NO IDEA HOW HE GETS IT ALL DONE.
OH.
OH, NO...
DO YOU KNOW WHO PETER PARKER IS?
YES. HE'S ON THE TEAM.
PLEASE DON'T TELL HIM I SLIPPED JUST THERE AND USED HIS REAL NAME.
JUST DO ME A FAVOR AND THINK ABOUT IT.

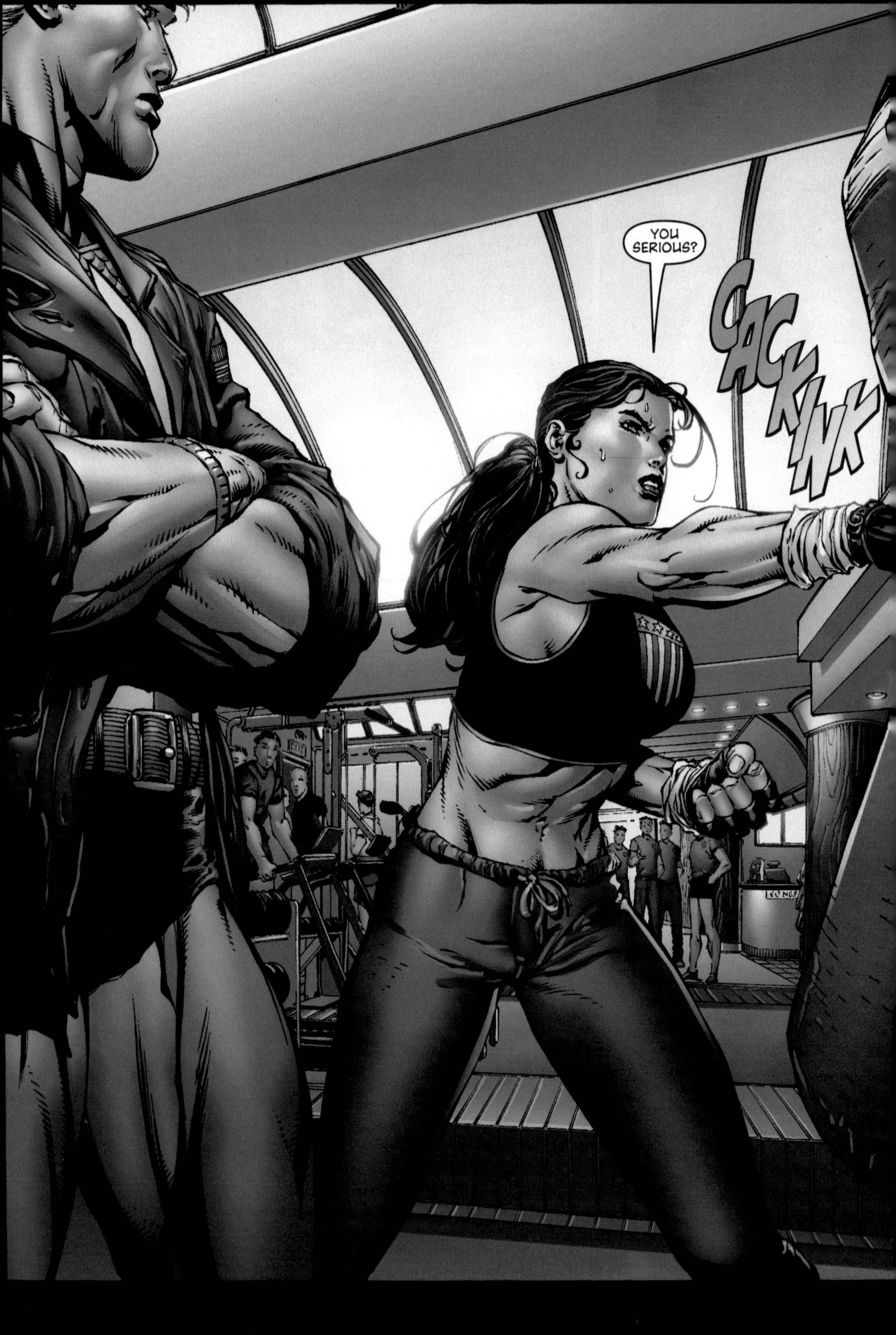
YOU SERIOUS?
CACKINK

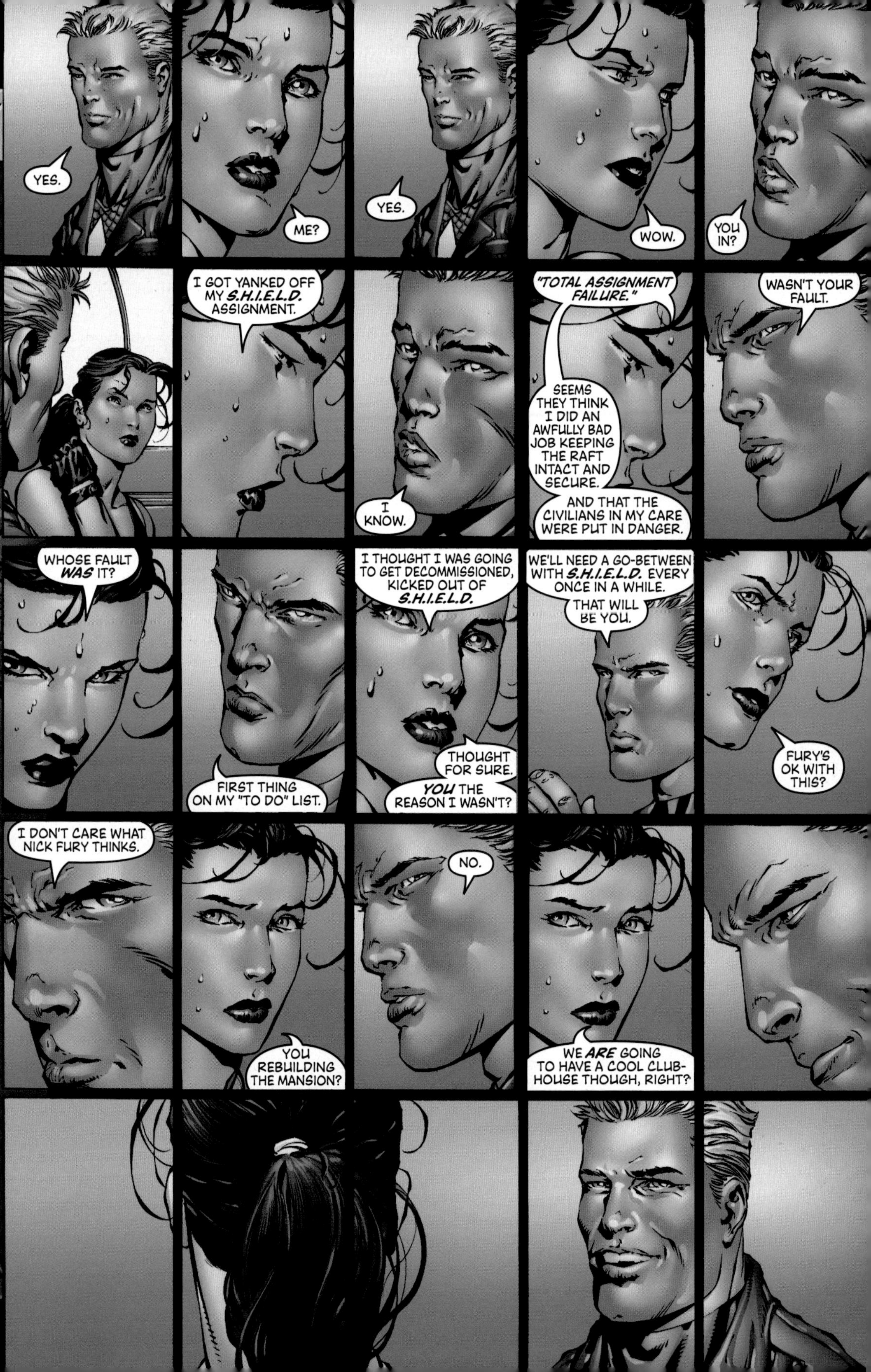
YES.
ME?
YES.
WOW.
YOU IN?
I GOT YANKED OFF MY S.H.I.E.L.D. ASSIGNMENT.
I KNOW.
"TOTAL ASSIGNMENT FAILURE."
SEEMS THEY THINK I DID AN AWFULLY BAD JOB KEEPING THE RAFT INTACT AND SECURE.
AND THAT THE CIVILIANS IN MY CARE WERE PUT IN DANGER.
WASN'T YOUR FAULT.
WHOSE FAULT WAS IT?
FIRST THING ON MY "TO DO" LIST.
I THOUGHT I WAS GOING TO GET DECOMMISSIONED, KICKED OUT OF S.H.I.E.L.D.
THOUGHT FOR SURE.
YOU THE REASON I WASN'T?
WE'LL NEED A GO-BETWEEN WITH S.H.I.E.L.D. EVERY ONCE IN A WHILE.
THAT WILL BE YOU.
FURY'S OK WITH THIS?
I DON'T CARE WHAT NICK FURY THINKS.
YOU REBUILDING THE MANSION?
NO.
WE ARE GOING TO HAVE A COOL CLUB-HOUSE THOUGH, RIGHT?

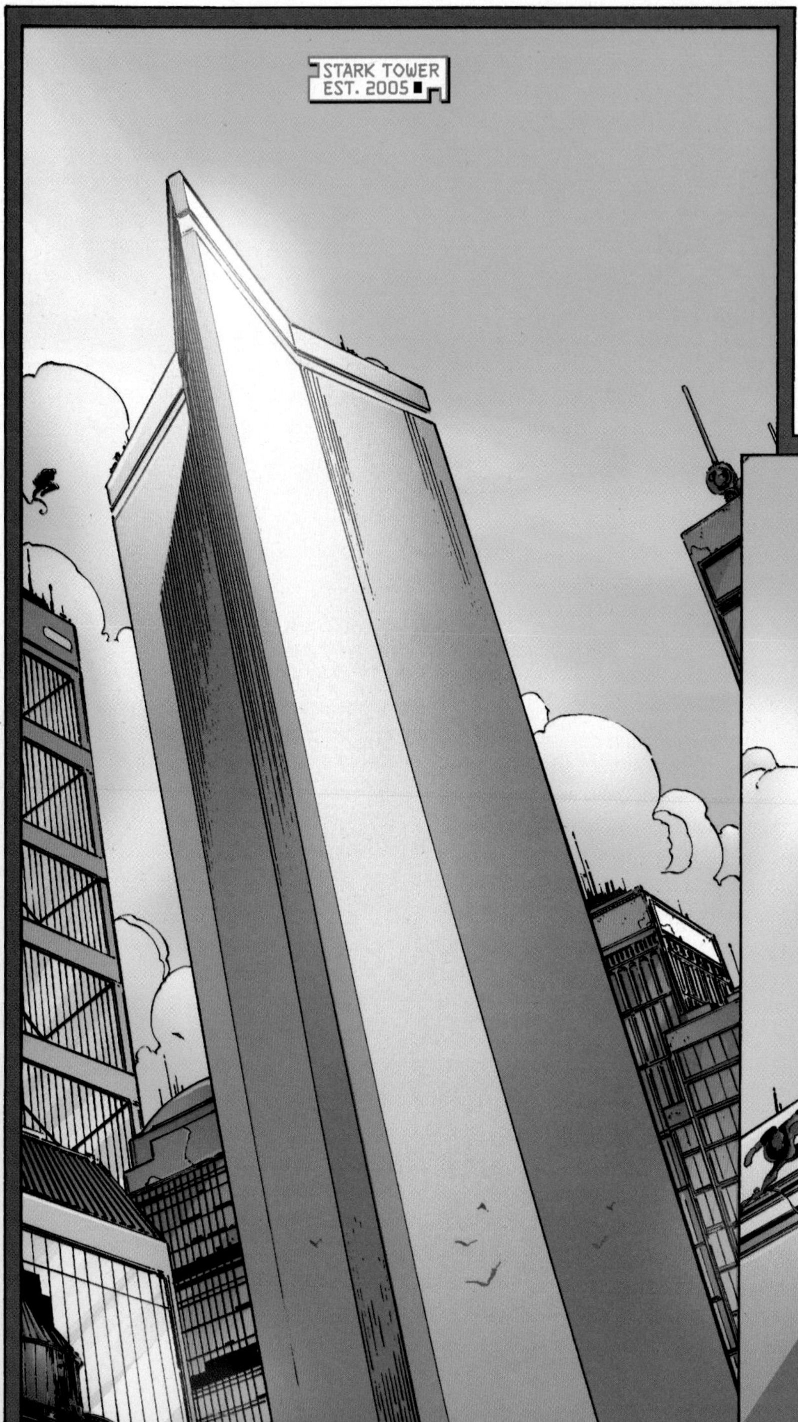
STARK TOWER
EST. 2005
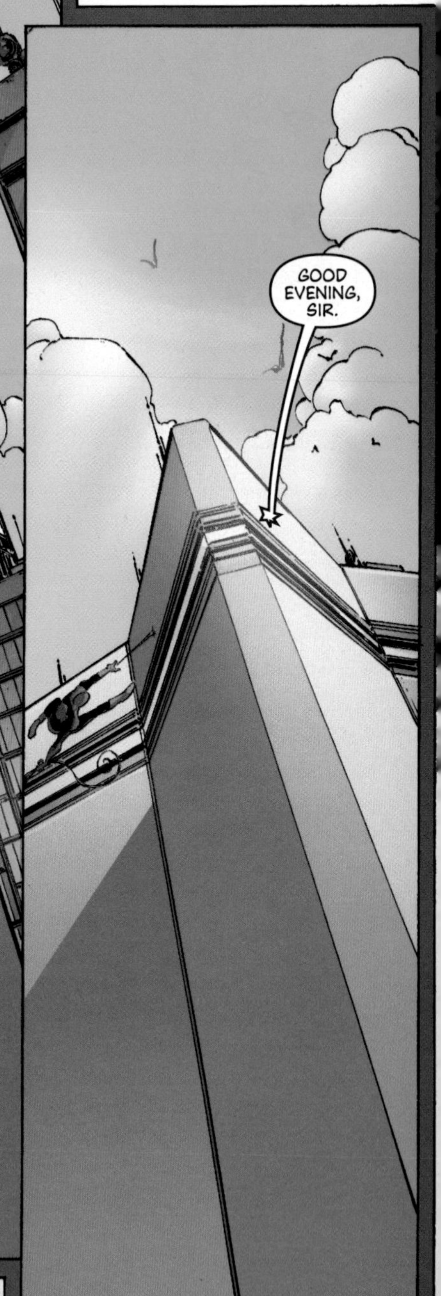
GOOD EVENING, SIR.

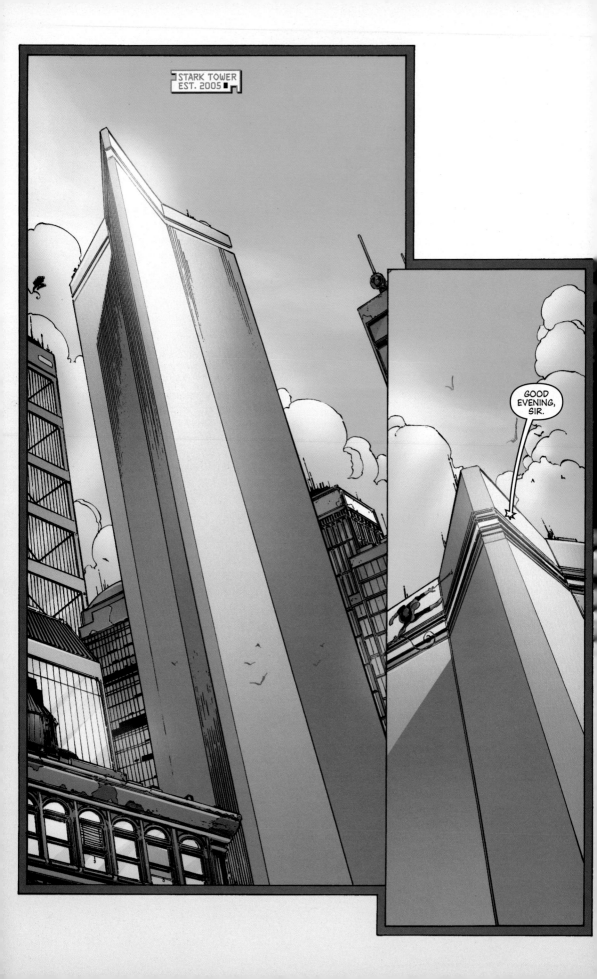

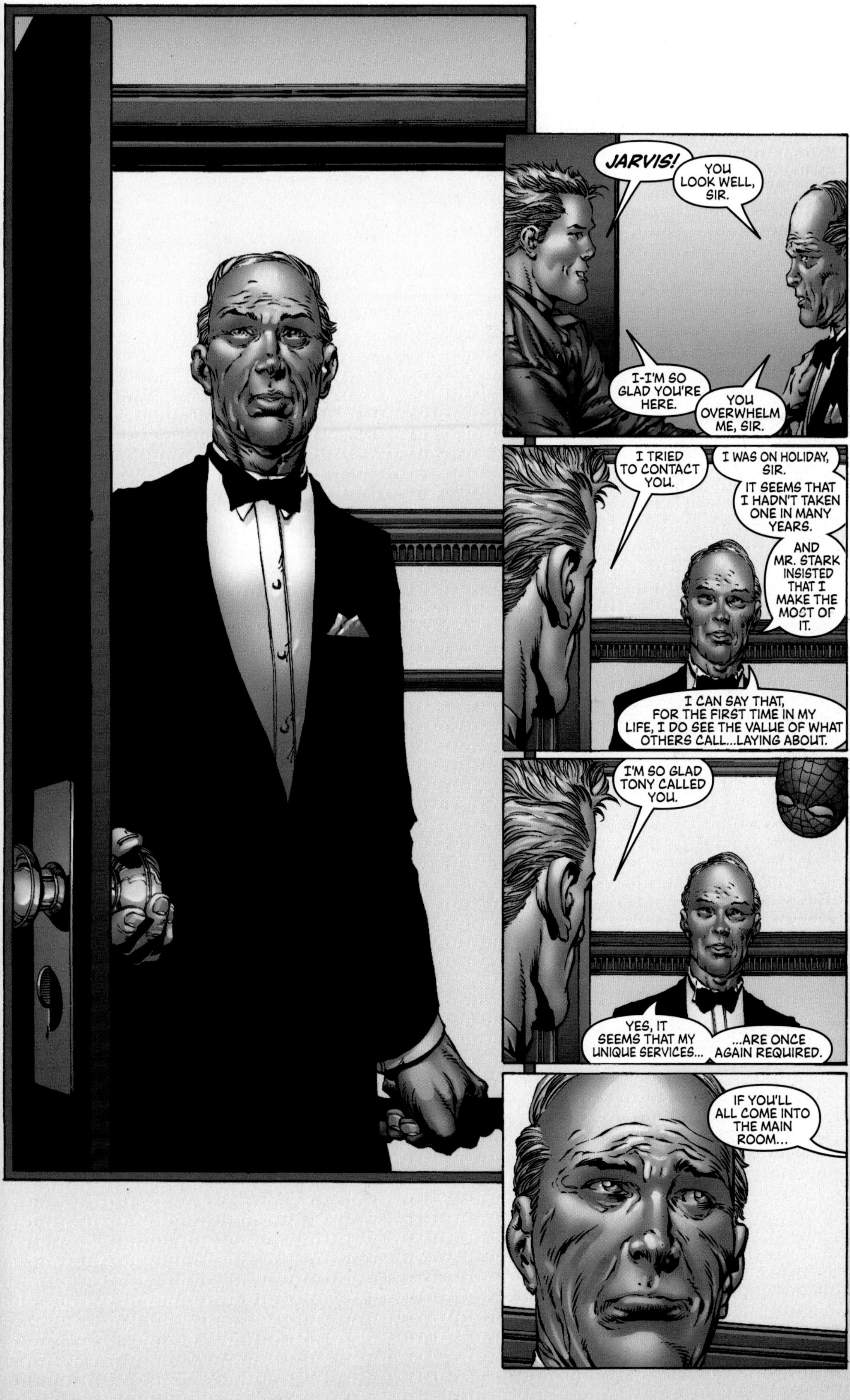
JARVIS!
YOU LOOK WELL, SIR.
I-I'M SO GLAD YOU'RE HERE.
YOU OVERWHELM ME, SIR.
I TRIED TO CONTACT YOU.
I WAS ON HOLIDAY, SIR.
IT SEEMS THAT I HADN'T TAKEN ONE IN MANY YEARS.
AND MR. STARK INSISTED THAT I MAKE THE MOST OF IT.
I CAN SAY THAT, FOR THE FIRST TIME IN MY LIFE, I DO SEE THE VALUE OF WHAT OTHERS CALL...LAYING ABOUT.
I'M SO GLAD TONY CALLED YOU.
YES, IT SEEMS THAT MY UNIQUE SERVICES...
...ARE ONCE AGAIN REQUIRED.
IF YOU'LL ALL COME INTO THE MAIN ROOM...

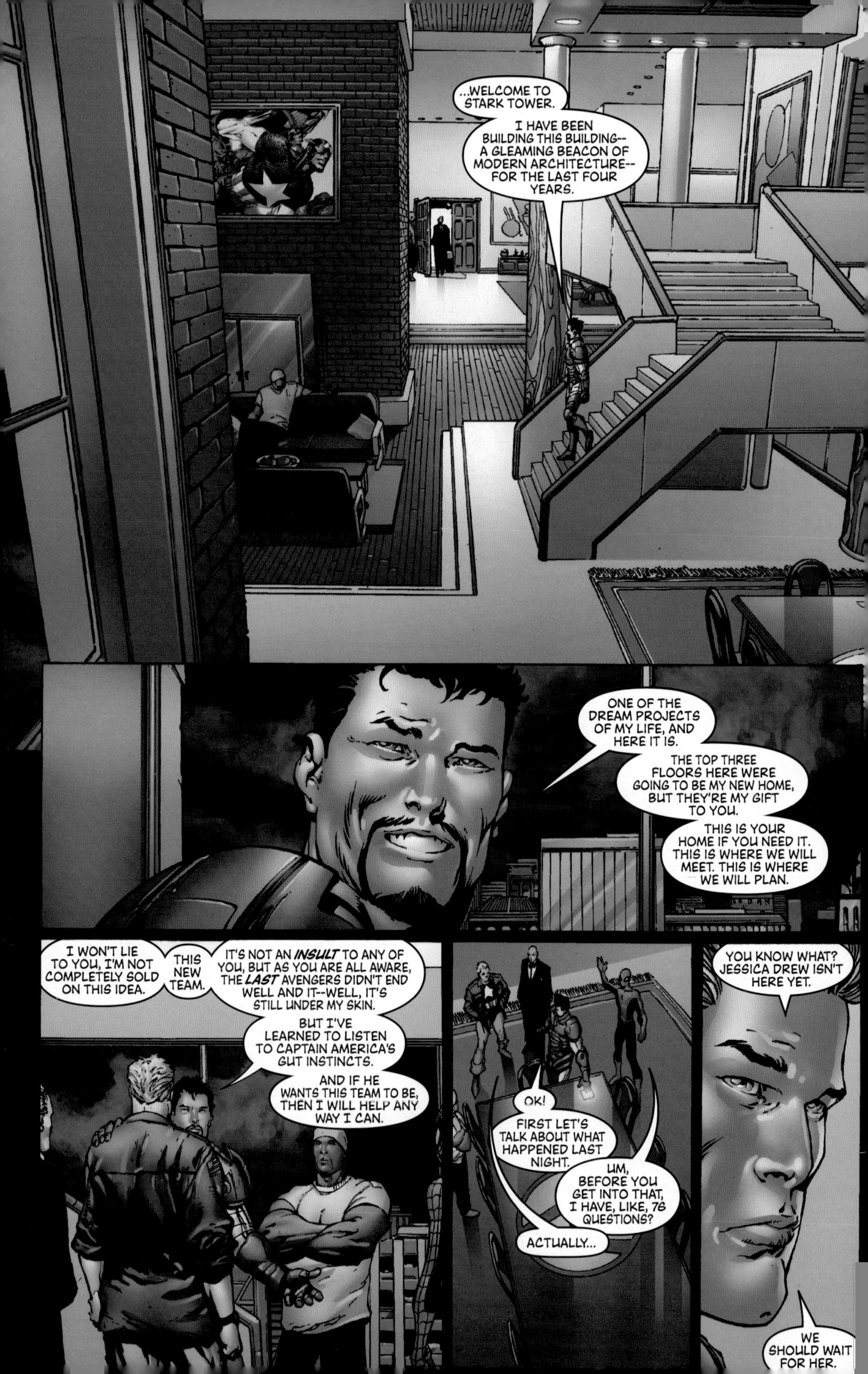

...WELCOME TO STARK TOWER.
I HAVE BEEN BUILDING THIS BUILDING-- A GLEAMING BEACON OF MODERN ARCHITECTURE-- FOR THE LAST FOUR YEARS.
ONE OF THE DREAM PROJECTS OF MY LIFE, AND HERE IT IS.
THE TOP THREE FLOORS HERE WERE GOING TO BE MY NEW HOME, BUT THEY'RE MY GIFT TO YOU.
THIS IS YOUR HOME IF YOU NEED IT. THIS IS WHERE WE WILL MEET. THIS IS WHERE WE WILL PLAN.
I WON'T LIE TO YOU, I'M NOT COMPLETELY SOLD ON THIS IDEA.
THIS NEW TEAM.
IT'S NOT AN *INSULT* TO ANY OF YOU, BUT AS YOU ARE ALL AWARE, THE *LAST* AVENGERS DIDN'T END WELL AND IT--WELL, IT'S STILL UNDER MY SKIN.
BUT I'VE LEARNED TO LISTEN TO CAPTAIN AMERICA'S GUT INSTINCTS.
AND IF HE WANTS THIS TEAM TO BE, THEN I WILL HELP ANY WAY I CAN.
OK!
FIRST LET'S TALK ABOUT WHAT HAPPENED LAST NIGHT.
UM, BEFORE YOU GET INTO THAT, I HAVE, LIKE, 76 QUESTIONS?
ACTUALLY...
YOU KNOW WHAT? JESSICA DREW ISN'T HERE YET.
WE SHOULD WAIT FOR HER.

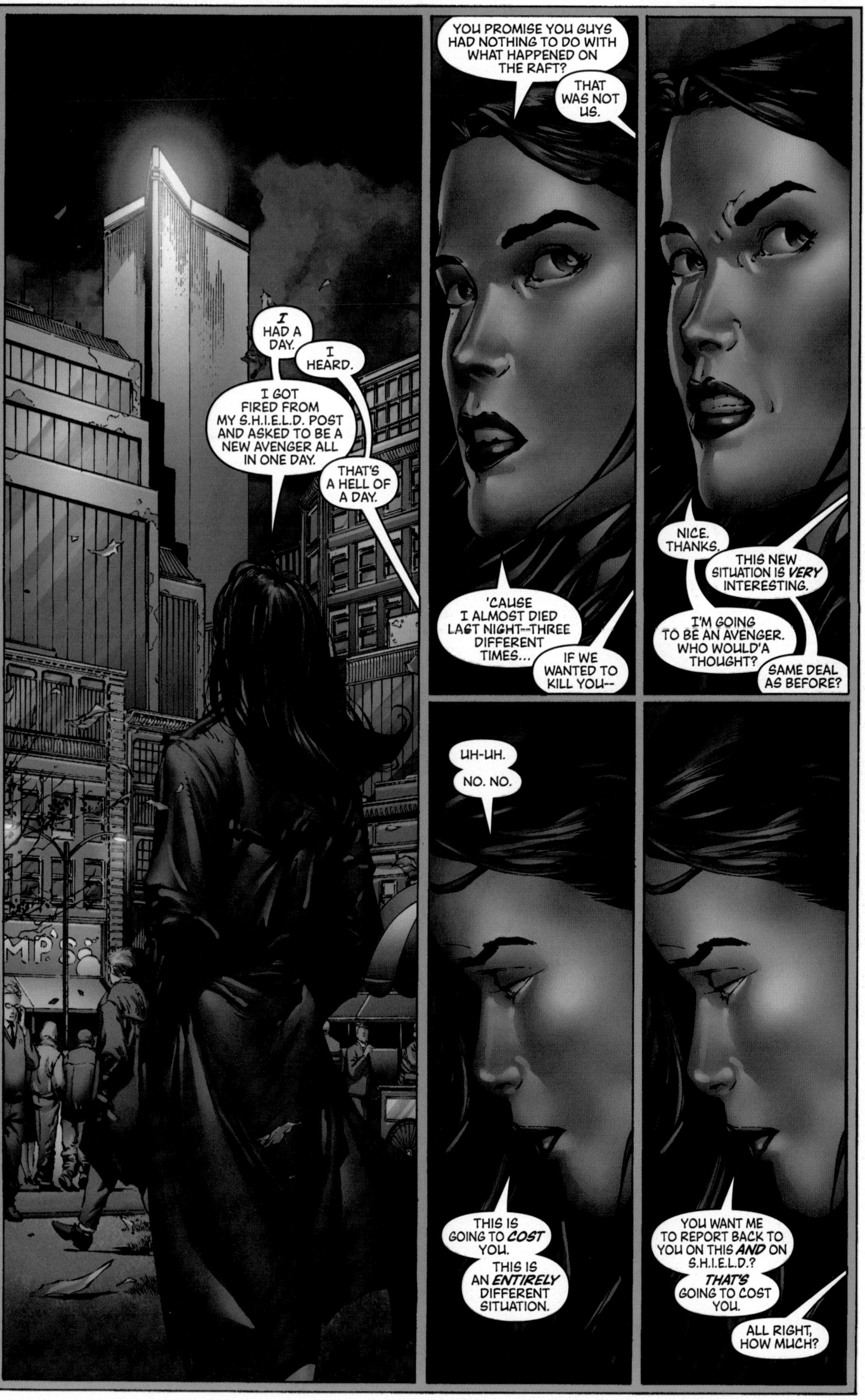
I HAD A DAY.
I HEARD.
I GOT FIRED FROM MY S.H.I.E.L.D. POST AND ASKED TO BE A NEW AVENGER ALL IN ONE DAY.
THAT'S A HELL OF A DAY.
YOU PROMISE YOU GUYS HAD NOTHING TO DO WITH WHAT HAPPENED ON THE RAFT?
THAT WAS NOT US.
'CAUSE I ALMOST DIED LAST NIGHT--THREE DIFFERENT TIMES...
IF WE WANTED TO KILL YOU--
NICE. THANKS.
THIS NEW SITUATION IS VERY INTERESTING.
I'M GOING TO BE AN AVENGER. WHO WOULD'A THOUGHT?
SAME DEAL AS BEFORE?
UH-UH.
NO. NO.
THIS IS GOING TO COST YOU.
THIS IS AN ENTIRELY DIFFERENT SITUATION.
YOU WANT ME TO REPORT BACK TO YOU ON THIS AND ON S.H.I.E.L.D.?
THAT'S GOING TO COST YOU.
ALL RIGHT, HOW MUCH?

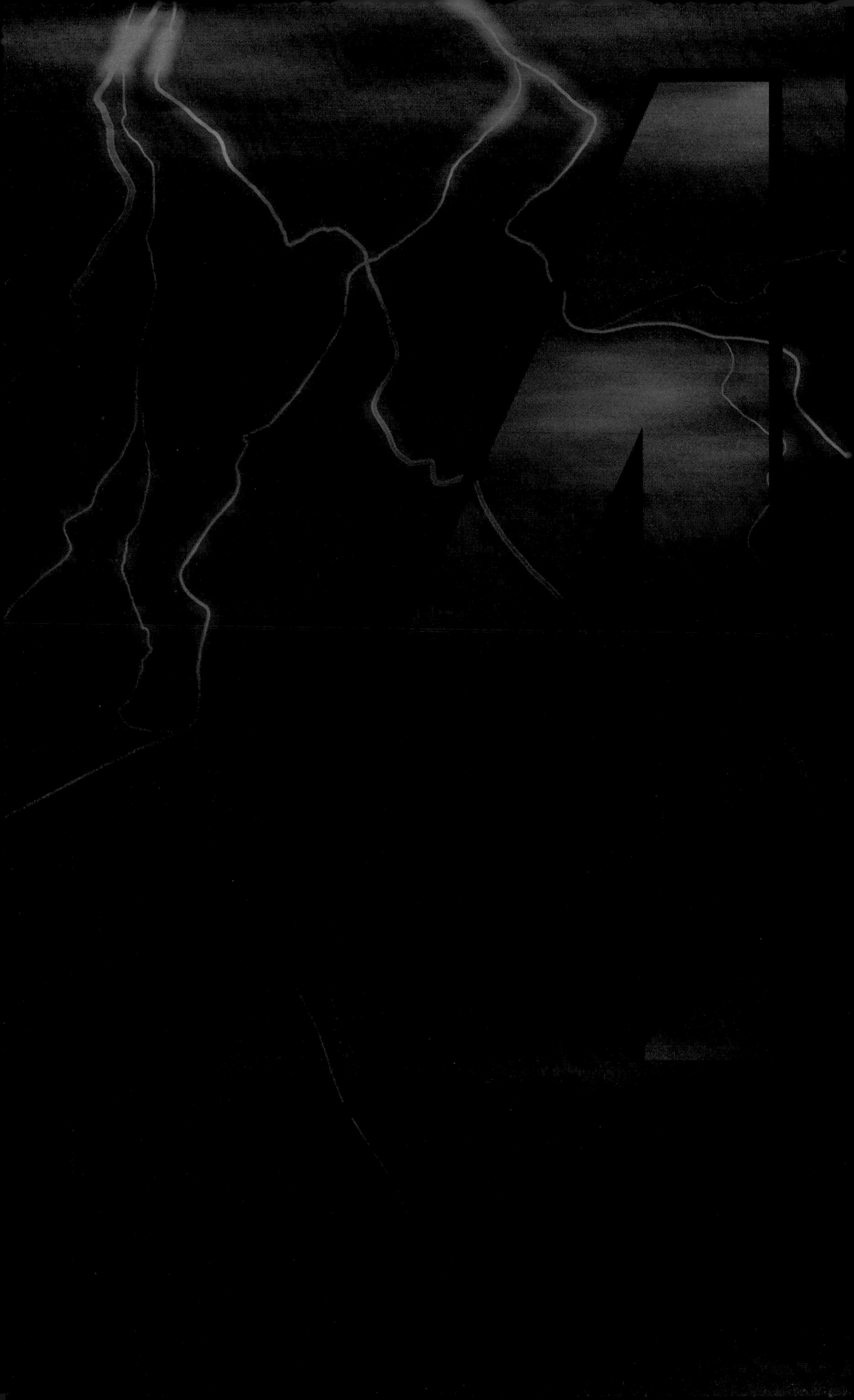

#4

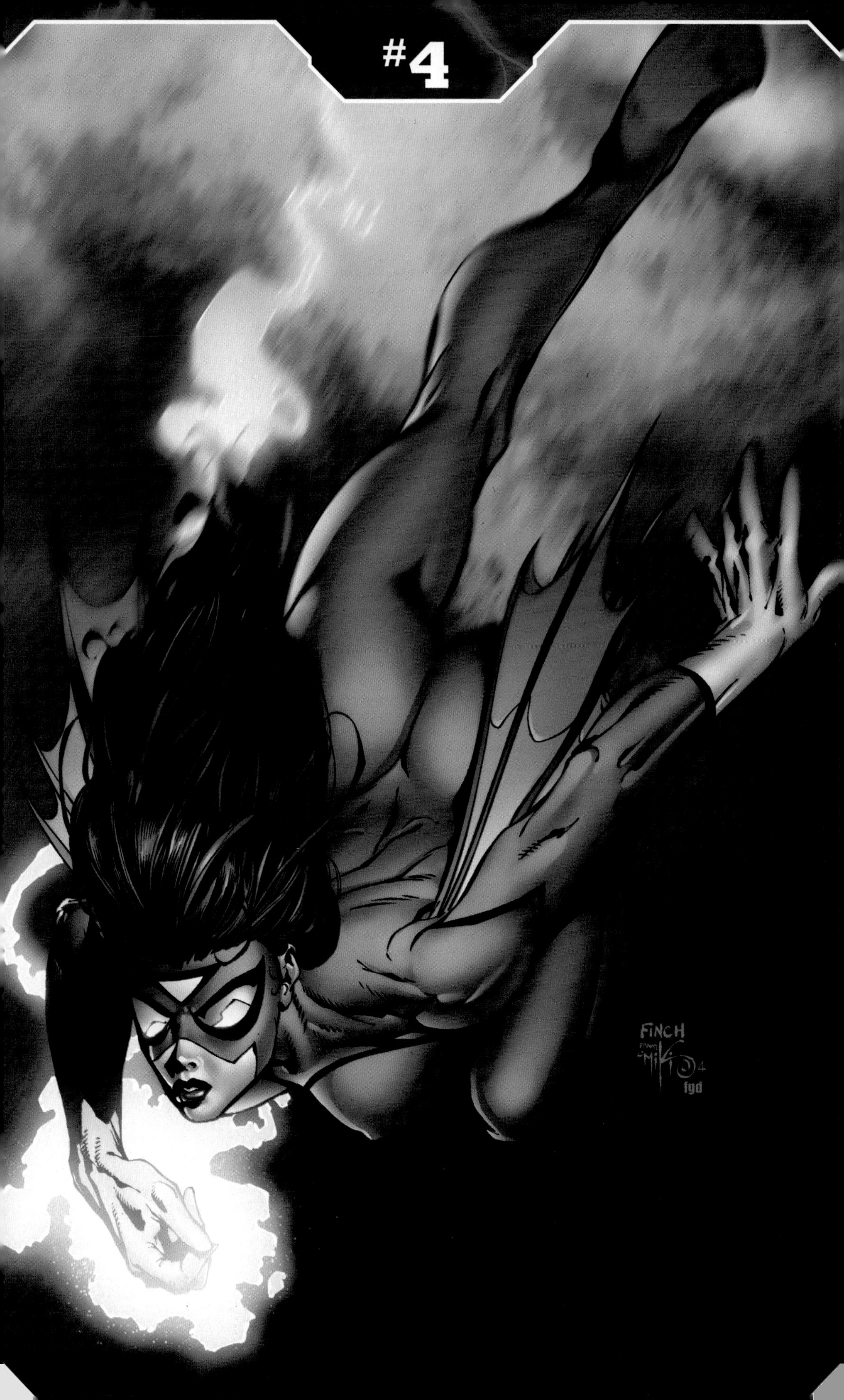
FINCH

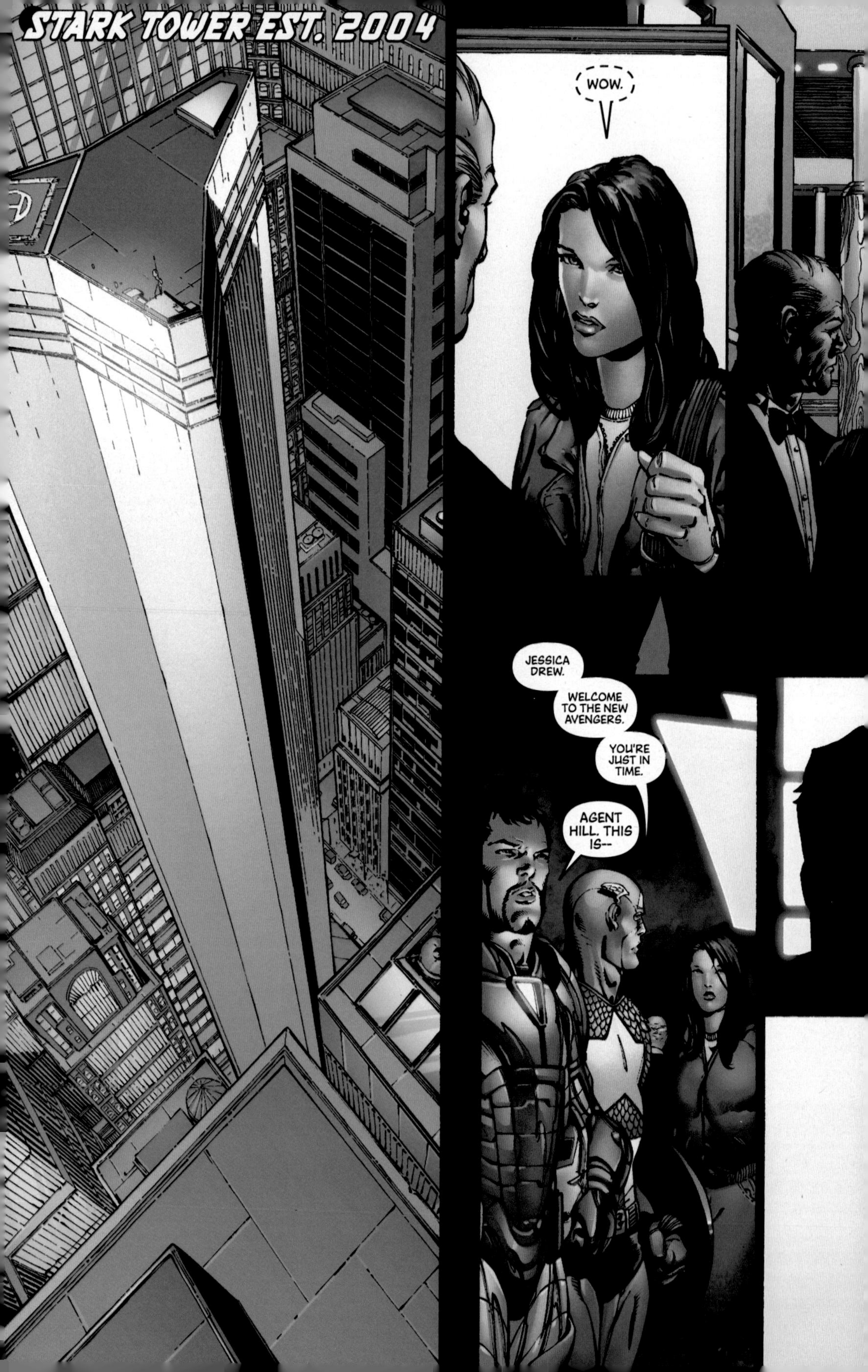
STARK TOWER EST. 2004
WOW.
JESSICA DREW.
WELCOME TO THE NEW AVENGERS.
YOU'RE JUST IN TIME.
AGENT HILL. THIS IS--

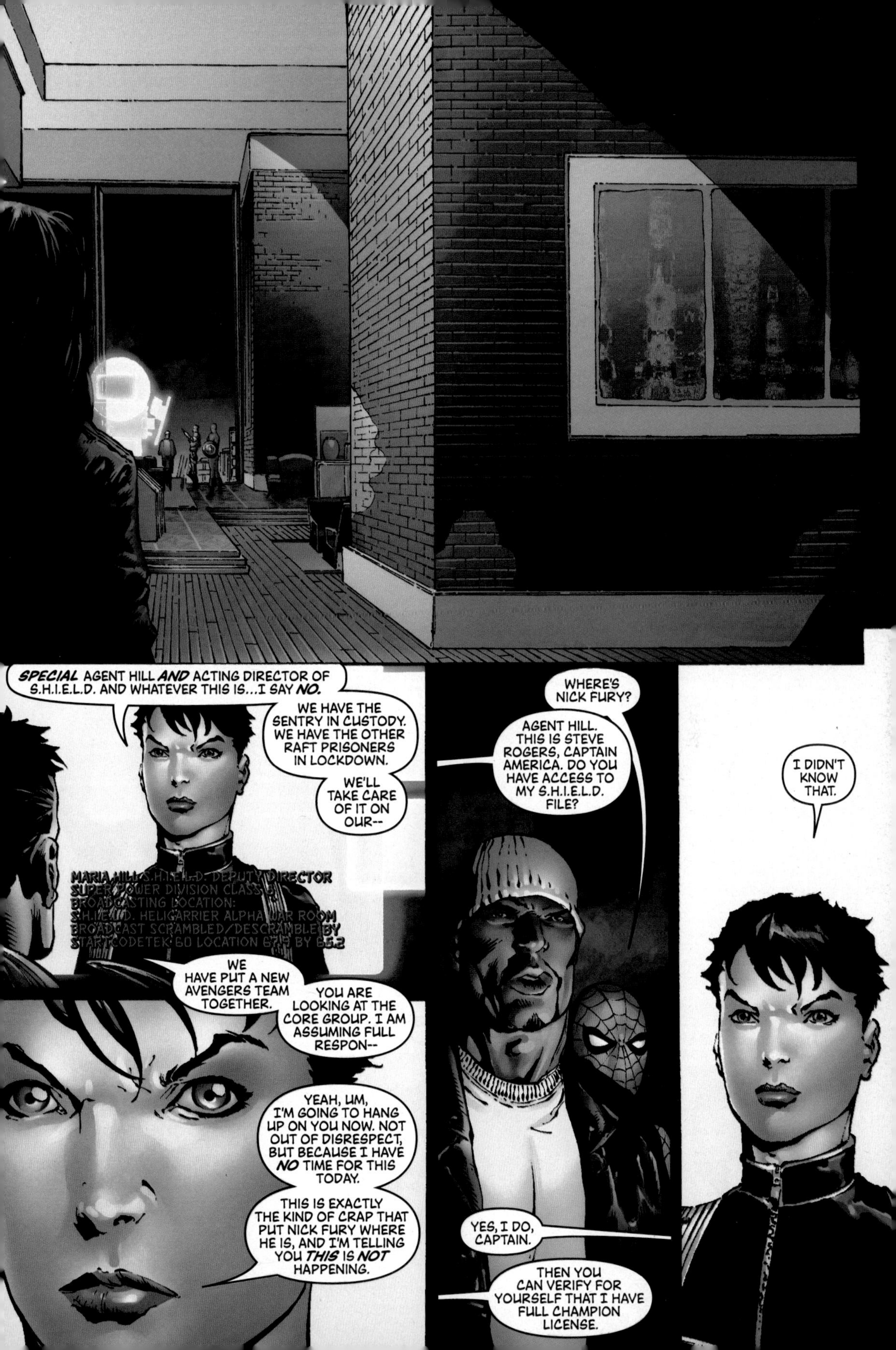
SPECIAL AGENT HILL AND ACTING DIRECTOR OF S.H.I.E.L.D. AND WHATEVER THIS IS...I SAY NO.
WE HAVE THE SENTRY IN CUSTODY. WE HAVE THE OTHER RAFT PRISONERS IN LOCKDOWN.
WE'LL TAKE CARE OF IT ON OUR--
MARIA HILL S.H.I.E.L.D. DEPUTY DIRECTOR
SUPER POWER DIVISION CLASS B
BROADCASTING LOCATION:
S.H.I.E.L.D. HELICARRIER ALPHA WAR ROOM
BROADCAST SCRAMBLED/DESCRAMBLE BY
STARTCODETEK 60 LOCATION 67.9 BY 65.2
WE HAVE PUT A NEW AVENGERS TEAM TOGETHER.
YOU ARE LOOKING AT THE CORE GROUP. I AM ASSUMING FULL RESPON--
YEAH, UM, I'M GOING TO HANG UP ON YOU NOW. NOT OUT OF DISRESPECT, BUT BECAUSE I HAVE NO TIME FOR THIS TODAY.
THIS IS EXACTLY THE KIND OF CRAP THAT PUT NICK FURY WHERE HE IS, AND I'M TELLING YOU THIS IS NOT HAPPENING.
WHERE'S NICK FURY?
AGENT HILL. THIS IS STEVE ROGERS, CAPTAIN AMERICA. DO YOU HAVE ACCESS TO MY S.H.I.E.L.D. FILE?
YES, I DO, CAPTAIN.
THEN YOU CAN VERIFY FOR YOURSELF THAT I HAVE FULL CHAMPION LICENSE.
I DIDN'T KNOW THAT.

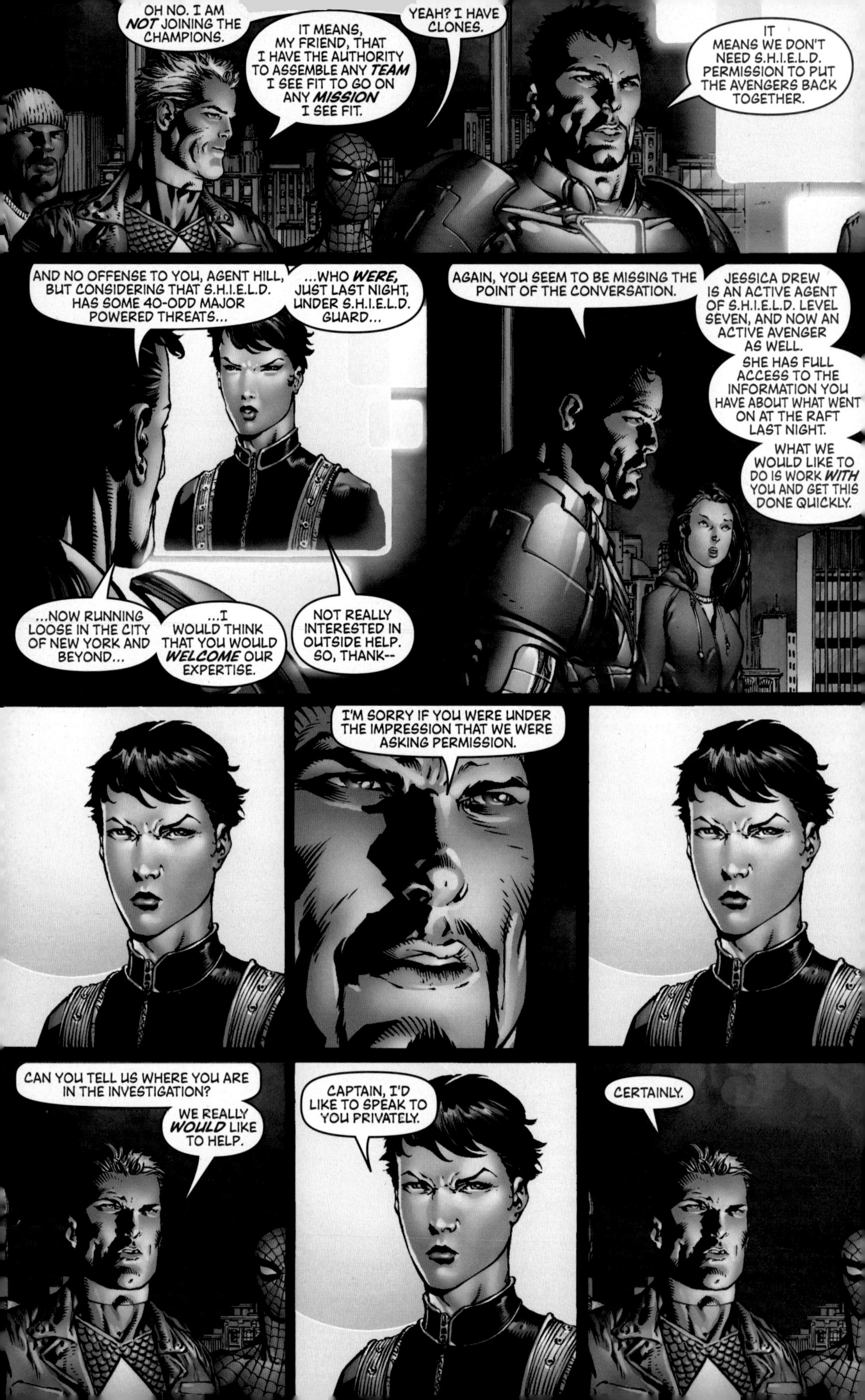
OH NO. I AM NOT JOINING THE CHAMPIONS.
IT MEANS, MY FRIEND, THAT I HAVE THE AUTHORITY TO ASSEMBLE ANY TEAM I SEE FIT TO GO ON ANY MISSION I SEE FIT.
YEAH? I HAVE CLONES.
IT MEANS WE DON'T NEED S.H.I.E.L.D. PERMISSION TO PUT THE AVENGERS BACK TOGETHER.
AND NO OFFENSE TO YOU, AGENT HILL, BUT CONSIDERING THAT S.H.I.E.L.D. HAS SOME 40-ODD MAJOR POWERED THREATS...
...WHO WERE, JUST LAST NIGHT, UNDER S.H.I.E.L.D. GUARD...
...NOW RUNNING LOOSE IN THE CITY OF NEW YORK AND BEYOND...
...I WOULD THINK THAT YOU WOULD WELCOME OUR EXPERTISE.
NOT REALLY INTERESTED IN OUTSIDE HELP. SO, THANK--
AGAIN, YOU SEEM TO BE MISSING THE POINT OF THE CONVERSATION.
JESSICA DREW IS AN ACTIVE AGENT OF S.H.I.E.L.D. LEVEL SEVEN, AND NOW AN ACTIVE AVENGER AS WELL.
SHE HAS FULL ACCESS TO THE INFORMATION YOU HAVE ABOUT WHAT WENT ON AT THE RAFT LAST NIGHT.
WHAT WE WOULD LIKE TO DO IS WORK WITH YOU AND GET THIS DONE QUICKLY.
I'M SORRY IF YOU WERE UNDER THE IMPRESSION THAT WE WERE ASKING PERMISSION.
CAN YOU TELL US WHERE YOU ARE IN THE INVESTIGATION?
WE REALLY WOULD LIKE TO HELP.
CAPTAIN, I'D LIKE TO SPEAK TO YOU PRIVATELY.
CERTAINLY.

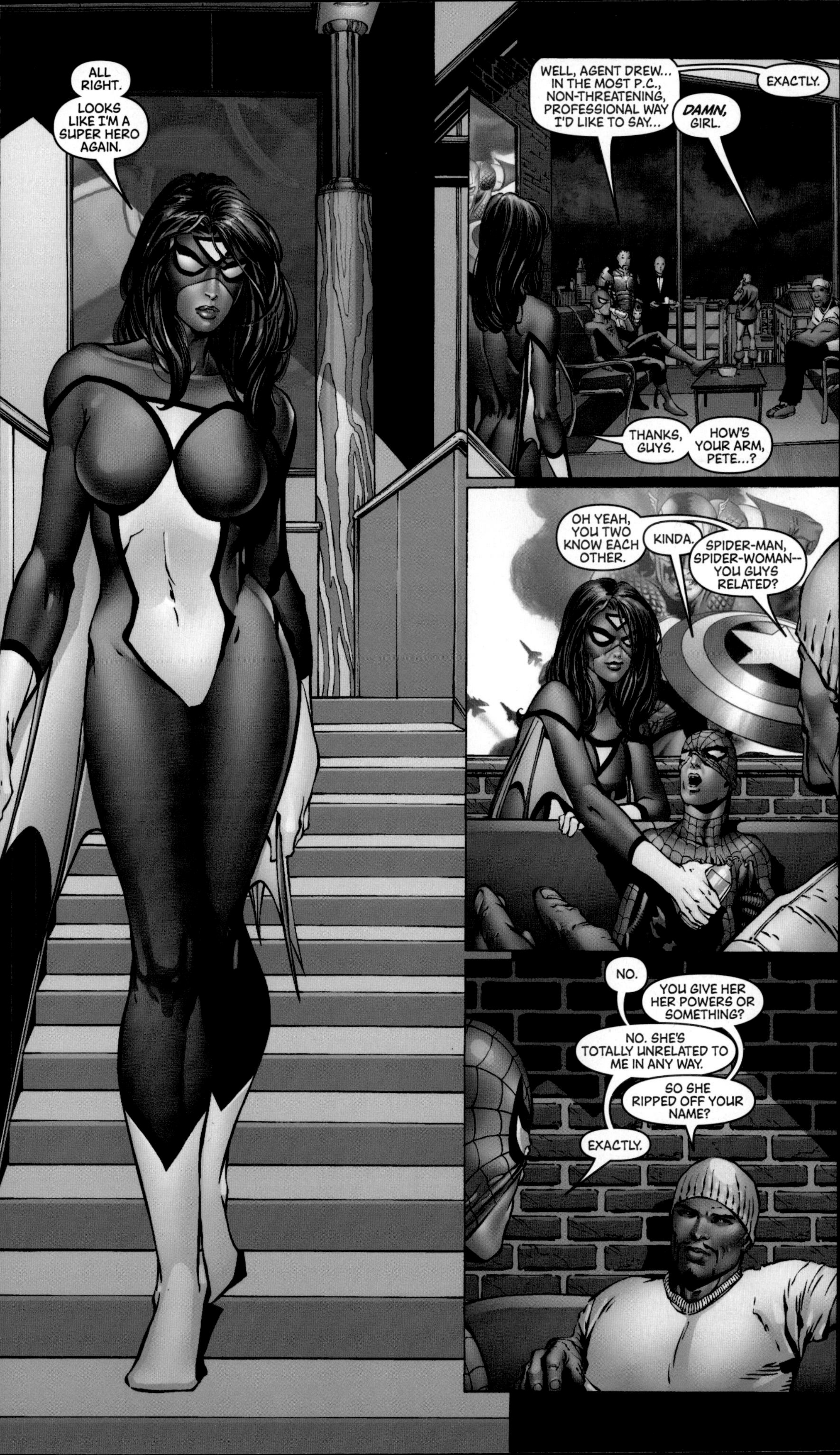
ALL RIGHT.
LOOKS LIKE I'M A SUPER HERO AGAIN.
WELL, AGENT DREW... IN THE MOST P.C., NON-THREATENING, PROFESSIONAL WAY I'D LIKE TO SAY...
EXACTLY.
DAMN, GIRL.
THANKS, GUYS.
HOW'S YOUR ARM, PETE...?
OH YEAH, YOU TWO KNOW EACH OTHER.
KINDA.
SPIDER-MAN, SPIDER-WOMAN-- YOU GUYS RELATED?
NO.
YOU GIVE HER HER POWERS OR SOMETHING?
NO. SHE'S TOTALLY UNRELATED TO ME IN ANY WAY.
SO SHE RIPPED OFF YOUR NAME?
EXACTLY.

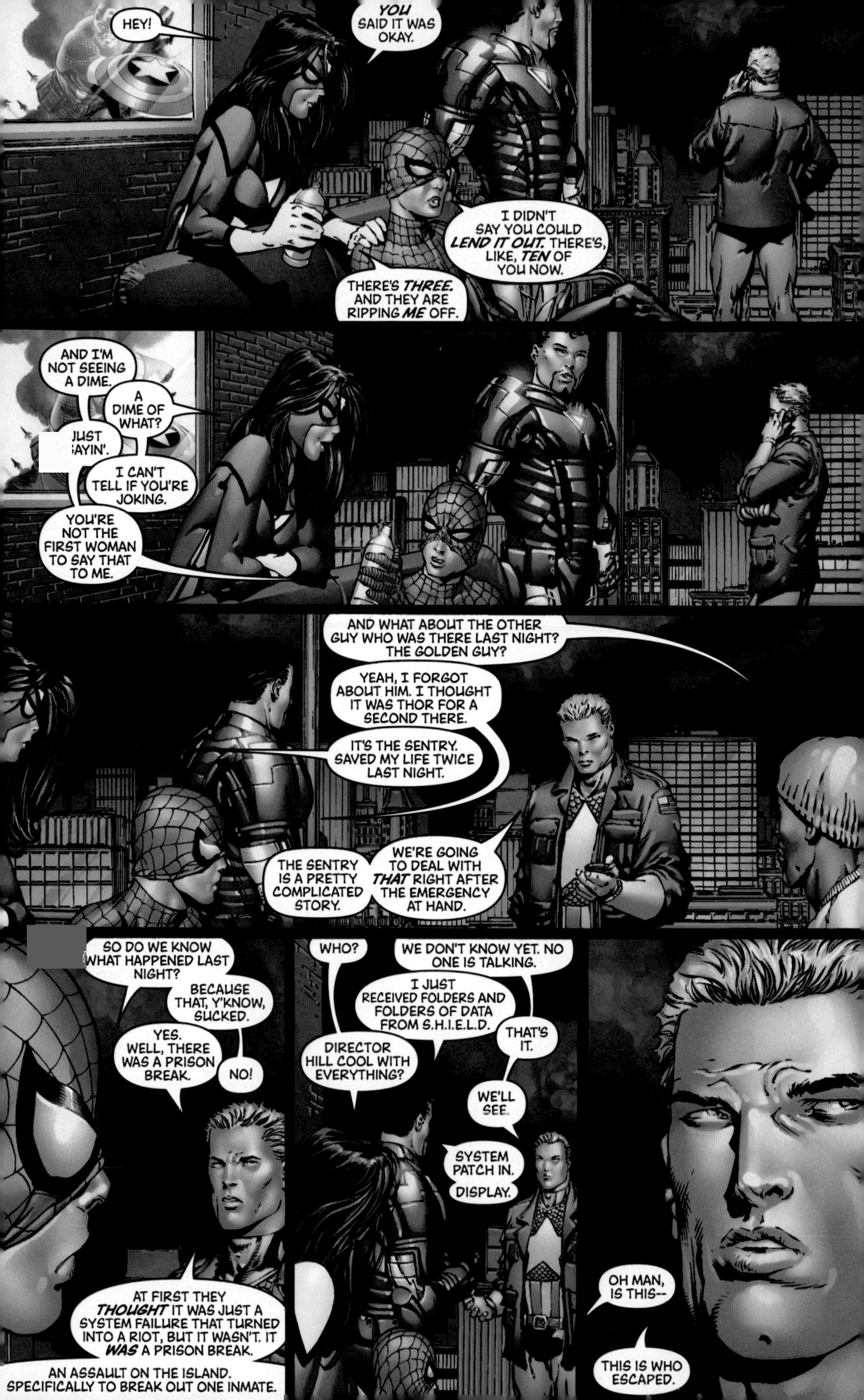
HEY!
YOU SAID IT WAS OKAY.
I DIDN'T SAY YOU COULD LEND IT OUT. THERE'S, LIKE, TEN OF YOU NOW.
THERE'S THREE. AND THEY ARE RIPPING ME OFF.
AND I'M NOT SEEING A DIME.
A DIME OF WHAT?
JUST AYIN'.
I CAN'T TELL IF YOU'RE JOKING.
YOU'RE NOT THE FIRST WOMAN TO SAY THAT TO ME.
AND WHAT ABOUT THE OTHER GUY WHO WAS THERE LAST NIGHT? THE GOLDEN GUY?
YEAH, I FORGOT ABOUT HIM. I THOUGHT IT WAS THOR FOR A SECOND THERE.
IT'S THE SENTRY. SAVED MY LIFE TWICE LAST NIGHT.
THE SENTRY IS A PRETTY COMPLICATED STORY.
WE'RE GOING TO DEAL WITH THAT RIGHT AFTER THE EMERGENCY AT HAND.
SO DO WE KNOW WHAT HAPPENED LAST NIGHT?
BECAUSE THAT, Y'KNOW, SUCKED.
YES. WELL, THERE WAS A PRISON BREAK.
NO!
AT FIRST THEY THOUGHT IT WAS JUST A SYSTEM FAILURE THAT TURNED INTO A RIOT, BUT IT WASN'T. IT WAS A PRISON BREAK.
AN ASSAULT ON THE ISLAND. SPECIFICALLY TO BREAK OUT ONE INMATE.
WHO?
WE DON'T KNOW YET. NO ONE IS TALKING.
I JUST RECEIVED FOLDERS AND FOLDERS OF DATA FROM S.H.I.E.L.D.
THAT'S IT.
DIRECTOR HILL COOL WITH EVERYTHING?
WE'LL SEE.
SYSTEM PATCH IN.
DISPLAY.
OH MAN, IS THIS--
THIS IS WHO ESCAPED.

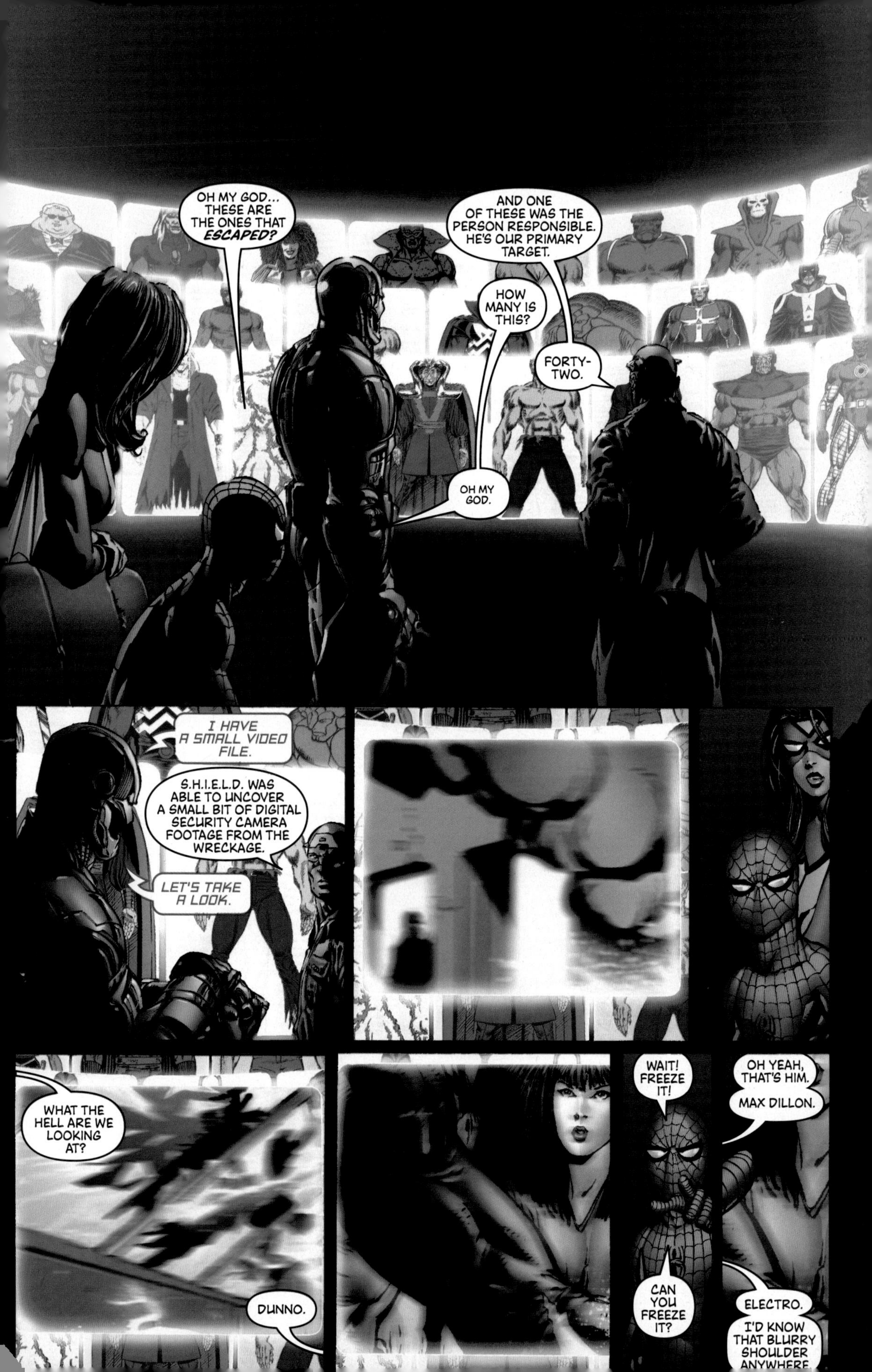
OH MY GOD... THESE ARE THE ONES THAT ESCAPED?
AND ONE OF THESE WAS THE PERSON RESPONSIBLE. HE'S OUR PRIMARY TARGET.
HOW MANY IS THIS?
FORTY-TWO.
OH MY GOD.
I HAVE A SMALL VIDEO FILE.
S.H.I.E.L.D. WAS ABLE TO UNCOVER A SMALL BIT OF DIGITAL SECURITY CAMERA FOOTAGE FROM THE WRECKAGE.
LET'S TAKE A LOOK.
WHAT THE HELL ARE WE LOOKING AT?
DUNNO.
WAIT! FREEZE IT!
CAN YOU FREEZE IT?
OH YEAH, THAT'S HIM.
MAX DILLON.
ELECTRO.
I'D KNOW THAT BLURRY SHOULDER ANYWHERE.

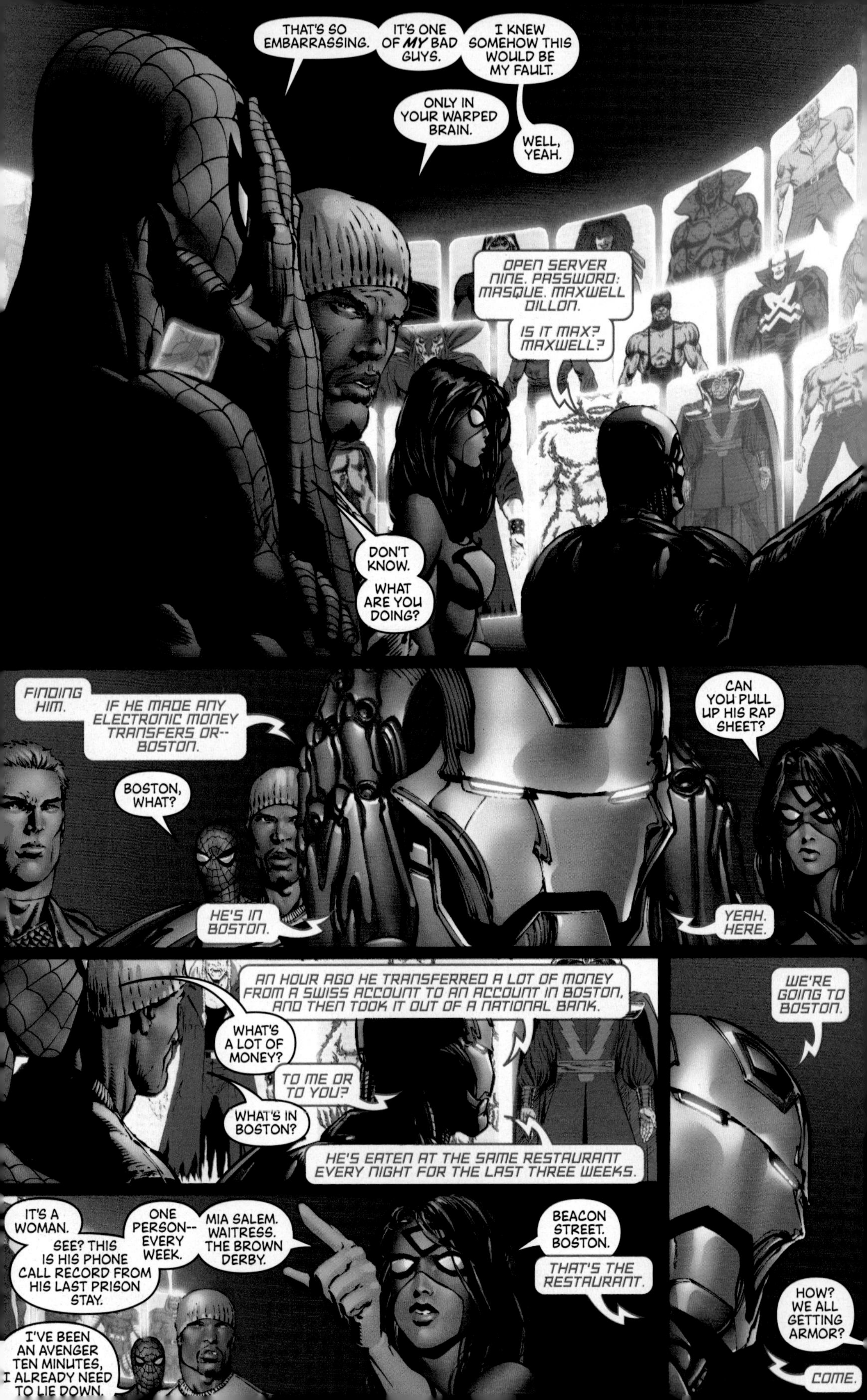

THAT'S SO EMBARRASSING.
IT'S ONE OF MY BAD GUYS.
I KNEW SOMEHOW THIS WOULD BE MY FAULT.
ONLY IN YOUR WARPED BRAIN.
WELL, YEAH.
OPEN SERVER NINE. PASSWORD: MASQUE. MAXWELL DILLON.
IS IT MAX? MAXWELL?
DON'T KNOW.
WHAT ARE YOU DOING?
FINDING HIM.
IF HE MADE ANY ELECTRONIC MONEY TRANSFERS OR-- BOSTON.
BOSTON, WHAT?
HE'S IN BOSTON.
CAN YOU PULL UP HIS RAP SHEET?
YEAH. HERE.
AN HOUR AGO HE TRANSFERRED A LOT OF MONEY FROM A SWISS ACCOUNT TO AN ACCOUNT IN BOSTON, AND THEN TOOK IT OUT OF A NATIONAL BANK.
WHAT'S A LOT OF MONEY?
TO ME OR TO YOU?
WHAT'S IN BOSTON?
HE'S EATEN AT THE SAME RESTAURANT EVERY NIGHT FOR THE LAST THREE WEEKS.
WE'RE GOING TO BOSTON.
IT'S A WOMAN.
SEE? THIS IS HIS PHONE CALL RECORD FROM HIS LAST PRISON STAY.
ONE PERSON-- EVERY WEEK.
MIA SALEM. WAITRESS. THE BROWN DERBY.
BEACON STREET. BOSTON.
THAT'S THE RESTAURANT.
I'VE BEEN AN AVENGER TEN MINUTES, I ALREADY NEED TO LIE DOWN.
HOW? WE ALL GETTING ARMOR?
COME.

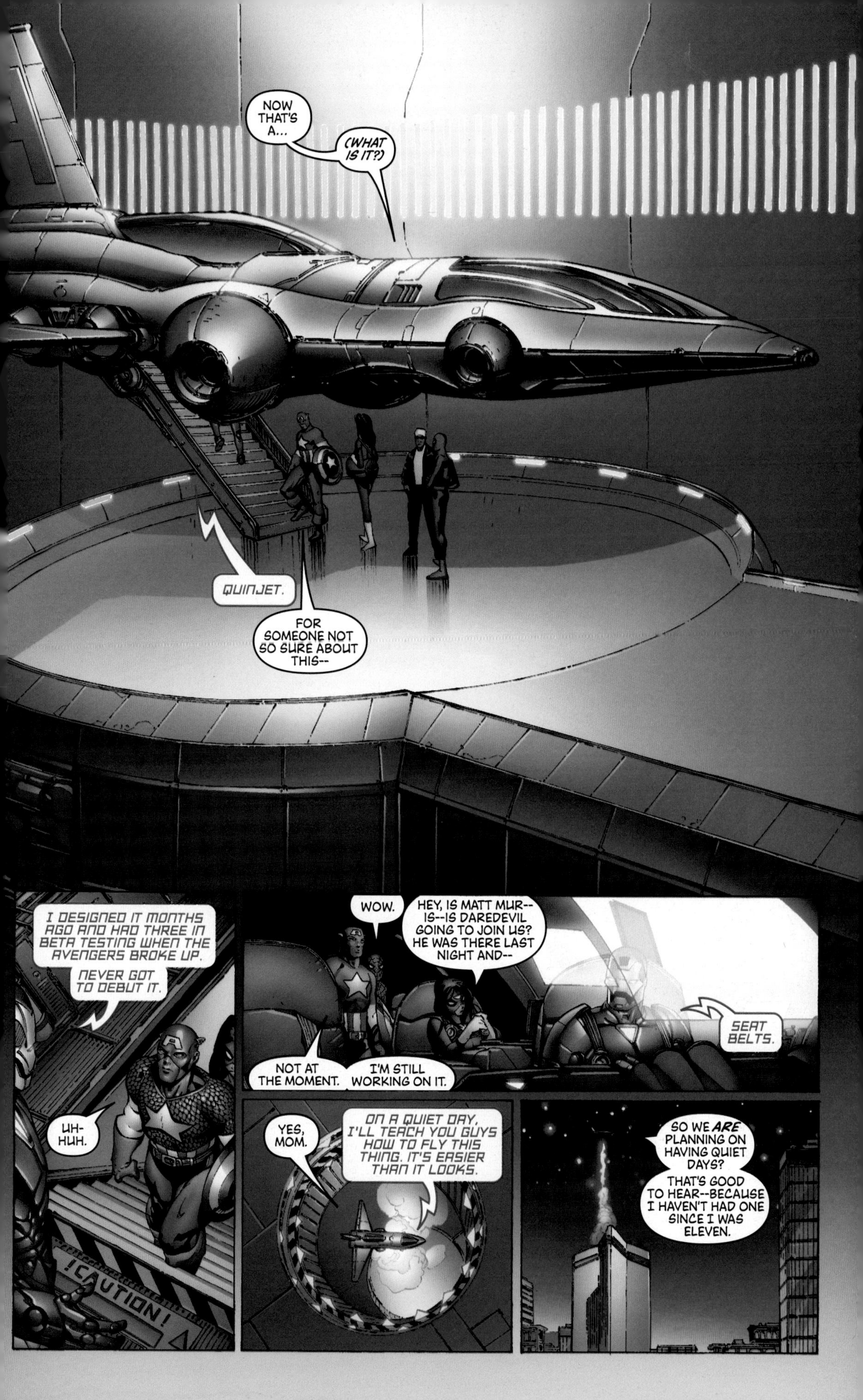
NOW THAT'S A...
(WHAT IS IT?)
QUINJET.
FOR SOMEONE NOT SO SURE ABOUT THIS--
I DESIGNED IT MONTHS AGO AND HAD THREE IN BETA TESTING WHEN THE AVENGERS BROKE UP.
NEVER GOT TO DEBUT IT.
UH-HUH.
!CAUTION!
WOW.
HEY, IS MATT MUR-- IS--IS DAREDEVIL GOING TO JOIN US? HE WAS THERE LAST NIGHT AND--
NOT AT THE MOMENT.
I'M STILL WORKING ON IT.
SEAT BELTS.
YES, MOM.
ON A QUIET DAY, I'LL TEACH YOU GUYS HOW TO FLY THIS THING. IT'S EASIER THAN IT LOOKS.
SO WE ARE PLANNING ON HAVING QUIET DAYS?
THAT'S GOOD TO HEAR--BECAUSE I HAVEN'T HAD ONE SINCE I WAS ELEVEN.

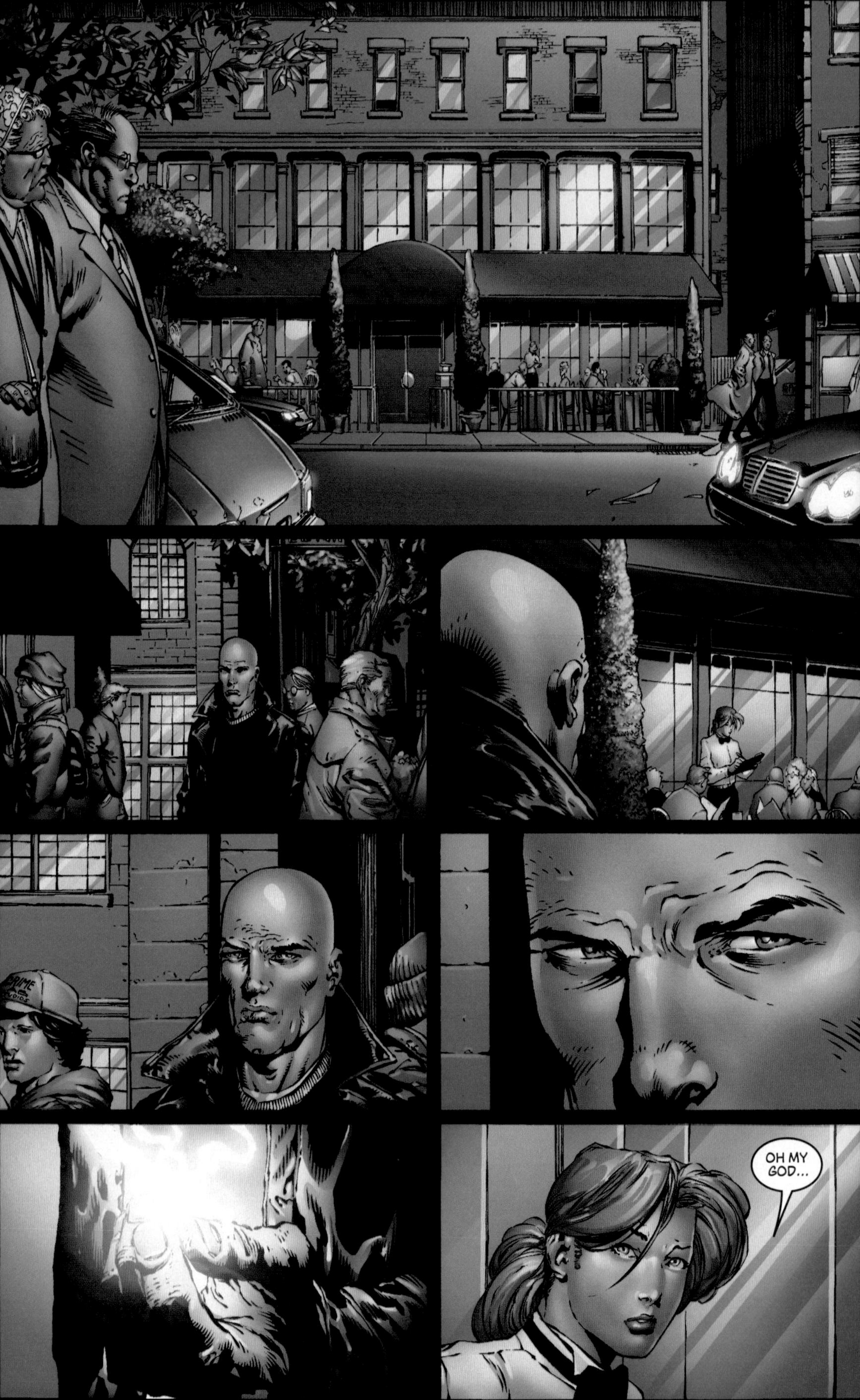
OH MY GOD...

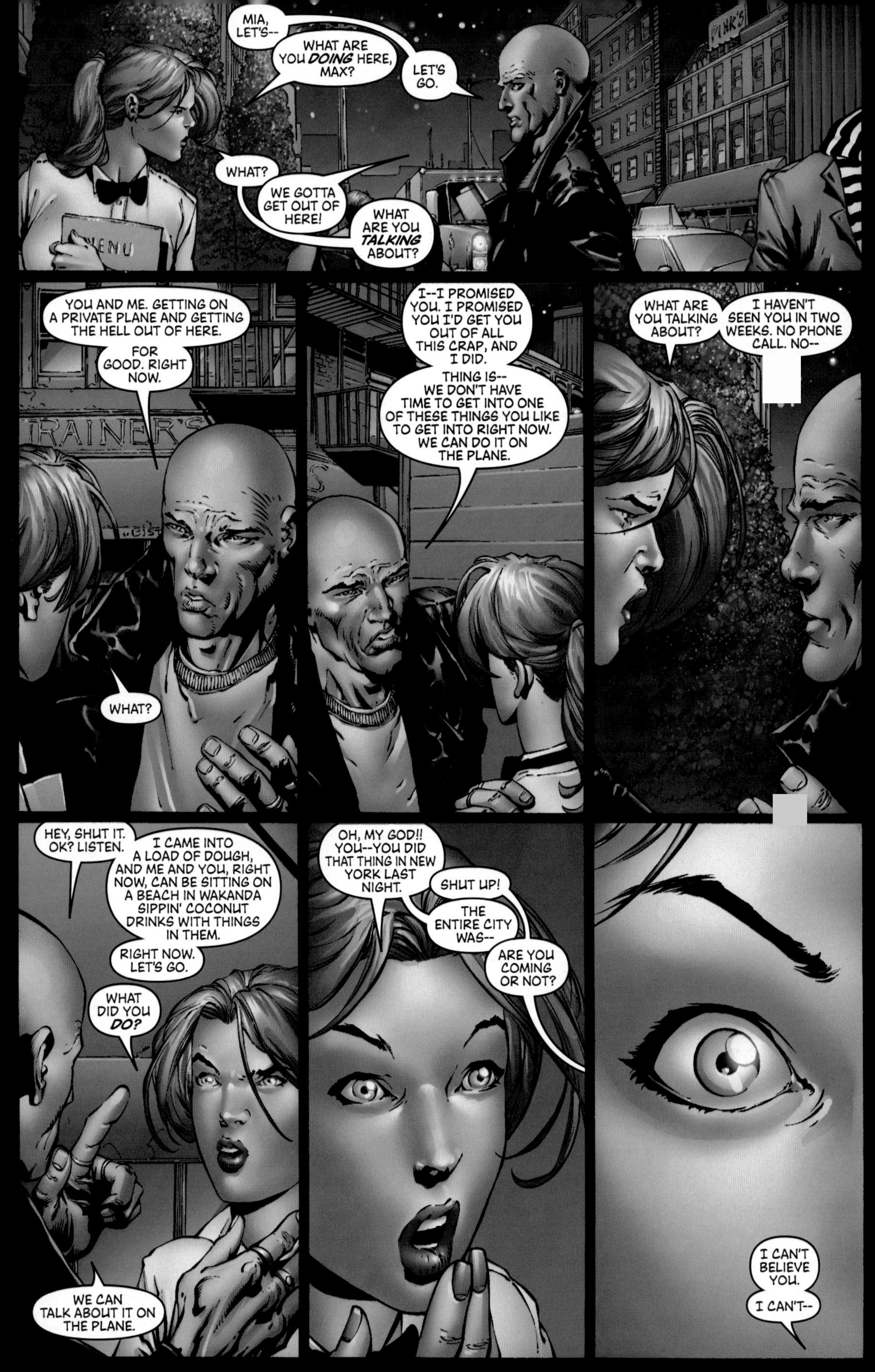
MIA, LET'S--
WHAT ARE YOU *DOING* HERE, MAX?
LET'S GO.
PINK'S
WHAT?
WE GOTTA GET OUT OF HERE!
WHAT ARE YOU *TALKING* ABOUT?
MENU
YOU AND ME. GETTING ON A PRIVATE PLANE AND GETTING THE HELL OUT OF HERE.
FOR GOOD. RIGHT NOW.
TRAINER'S
WHAT?
I--I PROMISED YOU. I PROMISED YOU I'D GET YOU OUT OF ALL THIS CRAP, AND I DID.
THING IS-- WE DON'T HAVE TIME TO GET INTO ONE OF THESE THINGS YOU LIKE TO GET INTO RIGHT NOW. WE CAN DO IT ON THE PLANE.
WHAT ARE YOU TALKING ABOUT?
I HAVEN'T SEEN YOU IN TWO WEEKS. NO PHONE CALL. NO--
HEY, SHUT IT. OK? LISTEN.
I CAME INTO A LOAD OF DOUGH, AND ME AND YOU, RIGHT NOW, CAN BE SITTING ON A BEACH IN WAKANDA SIPPIN' COCONUT DRINKS WITH THINGS IN THEM.
RIGHT NOW. LET'S GO.
WHAT DID YOU *DO?*
WE CAN TALK ABOUT IT ON THE PLANE.
OH, MY GOD!! YOU--YOU DID THAT THING IN NEW YORK LAST NIGHT.
SHUT UP!
THE ENTIRE CITY WAS--
ARE YOU COMING OR NOT?
I CAN'T BELIEVE YOU.
I CAN'T--

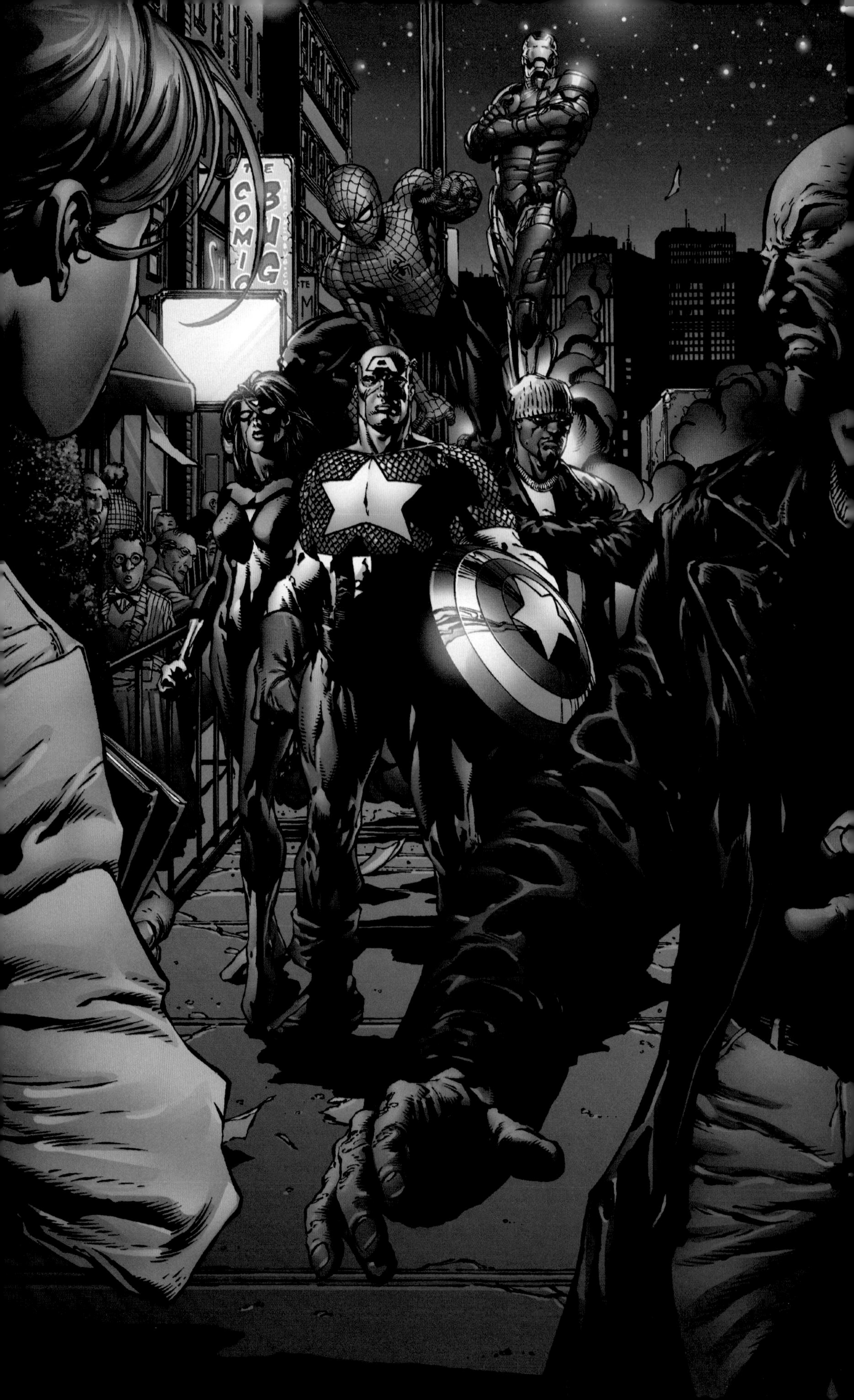
BUG

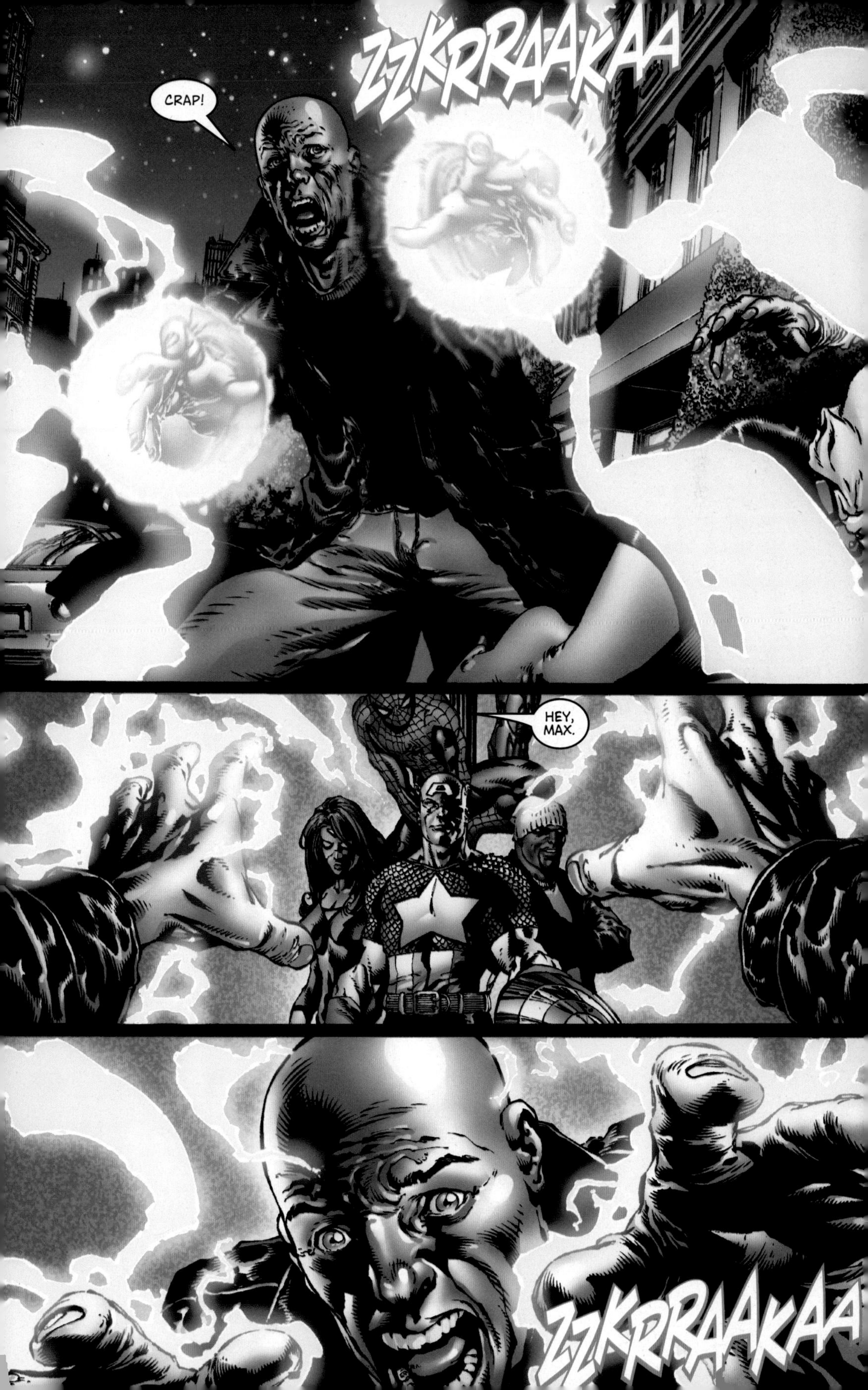
ZZKRRAAKAA
CRAP!
HEY, MAX.
ZZKRRAAKAA

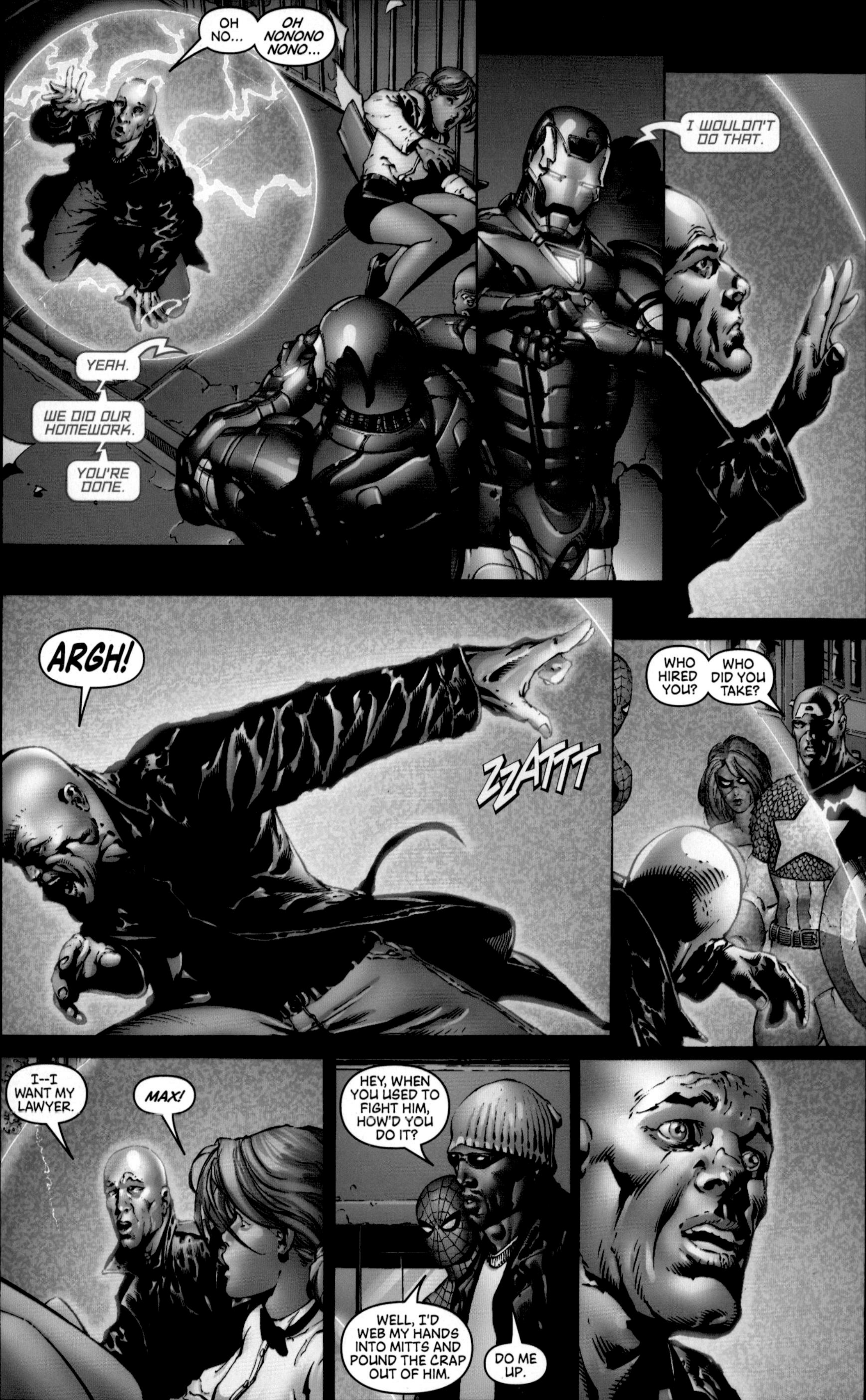

OH NO... OH NONONO NONO...
I WOULDN'T DO THAT.
YEAH.
WE DID OUR HOMEWORK.
YOU'RE DONE.
ARGH!
ZZATTT
WHO HIRED YOU?
WHO DID YOU TAKE?
I--I WANT MY LAWYER.
MAX!
HEY, WHEN YOU USED TO FIGHT HIM, HOW'D YOU DO IT?
WELL, I'D WEB MY HANDS INTO MITTS AND POUND THE CRAP OUT OF HIM.
DO ME UP.

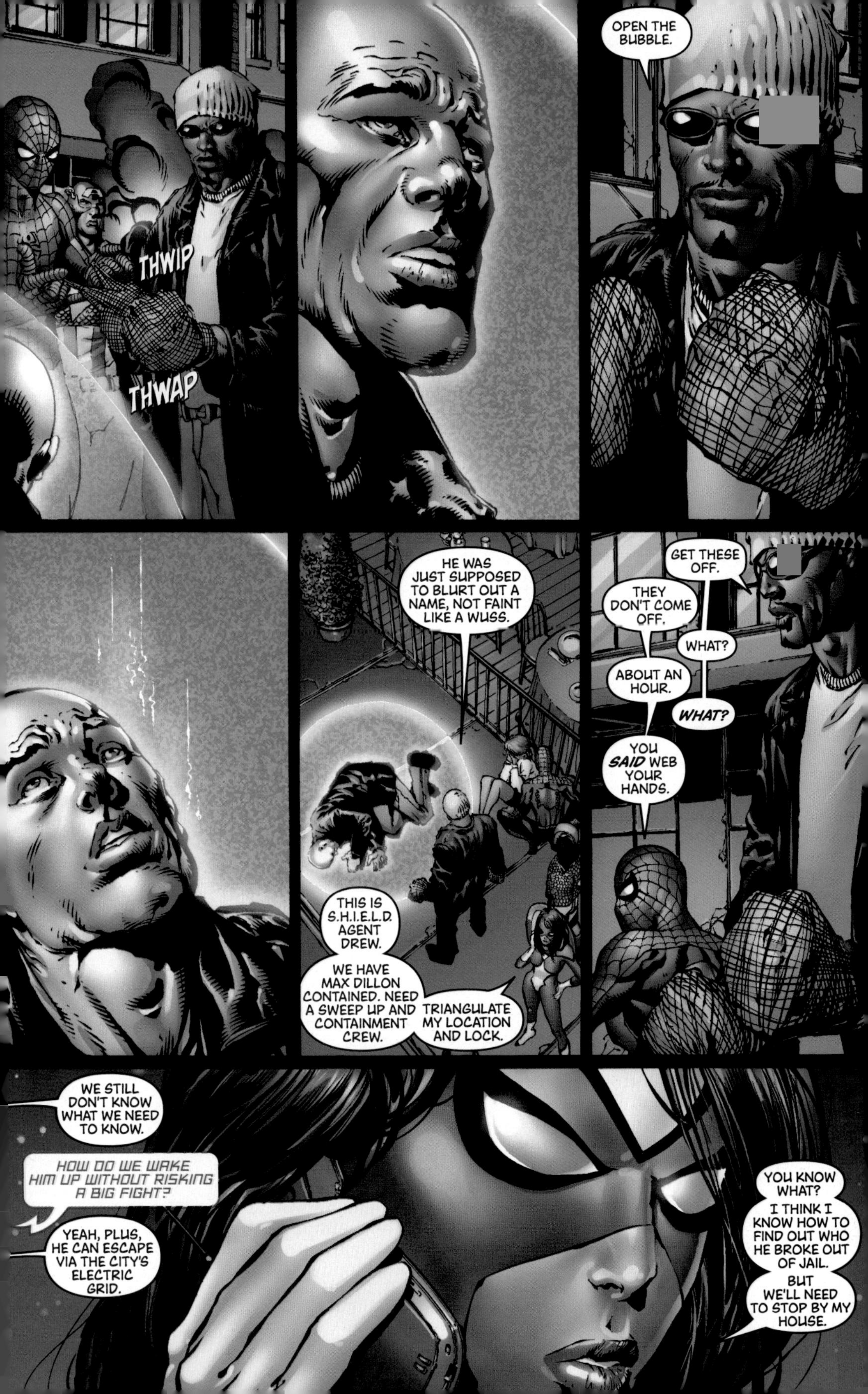
THWIP
THWAP
OPEN THE BUBBLE.
HE WAS JUST SUPPOSED TO BLURT OUT A NAME, NOT FAINT LIKE A WUSS.
THIS IS S.H.I.E.L.D. AGENT DREW.
WE HAVE MAX DILLON CONTAINED. NEED A SWEEP UP AND CONTAINMENT CREW.
TRIANGULATE MY LOCATION AND LOCK.
GET THESE OFF.
THEY DON'T COME OFF.
WHAT?
ABOUT AN HOUR.
WHAT?
YOU SAID WEB YOUR HANDS.
WE STILL DON'T KNOW WHAT WE NEED TO KNOW.
HOW DO WE WAKE HIM UP WITHOUT RISKING A BIG FIGHT?
YEAH, PLUS, HE CAN ESCAPE VIA THE CITY'S ELECTRIC GRID.
YOU KNOW WHAT?
I THINK I KNOW HOW TO FIND OUT WHO HE BROKE OUT OF JAIL.
BUT WE'LL NEED TO STOP BY MY HOUSE.

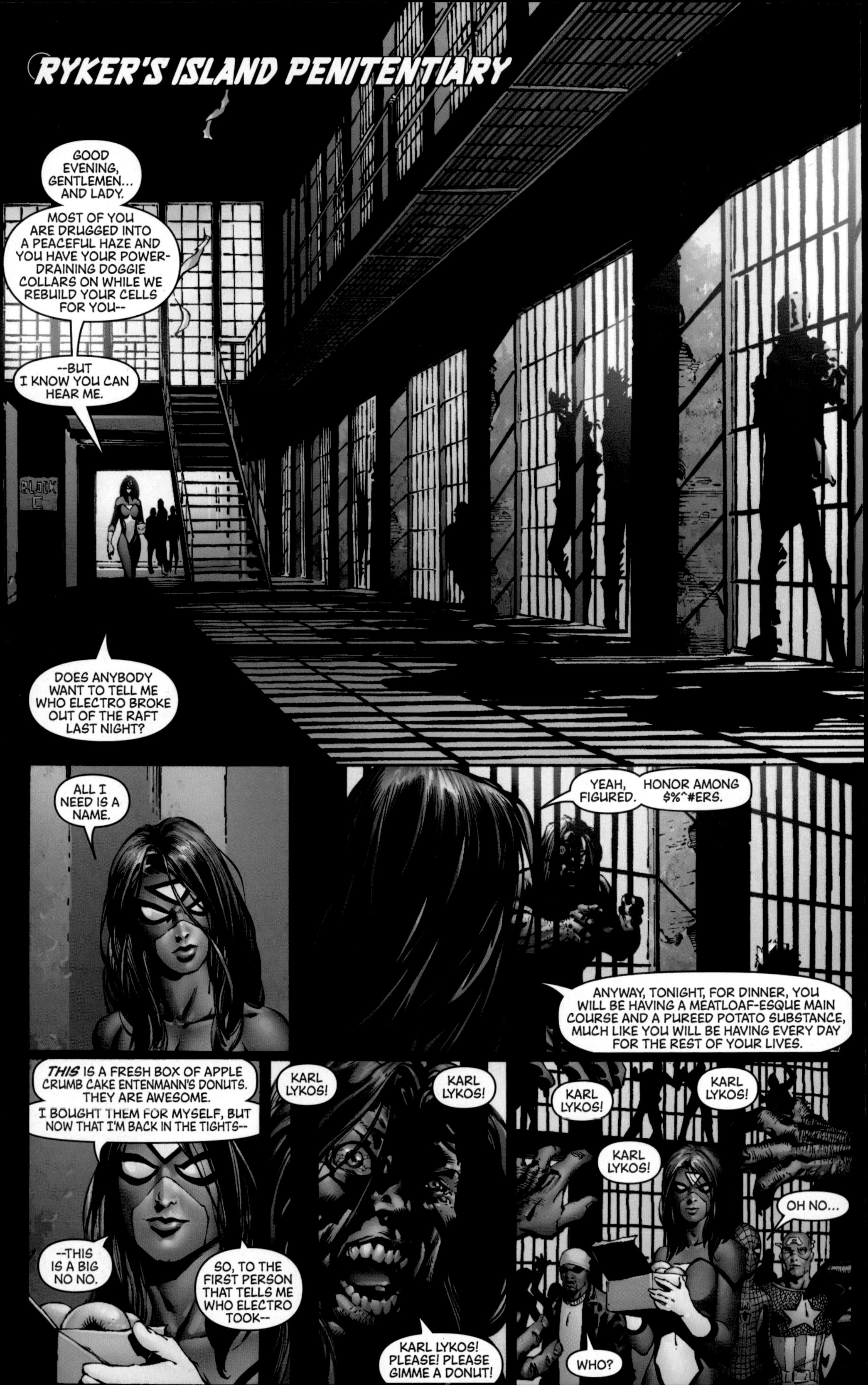
RYKER'S ISLAND PENITENTIARY
GOOD EVENING, GENTLEMEN... AND LADY.
MOST OF YOU ARE DRUGGED INTO A PEACEFUL HAZE AND YOU HAVE YOUR POWER-DRAINING DOGGIE COLLARS ON WHILE WE REBUILD YOUR CELLS FOR YOU--
--BUT I KNOW YOU CAN HEAR ME.
BLOCK C
DOES ANYBODY WANT TO TELL ME WHO ELECTRO BROKE OUT OF THE RAFT LAST NIGHT?
ALL I NEED IS A NAME.
YEAH, FIGURED.
HONOR AMONG $%^#ERS.
ANYWAY, TONIGHT, FOR DINNER, YOU WILL BE HAVING A MEATLOAF-ESQUE MAIN COURSE AND A PUREED POTATO SUBSTANCE, MUCH LIKE YOU WILL BE HAVING EVERY DAY FOR THE REST OF YOUR LIVES.
THIS IS A FRESH BOX OF APPLE CRUMB CAKE ENTENMANN'S DONUTS. THEY ARE AWESOME.
I BOUGHT THEM FOR MYSELF, BUT NOW THAT I'M BACK IN THE TIGHTS--
--THIS IS A BIG NO NO.
SO, TO THE FIRST PERSON THAT TELLS ME WHO ELECTRO TOOK--
KARL LYKOS!
KARL LYKOS!
KARL LYKOS! PLEASE! PLEASE GIMME A DONUT!
KARL LYKOS!
KARL LYKOS!
KARL LYKOS!
OH NO...
WHO?

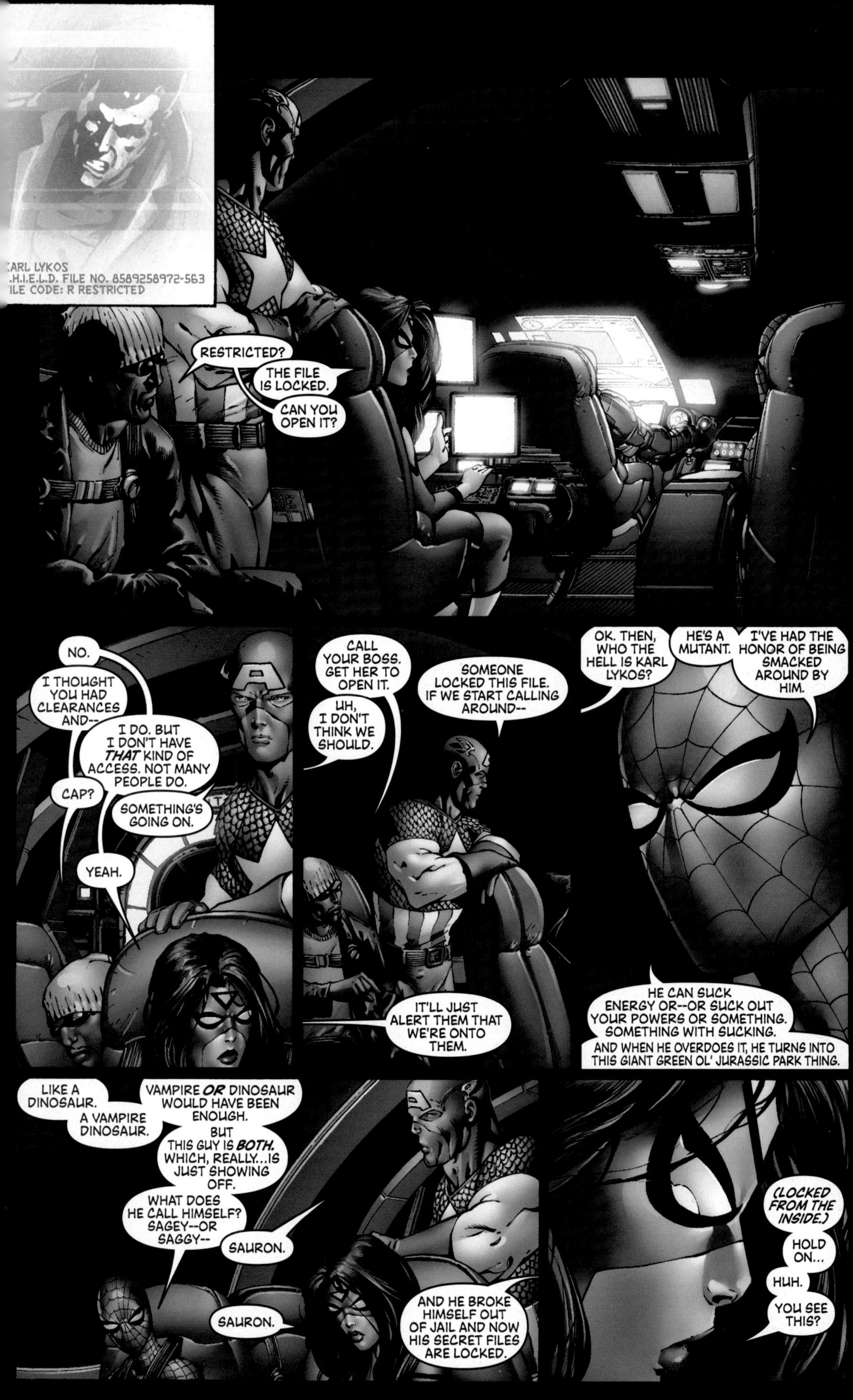

KARL LYKOS
.H.I.E.L.D. FILE NO. 8589258972-563
ILE CODE: R RESTRICTED
RESTRICTED?
THE FILE IS LOCKED.
CAN YOU OPEN IT?
NO.
I THOUGHT YOU HAD CLEARANCES AND--
I DO. BUT I DON'T HAVE *THAT* KIND OF ACCESS. NOT MANY PEOPLE DO.
CAP?
SOMETHING'S GOING ON.
YEAH.
CALL YOUR BOSS. GET HER TO OPEN IT.
UH, I DON'T THINK WE SHOULD.
SOMEONE LOCKED THIS FILE. IF WE START CALLING AROUND--
IT'LL JUST ALERT THEM THAT WE'RE ONTO THEM.
OK. THEN, WHO THE HELL IS KARL LYKOS?
HE'S A MUTANT.
I'VE HAD THE HONOR OF BEING SMACKED AROUND BY HIM.
HE CAN SUCK ENERGY OR--OR SUCK OUT YOUR POWERS OR SOMETHING. SOMETHING WITH SUCKING.
AND WHEN HE OVERDOES IT, HE TURNS INTO THIS GIANT GREEN OL' JURASSIC PARK THING.
LIKE A DINOSAUR.
A VAMPIRE DINOSAUR.
VAMPIRE *OR* DINOSAUR WOULD HAVE BEEN ENOUGH.
BUT THIS GUY IS *BOTH.* WHICH, REALLY...IS JUST SHOWING OFF.
WHAT DOES HE CALL HIMSELF? SAGEY--OR SAGGY--
SAURON.
SAURON.
AND HE BROKE HIMSELF OUT OF JAIL AND NOW HIS SECRET FILES ARE LOCKED.
(LOCKED FROM THE INSIDE.)
HOLD ON...
HUH.
YOU SEE THIS?

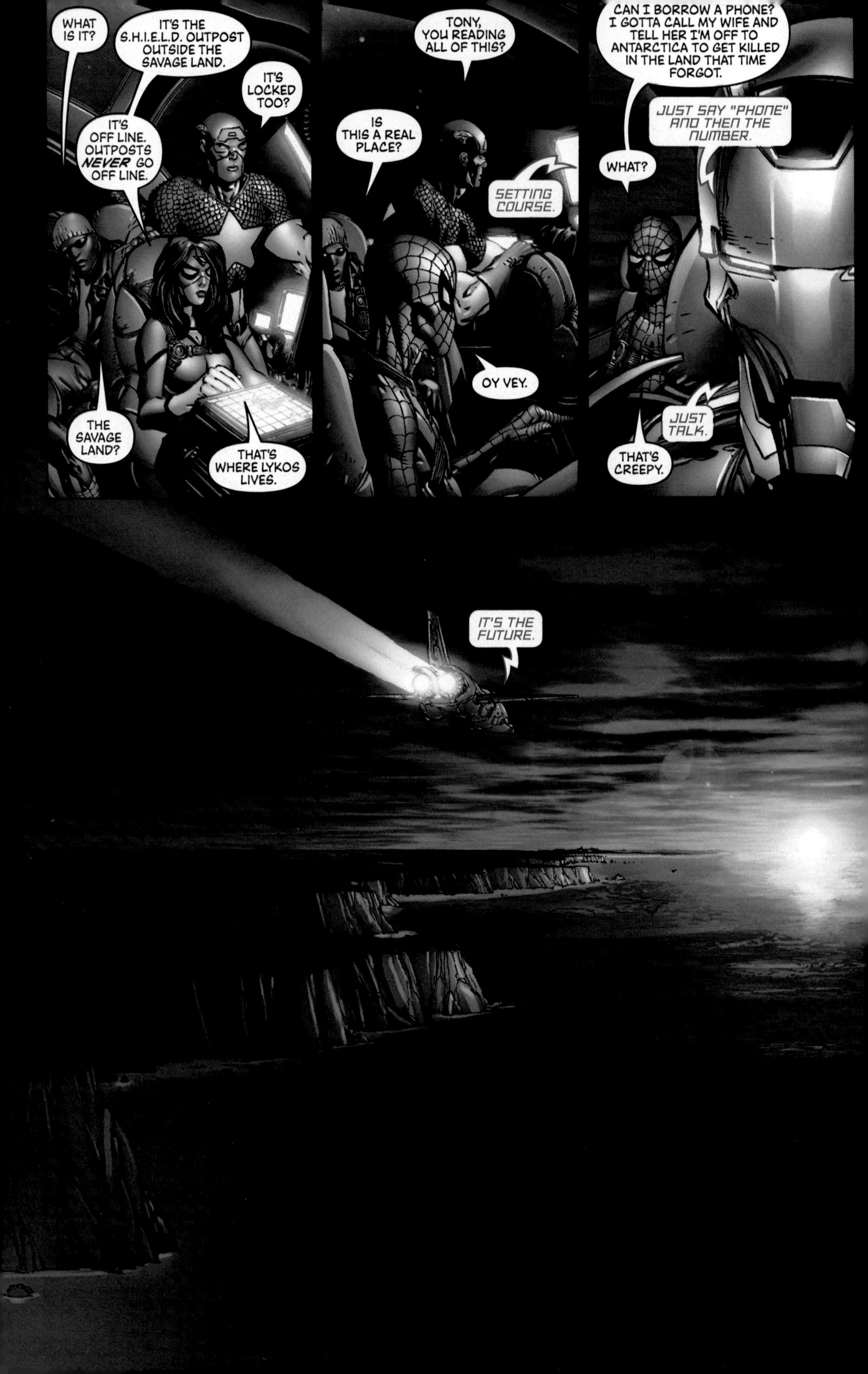
WHAT IS IT?
IT'S THE S.H.I.E.L.D. OUTPOST OUTSIDE THE SAVAGE LAND.
IT'S LOCKED TOO?
IT'S OFF LINE. OUTPOSTS NEVER GO OFF LINE.
THE SAVAGE LAND?
THAT'S WHERE LYKOS LIVES.
TONY, YOU READING ALL OF THIS?
IS THIS A REAL PLACE?
SETTING COURSE.
OY VEY.
CAN I BORROW A PHONE? I GOTTA CALL MY WIFE AND TELL HER I'M OFF TO ANTARCTICA TO GET KILLED IN THE LAND THAT TIME FORGOT.
JUST SAY "PHONE" AND THEN THE NUMBER.
WHAT?
JUST TALK.
THAT'S CREEPY.
IT'S THE FUTURE.

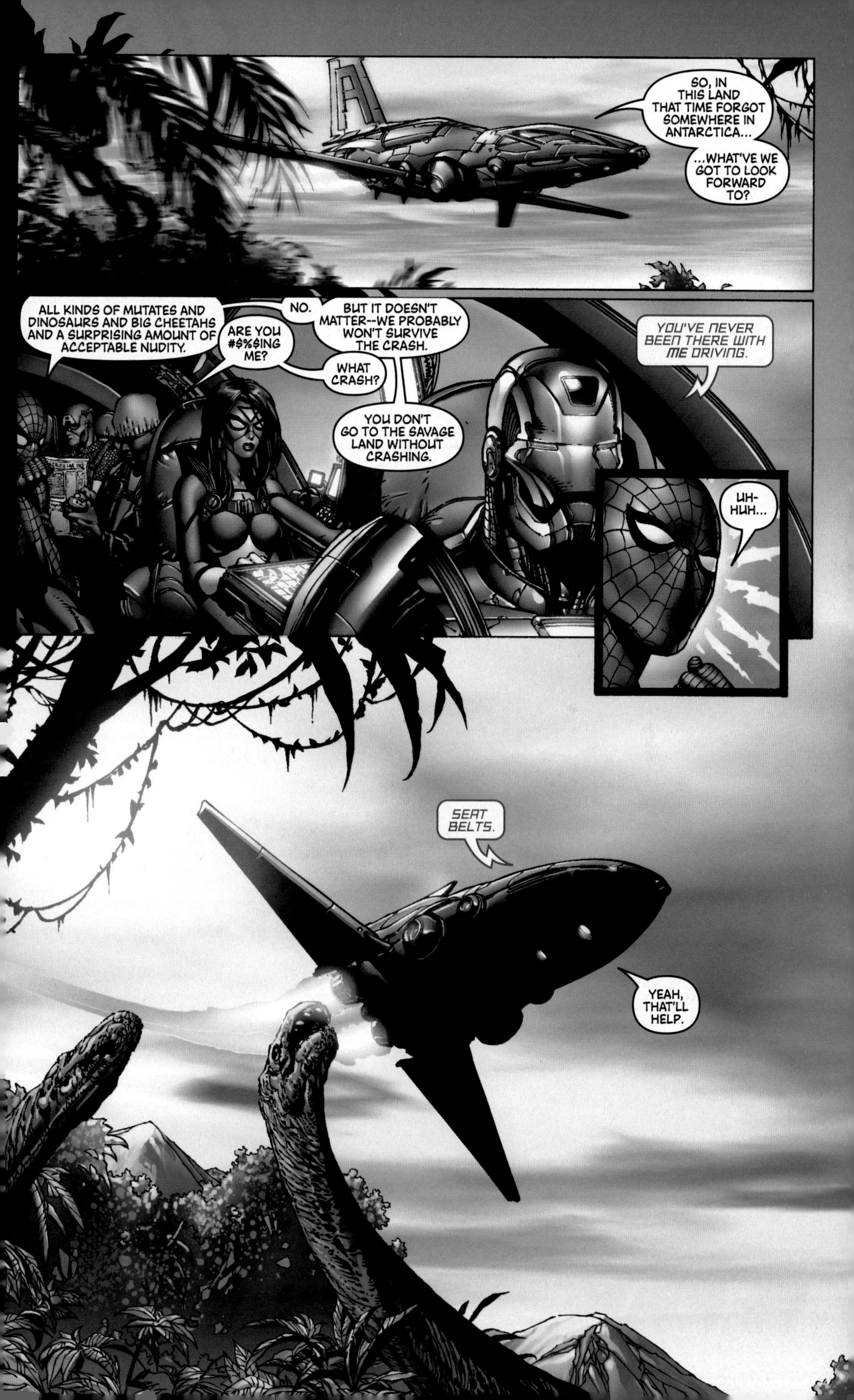
SO, IN THIS LAND THAT TIME FORGOT SOMEWHERE IN ANTARCTICA...
...WHAT'VE WE GOT TO LOOK FORWARD TO?
ALL KINDS OF MUTATES AND DINOSAURS AND BIG CHEETAHS AND A SURPRISING AMOUNT OF ACCEPTABLE NUDITY.
ARE YOU #$%$ING ME?
NO.
BUT IT DOESN'T MATTER--WE PROBABLY WON'T SURVIVE THE CRASH.
WHAT CRASH?
YOU DON'T GO TO THE SAVAGE LAND WITHOUT CRASHING.
YOU'VE NEVER BEEN THERE WITH ME DRIVING.
UH-HUH...
SEAT BELTS.
YEAH, THAT'LL HELP.

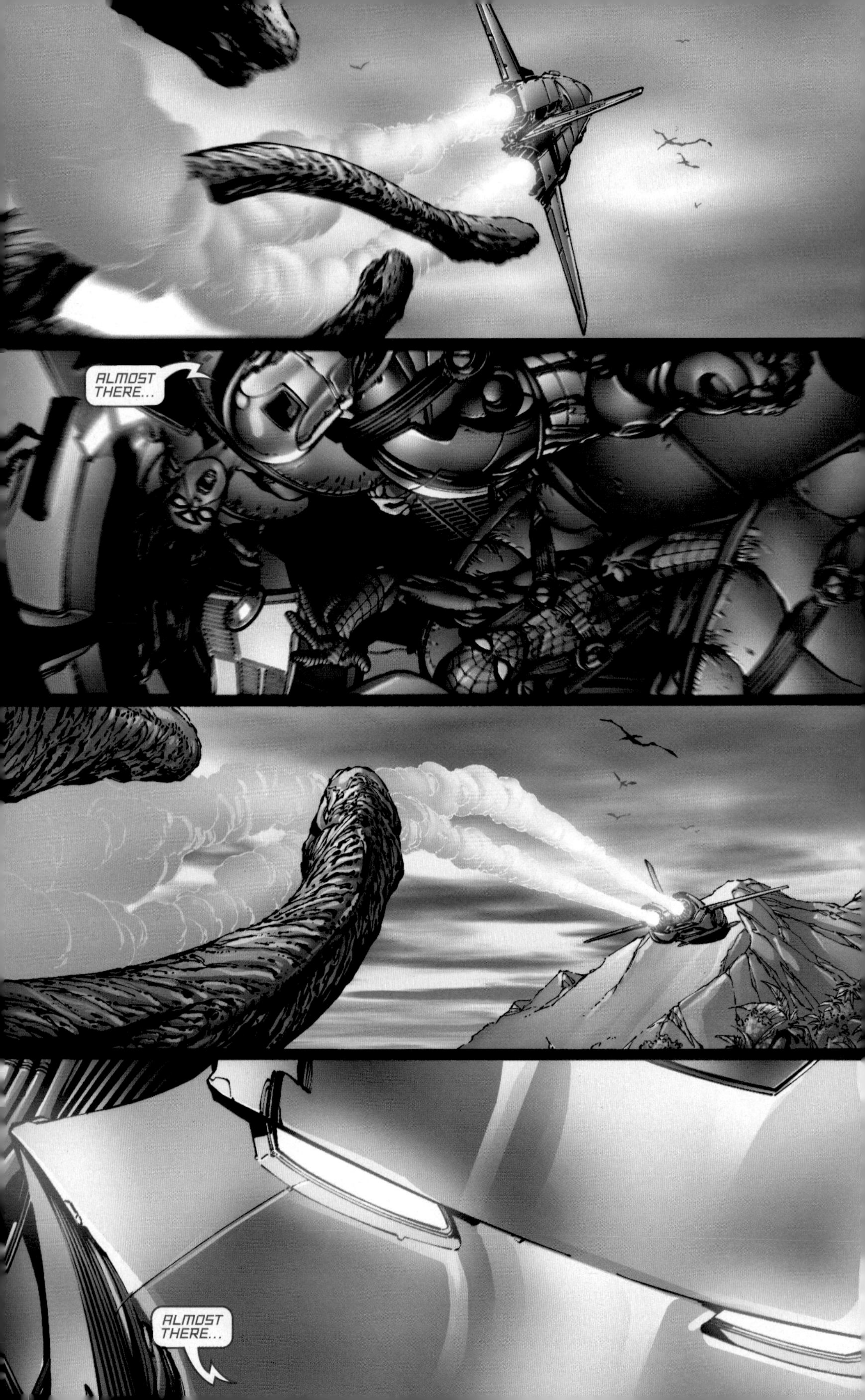
ALMOST THERE...
ALMOST THERE...

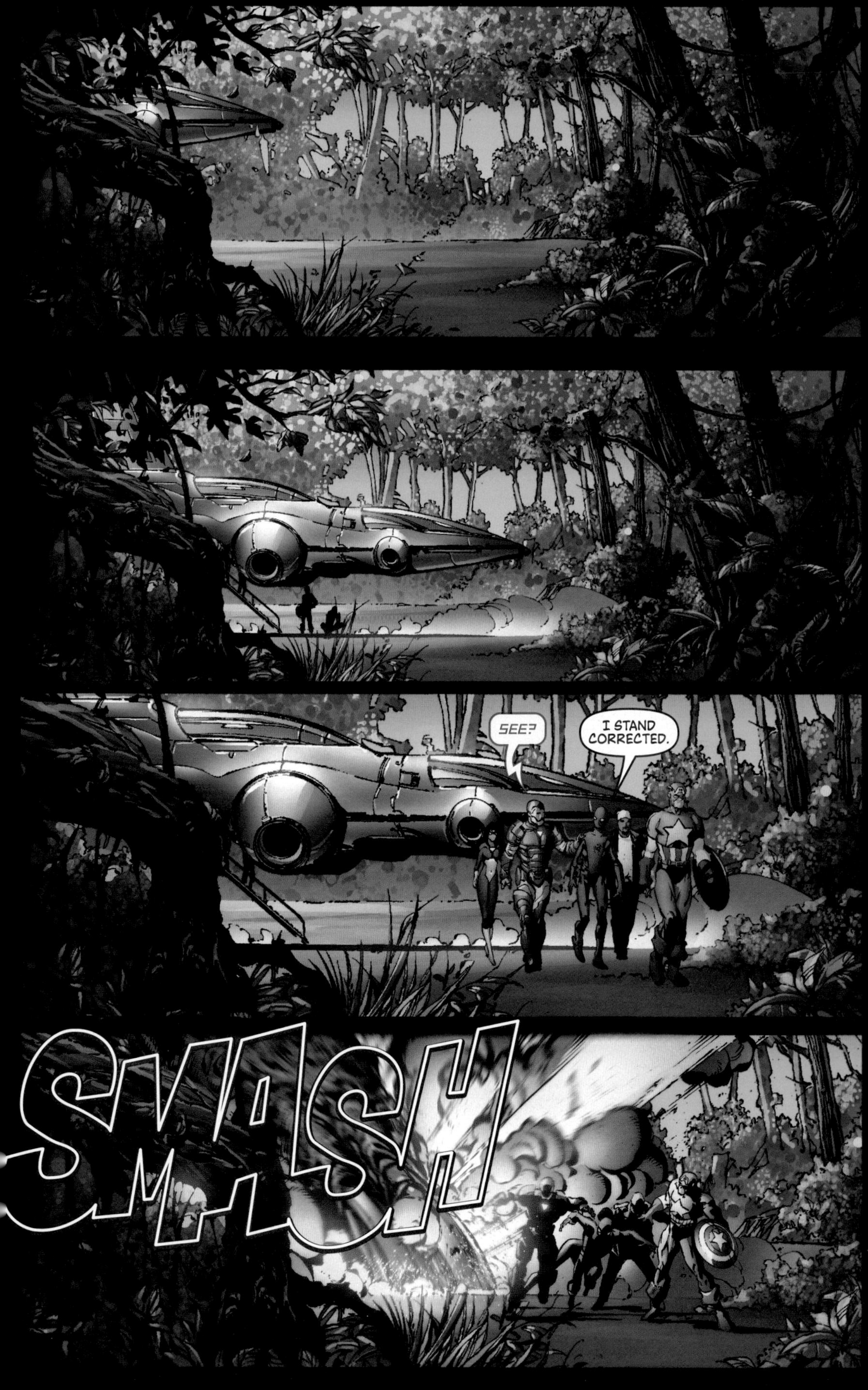
SEE?
I STAND CORRECTED.
SMASH

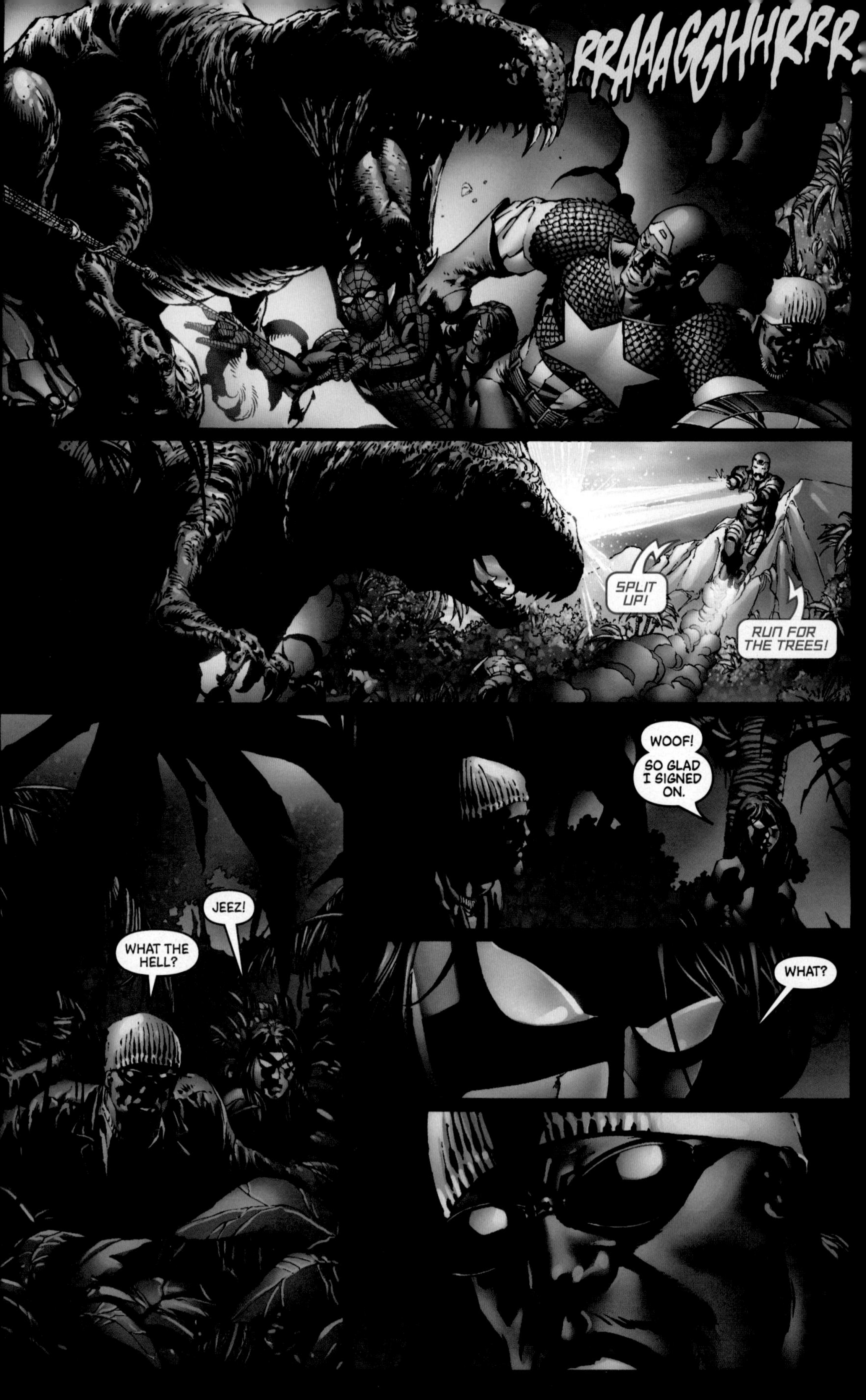
RRAAAGGHHRRR!
SPLIT UP!
RUN FOR THE TREES!
WOOF! SO GLAD I SIGNED ON.
WHAT THE HELL?
JEEZ!
WHAT?

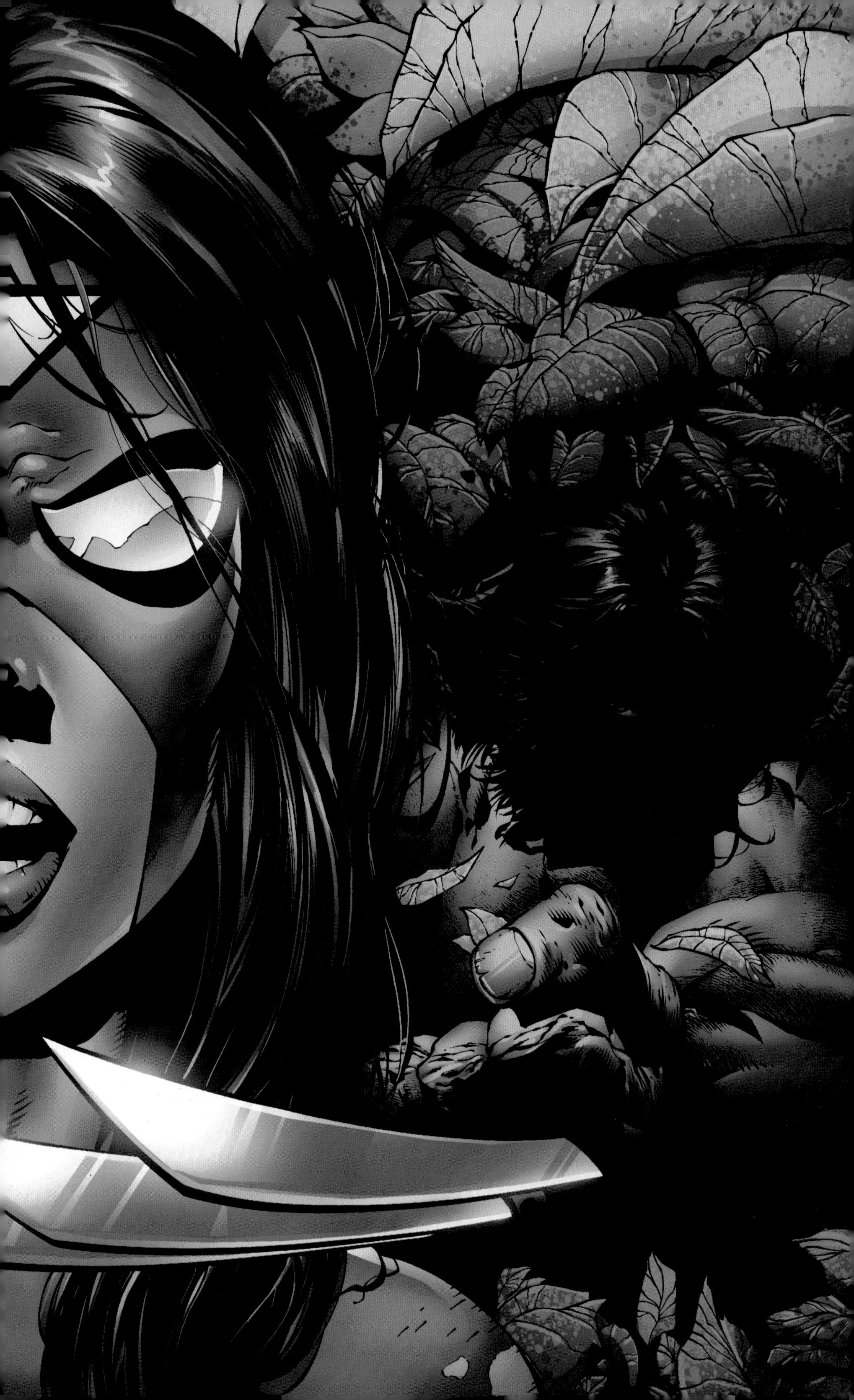

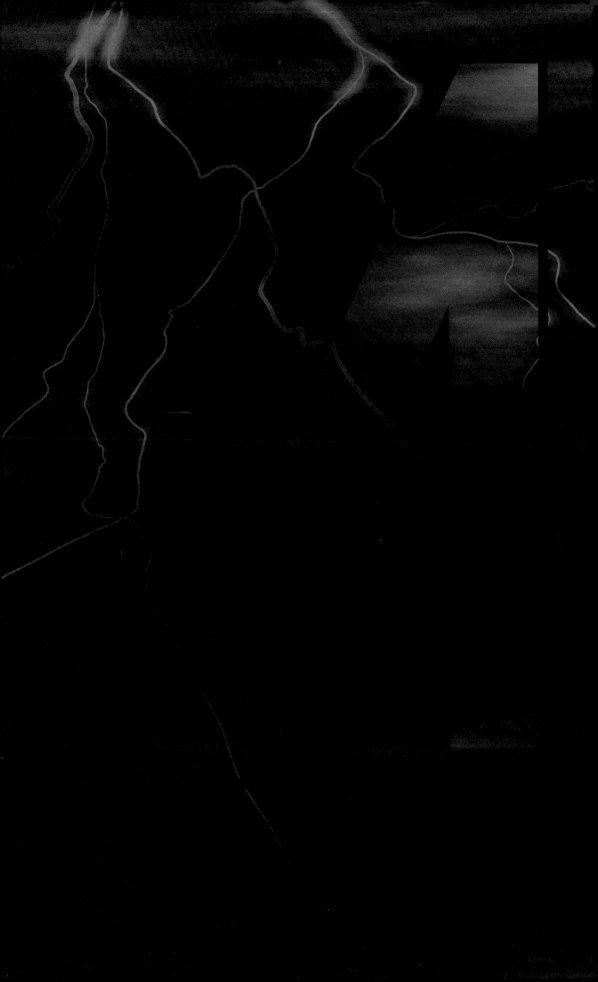

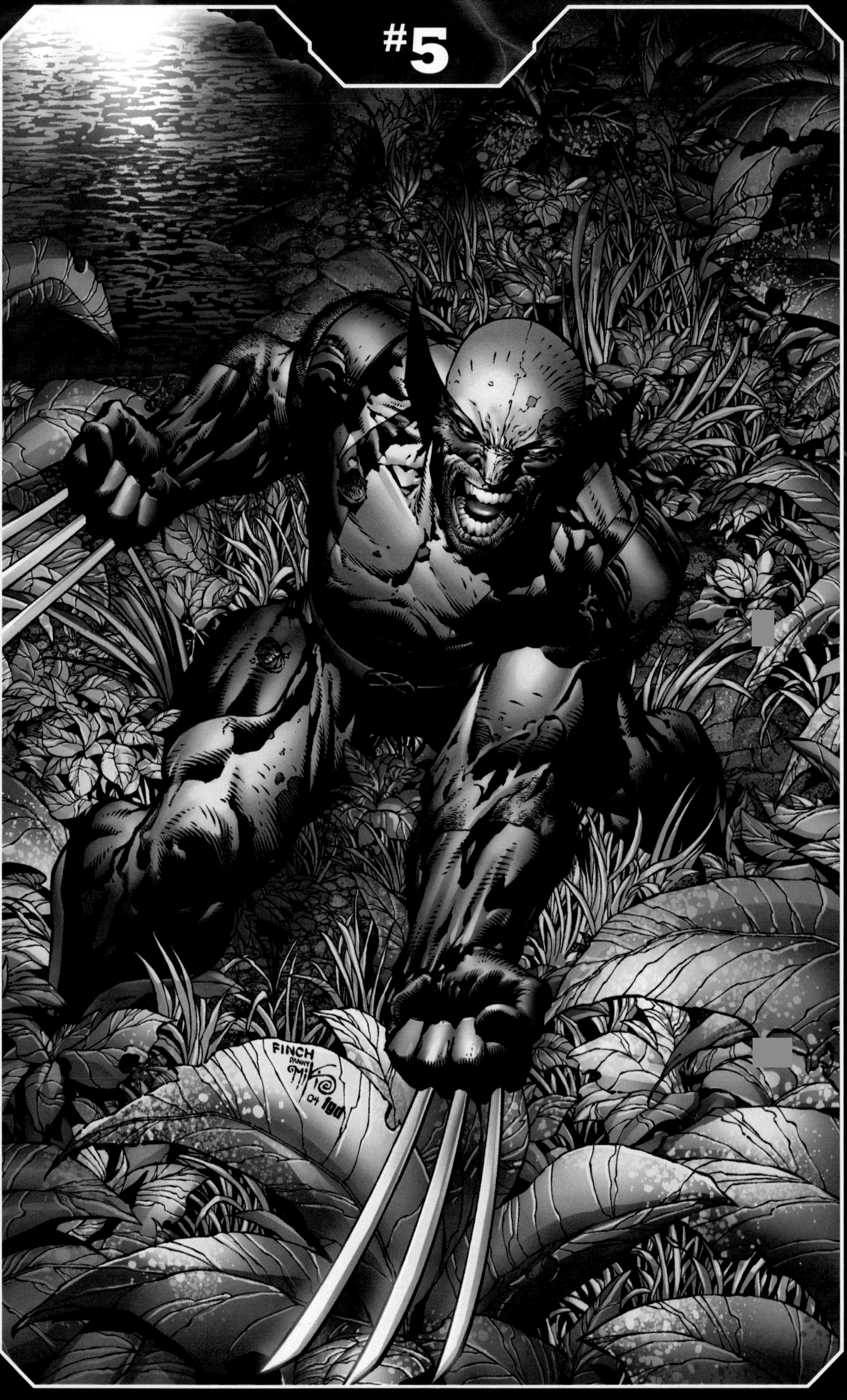
#5

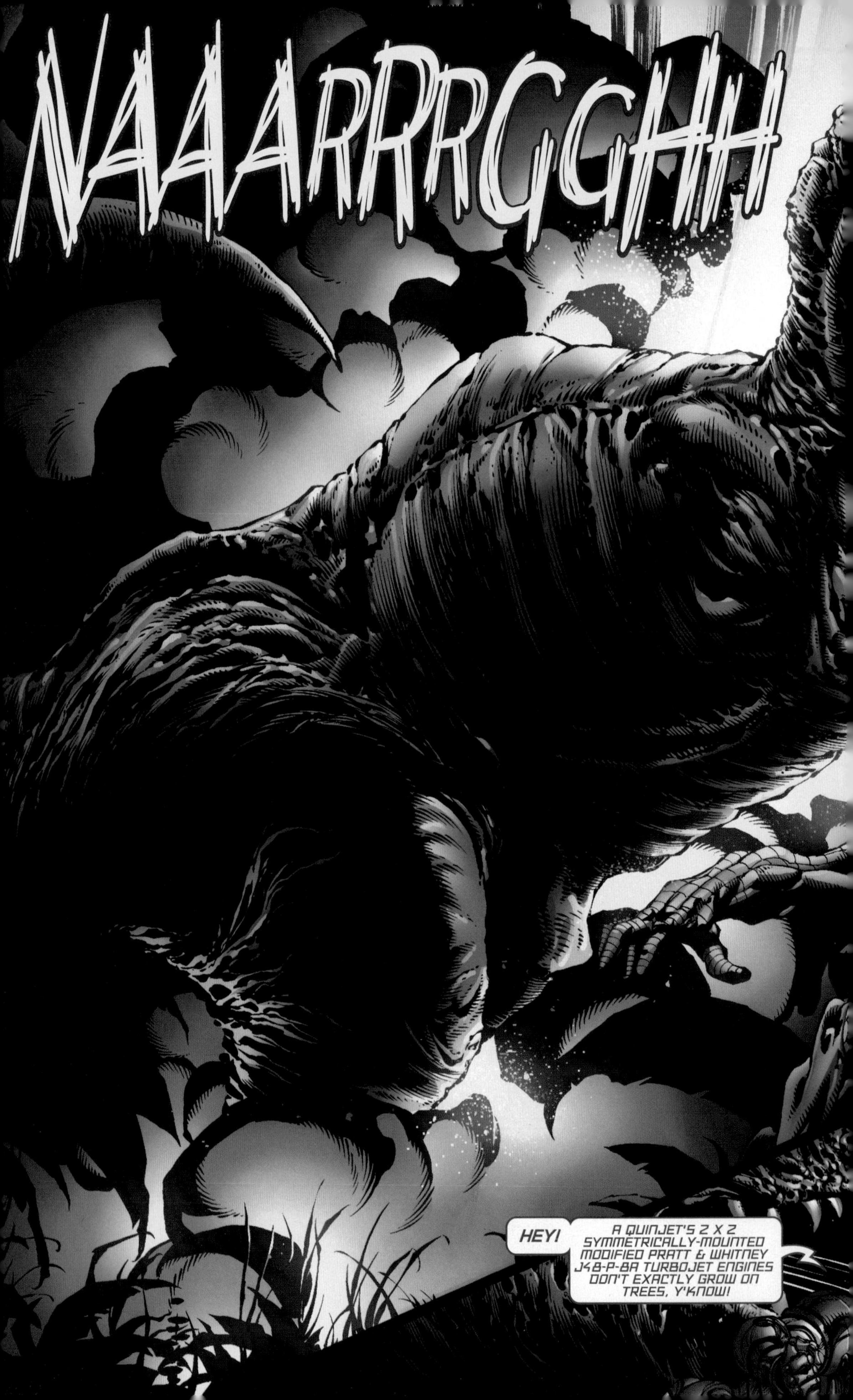
NAAARRRGGHH
HEY!
A QUINJET'S 2 X 2 SYMMETRICALLY-MOUNTED MODIFIED PRATT & WHITNEY J48-P-8A TURBOJET ENGINES DON'T EXACTLY GROW ON TREES, Y'KNOW!

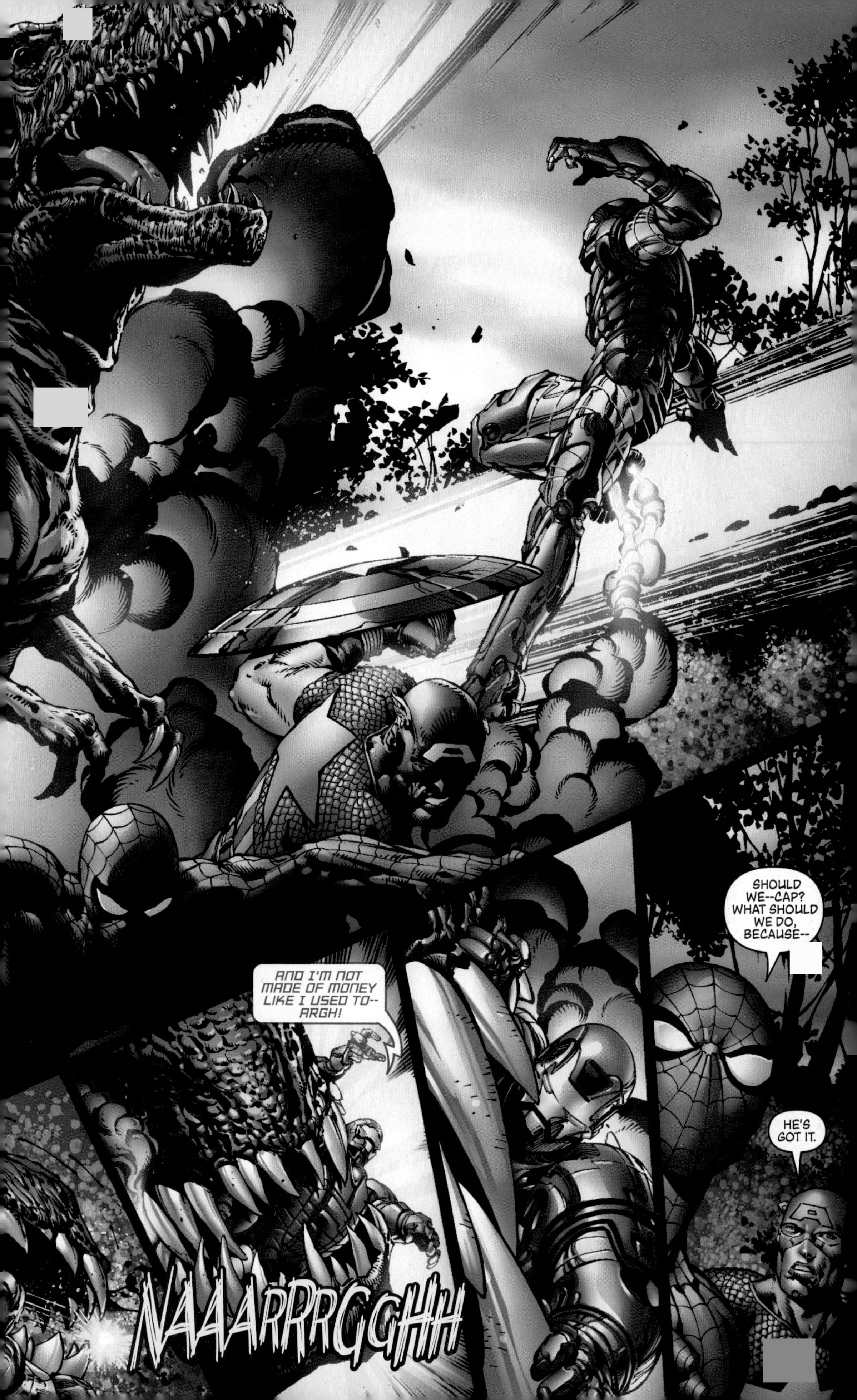
AND I'M NOT MADE OF MONEY LIKE I USED TO-- ARGH!
NAAARRRGGHH
SHOULD WE--CAP? WHAT SHOULD WE DO, BECAUSE--
HE'S GOT IT.

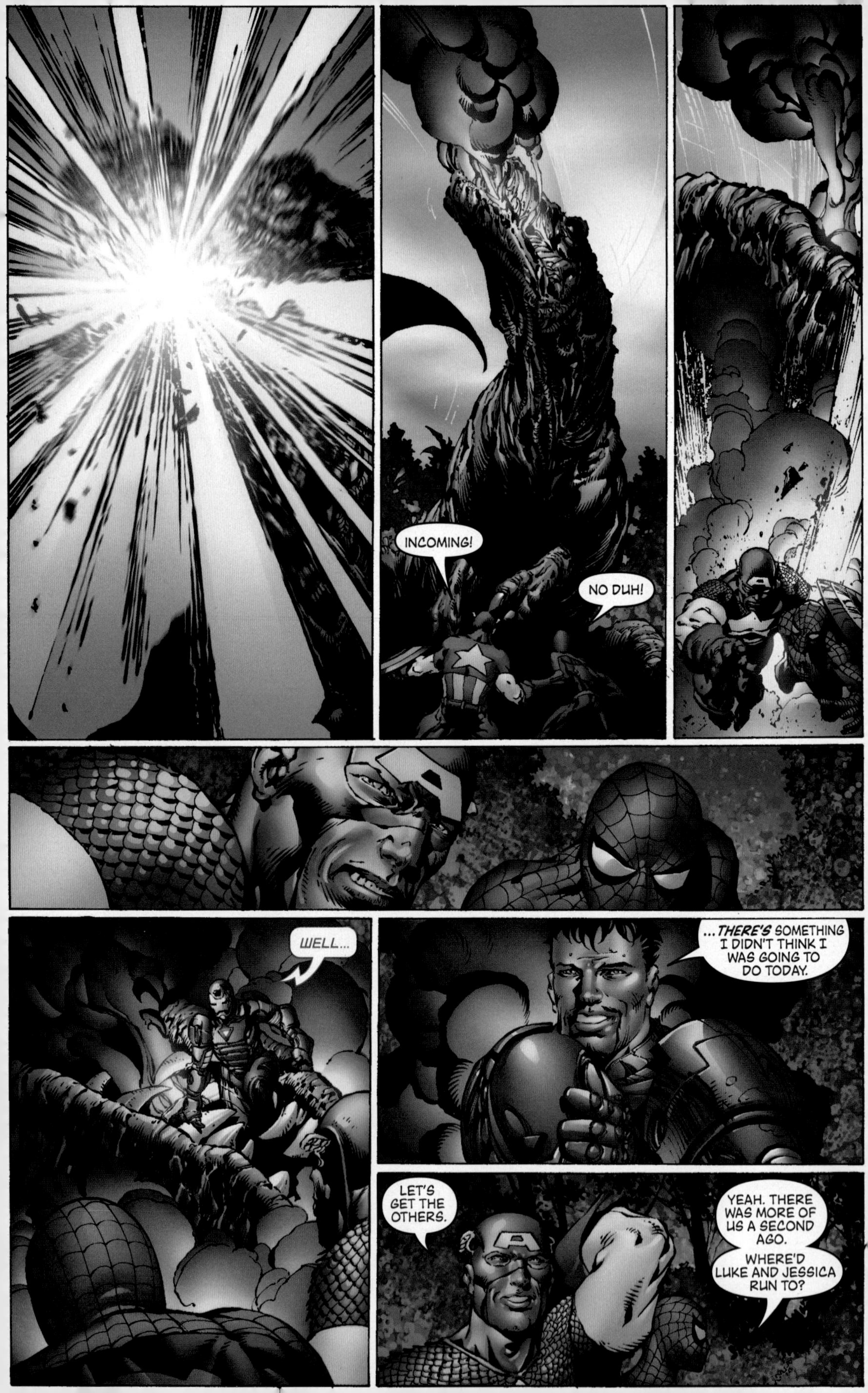
INCOMING!
NO DUH!
WELL...
...THERE'S SOMETHING I DIDN'T THINK I WAS GOING TO DO TODAY.
LET'S GET THE OTHERS.
YEAH. THERE WAS MORE OF US A SECOND AGO.
WHERE'D LUKE AND JESSICA RUN TO?

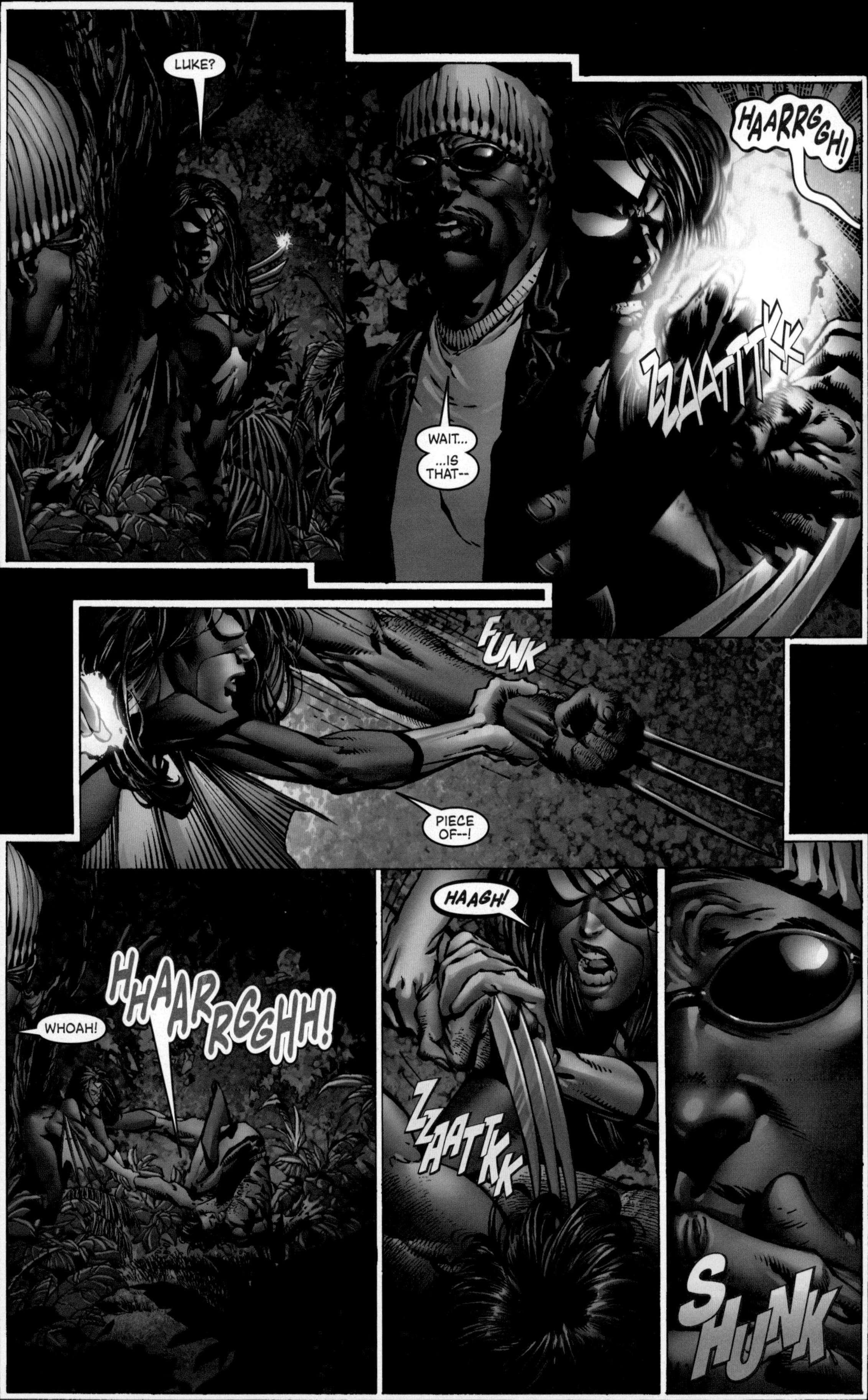

LUKE?
WAIT...
...IS THAT--
HAARRGGH!
ZZAATTTKK
FUNK
PIECE OF--!
WHOAH!
HHAARRGGHH!
HAAGH!
ZZAATTKK
SHUNK

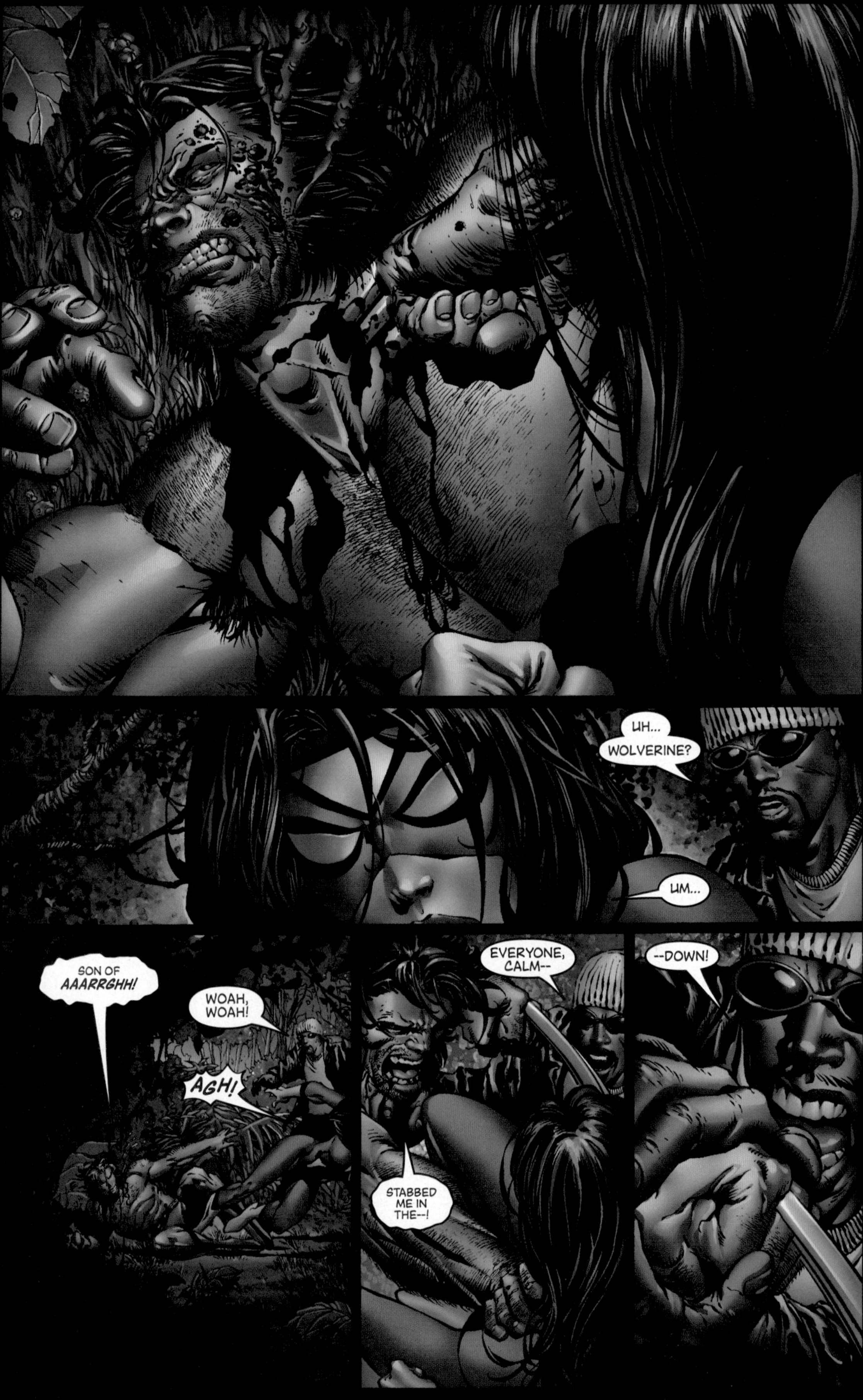
UH... WOLVERINE?
UM...
SON OF AAARRGHH!
WOAH, WOAH!
AGH!
EVERYONE, CALM--
STABBED ME IN THE--!
--DOWN!

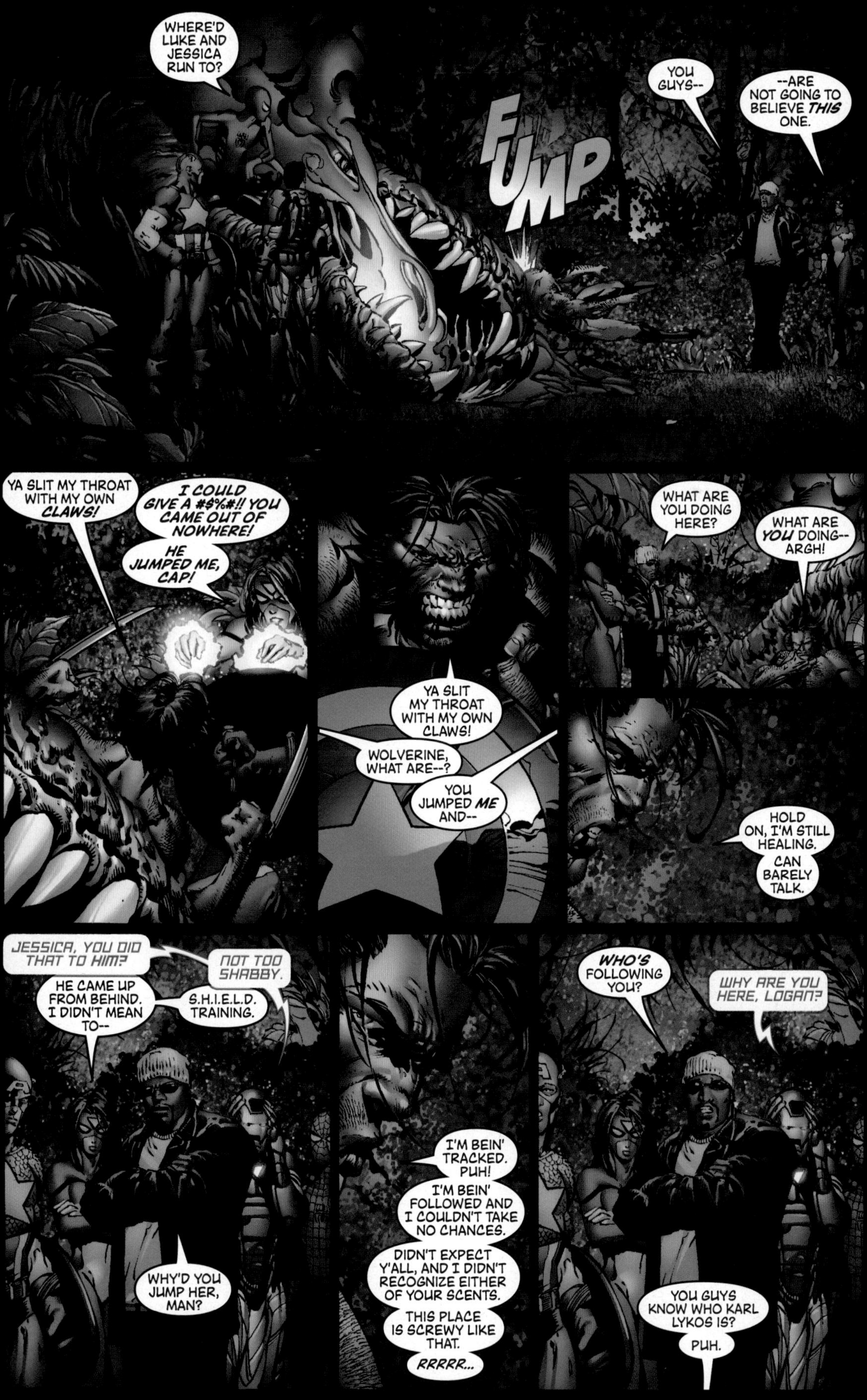

WHERE'D LUKE AND JESSICA RUN TO?
FUMP
YOU GUYS--
--ARE NOT GOING TO BELIEVE THIS ONE.
YA SLIT MY THROAT WITH MY OWN CLAWS!
I COULD GIVE A #$%#!! YOU CAME OUT OF NOWHERE!
HE JUMPED ME, CAP!
YA SLIT MY THROAT WITH MY OWN CLAWS!
WOLVERINE, WHAT ARE--?
YOU JUMPED ME AND--
WHAT ARE YOU DOING HERE?
WHAT ARE YOU DOING-- ARGH!
HOLD ON, I'M STILL HEALING.
CAN BARELY TALK.
JESSICA, YOU DID THAT TO HIM?
NOT TOO SHABBY.
HE CAME UP FROM BEHIND. I DIDN'T MEAN TO--
S.H.I.E.L.D. TRAINING.
WHY'D YOU JUMP HER, MAN?
I'M BEIN' TRACKED. PUH!
I'M BEIN' FOLLOWED AND I COULDN'T TAKE NO CHANCES.
DIDN'T EXPECT Y'ALL, AND I DIDN'T RECOGNIZE EITHER OF YOUR SCENTS.
THIS PLACE IS SCREWY LIKE THAT.
RRRRR...
WHO'S FOLLOWING YOU?
WHY ARE YOU HERE, LOGAN?
YOU GUYS KNOW WHO KARL LYKOS IS?
PUH.

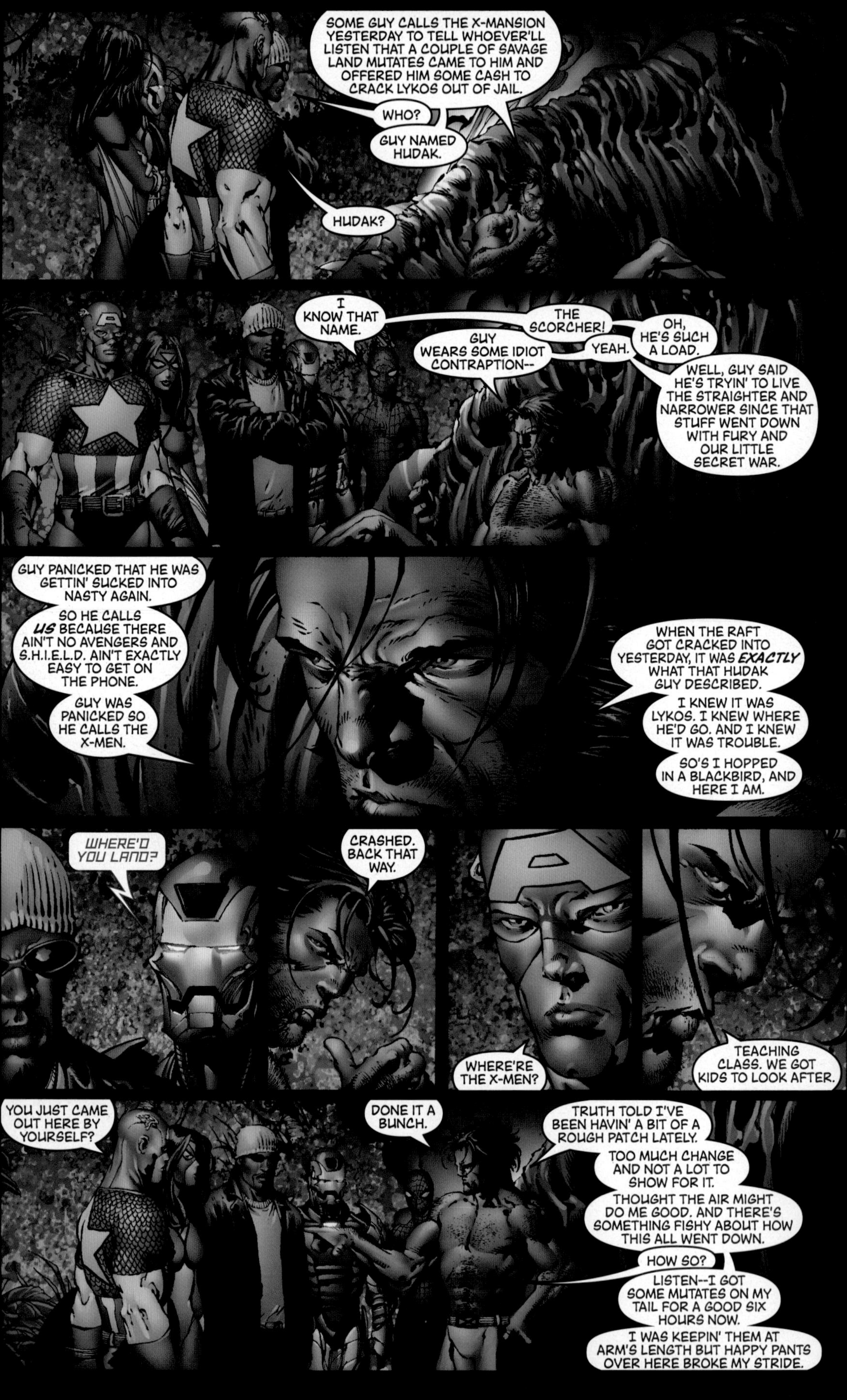
SOME GUY CALLS THE X-MANSION YESTERDAY TO TELL WHOEVER'LL LISTEN THAT A COUPLE OF SAVAGE LAND MUTATES CAME TO HIM AND OFFERED HIM SOME CASH TO CRACK LYKOS OUT OF JAIL.
WHO?
GUY NAMED HUDAK.
HUDAK?
I KNOW THAT NAME.
THE SCORCHER!
OH, HE'S SUCH A LOAD.
GUY WEARS SOME IDIOT CONTRAPTION--
YEAH.
WELL, GUY SAID HE'S TRYIN' TO LIVE THE STRAIGHTER AND NARROWER SINCE THAT STUFF WENT DOWN WITH FURY AND OUR LITTLE SECRET WAR.
GUY PANICKED THAT HE WAS GETTIN' SUCKED INTO NASTY AGAIN.
SO HE CALLS *US* BECAUSE THERE AIN'T NO AVENGERS AND S.H.I.E.L.D. AIN'T EXACTLY EASY TO GET ON THE PHONE.
GUY WAS PANICKED SO HE CALLS THE X-MEN.
WHEN THE RAFT GOT CRACKED INTO YESTERDAY, IT WAS *EXACTLY* WHAT THAT HUDAK GUY DESCRIBED.
I KNEW IT WAS LYKOS. I KNEW WHERE HE'D GO. AND I KNEW IT WAS TROUBLE.
SO'S I HOPPED IN A BLACKBIRD, AND HERE I AM.
WHERE'D YOU LAND?
CRASHED. BACK THAT WAY.
WHERE'RE THE X-MEN?
TEACHING CLASS. WE GOT KIDS TO LOOK AFTER.
YOU JUST CAME OUT HERE BY YOURSELF?
DONE IT A BUNCH.
TRUTH TOLD I'VE BEEN HAVIN' A BIT OF A ROUGH PATCH LATELY.
TOO MUCH CHANGE AND NOT A LOT TO SHOW FOR IT.
THOUGHT THE AIR MIGHT DO ME GOOD. AND THERE'S SOMETHING FISHY ABOUT HOW THIS ALL WENT DOWN.
HOW SO?
LISTEN--I GOT SOME MUTATES ON MY TAIL FOR A GOOD SIX HOURS NOW.
I WAS KEEPIN' THEM AT ARM'S LENGTH BUT HAPPY PANTS OVER HERE BROKE MY STRIDE.

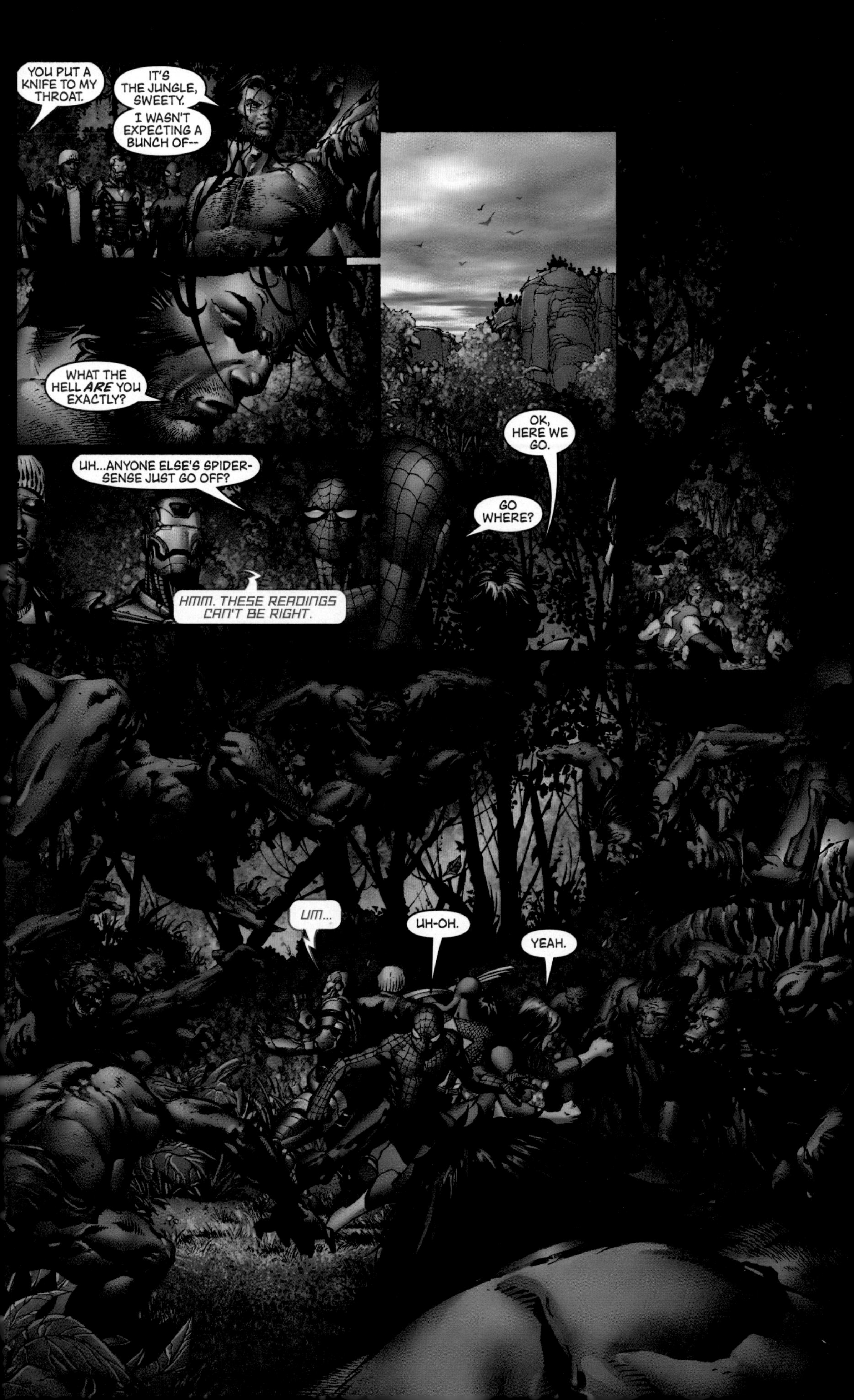
YOU PUT A KNIFE TO MY THROAT.
IT'S THE JUNGLE, SWEETY.
I WASN'T EXPECTING A BUNCH OF--
WHAT THE HELL *ARE* YOU EXACTLY?
UH...ANYONE ELSE'S SPIDER-SENSE JUST GO OFF?
HMM. THESE READINGS CAN'T BE RIGHT.
OK, HERE WE GO.
GO WHERE?
UM...
UH-OH.
YEAH.

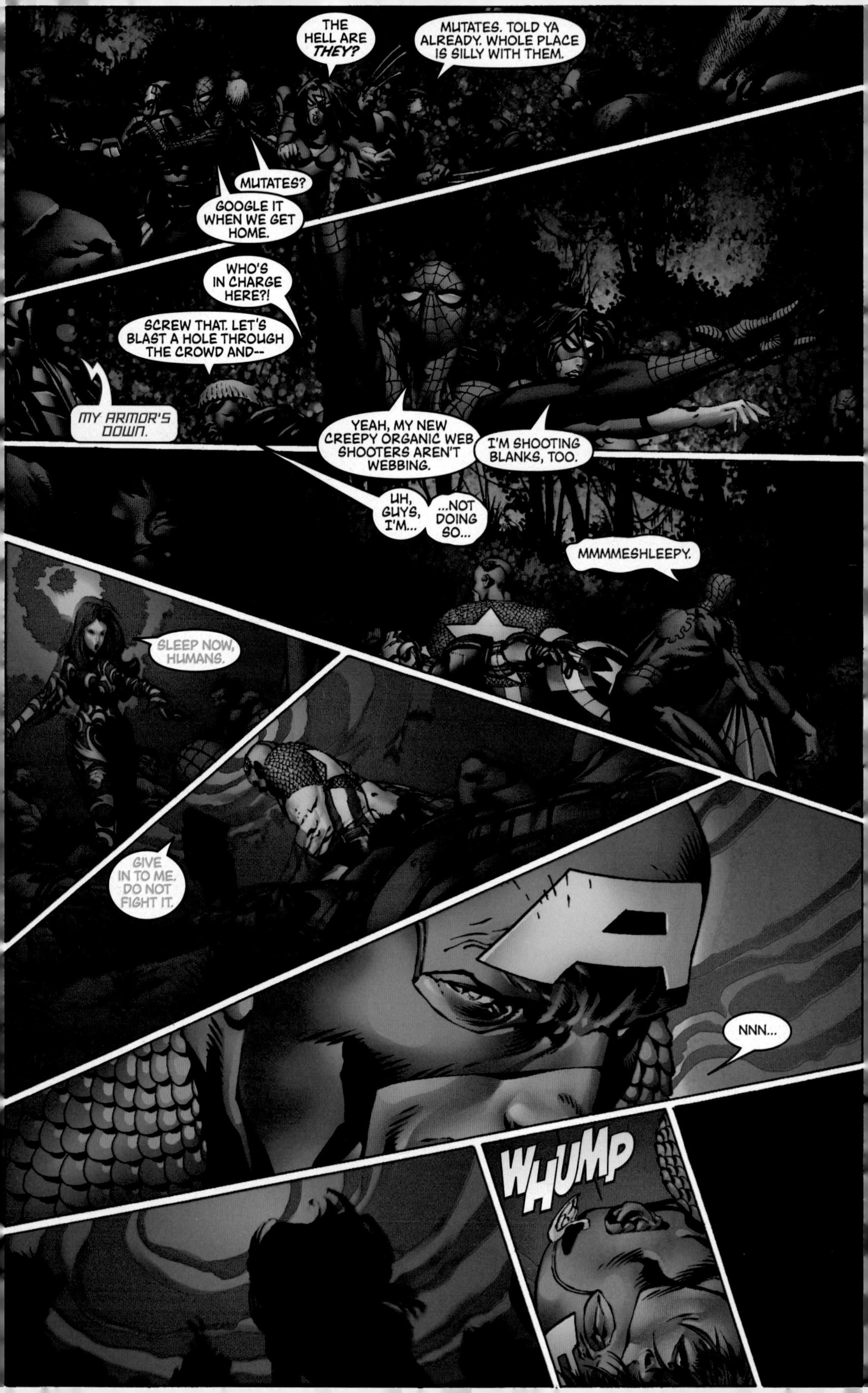
THE HELL ARE *THEY?*
MUTATES. TOLD YA ALREADY. WHOLE PLACE IS SILLY WITH THEM.
MUTATES?
GOOGLE IT WHEN WE GET HOME.
WHO'S IN CHARGE HERE?!
SCREW THAT. LET'S BLAST A HOLE THROUGH THE CROWD AND--
MY ARMOR'S DOWN.
YEAH, MY NEW CREEPY ORGANIC WEB SHOOTERS AREN'T WEBBING.
I'M SHOOTING BLANKS, TOO.
UH, GUYS, I'M...
...NOT DOING SO...
MMMMESHLEEPY.
SLEEP NOW, HUMANS.
GIVE IN TO ME. DO NOT FIGHT IT.
NNN...
WHUMP

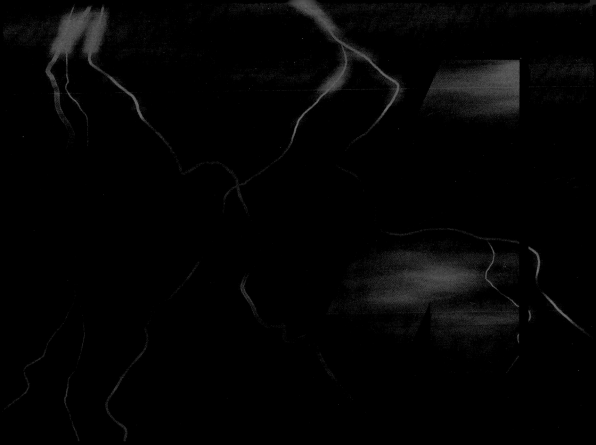

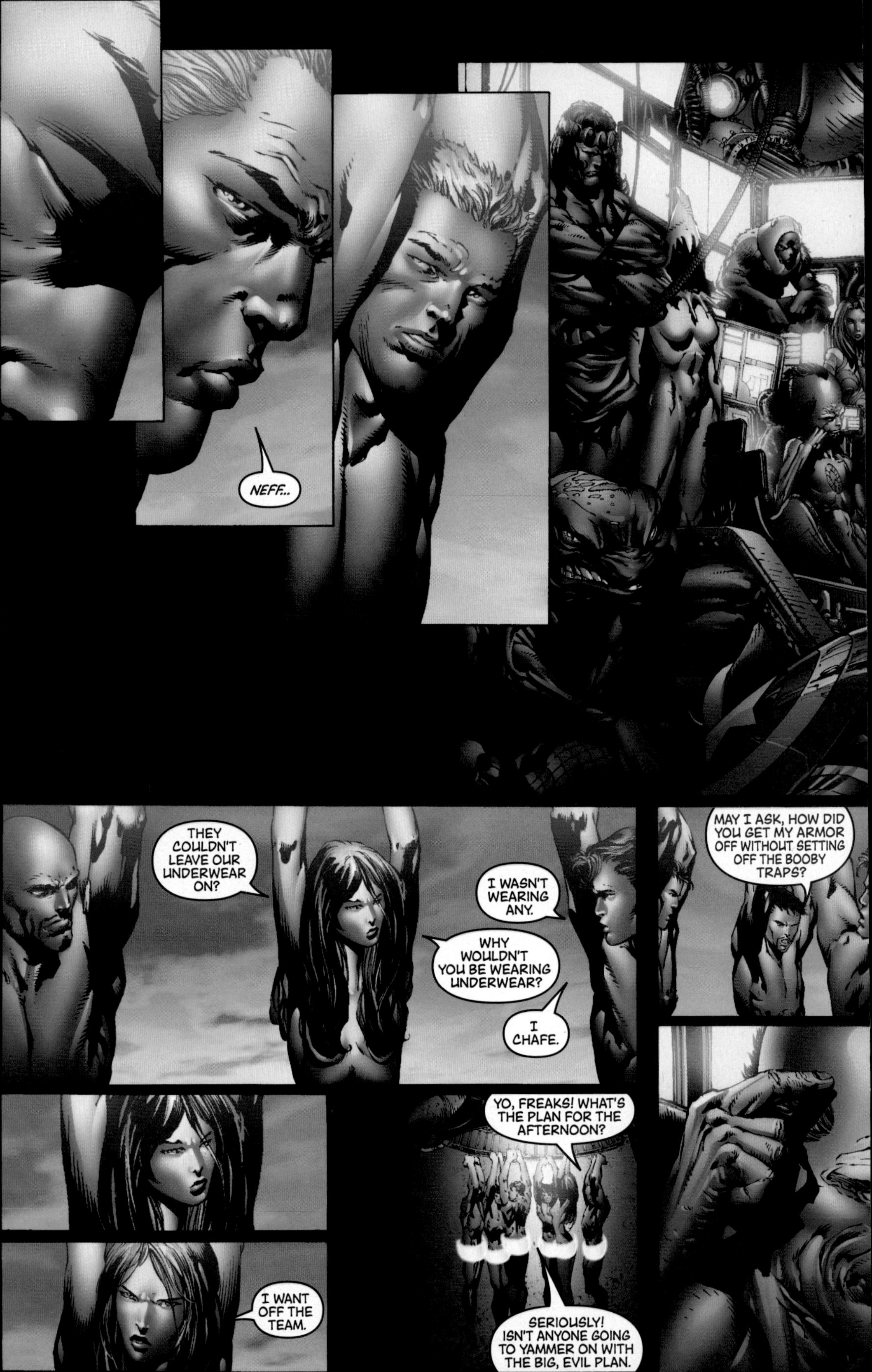
NEFF...
THEY COULDN'T LEAVE OUR UNDERWEAR ON?
I WASN'T WEARING ANY.
WHY WOULDN'T YOU BE WEARING UNDERWEAR?
I CHAFE.
MAY I ASK, HOW DID YOU GET MY ARMOR OFF WITHOUT SETTING OFF THE BOOBY TRAPS?
YO, FREAKS! WHAT'S THE PLAN FOR THE AFTERNOON?
SERIOUSLY! ISN'T ANYONE GOING TO YAMMER ON WITH THE BIG, EVIL PLAN.
I WANT OFF THE TEAM.

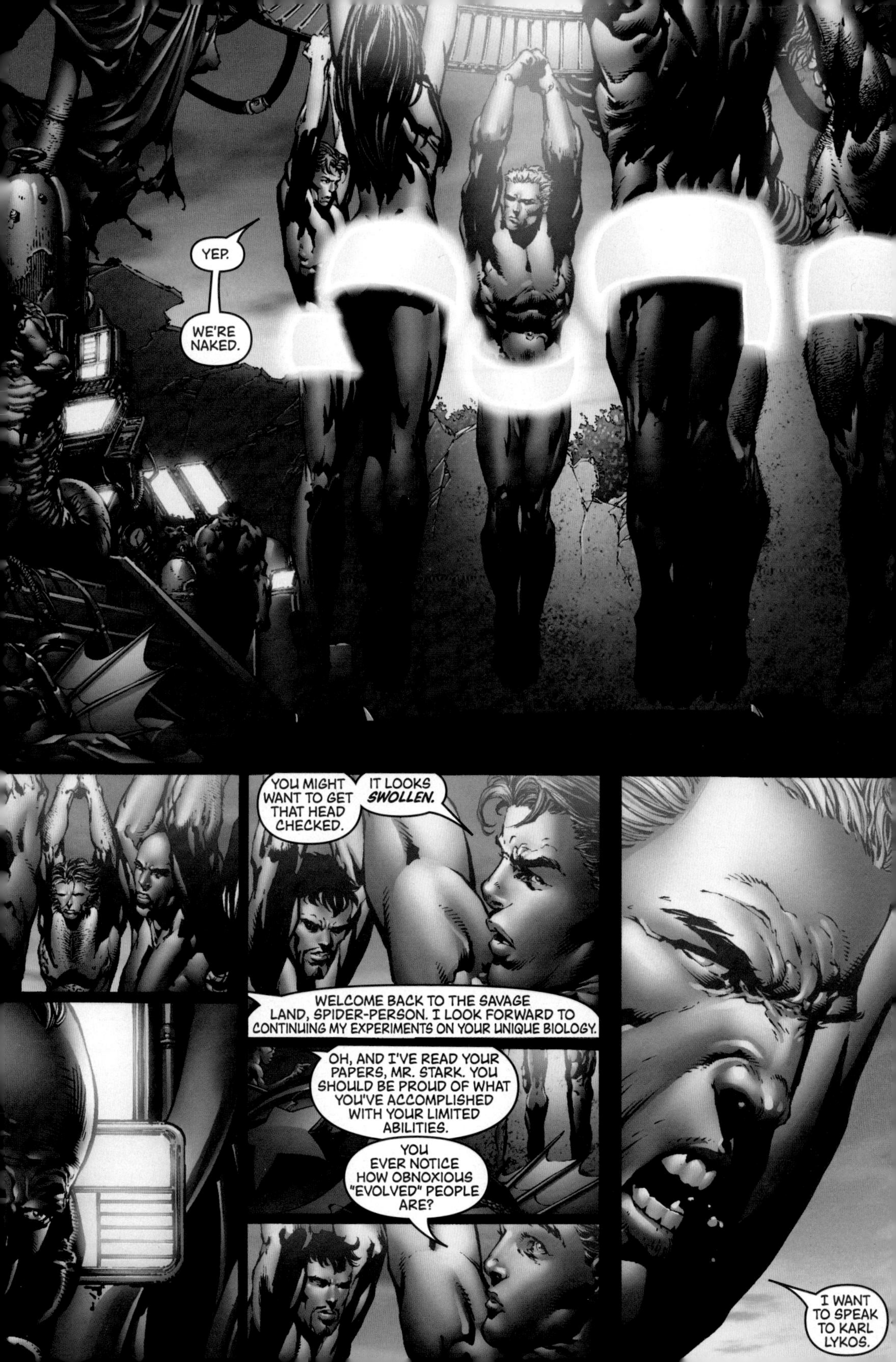
YEP.
WE'RE NAKED.
YOU MIGHT WANT TO GET THAT HEAD CHECKED.
IT LOOKS *SWOLLEN.*
WELCOME BACK TO THE SAVAGE LAND, SPIDER-PERSON. I LOOK FORWARD TO CONTINUING MY EXPERIMENTS ON YOUR UNIQUE BIOLOGY.
OH, AND I'VE READ YOUR PAPERS, MR. STARK. YOU SHOULD BE PROUD OF WHAT YOU'VE ACCOMPLISHED WITH YOUR LIMITED ABILITIES.
YOU EVER NOTICE HOW OBNOXIOUS "EVOLVED" PEOPLE ARE?
I WANT TO SPEAK TO KARL LYKOS.

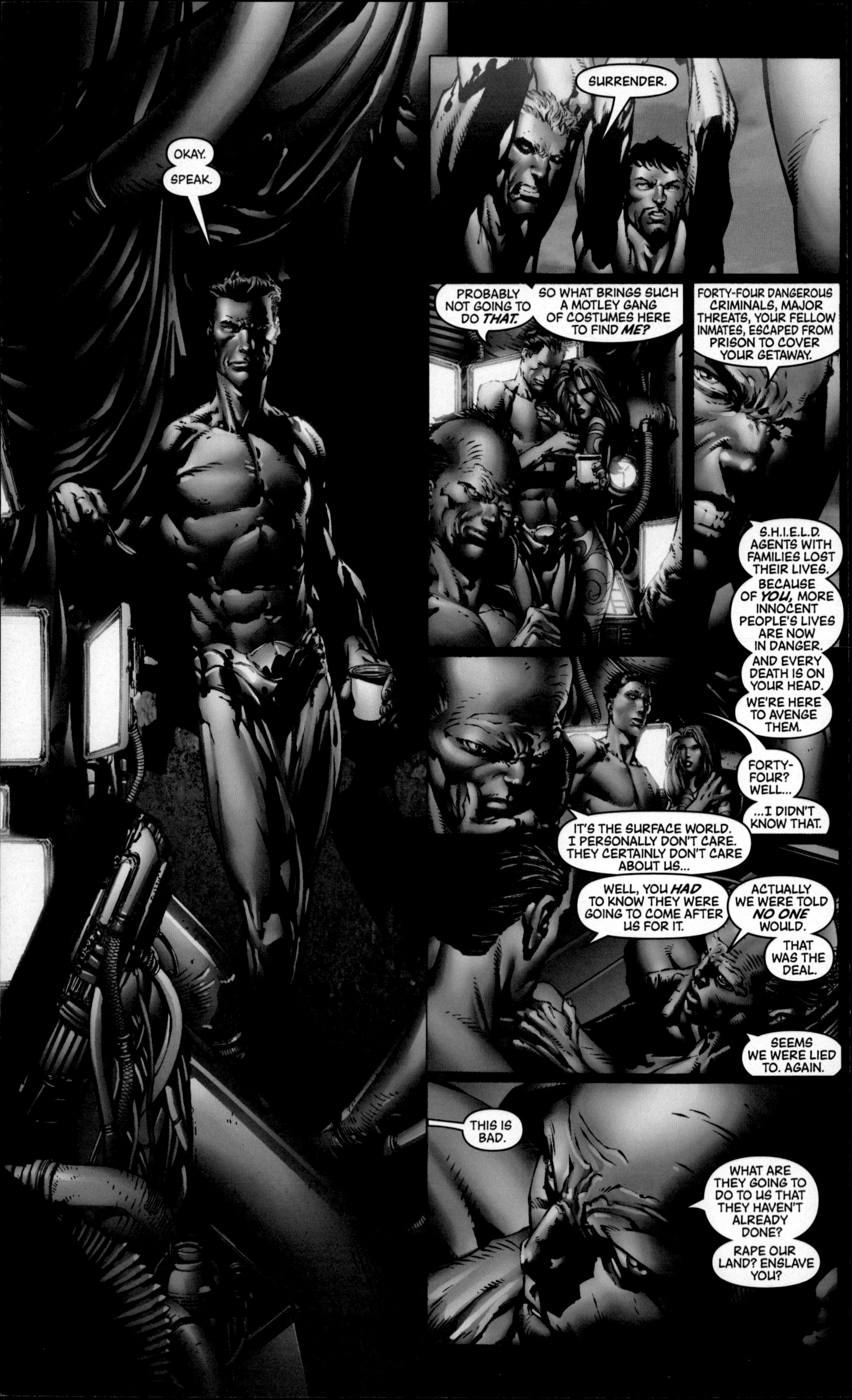

OKAY.
SPEAK.
SURRENDER.
PROBABLY NOT GOING TO DO *THAT.*
SO WHAT BRINGS SUCH A MOTLEY GANG OF COSTUMES HERE TO FIND *ME?*
FORTY-FOUR DANGEROUS CRIMINALS, MAJOR THREATS, YOUR FELLOW INMATES, ESCAPED FROM PRISON TO COVER YOUR GETAWAY.
S.H.I.E.L.D. AGENTS WITH FAMILIES LOST THEIR LIVES.
BECAUSE OF *YOU,* MORE INNOCENT PEOPLE'S LIVES ARE NOW IN DANGER.
AND EVERY DEATH IS ON YOUR HEAD.
WE'RE HERE TO AVENGE THEM.
FORTY-FOUR? WELL...
...I DIDN'T KNOW THAT.
IT'S THE SURFACE WORLD. I PERSONALLY DON'T CARE. THEY CERTAINLY DON'T CARE ABOUT US...
WELL, YOU *HAD* TO KNOW THEY WERE GOING TO COME AFTER US FOR IT.
ACTUALLY WE WERE TOLD *NO ONE* WOULD.
THAT WAS THE DEAL.
SEEMS WE WERE LIED TO. AGAIN.
THIS IS BAD.
WHAT ARE THEY GOING TO DO TO US THAT THEY HAVEN'T ALREADY DONE?
RAPE OUR LAND? ENSLAVE YOU?

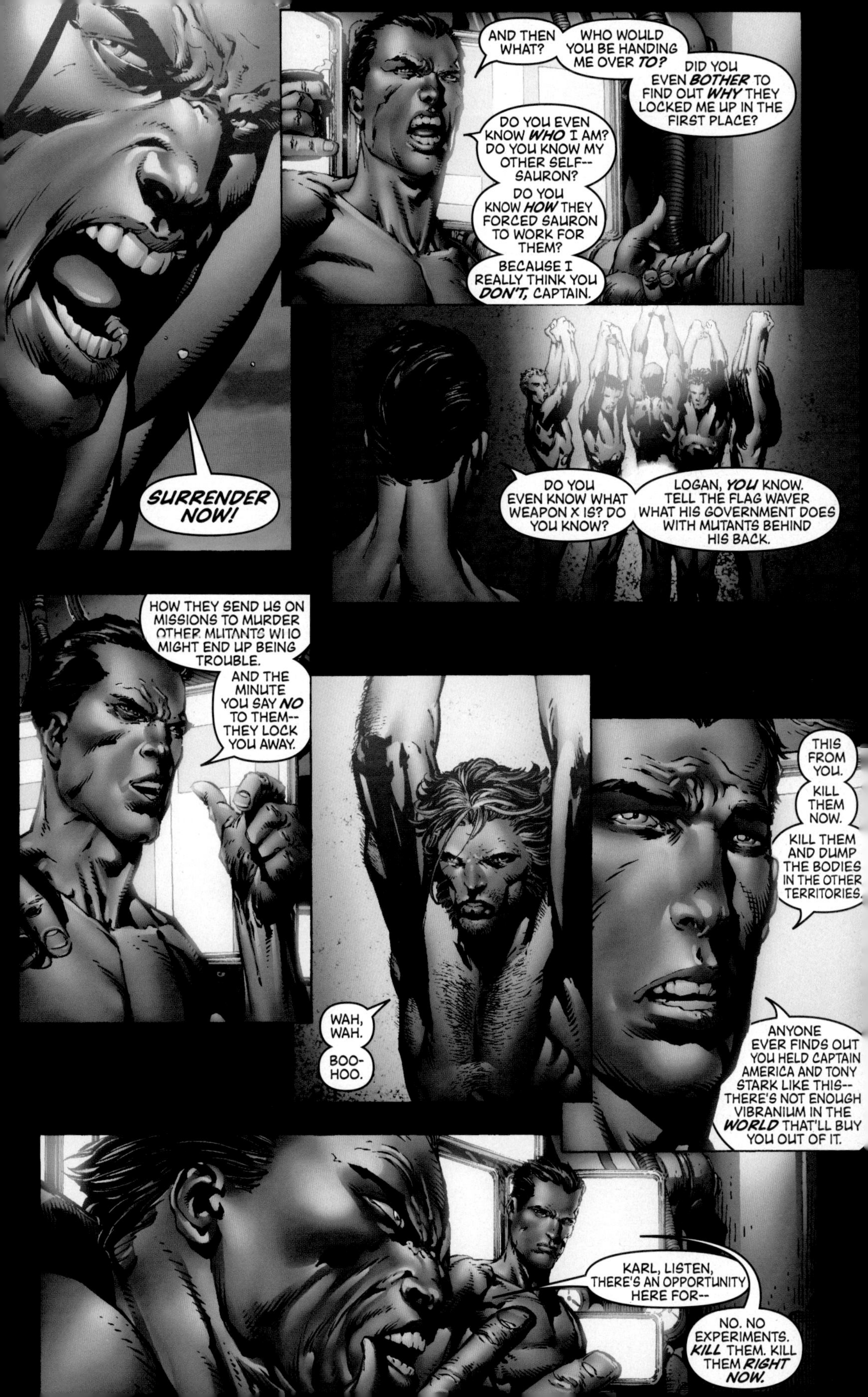

SURRENDER NOW!
AND THEN WHAT?
WHO WOULD YOU BE HANDING ME OVER TO?
DID YOU EVEN BOTHER TO FIND OUT WHY THEY LOCKED ME UP IN THE FIRST PLACE?
DO YOU EVEN KNOW WHO I AM? DO YOU KNOW MY OTHER SELF-- SAURON?
DO YOU KNOW HOW THEY FORCED SAURON TO WORK FOR THEM?
BECAUSE I REALLY THINK YOU DON'T, CAPTAIN.
DO YOU EVEN KNOW WHAT WEAPON X IS? DO YOU KNOW?
LOGAN, YOU KNOW. TELL THE FLAG WAVER WHAT HIS GOVERNMENT DOES WITH MUTANTS BEHIND HIS BACK.
HOW THEY SEND US ON MISSIONS TO MURDER OTHER MUTANTS WHO MIGHT END UP BEING TROUBLE.
AND THE MINUTE YOU SAY NO TO THEM-- THEY LOCK YOU AWAY.
WAH, WAH.
BOO-HOO.
THIS FROM YOU.
KILL THEM NOW.
KILL THEM AND DUMP THE BODIES IN THE OTHER TERRITORIES.
ANYONE EVER FINDS OUT YOU HELD CAPTAIN AMERICA AND TONY STARK LIKE THIS-- THERE'S NOT ENOUGH VIBRANIUM IN THE WORLD THAT'LL BUY YOU OUT OF IT.
KARL, LISTEN, THERE'S AN OPPORTUNITY HERE FOR--
NO. NO EXPERIMENTS. KILL THEM. KILL THEM RIGHT NOW.

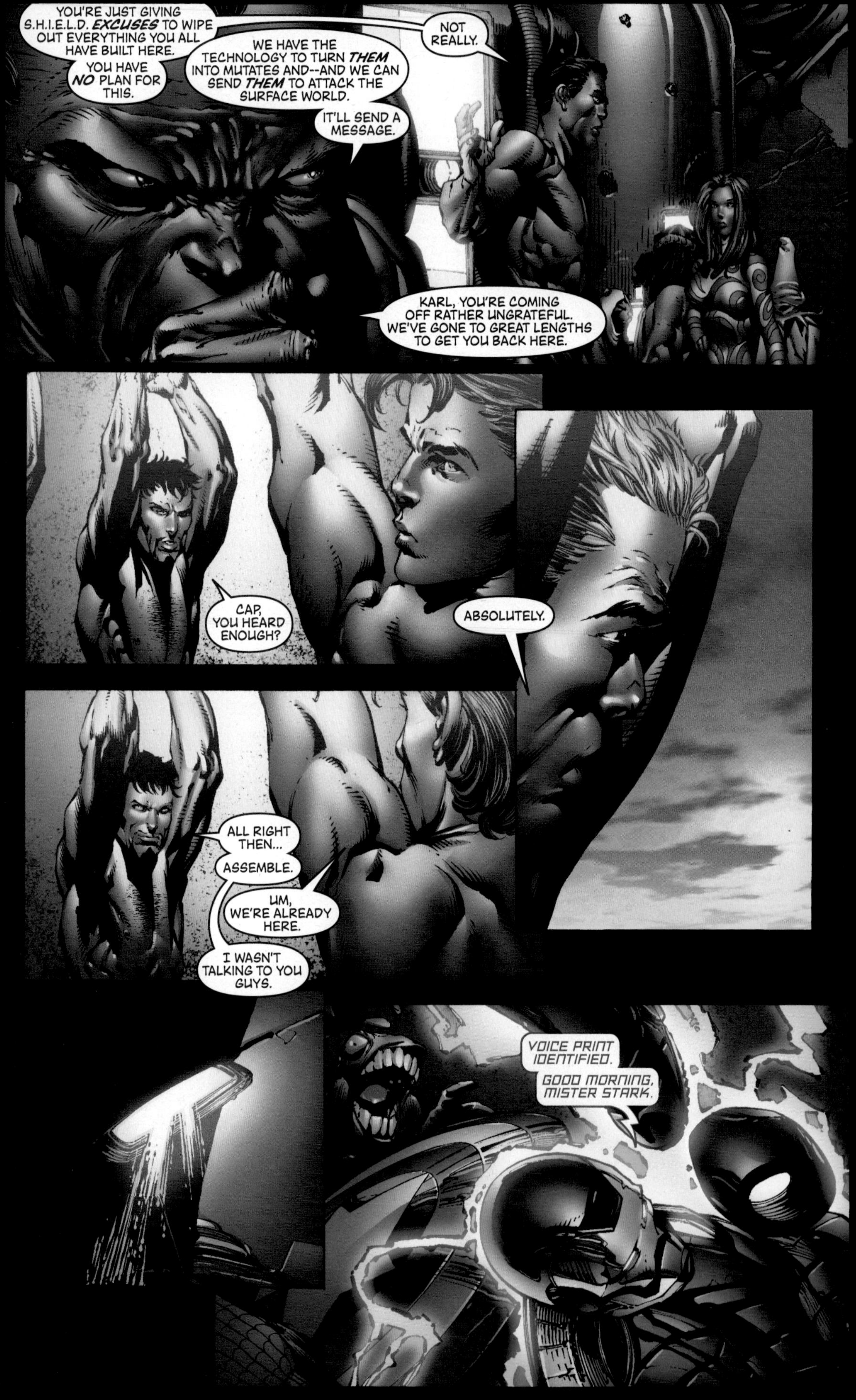
YOU'RE JUST GIVING S.H.I.E.L.D. EXCUSES TO WIPE OUT EVERYTHING YOU ALL HAVE BUILT HERE.
YOU HAVE NO PLAN FOR THIS.
NOT REALLY.
WE HAVE THE TECHNOLOGY TO TURN THEM INTO MUTATES AND--AND WE CAN SEND THEM TO ATTACK THE SURFACE WORLD.
IT'LL SEND A MESSAGE.
KARL, YOU'RE COMING OFF RATHER UNGRATEFUL. WE'VE GONE TO GREAT LENGTHS TO GET YOU BACK HERE.
CAP, YOU HEARD ENOUGH?
ABSOLUTELY.
ALL RIGHT THEN...
ASSEMBLE.
UM, WE'RE ALREADY HERE.
I WASN'T TALKING TO YOU GUYS.
VOICE PRINT IDENTIFIED.
GOOD MORNING, MISTER STARK.

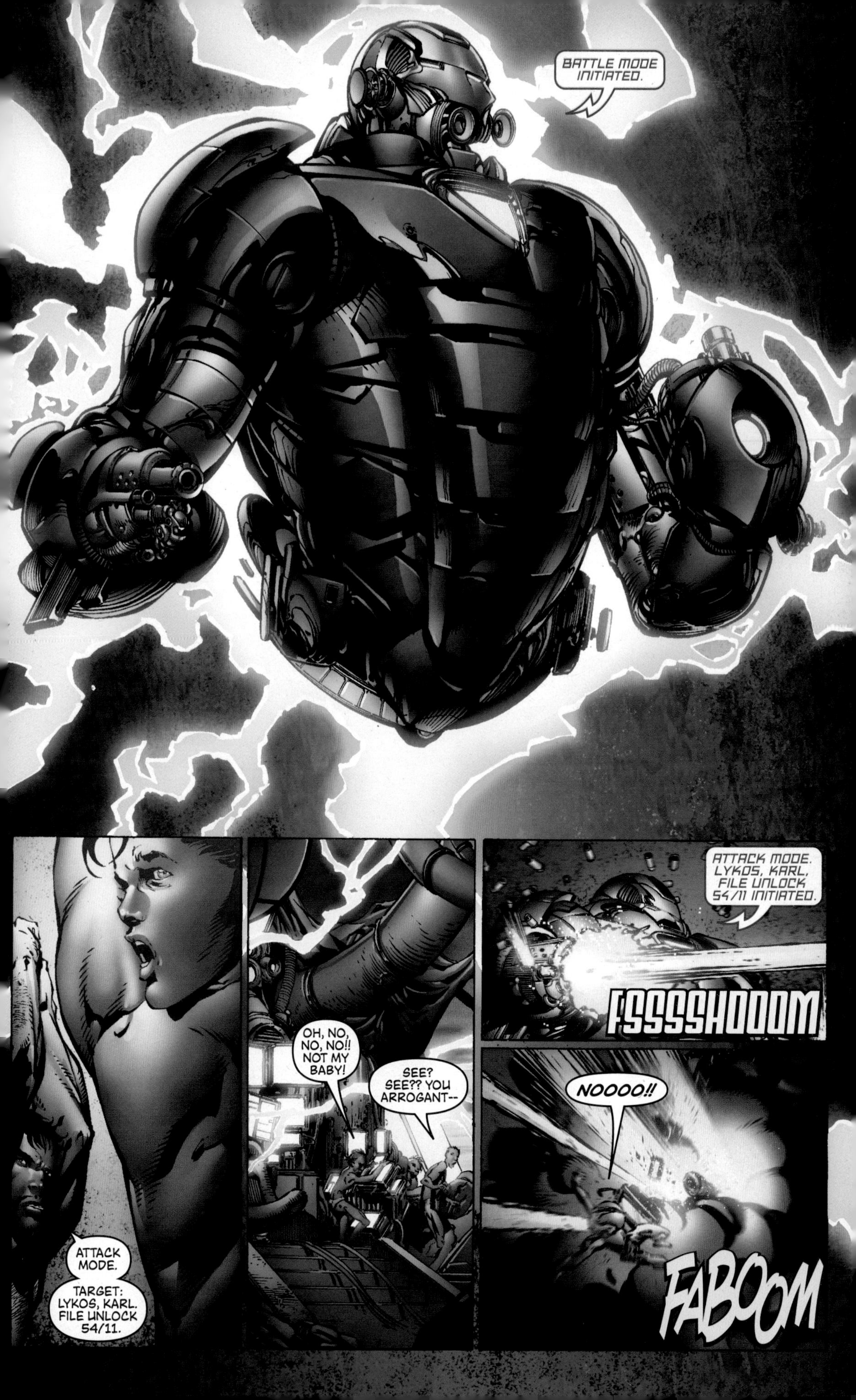
BATTLE MODE INITIATED.
ATTACK MODE.
TARGET: LYKOS, KARL. FILE UNLOCK 54/11.
OH, NO, NO, NO!! NOT MY BABY!
SEE? SEE?? YOU ARROGANT--
ATTACK MODE. LYKOS, KARL, FILE UNLOCK 54/11 INITIATED.
FSSSSHOOOM
NOOOO!!
FABOOM

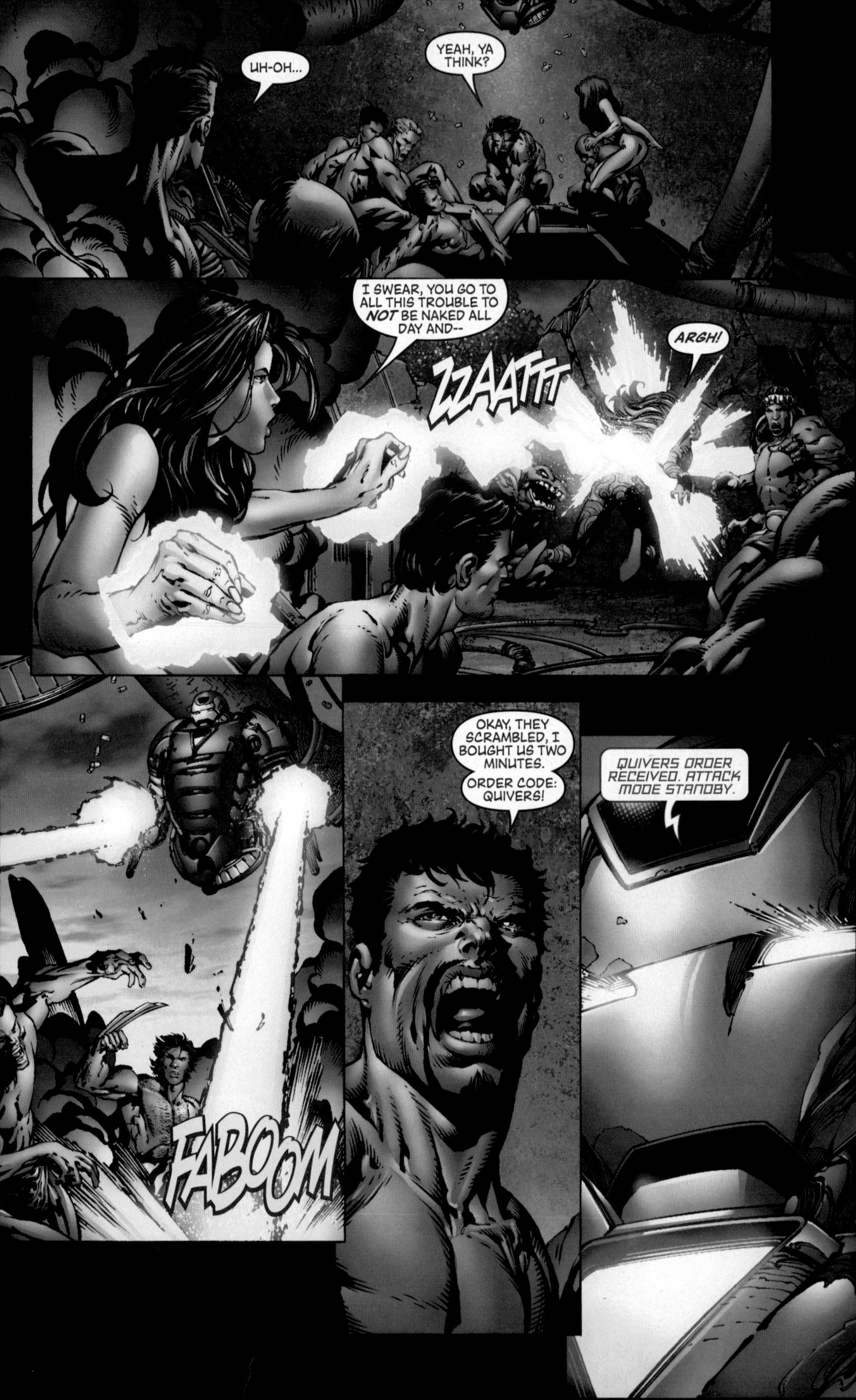
UH-OH...
YEAH, YA THINK?
I SWEAR, YOU GO TO ALL THIS TROUBLE TO NOT BE NAKED ALL DAY AND--
ZZAATTT
ARGH!
FABOOM
OKAY, THEY SCRAMBLED, I BOUGHT US TWO MINUTES.
ORDER CODE: QUIVERS!
QUIVERS ORDER RECEIVED. ATTACK MODE STANDBY.

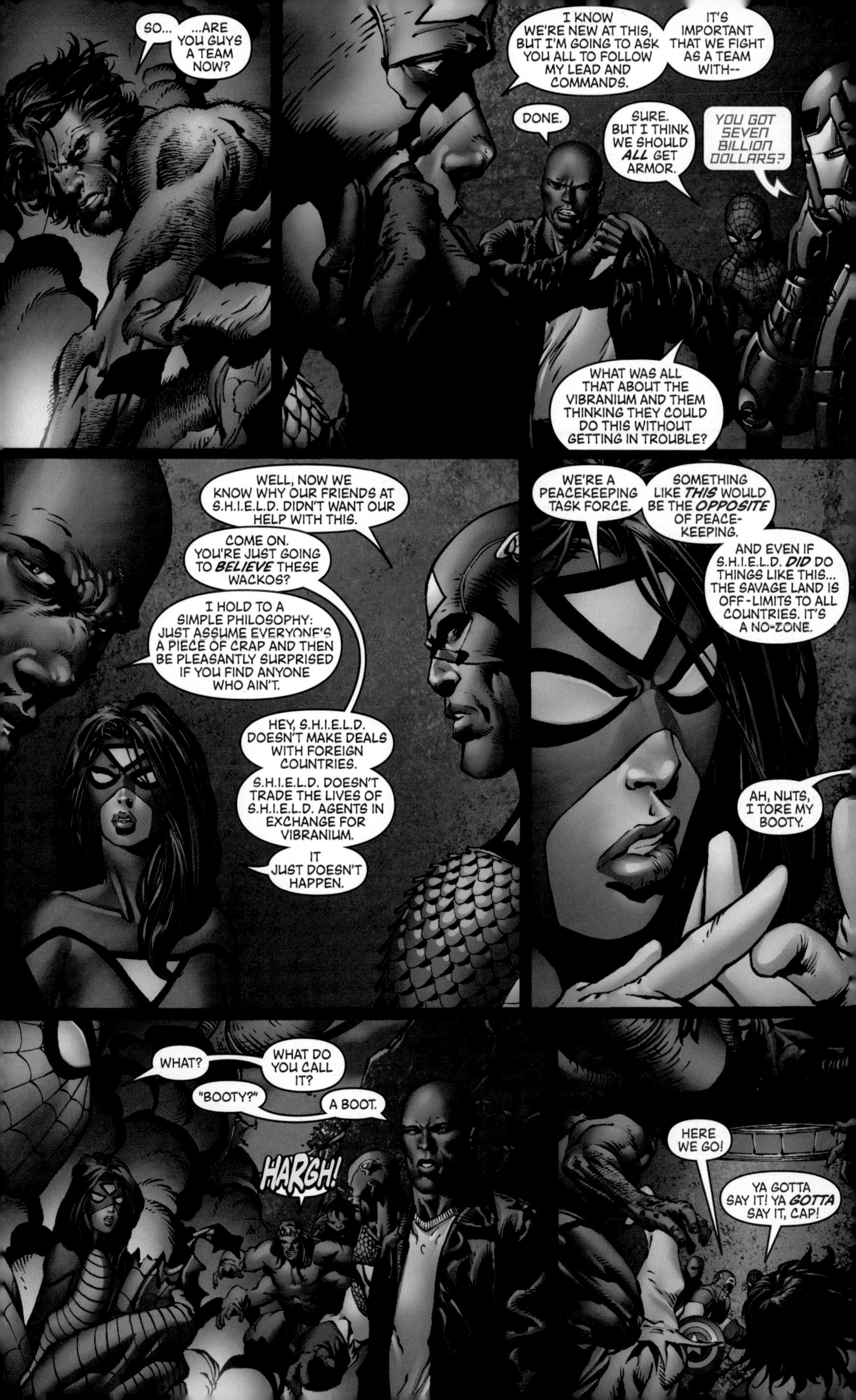
SO... ...ARE YOU GUYS A TEAM NOW?
I KNOW WE'RE NEW AT THIS, BUT I'M GOING TO ASK YOU ALL TO FOLLOW MY LEAD AND COMMANDS.
IT'S IMPORTANT THAT WE FIGHT AS A TEAM WITH--
DONE.
SURE. BUT I THINK WE SHOULD ALL GET ARMOR.
YOU GOT SEVEN BILLION DOLLARS?
WHAT WAS ALL THAT ABOUT THE VIBRANIUM AND THEM THINKING THEY COULD DO THIS WITHOUT GETTING IN TROUBLE?
WELL, NOW WE KNOW WHY OUR FRIENDS AT S.H.I.E.L.D. DIDN'T WANT OUR HELP WITH THIS.
COME ON. YOU'RE JUST GOING TO BELIEVE THESE WACKOS?
I HOLD TO A SIMPLE PHILOSOPHY: JUST ASSUME EVERYONE'S A PIECE OF CRAP AND THEN BE PLEASANTLY SURPRISED IF YOU FIND ANYONE WHO AIN'T.
HEY, S.H.I.E.L.D. DOESN'T MAKE DEALS WITH FOREIGN COUNTRIES.
S.H.I.E.L.D. DOESN'T TRADE THE LIVES OF S.H.I.E.L.D. AGENTS IN EXCHANGE FOR VIBRANIUM.
IT JUST DOESN'T HAPPEN.
WE'RE A PEACEKEEPING TASK FORCE.
SOMETHING LIKE THIS WOULD BE THE OPPOSITE OF PEACE-KEEPING.
AND EVEN IF S.H.I.E.L.D. DID DO THINGS LIKE THIS... THE SAVAGE LAND IS OFF-LIMITS TO ALL COUNTRIES. IT'S A NO-ZONE.
AH, NUTS, I TORE MY BOOTY.
WHAT?
WHAT DO YOU CALL IT?
"BOOTY?"
A BOOT.
HARGH!
HERE WE GO!
YA GOTTA SAY IT! YA GOTTA SAY IT, CAP!

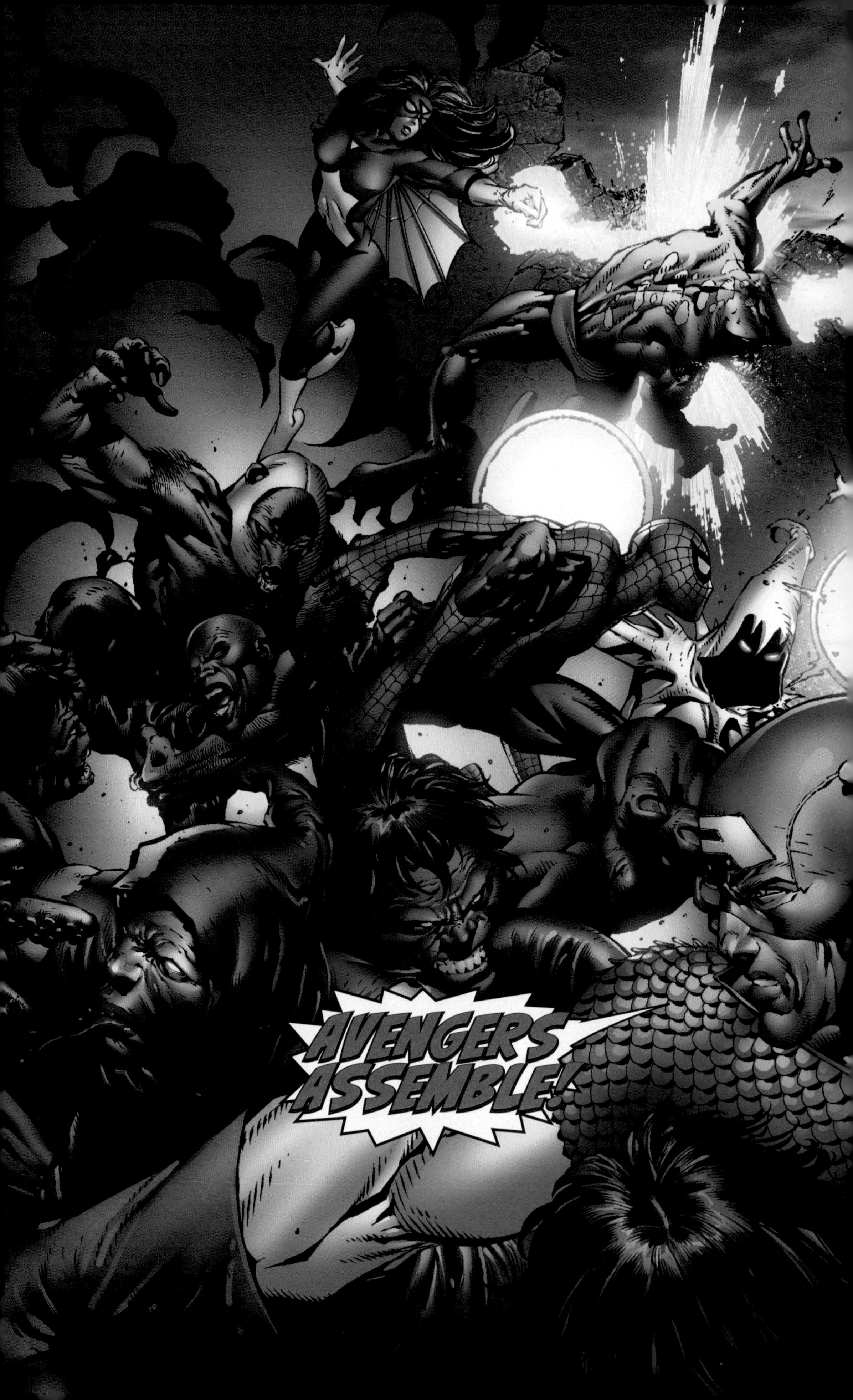
AVENGERS ASSEMBLE!

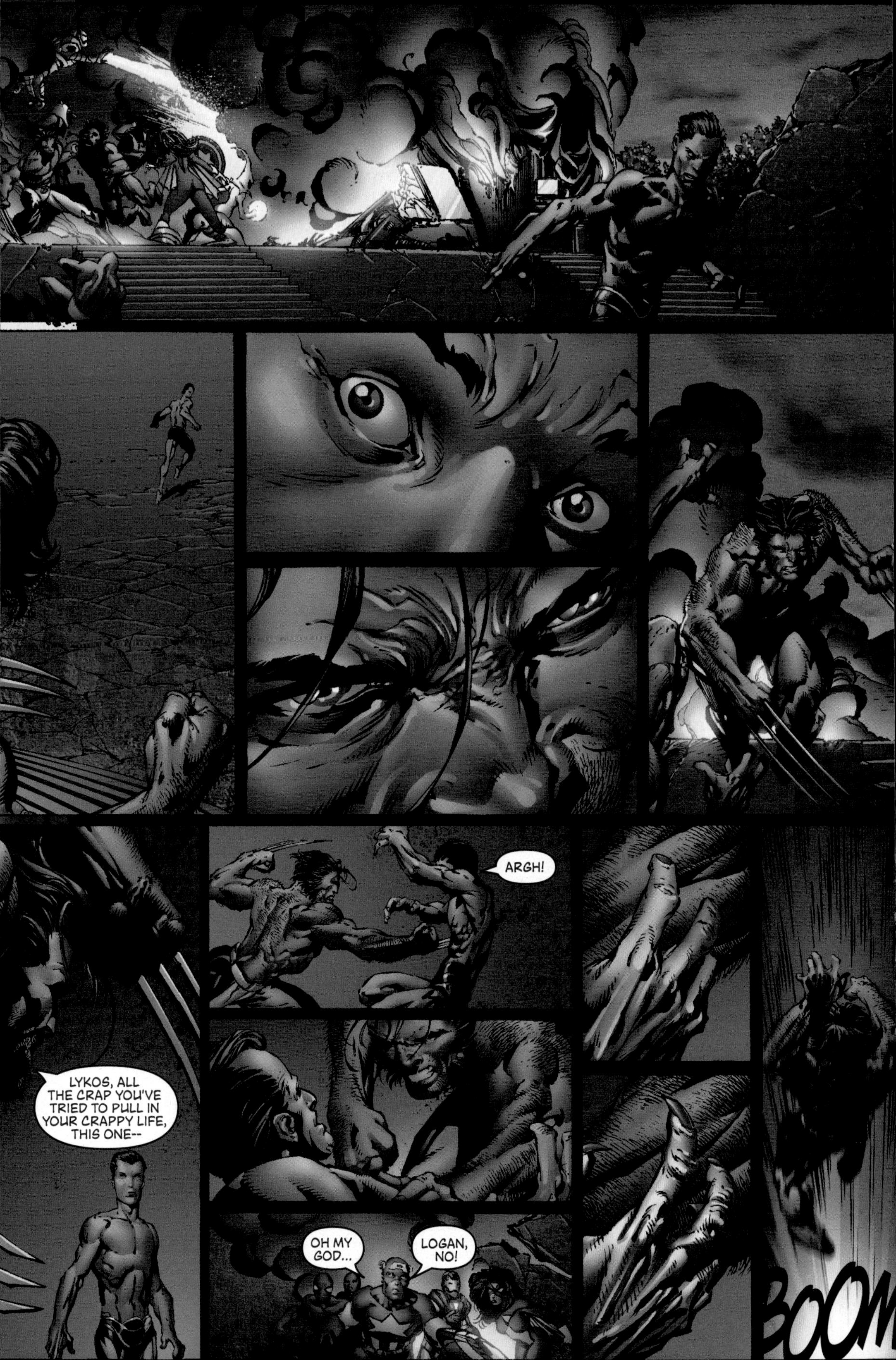
ARGH!
LYKOS, ALL THE CRAP YOU'VE TRIED TO PULL IN YOUR CRAPPY LIFE, THIS ONE--
OH MY GOD...
LOGAN, NO!
BOOM

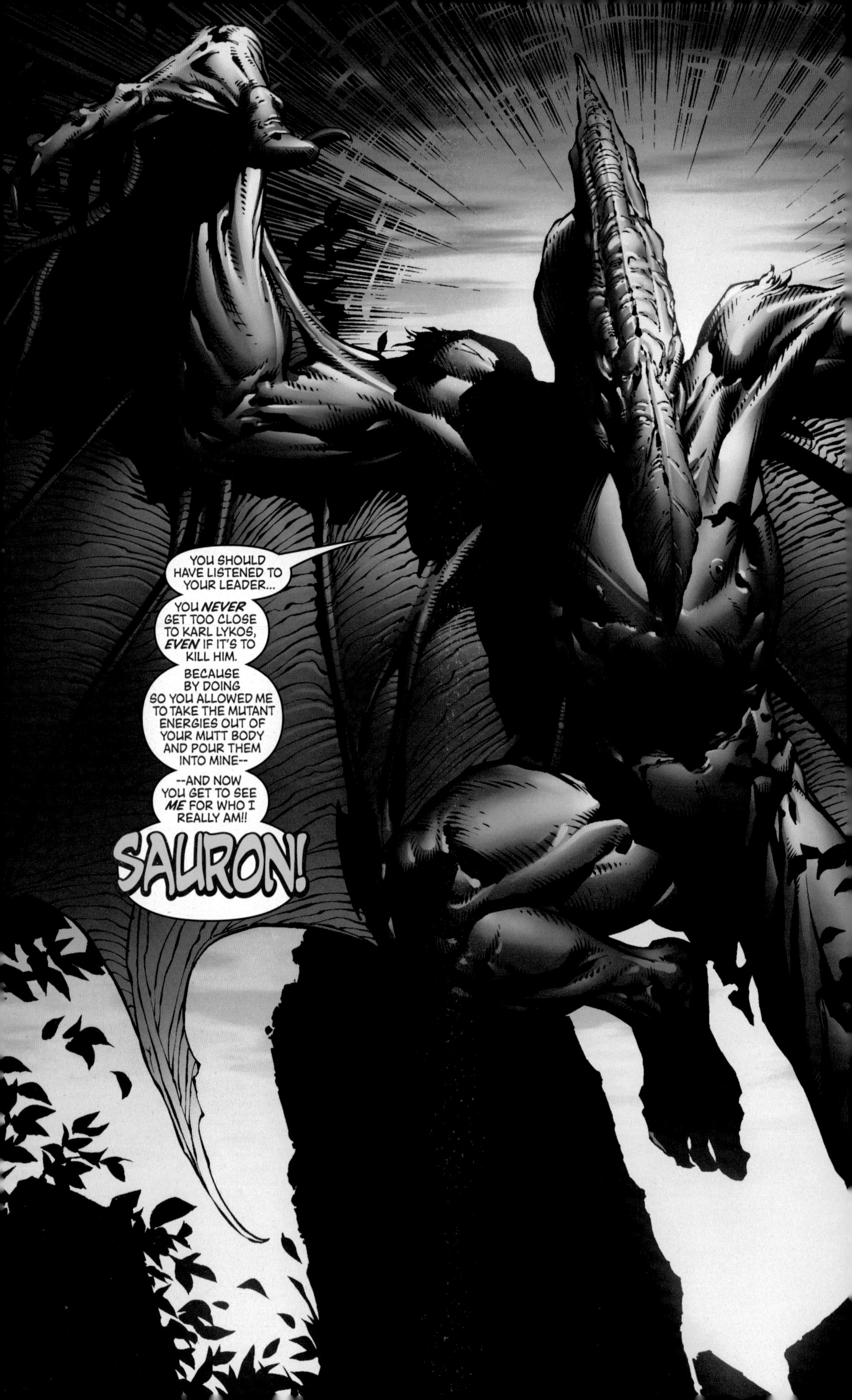

YOU SHOULD HAVE LISTENED TO YOUR LEADER...
YOU NEVER GET TOO CLOSE TO KARL LYKOS, EVEN IF IT'S TO KILL HIM.
BECAUSE BY DOING SO YOU ALLOWED ME TO TAKE THE MUTANT ENERGIES OUT OF YOUR MUTT BODY AND POUR THEM INTO MINE--
--AND NOW YOU GET TO SEE ME FOR WHO I REALLY AM!!
SAURON!

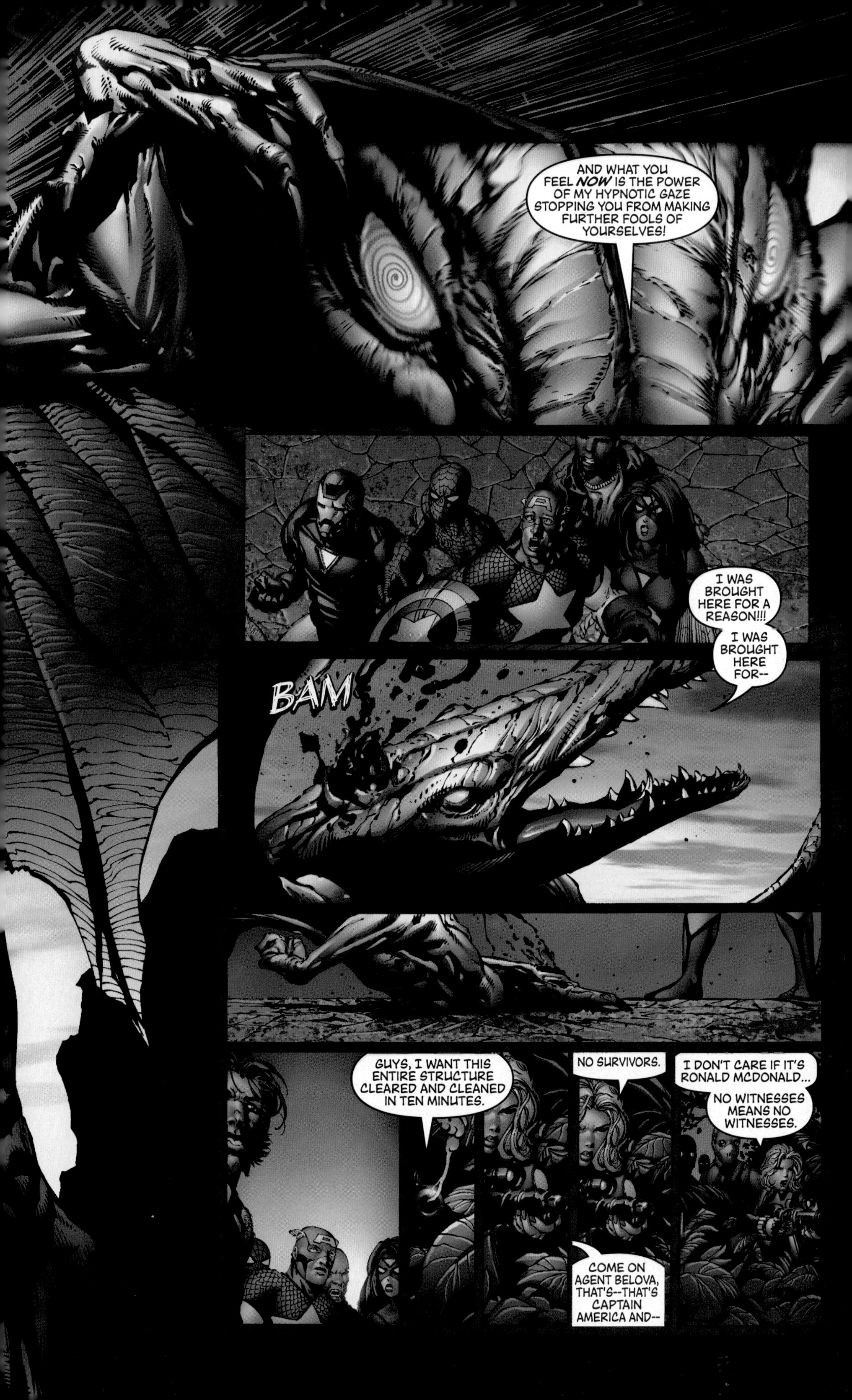
AND WHAT YOU FEEL NOW IS THE POWER OF MY HYPNOTIC GAZE STOPPING YOU FROM MAKING FURTHER FOOLS OF YOURSELVES!
I WAS BROUGHT HERE FOR A REASON!!!
I WAS BROUGHT HERE FOR--
BAM
GUYS, I WANT THIS ENTIRE STRUCTURE CLEARED AND CLEANED IN TEN MINUTES.
NO SURVIVORS.
COME ON AGENT BELOVA, THAT'S--THAT'S CAPTAIN AMERICA AND--
I DON'T CARE IF IT'S RONALD MCDONALD...
NO WITNESSES MEANS NO WITNESSES.

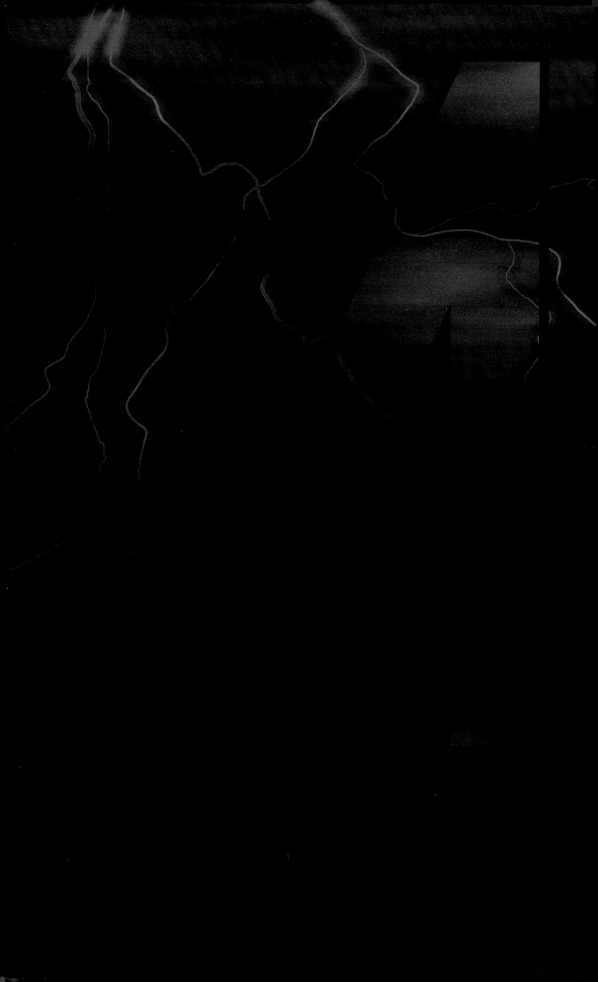

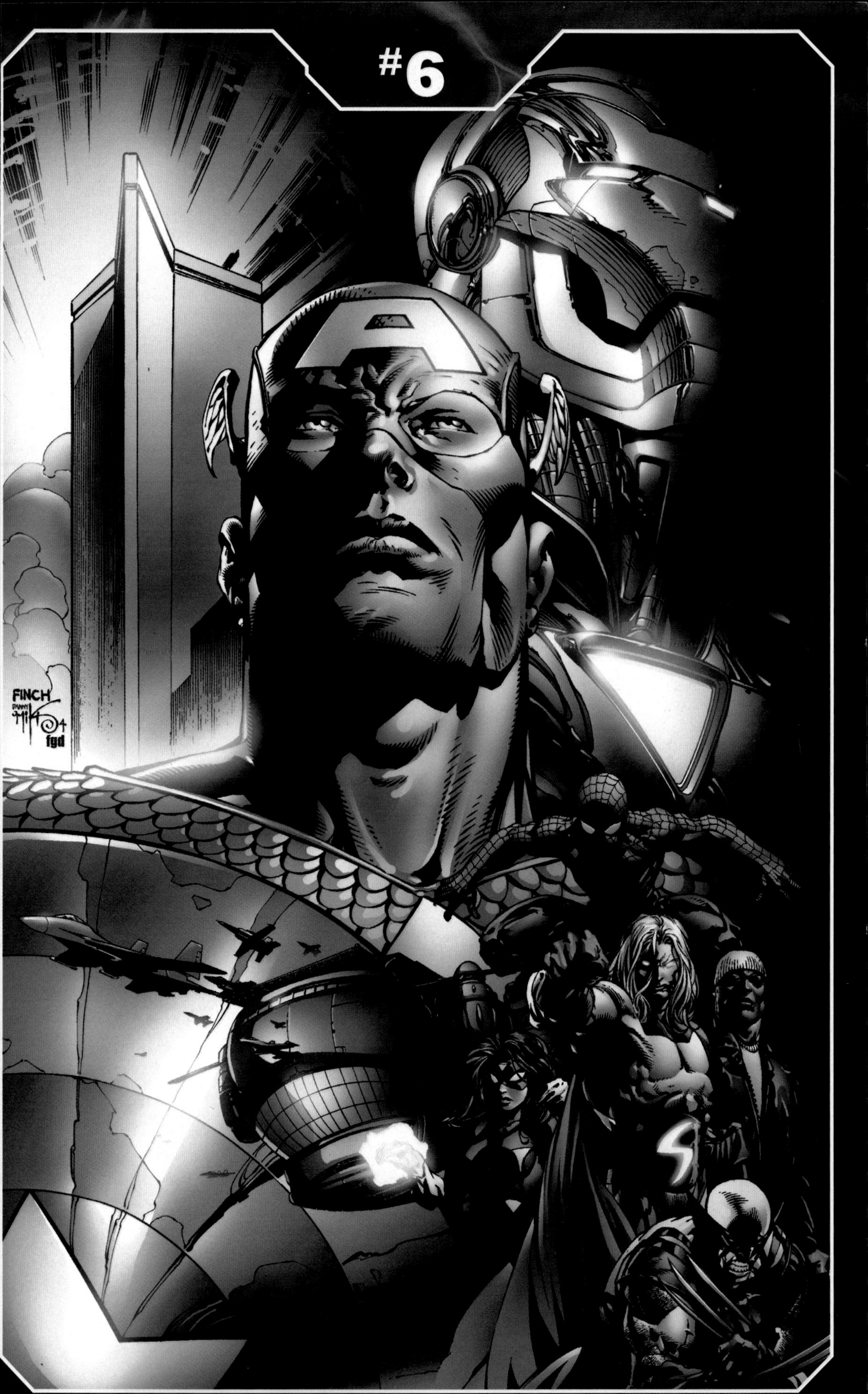
#6
FINCH
fgd

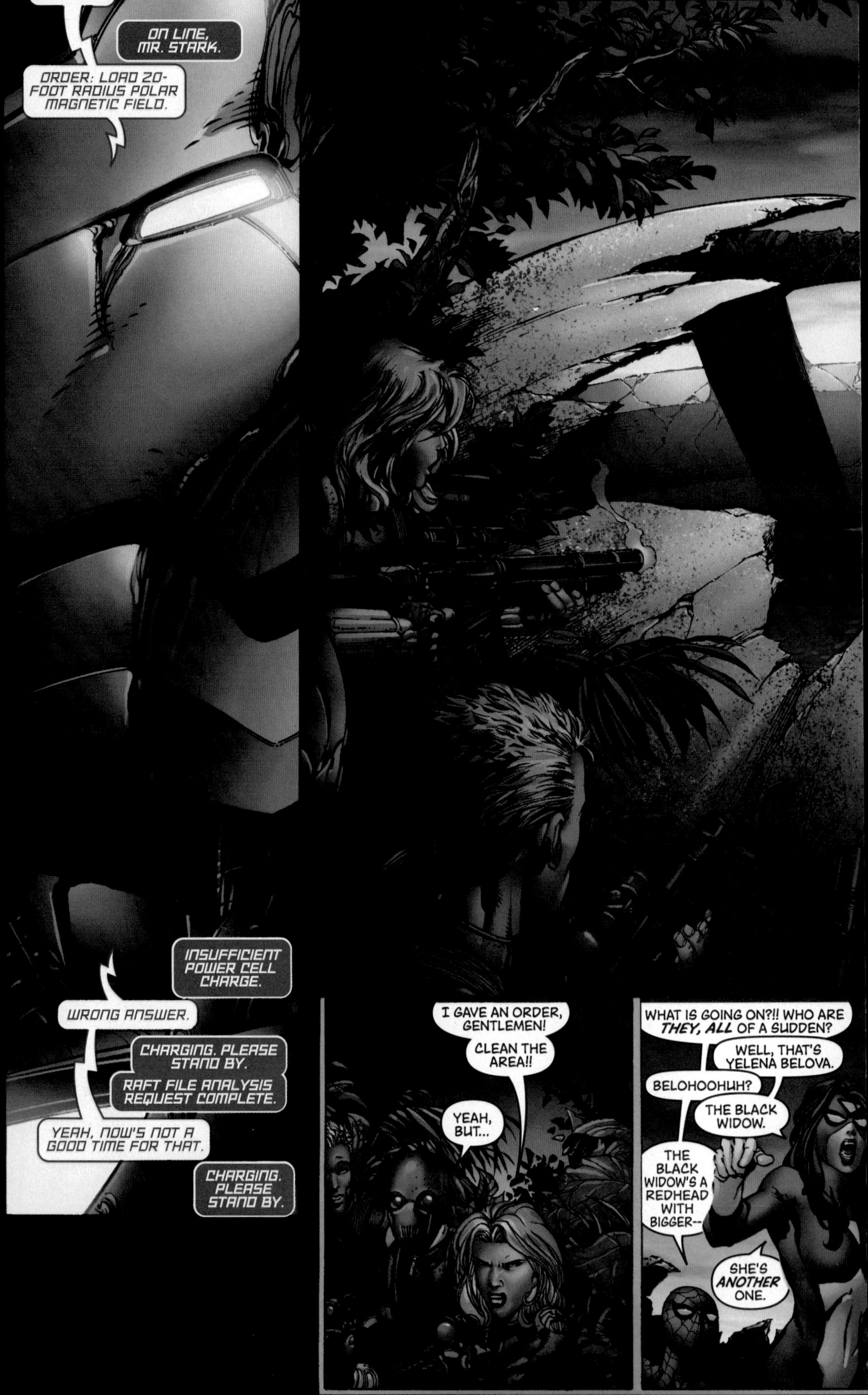
ON LINE, MR. STARK.
ORDER: LOAD 20-FOOT RADIUS POLAR MAGNETIC FIELD.
INSUFFICIENT POWER CELL CHARGE.
WRONG ANSWER.
CHARGING. PLEASE STAND BY.
RAFT FILE ANALYSIS REQUEST COMPLETE.
YEAH, NOW'S NOT A GOOD TIME FOR THAT.
CHARGING. PLEASE STAND BY.
I GAVE AN ORDER, GENTLEMEN!
CLEAN THE AREA!!
YEAH, BUT...
WHAT IS GOING ON?!! WHO ARE *THEY, ALL* OF A SUDDEN?
WELL, THAT'S YELENA BELOVA.
BELOHOOHUH?
THE BLACK WIDOW.
THE BLACK WIDOW'S A REDHEAD WITH BIGGER--
SHE'S *ANOTHER* ONE.

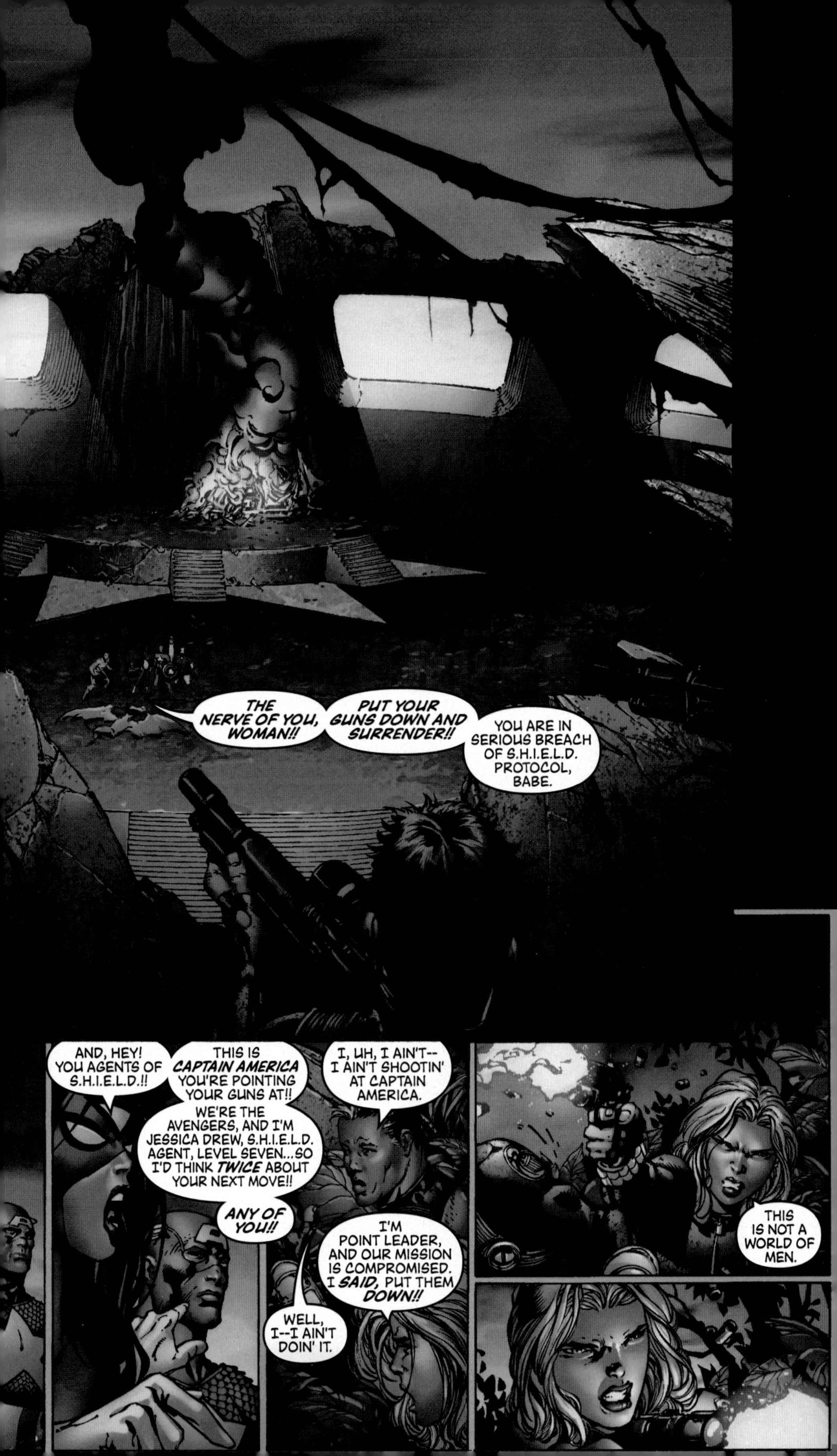
THE NERVE OF YOU, WOMAN!!
PUT YOUR GUNS DOWN AND SURRENDER!!
YOU ARE IN SERIOUS BREACH OF S.H.I.E.L.D. PROTOCOL, BABE.
AND, HEY! YOU AGENTS OF S.H.I.E.L.D.!!
THIS IS CAPTAIN AMERICA YOU'RE POINTING YOUR GUNS AT!!
WE'RE THE AVENGERS, AND I'M JESSICA DREW, S.H.I.E.L.D. AGENT, LEVEL SEVEN...SO I'D THINK TWICE ABOUT YOUR NEXT MOVE!!
ANY OF YOU!!
I, UH, I AIN'T-- I AIN'T SHOOTIN' AT CAPTAIN AMERICA.
I'M POINT LEADER, AND OUR MISSION IS COMPROMISED. I SAID, PUT THEM DOWN!!
WELL, I--I AIN'T DOIN' IT.
THIS IS NOT A WORLD OF MEN.

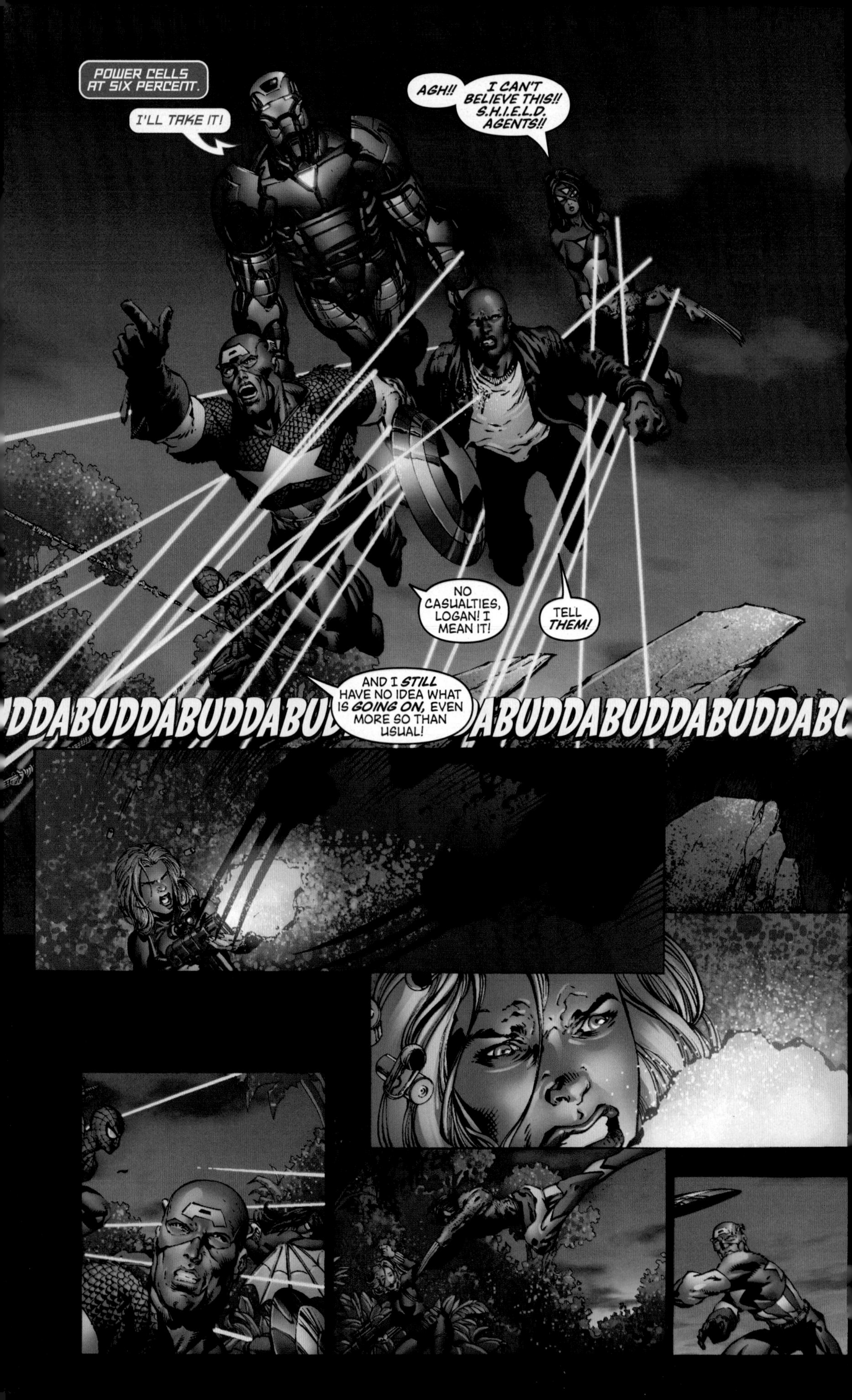
POWER CELLS AT SIX PERCENT.
I'LL TAKE IT!
AGH!! I CAN'T BELIEVE THIS!! S.H.I.E.L.D. AGENTS!!
NO CASUALTIES, LOGAN! I MEAN IT!
TELL *THEM!*
AND I *STILL* HAVE NO IDEA WHAT IS *GOING ON,* EVEN MORE SO THAN USUAL!
DDABUDDABUDDABUD ABUDDABUDDABUDDABU

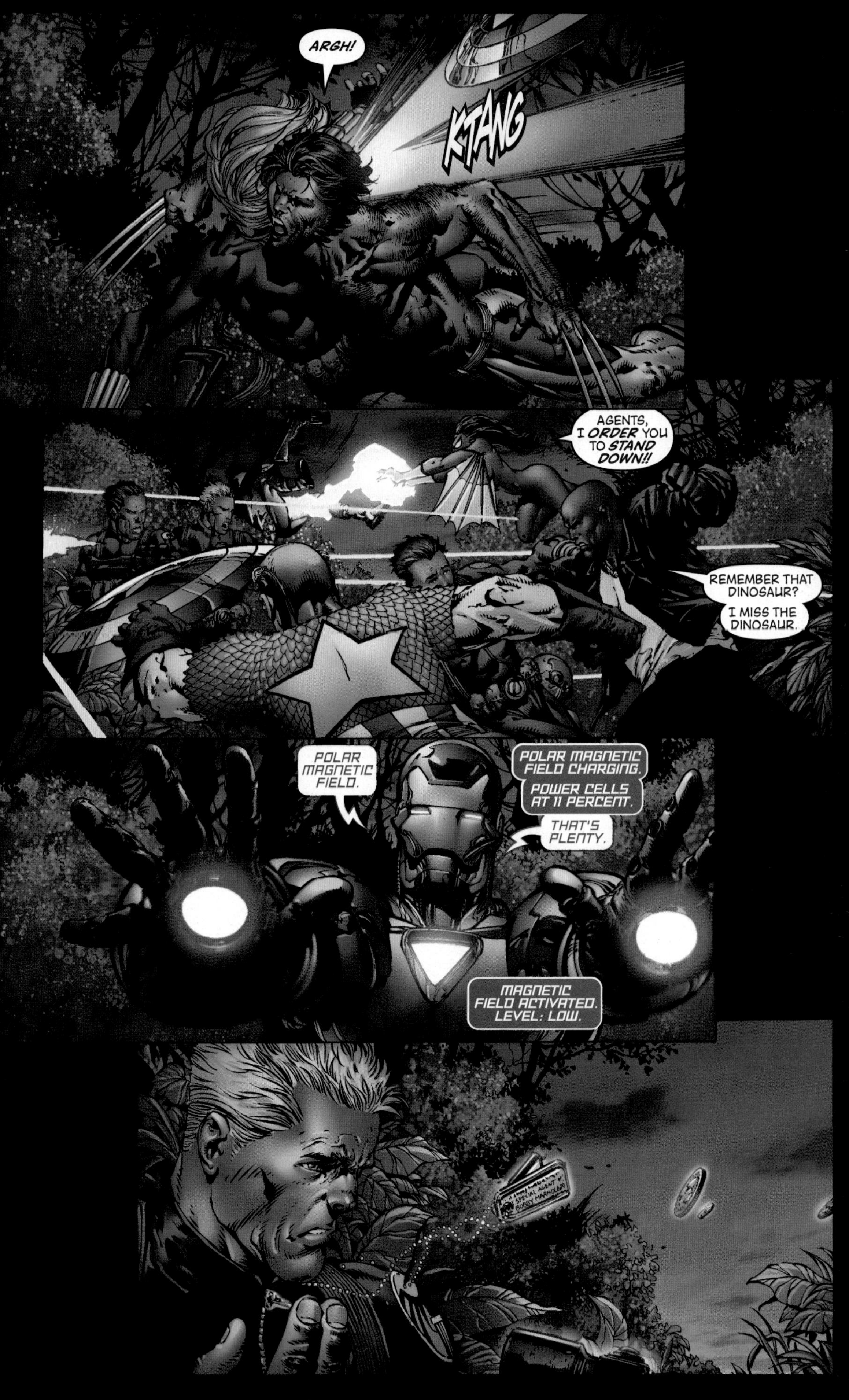
ARGH!
KTANG
AGENTS, I ORDER YOU TO STAND DOWN!!
REMEMBER THAT DINOSAUR?
I MISS THE DINOSAUR.
POLAR MAGNETIC FIELD.
POLAR MAGNETIC FIELD CHARGING.
POWER CELLS AT 11 PERCENT.
THAT'S PLENTY.
MAGNETIC FIELD ACTIVATED. LEVEL: LOW.

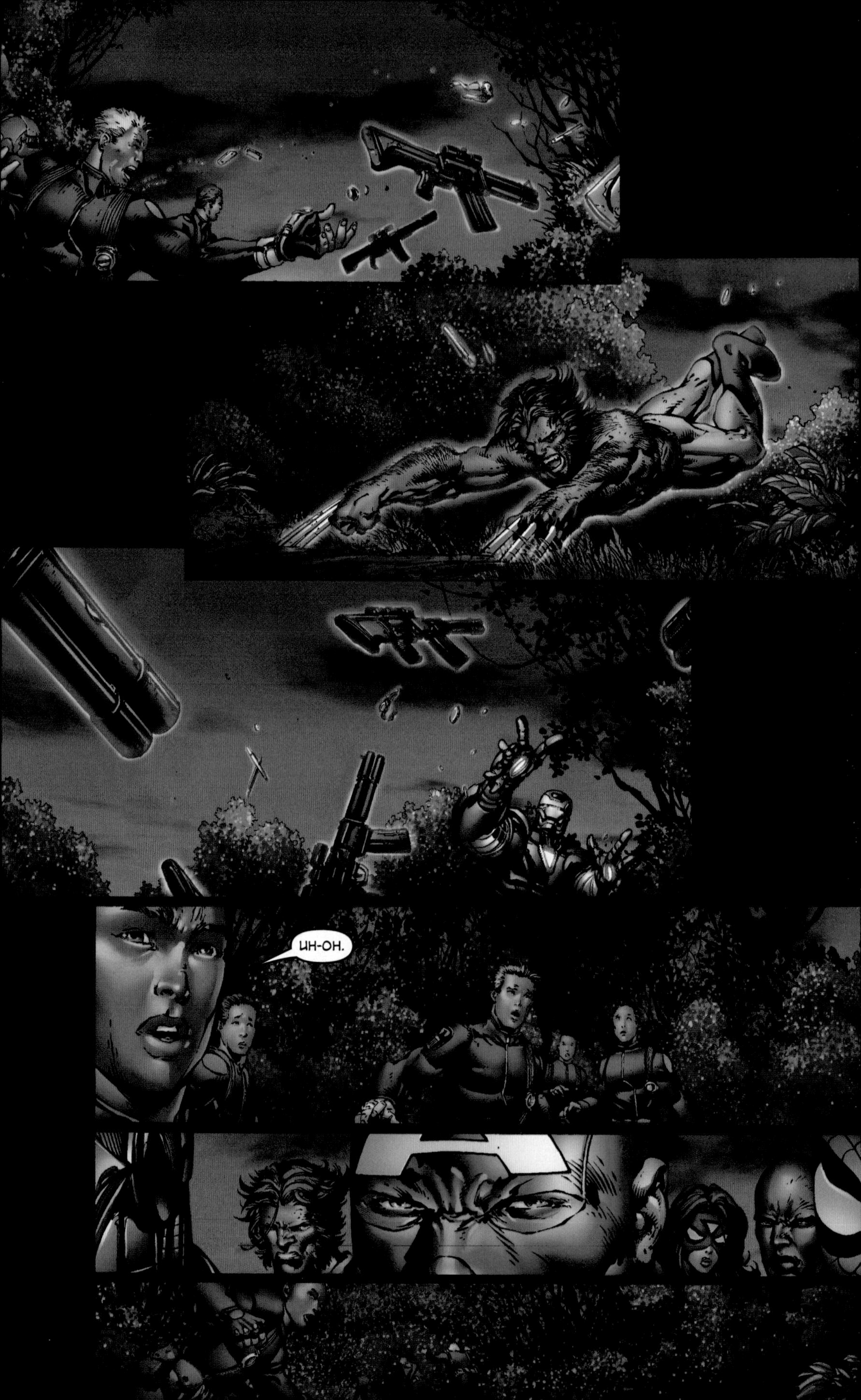
UH-OH.

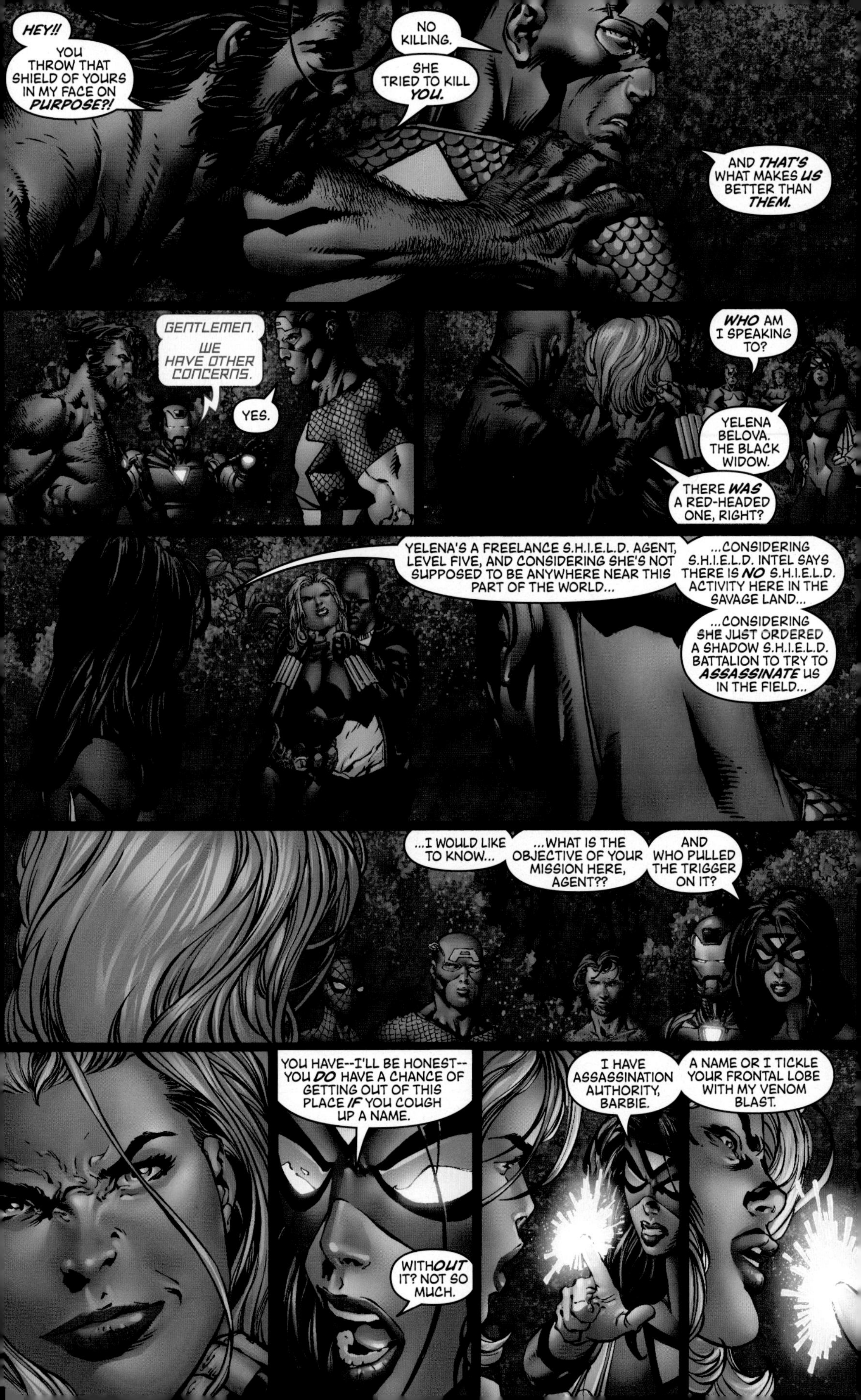
HEY!! YOU THROW THAT SHIELD OF YOURS IN MY FACE ON PURPOSE?!
NO KILLING.
SHE TRIED TO KILL YOU.
AND THAT'S WHAT MAKES US BETTER THAN THEM.
GENTLEMEN. WE HAVE OTHER CONCERNS.
YES.
WHO AM I SPEAKING TO?
YELENA BELOVA. THE BLACK WIDOW.
THERE WAS A RED-HEADED ONE, RIGHT?
YELENA'S A FREELANCE S.H.I.E.L.D. AGENT, LEVEL FIVE, AND CONSIDERING SHE'S NOT SUPPOSED TO BE ANYWHERE NEAR THIS PART OF THE WORLD...
...CONSIDERING S.H.I.E.L.D. INTEL SAYS THERE IS NO S.H.I.E.L.D. ACTIVITY HERE IN THE SAVAGE LAND...
...CONSIDERING SHE JUST ORDERED A SHADOW S.H.I.E.L.D. BATTALION TO TRY TO ASSASSINATE US IN THE FIELD...
...I WOULD LIKE TO KNOW...
...WHAT IS THE OBJECTIVE OF YOUR MISSION HERE, AGENT??
AND WHO PULLED THE TRIGGER ON IT?
YOU HAVE--I'LL BE HONEST--YOU DO HAVE A CHANCE OF GETTING OUT OF THIS PLACE IF YOU COUGH UP A NAME.
WITHOUT IT? NOT SO MUCH.
I HAVE ASSASSINATION AUTHORITY, BARBIE.
A NAME OR I TICKLE YOUR FRONTAL LOBE WITH MY VENOM BLAST.

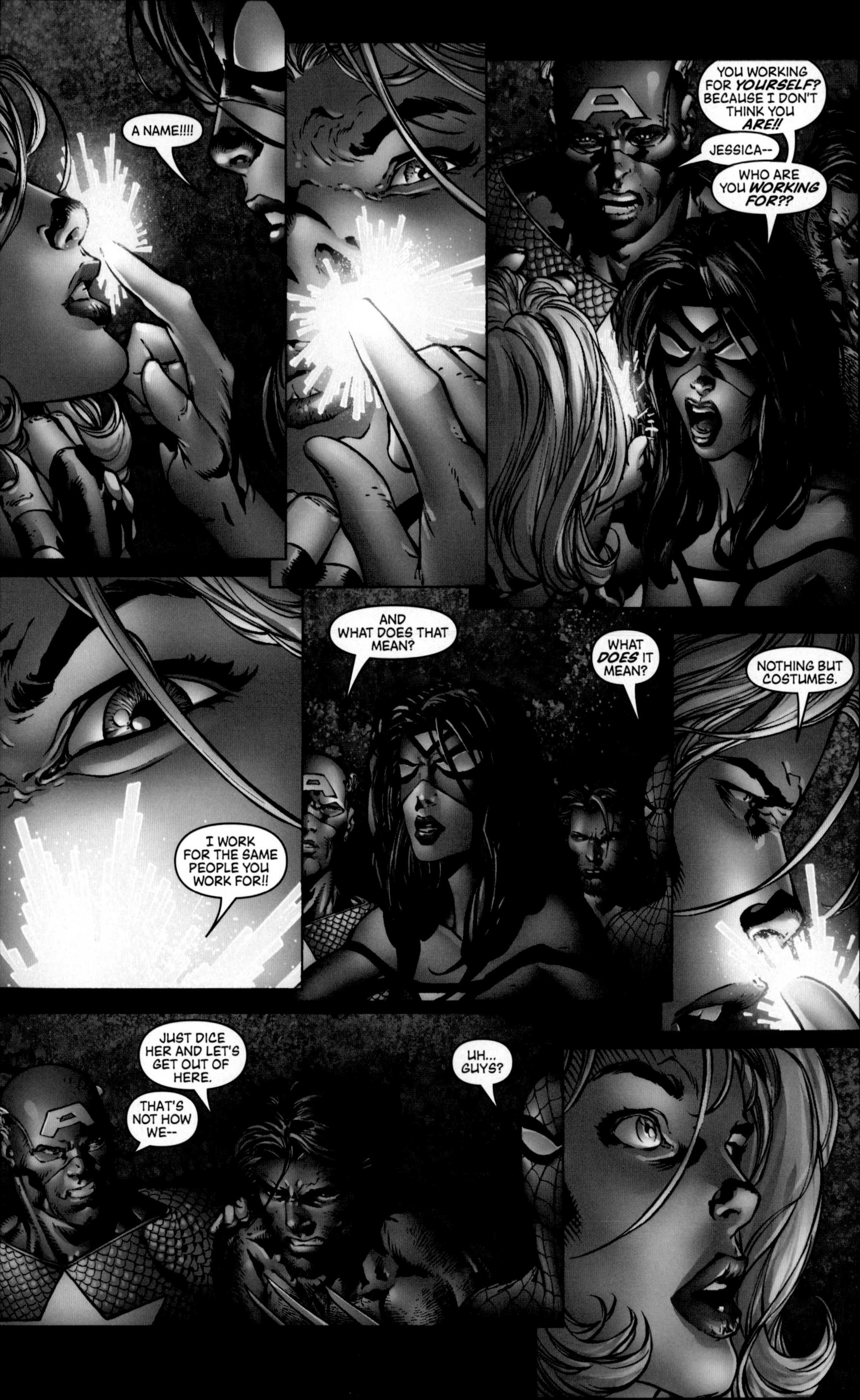
A NAME!!!!
YOU WORKING FOR YOURSELF? BECAUSE I DON'T THINK YOU ARE!!
JESSICA--
WHO ARE YOU WORKING FOR??
I WORK FOR THE SAME PEOPLE YOU WORK FOR!!
AND WHAT DOES THAT MEAN?
WHAT DOES IT MEAN?
NOTHING BUT COSTUMES.
JUST DICE HER AND LET'S GET OUT OF HERE.
THAT'S NOT HOW WE--
UH... GUYS?

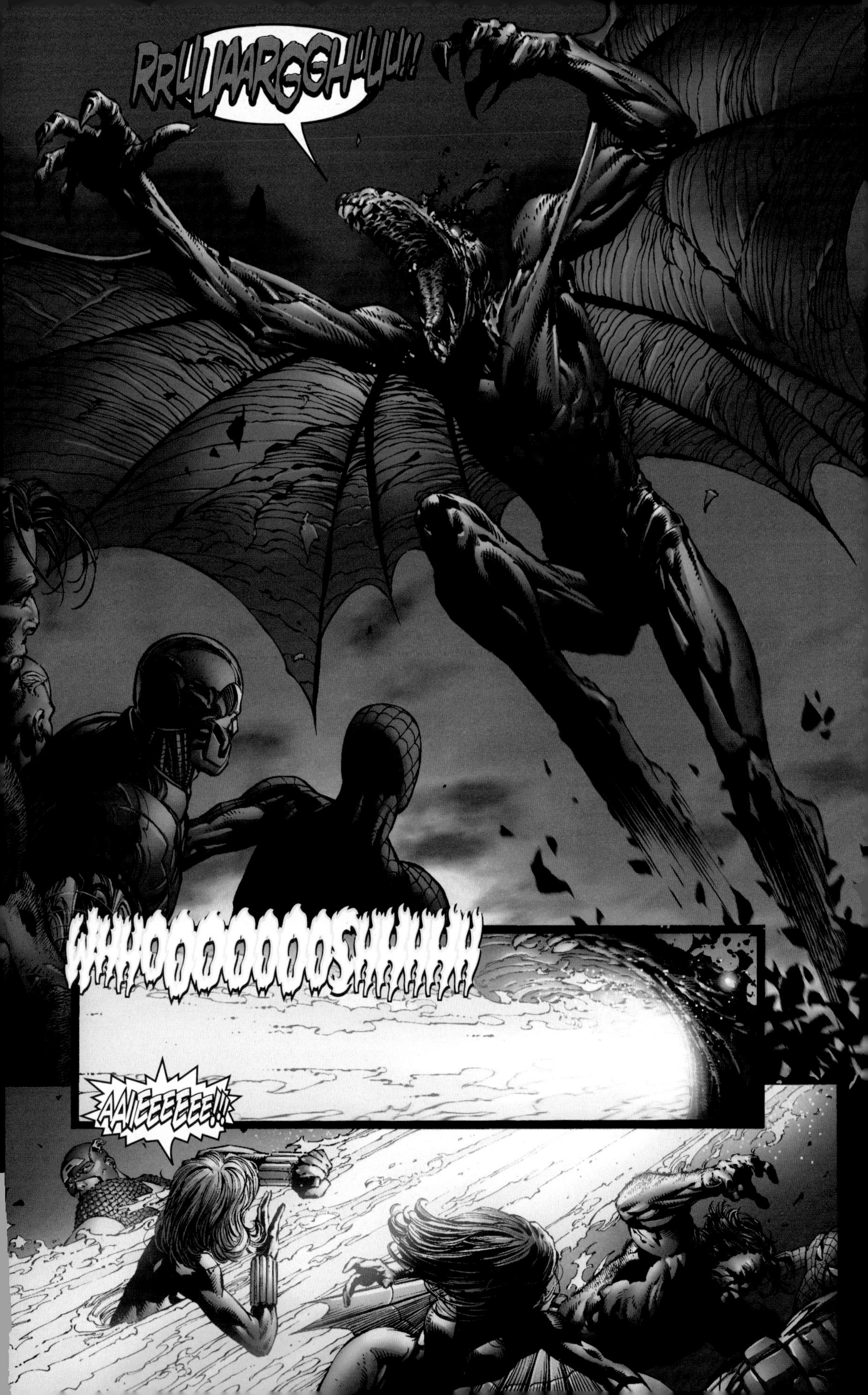
RRUUAARGGHUUUU!!
WHHOOOOOOOOSHHHHH
AAIIEEEEEEE!!!

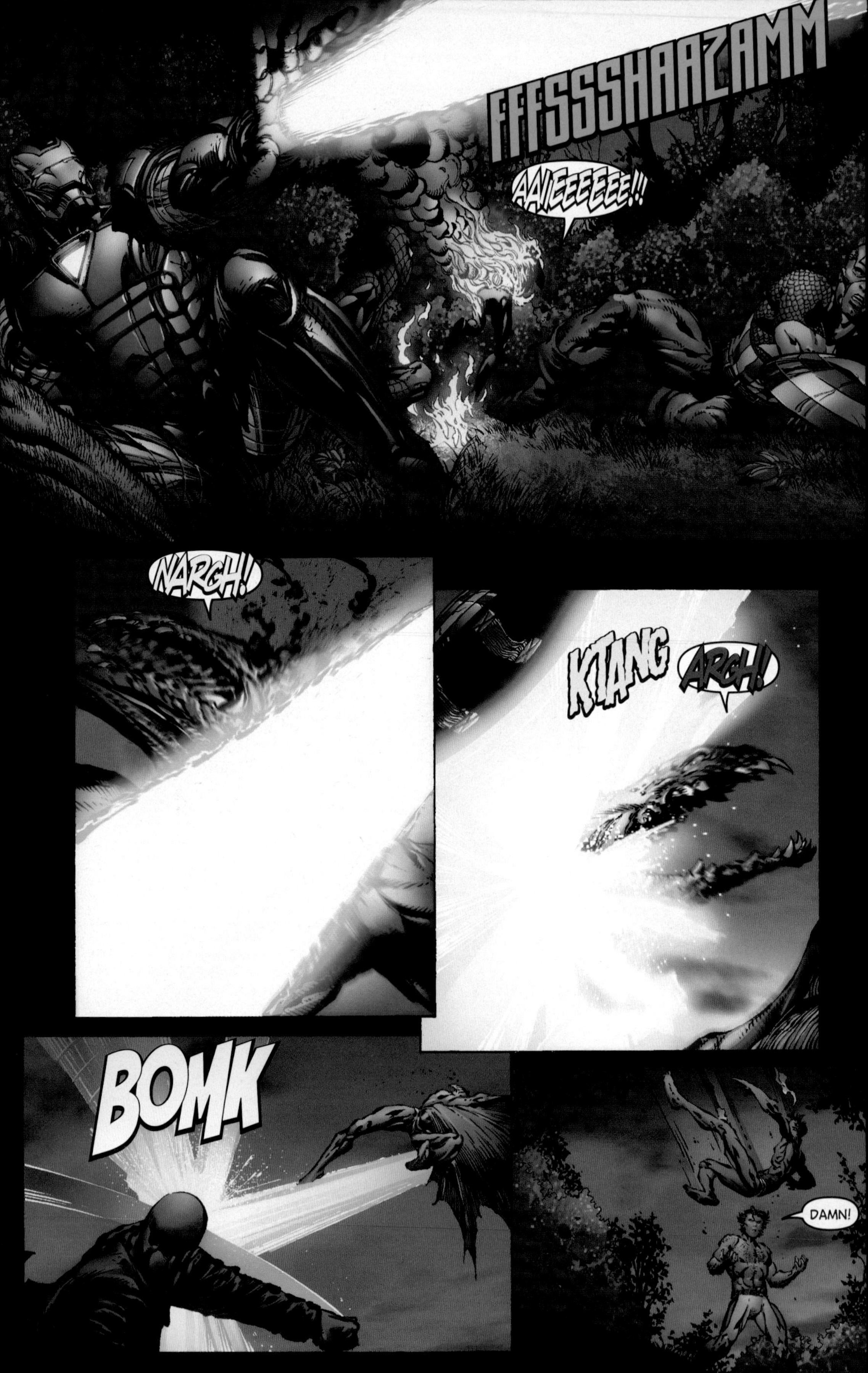
FFFSSSHAAZAMM
AAIIEEEEEEE!!!
NARGH!
KTANG
ARGH!
BOMK
DAMN!

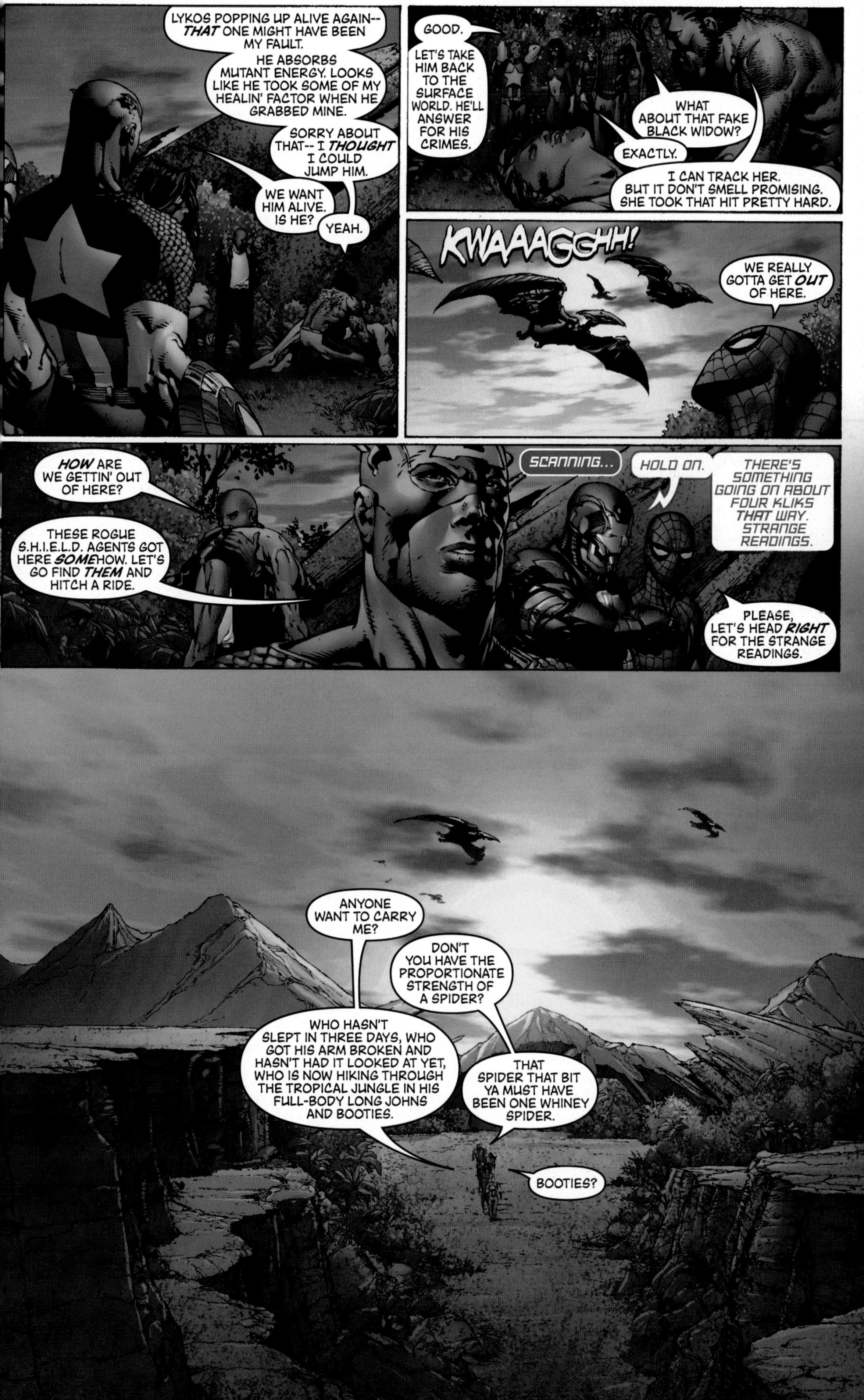
LYKOS POPPING UP ALIVE AGAIN-- THAT ONE MIGHT HAVE BEEN MY FAULT.
HE ABSORBS MUTANT ENERGY. LOOKS LIKE HE TOOK SOME OF MY HEALIN' FACTOR WHEN HE GRABBED MINE.
SORRY ABOUT THAT-- I THOUGHT I COULD JUMP HIM.
WE WANT HIM ALIVE. IS HE?
YEAH.
GOOD.
LET'S TAKE HIM BACK TO THE SURFACE WORLD. HE'LL ANSWER FOR HIS CRIMES.
WHAT ABOUT THAT FAKE BLACK WIDOW?
EXACTLY.
I CAN TRACK HER. BUT IT DON'T SMELL PROMISING. SHE TOOK THAT HIT PRETTY HARD.
KWAAAGGHH!
WE REALLY GOTTA GET OUT OF HERE.
HOW ARE WE GETTIN' OUT OF HERE?
THESE ROGUE S.H.I.E.L.D. AGENTS GOT HERE SOMEHOW. LET'S GO FIND THEM AND HITCH A RIDE.
SCANNING...
HOLD ON.
THERE'S SOMETHING GOING ON ABOUT FOUR KLIKS THAT WAY. STRANGE READINGS.
PLEASE, LET'S HEAD RIGHT FOR THE STRANGE READINGS.
ANYONE WANT TO CARRY ME?
DON'T YOU HAVE THE PROPORTIONATE STRENGTH OF A SPIDER?
WHO HASN'T SLEPT IN THREE DAYS, WHO GOT HIS ARM BROKEN AND HASN'T HAD IT LOOKED AT YET, WHO IS NOW HIKING THROUGH THE TROPICAL JUNGLE IN HIS FULL-BODY LONG JOHNS AND BOOTIES.
THAT SPIDER THAT BIT YA MUST HAVE BEEN ONE WHINEY SPIDER.
BOOTIES?

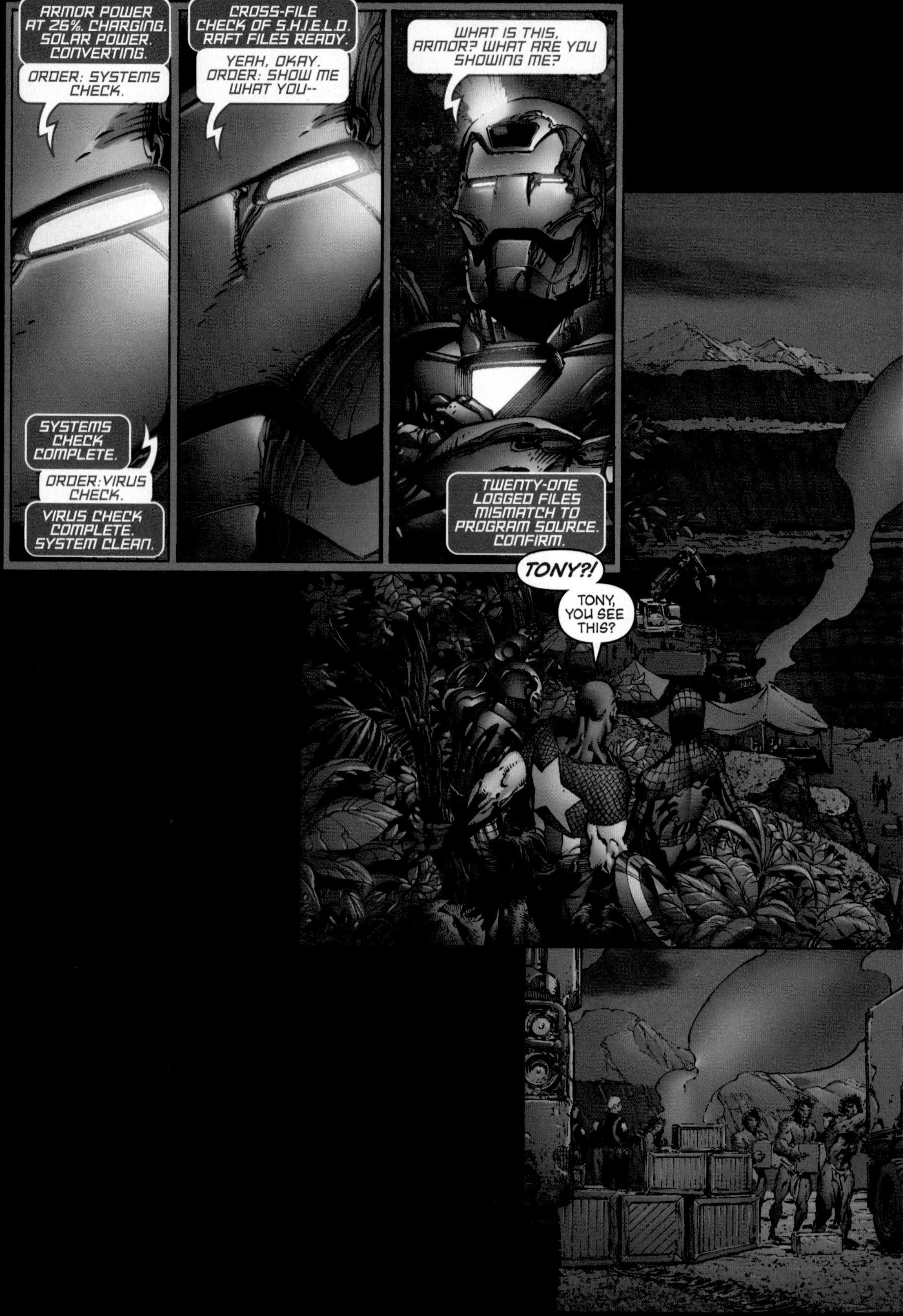
ARMOR POWER AT 26%. CHARGING. SOLAR POWER. CONVERTING.
ORDER: SYSTEMS CHECK.
SYSTEMS CHECK COMPLETE.
ORDER: VIRUS CHECK.
VIRUS CHECK COMPLETE. SYSTEM CLEAN.
CROSS-FILE CHECK OF S.H.I.E.L.D. RAFT FILES READY.
YEAH, OKAY. ORDER: SHOW ME WHAT YOU--
WHAT IS THIS, ARMOR? WHAT ARE YOU SHOWING ME?
TWENTY-ONE LOGGED FILES MISMATCH TO PROGRAM SOURCE. CONFIRM.
TONY?!
TONY, YOU SEE THIS?

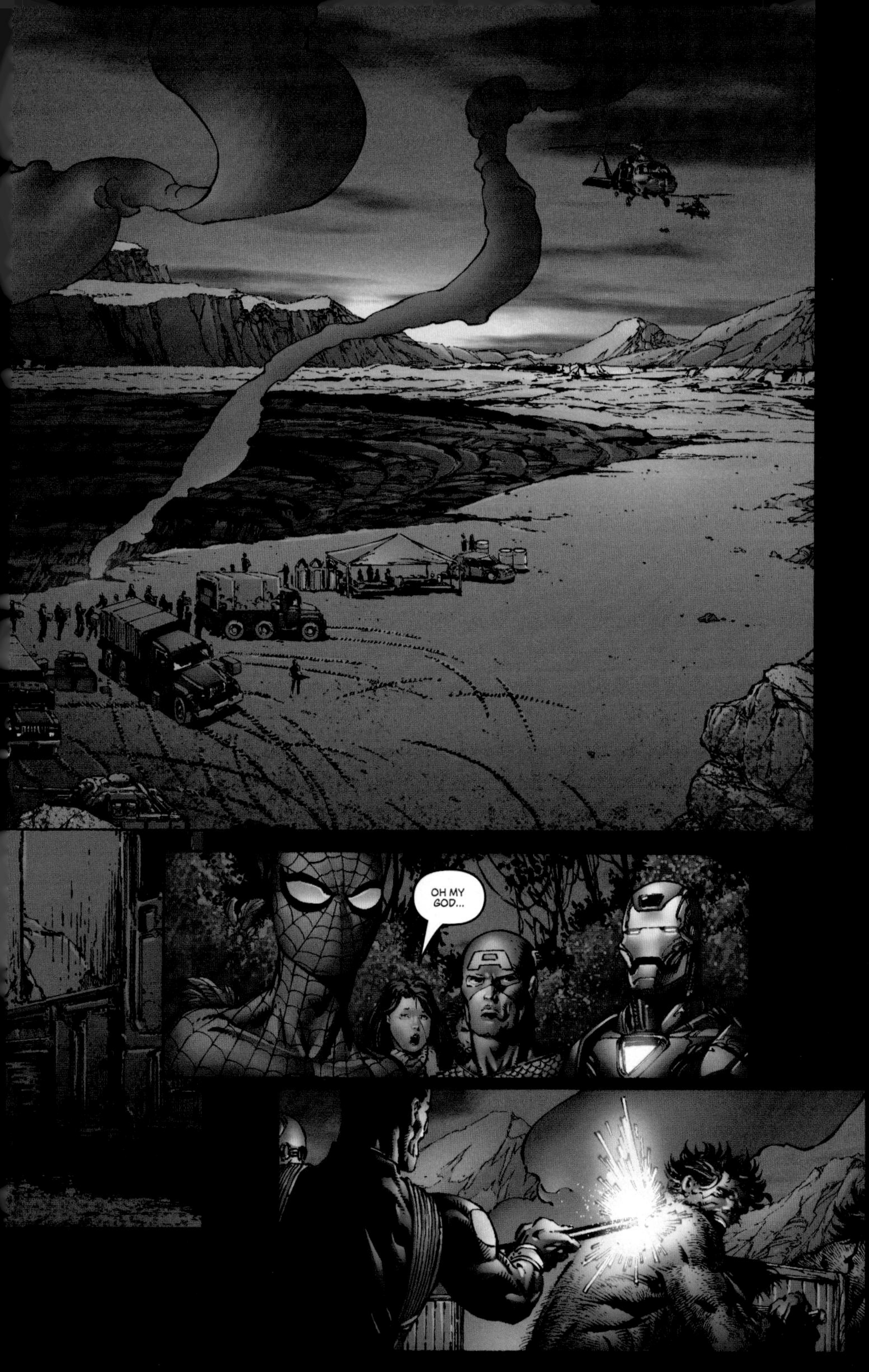
OH MY GOD...

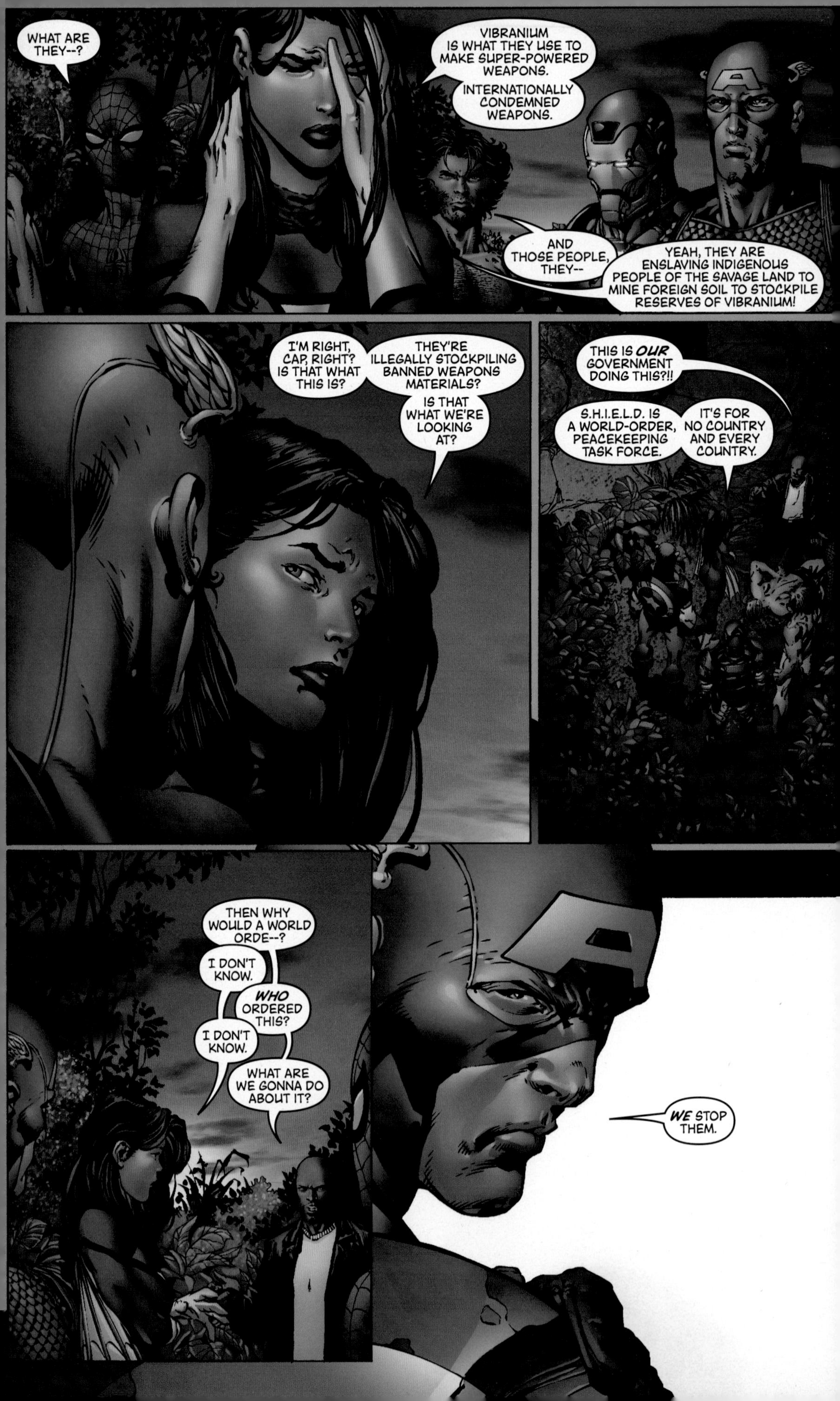

WHAT ARE THEY--?
VIBRANIUM IS WHAT THEY USE TO MAKE SUPER-POWERED WEAPONS.
INTERNATIONALLY CONDEMNED WEAPONS.
AND THOSE PEOPLE, THEY--
YEAH, THEY ARE ENSLAVING INDIGENOUS PEOPLE OF THE SAVAGE LAND TO MINE FOREIGN SOIL TO STOCKPILE RESERVES OF VIBRANIUM!
I'M RIGHT, CAP, RIGHT? IS THAT WHAT THIS IS?
THEY'RE ILLEGALLY STOCKPILING BANNED WEAPONS MATERIALS?
IS THAT WHAT WE'RE LOOKING AT?
THIS IS OUR GOVERNMENT DOING THIS?!!
S.H.I.E.L.D. IS A WORLD-ORDER, PEACEKEEPING TASK FORCE.
IT'S FOR NO COUNTRY AND EVERY COUNTRY.
THEN WHY WOULD A WORLD ORDE--?
I DON'T KNOW.
WHO ORDERED THIS?
I DON'T KNOW.
WHAT ARE WE GONNA DO ABOUT IT?
WE STOP THEM.

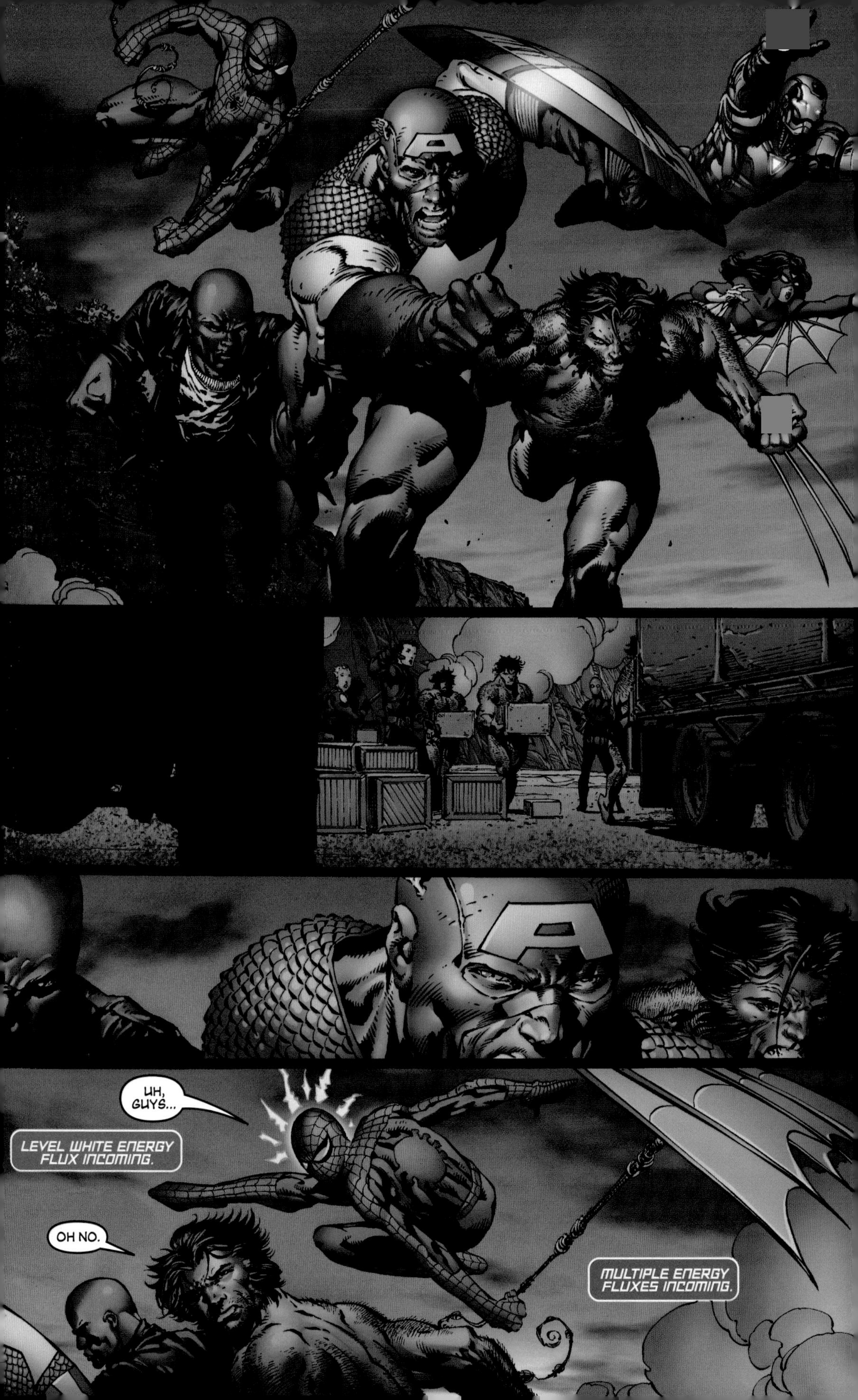
UH, GUYS...
LEVEL WHITE ENERGY FLUX INCOMING.
OH NO.
MULTIPLE ENERGY FLUXES INCOMING.

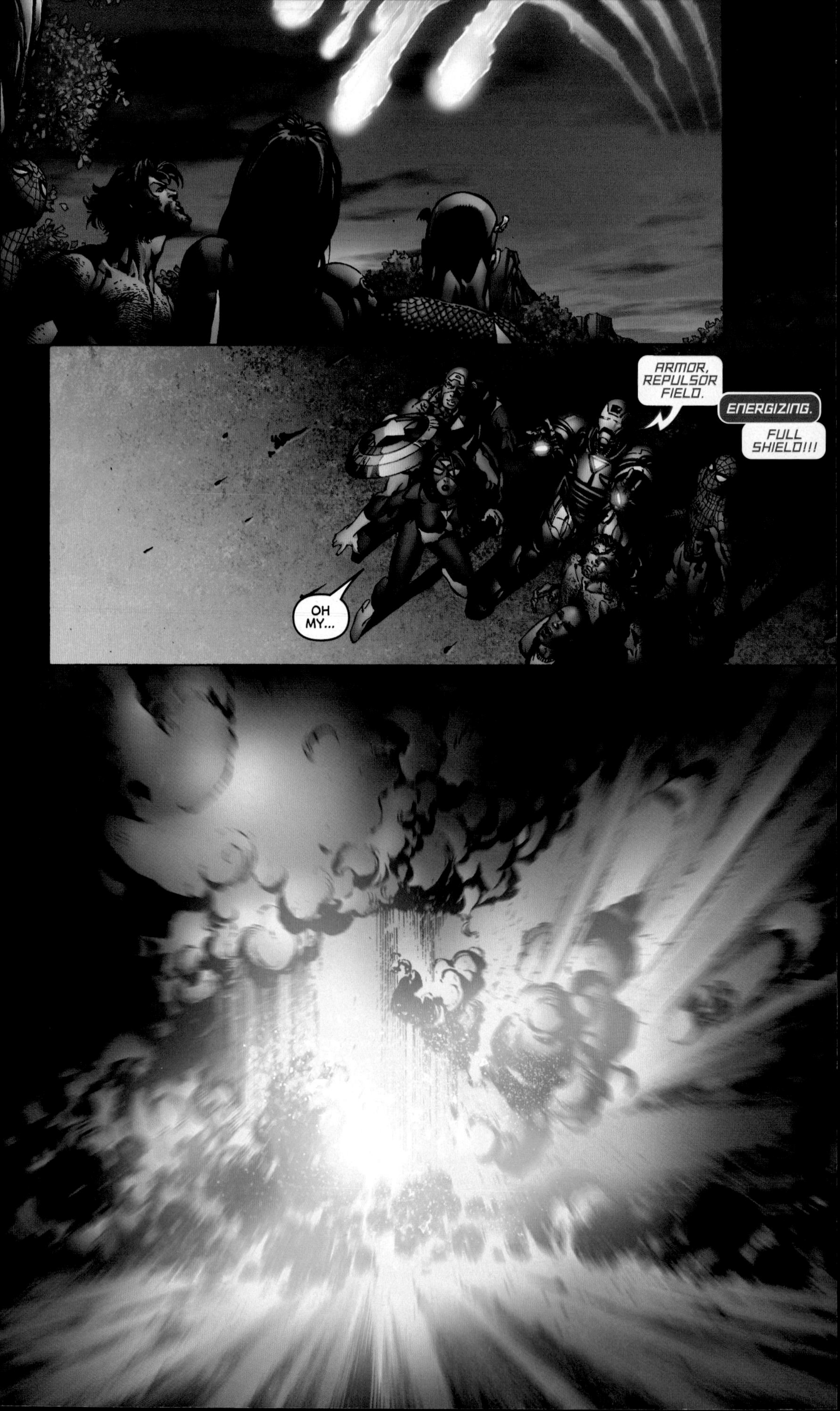
ARMOR, REPULSOR FIELD.
ENERGIZING.
FULL SHIELD!!!
OH MY...

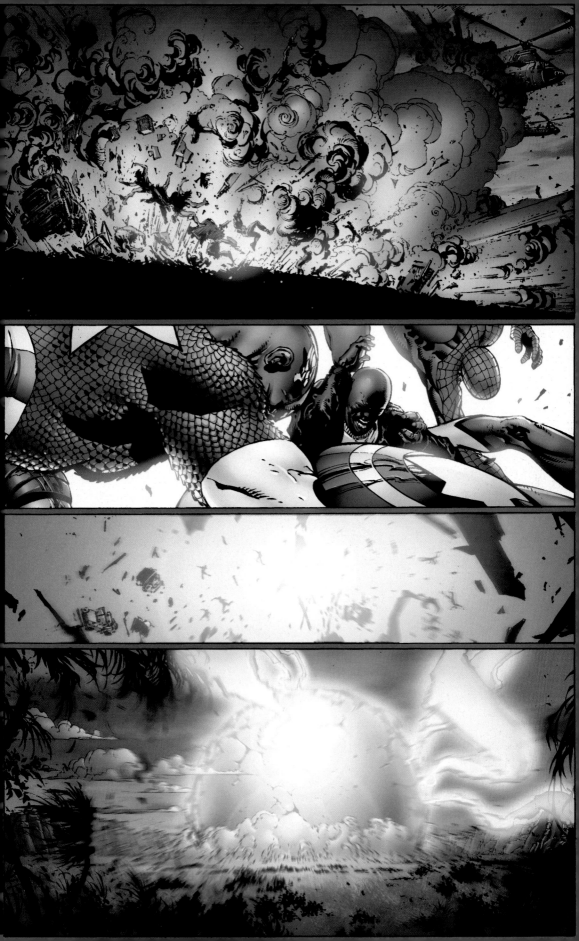

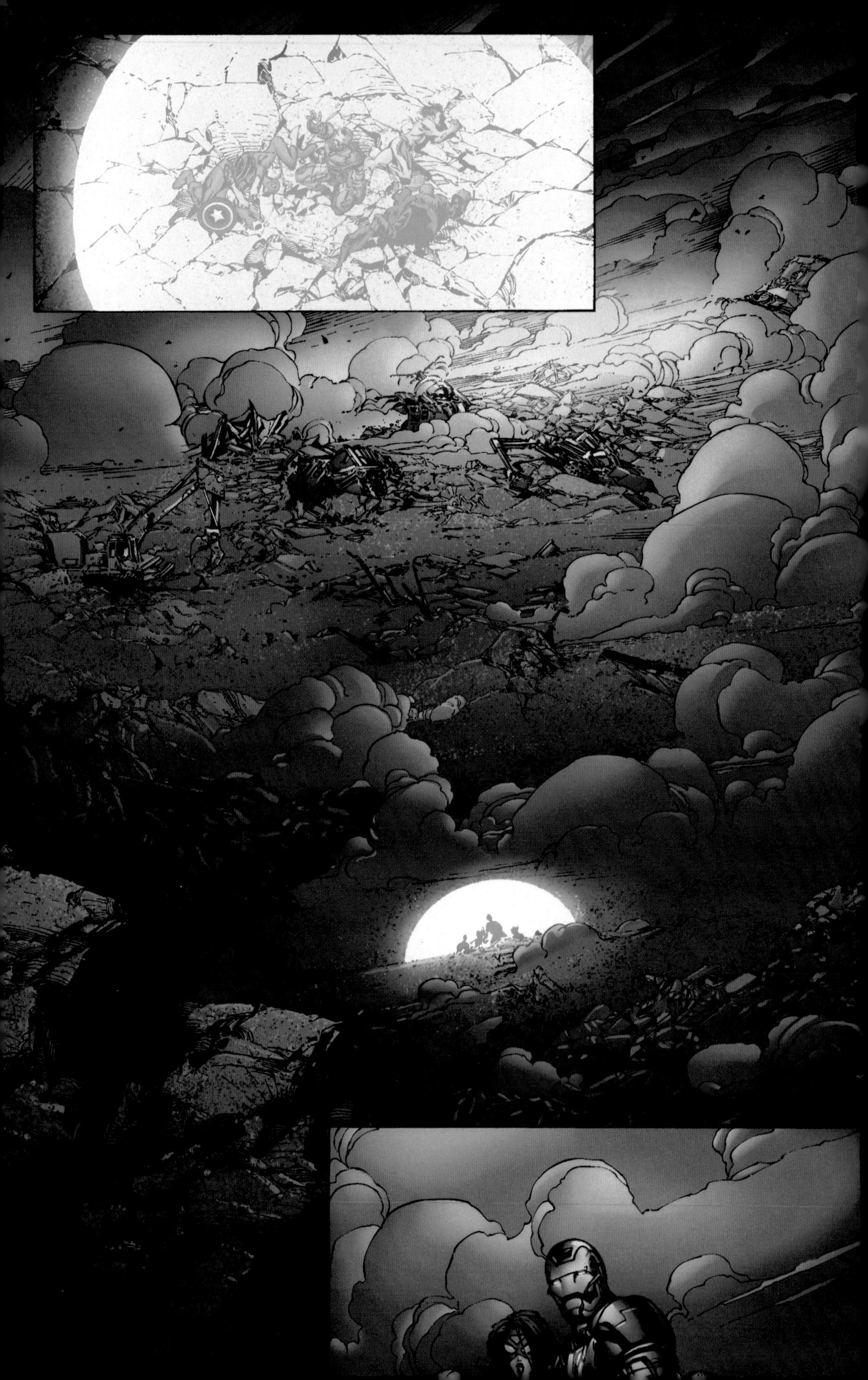

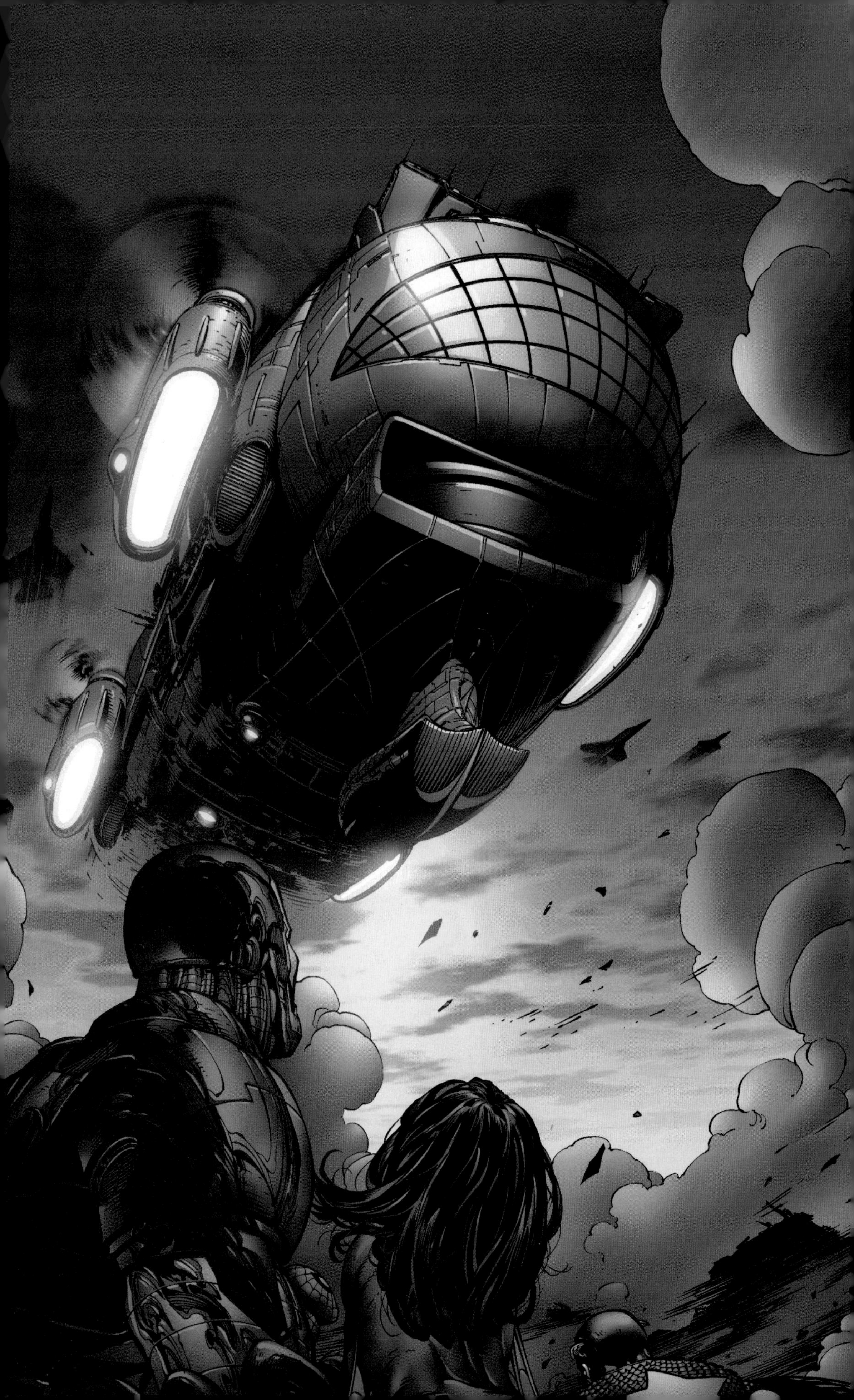

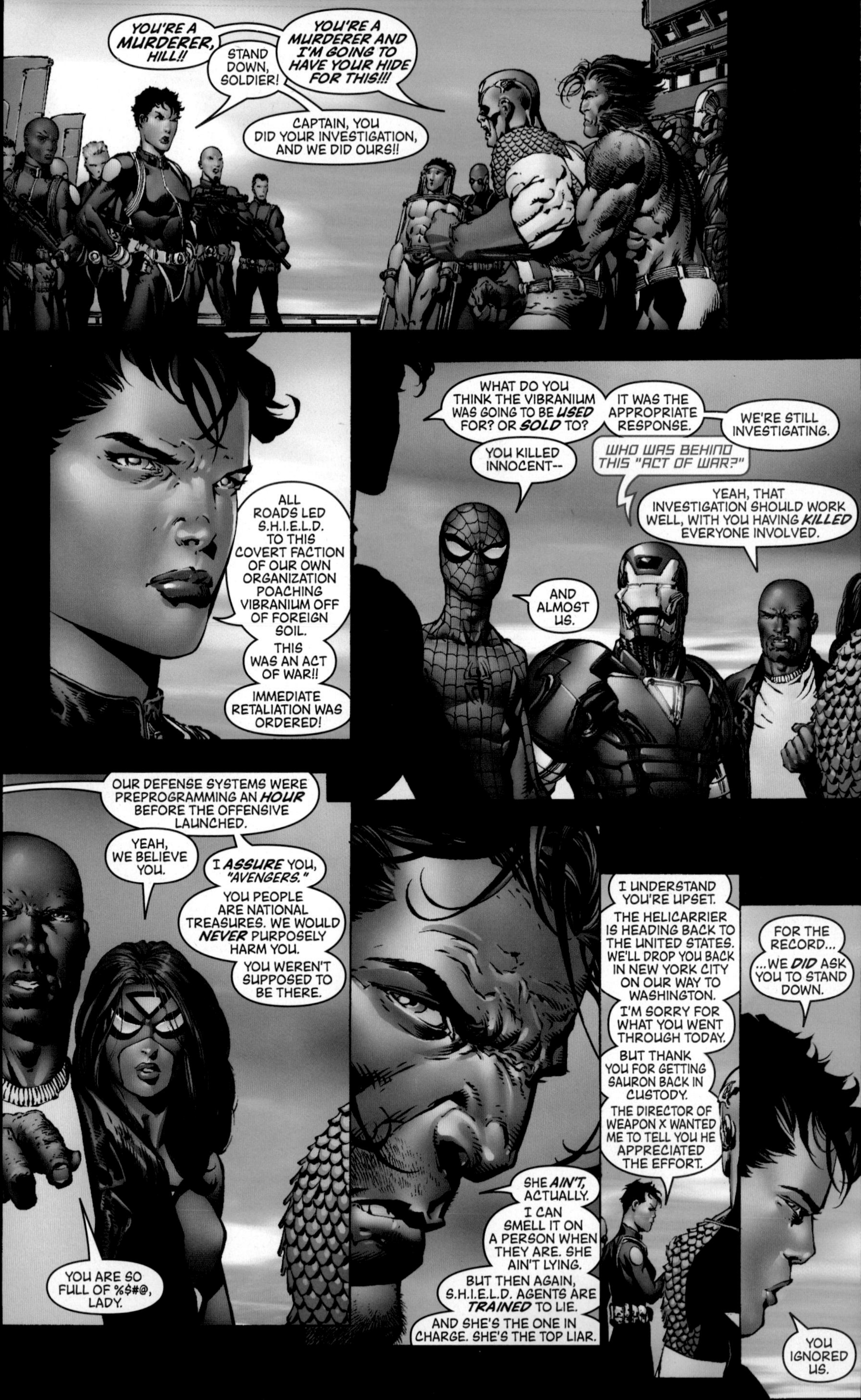
YOU'RE A MURDERER, HILL!!
STAND DOWN, SOLDIER!
YOU'RE A MURDERER AND I'M GOING TO HAVE YOUR HIDE FOR THIS!!!
CAPTAIN, YOU DID YOUR INVESTIGATION, AND WE DID OURS!!
ALL ROADS LED S.H.I.E.L.D. TO THIS COVERT FACTION OF OUR OWN ORGANIZATION POACHING VIBRANIUM OFF OF FOREIGN SOIL.
THIS WAS AN ACT OF WAR!!
IMMEDIATE RETALIATION WAS ORDERED!
WHAT DO YOU THINK THE VIBRANIUM WAS GOING TO BE USED FOR? OR SOLD TO?
YOU KILLED INNOCENT--
IT WAS THE APPROPRIATE RESPONSE.
WE'RE STILL INVESTIGATING.
WHO WAS BEHIND THIS "ACT OF WAR?"
YEAH, THAT INVESTIGATION SHOULD WORK WELL, WITH YOU HAVING KILLED EVERYONE INVOLVED.
AND ALMOST US.
OUR DEFENSE SYSTEMS WERE PREPROGRAMMING AN HOUR BEFORE THE OFFENSIVE LAUNCHED.
YEAH, WE BELIEVE YOU.
I ASSURE YOU, "AVENGERS."
YOU PEOPLE ARE NATIONAL TREASURES. WE WOULD NEVER PURPOSELY HARM YOU.
YOU WEREN'T SUPPOSED TO BE THERE.
YOU ARE SO FULL OF %$#@, LADY.
SHE AIN'T, ACTUALLY.
I CAN SMELL IT ON A PERSON WHEN THEY ARE. SHE AIN'T LYING.
BUT THEN AGAIN, S.H.I.E.L.D. AGENTS ARE TRAINED TO LIE.
AND SHE'S THE ONE IN CHARGE. SHE'S THE TOP LIAR.
I UNDERSTAND YOU'RE UPSET.
THE HELICARRIER IS HEADING BACK TO THE UNITED STATES. WE'LL DROP YOU BACK IN NEW YORK CITY ON OUR WAY TO WASHINGTON.
I'M SORRY FOR WHAT YOU WENT THROUGH TODAY.
BUT THANK YOU FOR GETTING SAURON BACK IN CUSTODY.
THE DIRECTOR OF WEAPON X WANTED ME TO TELL YOU HE APPRECIATED THE EFFORT.
FOR THE RECORD... ...WE DID ASK YOU TO STAND DOWN.
YOU IGNORED US.

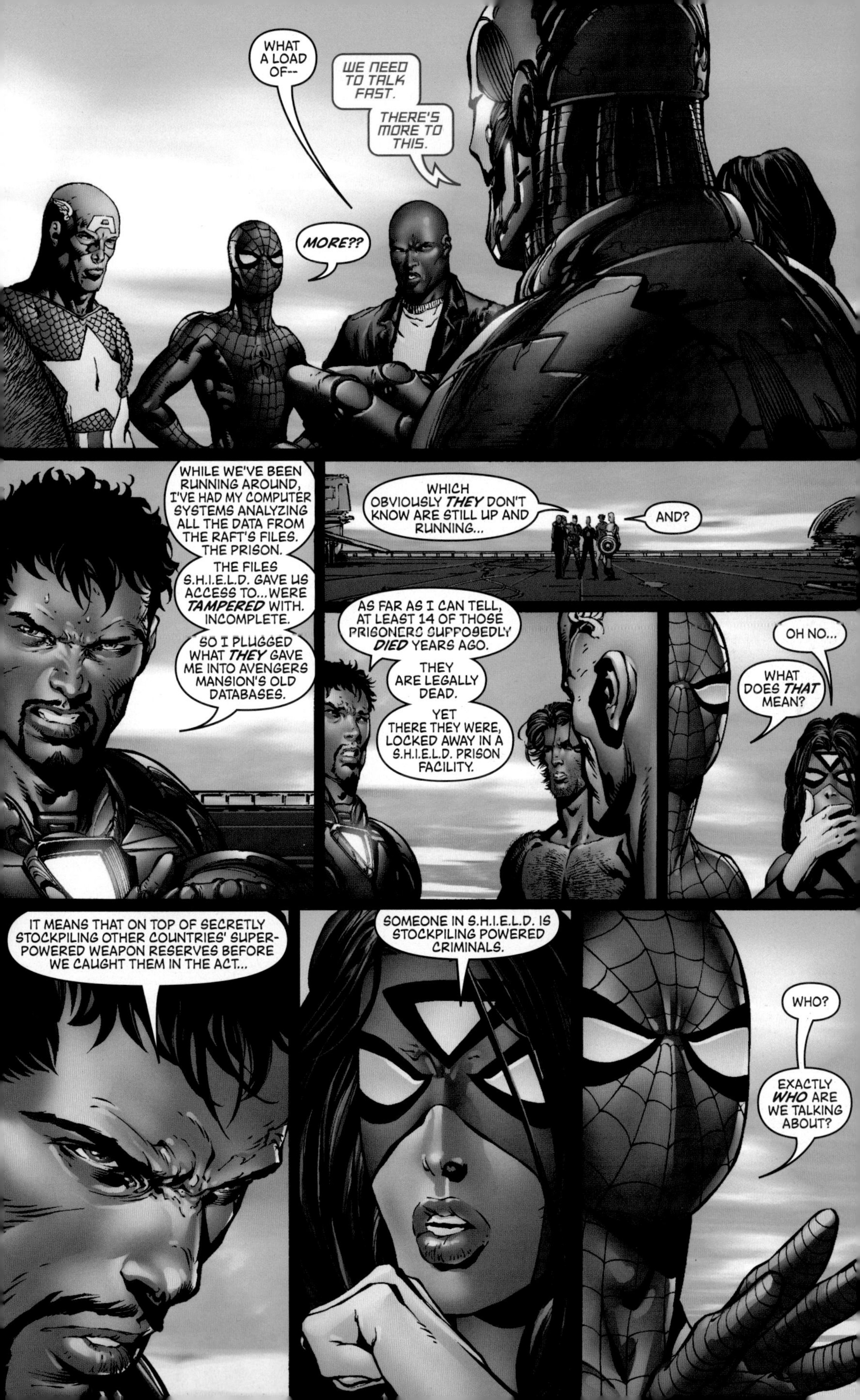
WHAT A LOAD OF--
WE NEED TO TALK FAST.
THERE'S MORE TO THIS.
MORE??
WHILE WE'VE BEEN RUNNING AROUND, I'VE HAD MY COMPUTER SYSTEMS ANALYZING ALL THE DATA FROM THE RAFT'S FILES. THE PRISON.
THE FILES S.H.I.E.L.D. GAVE US ACCESS TO...WERE TAMPERED WITH. INCOMPLETE.
SO I PLUGGED WHAT THEY GAVE ME INTO AVENGERS MANSION'S OLD DATABASES.
WHICH OBVIOUSLY THEY DON'T KNOW ARE STILL UP AND RUNNING...
AND?
AS FAR AS I CAN TELL, AT LEAST 14 OF THOSE PRISONERS SUPPOSEDLY DIED YEARS AGO.
THEY ARE LEGALLY DEAD.
YET THERE THEY WERE, LOCKED AWAY IN A S.H.I.E.L.D. PRISON FACILITY.
OH NO...
WHAT DOES THAT MEAN?
IT MEANS THAT ON TOP OF SECRETLY STOCKPILING OTHER COUNTRIES' SUPER-POWERED WEAPON RESERVES BEFORE WE CAUGHT THEM IN THE ACT...
SOMEONE IN S.H.I.E.L.D. IS STOCKPILING POWERED CRIMINALS.
WHO?
EXACTLY WHO ARE WE TALKING ABOUT?

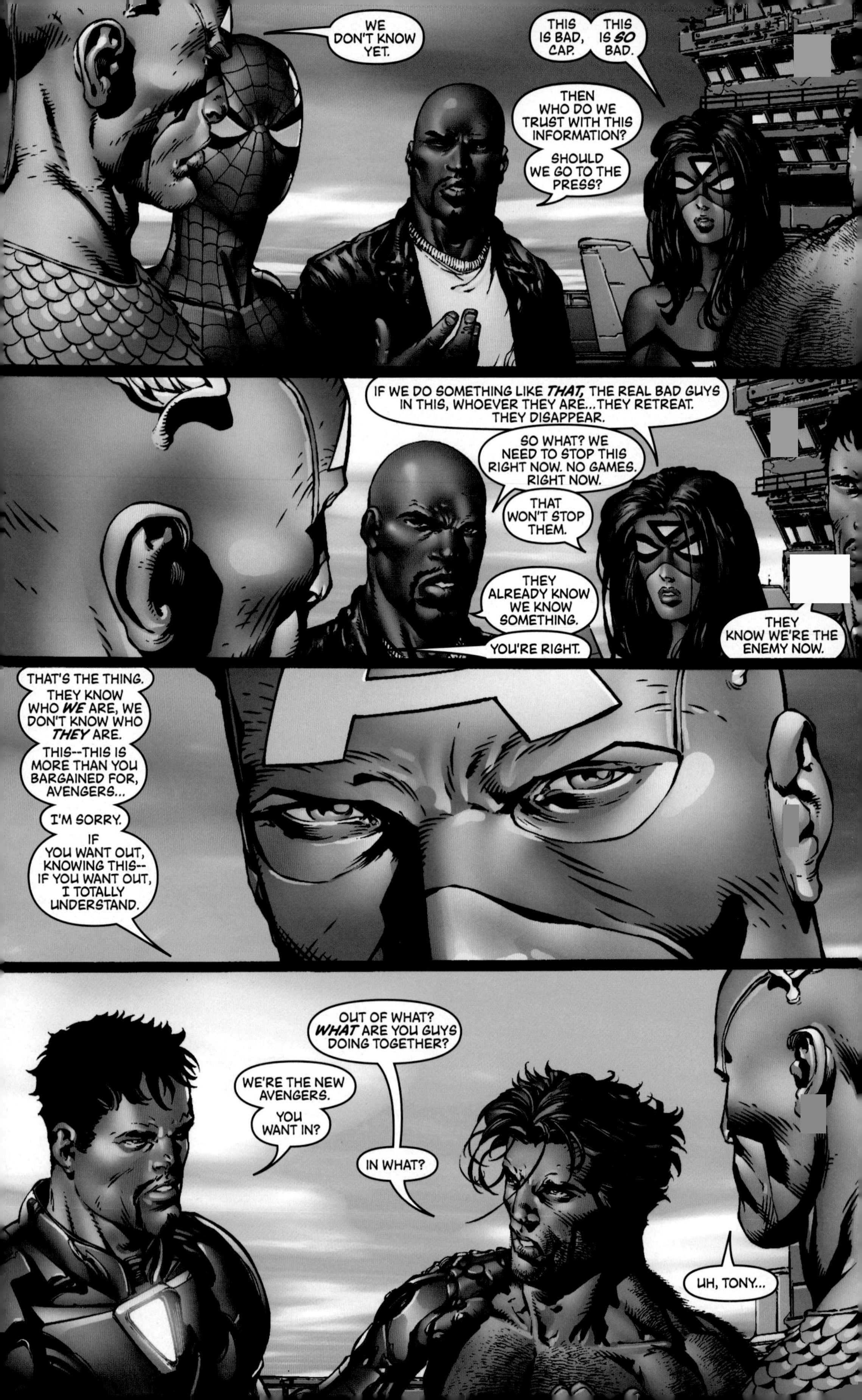
WE DON'T KNOW YET.
THIS IS BAD, CAP.
THIS IS *SO* BAD.
THEN WHO DO WE TRUST WITH THIS INFORMATION?
SHOULD WE GO TO THE PRESS?
IF WE DO SOMETHING LIKE *THAT,* THE REAL BAD GUYS IN THIS, WHOEVER THEY ARE...THEY RETREAT. THEY DISAPPEAR.
SO WHAT? WE NEED TO STOP THIS RIGHT NOW. NO GAMES. RIGHT NOW.
THAT WON'T STOP THEM.
THEY ALREADY KNOW WE KNOW SOMETHING.
YOU'RE RIGHT.
THEY KNOW WE'RE THE ENEMY NOW.
THAT'S THE THING.
THEY KNOW WHO *WE* ARE, WE DON'T KNOW WHO *THEY* ARE.
THIS--THIS IS MORE THAN YOU BARGAINED FOR, AVENGERS...
I'M SORRY.
IF YOU WANT OUT, KNOWING THIS-- IF YOU WANT OUT, I TOTALLY UNDERSTAND.
OUT OF WHAT? *WHAT* ARE YOU GUYS DOING TOGETHER?
WE'RE THE NEW AVENGERS.
YOU WANT IN?
IN WHAT?
UH, TONY...

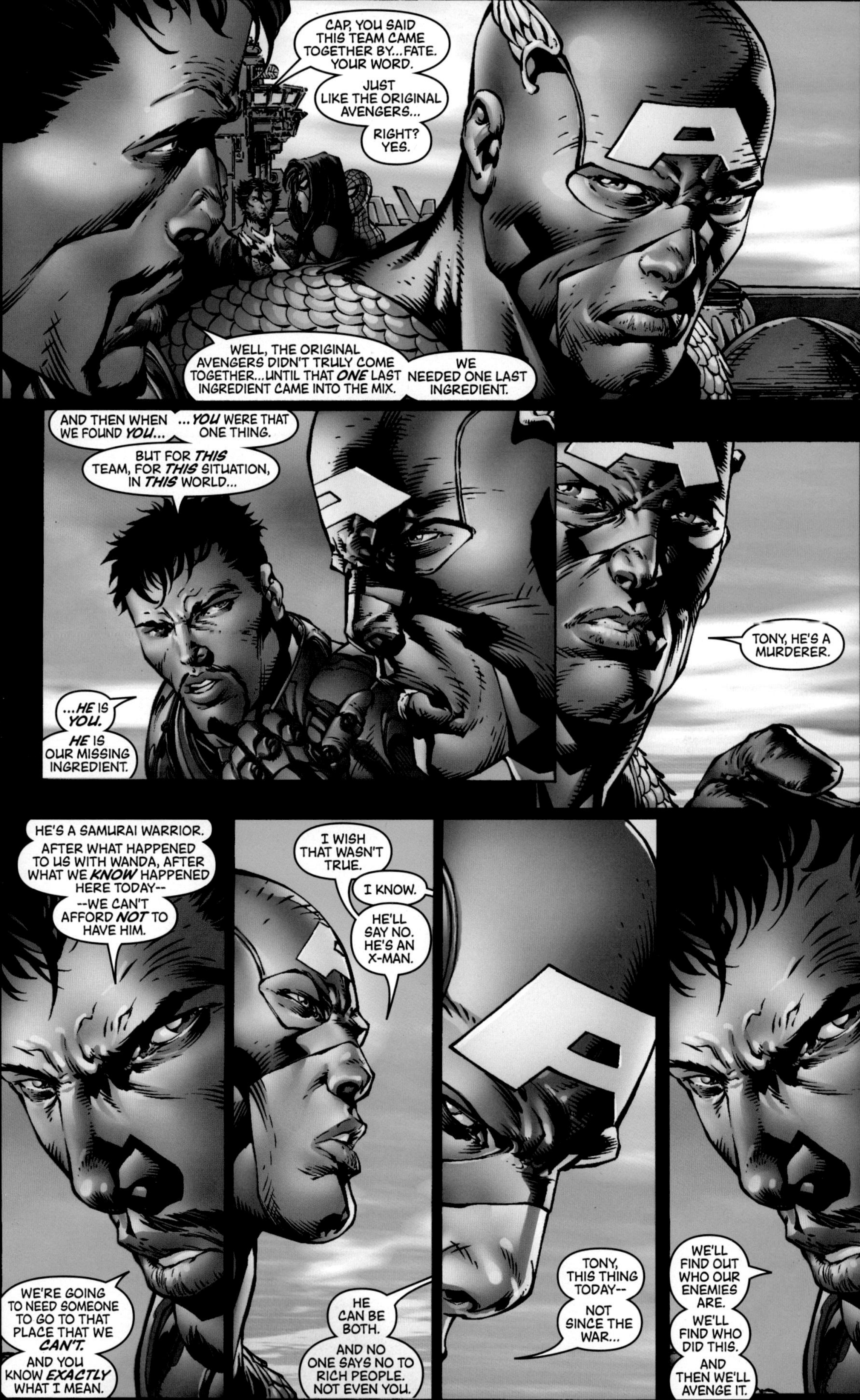
CAP, YOU SAID THIS TEAM CAME TOGETHER BY...FATE. YOUR WORD.
JUST LIKE THE ORIGINAL AVENGERS...
RIGHT? YES.
WELL, THE ORIGINAL AVENGERS DIDN'T TRULY COME TOGETHER...UNTIL THAT ONE LAST INGREDIENT CAME INTO THE MIX.
WE NEEDED ONE LAST INGREDIENT.
AND THEN WHEN WE FOUND YOU...
...YOU WERE THAT ONE THING.
BUT FOR THIS TEAM, FOR THIS SITUATION, IN THIS WORLD...
...HE IS YOU.
HE IS OUR MISSING INGREDIENT.
TONY, HE'S A MURDERER.
HE'S A SAMURAI WARRIOR.
AFTER WHAT HAPPENED TO US WITH WANDA, AFTER WHAT WE KNOW HAPPENED HERE TODAY--
--WE CAN'T AFFORD NOT TO HAVE HIM.
WE'RE GOING TO NEED SOMEONE TO GO TO THAT PLACE THAT WE CAN'T.
AND YOU KNOW EXACTLY WHAT I MEAN.
I WISH THAT WASN'T TRUE.
I KNOW.
HE'LL SAY NO. HE'S AN X-MAN.
HE CAN BE BOTH.
AND NO ONE SAYS NO TO RICH PEOPLE. NOT EVEN YOU.
TONY, THIS THING TODAY--
NOT SINCE THE WAR...
WE'LL FIND OUT WHO OUR ENEMIES ARE.
WE'LL FIND WHO DID THIS.
AND THEN WE'LL AVENGE IT.

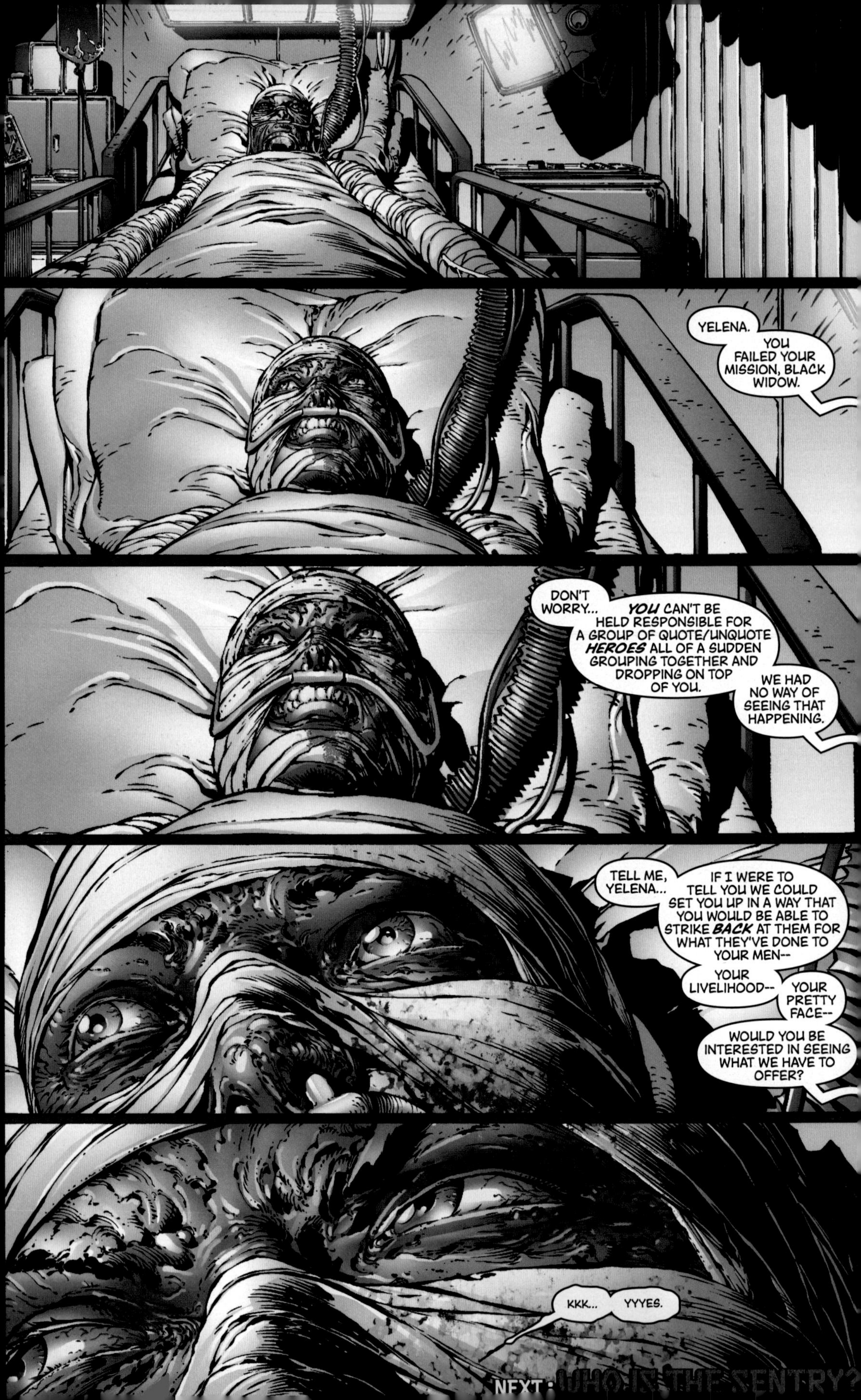
YELENA.
YOU FAILED YOUR MISSION, BLACK WIDOW.
DON'T WORRY...
YOU CAN'T BE HELD RESPONSIBLE FOR A GROUP OF QUOTE/UNQUOTE *HEROES* ALL OF A SUDDEN GROUPING TOGETHER AND DROPPING ON TOP OF YOU.
WE HAD NO WAY OF SEEING THAT HAPPENING.
TELL ME, YELENA...
IF I WERE TO TELL YOU WE COULD SET YOU UP IN A WAY THAT YOU WOULD BE ABLE TO STRIKE *BACK* AT THEM FOR WHAT THEY'VE DONE TO YOUR MEN--
YOUR LIVELIHOOD--
YOUR PRETTY FACE--
WOULD YOU BE INTERESTED IN SEEING WHAT WE HAVE TO OFFER?
KKK...
YYYES.
NEXT: WHO IS THE SENTRY?

#1A

by Steve McNiven

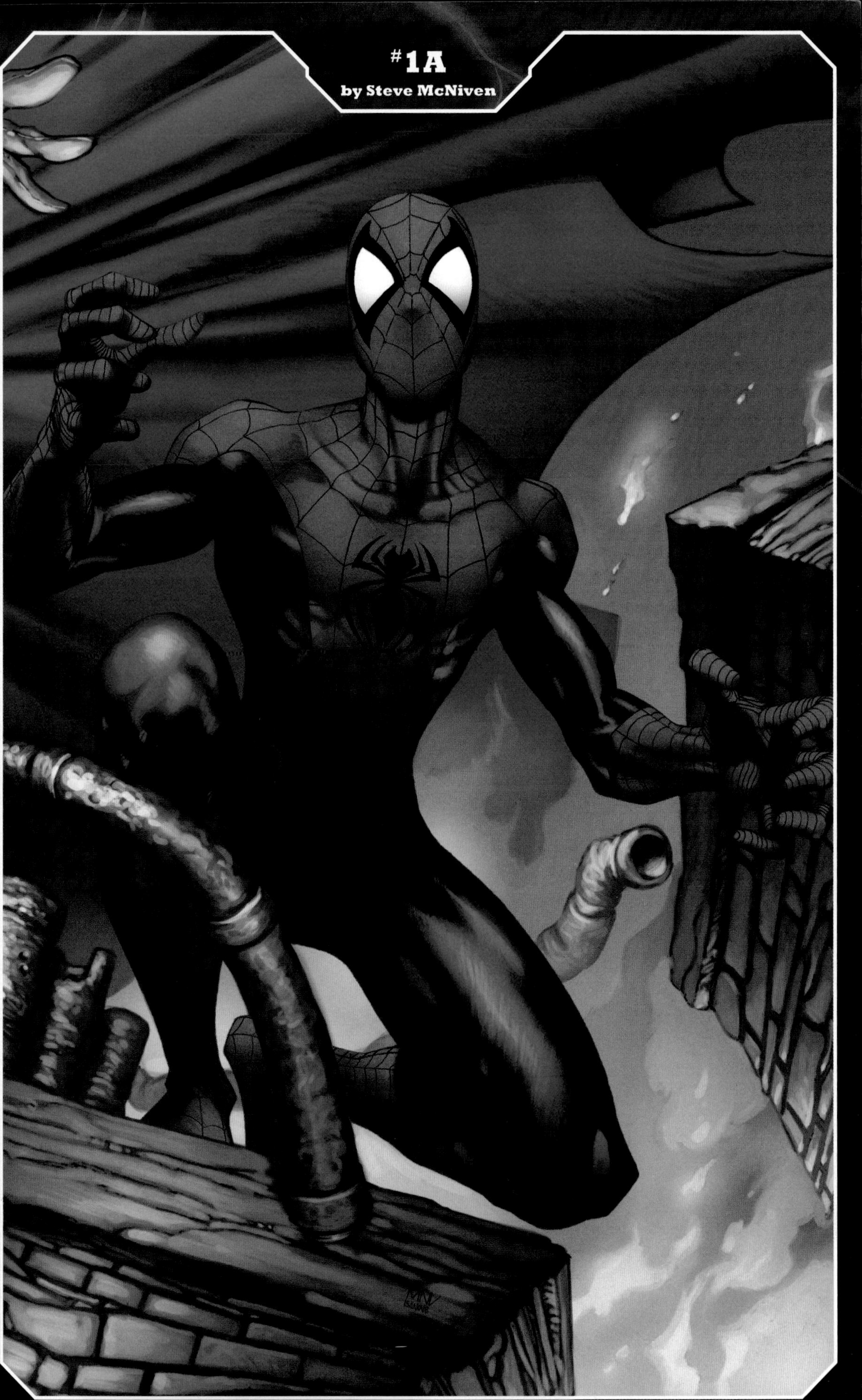

#1B
by Joe Quesada

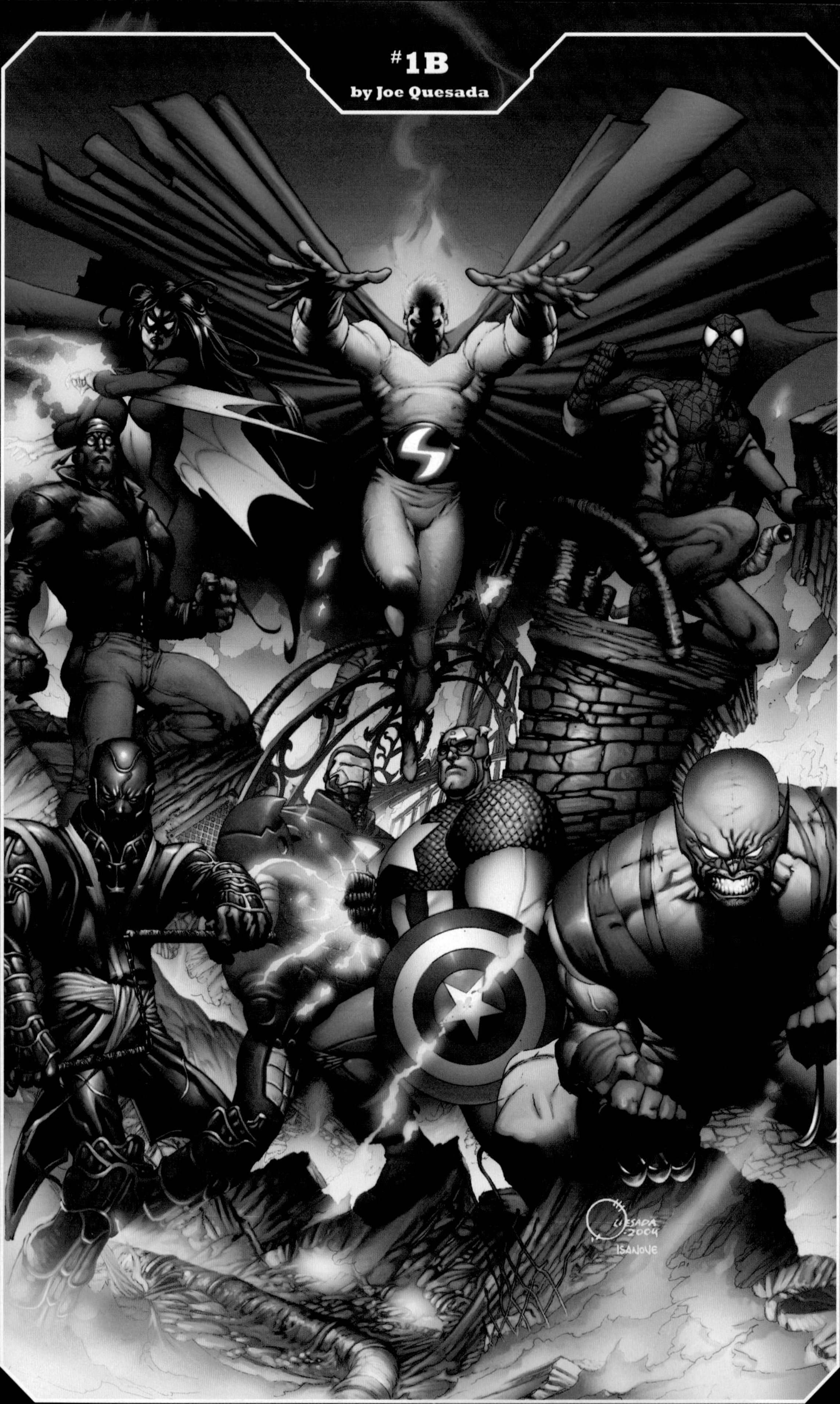
QUESADA
2004
ISANOVE

#1C

by David Finch

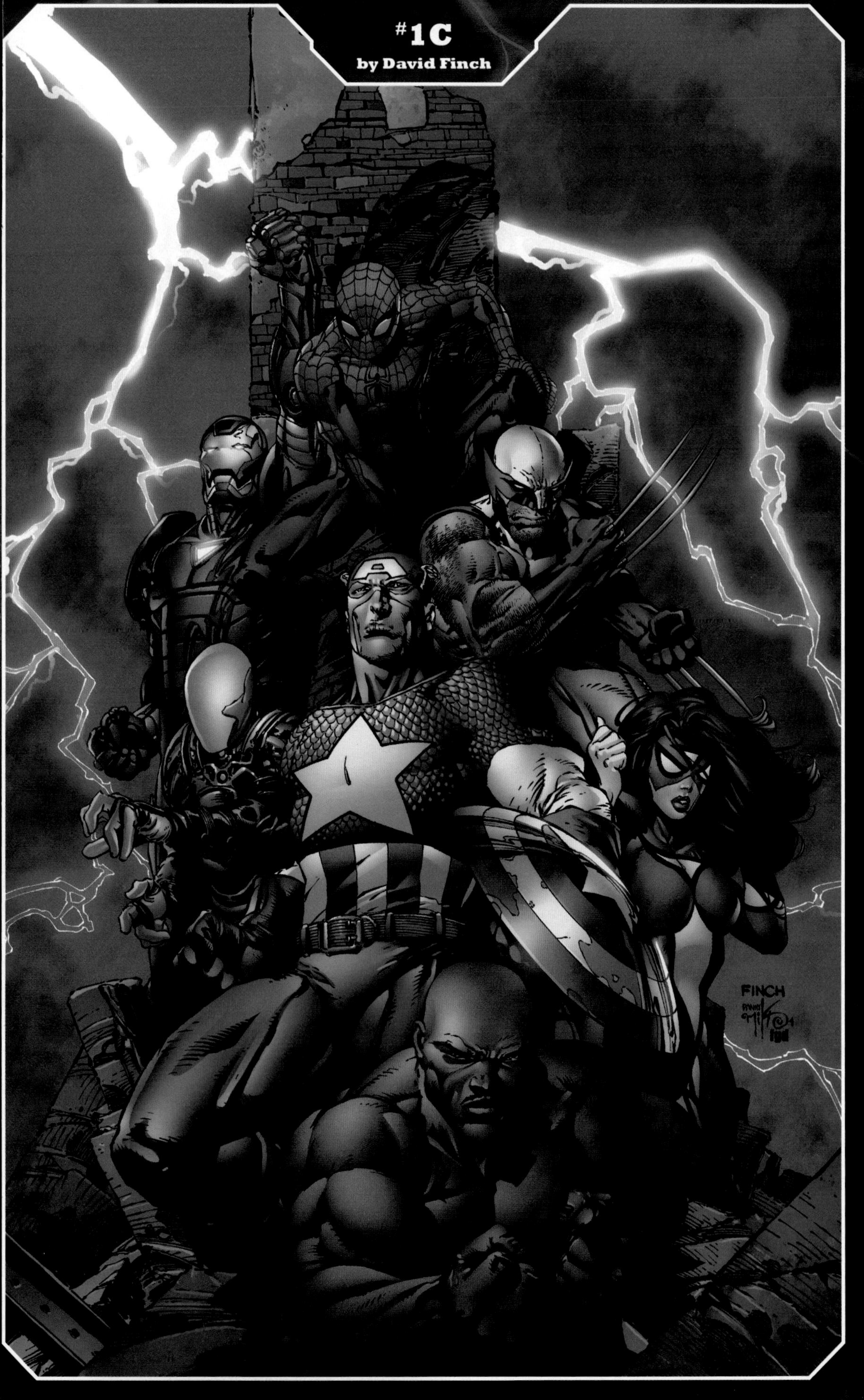
FINCH

#2A

by Trevor Hairsine

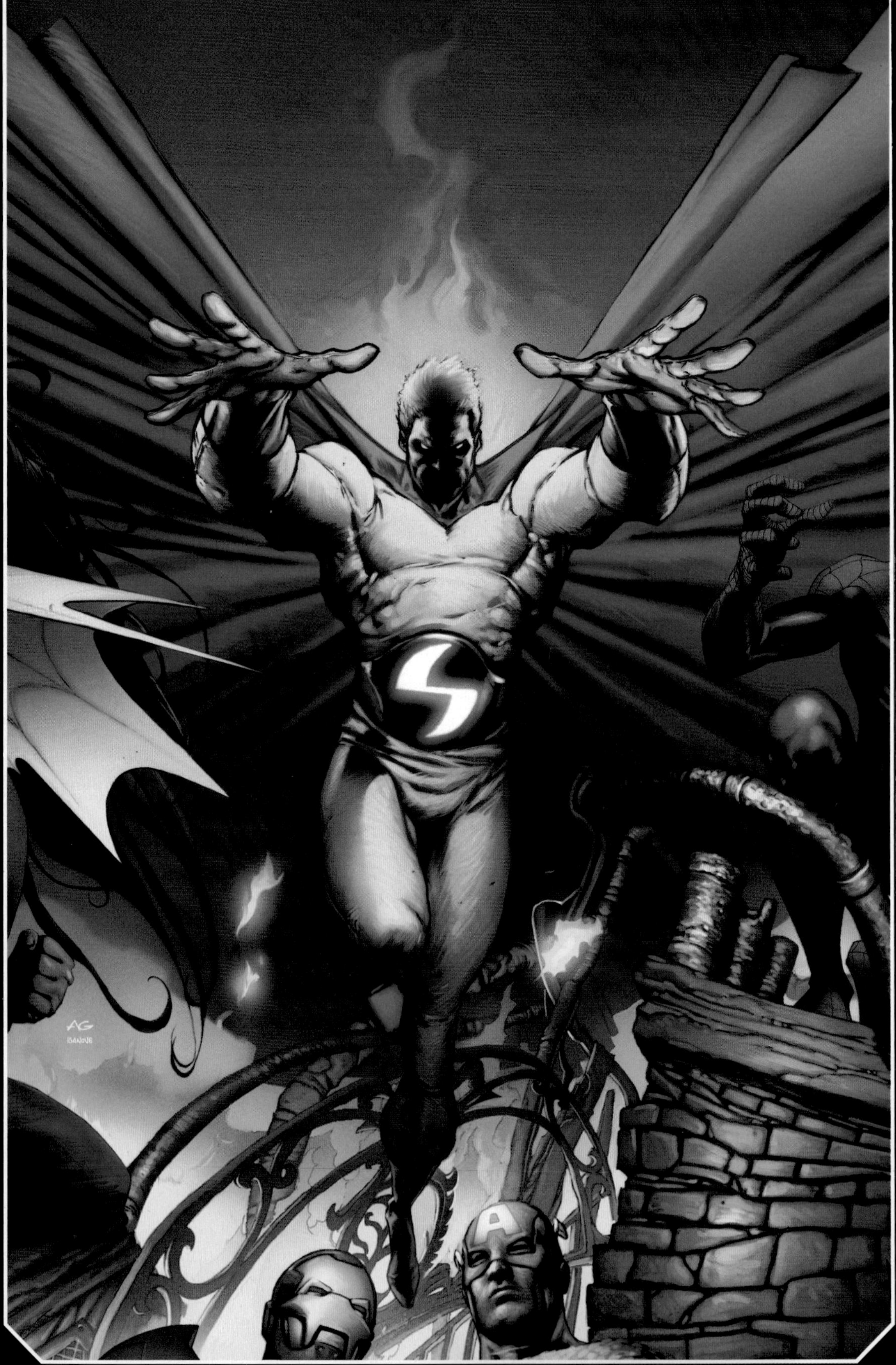

#3A

by Olivier Coipel

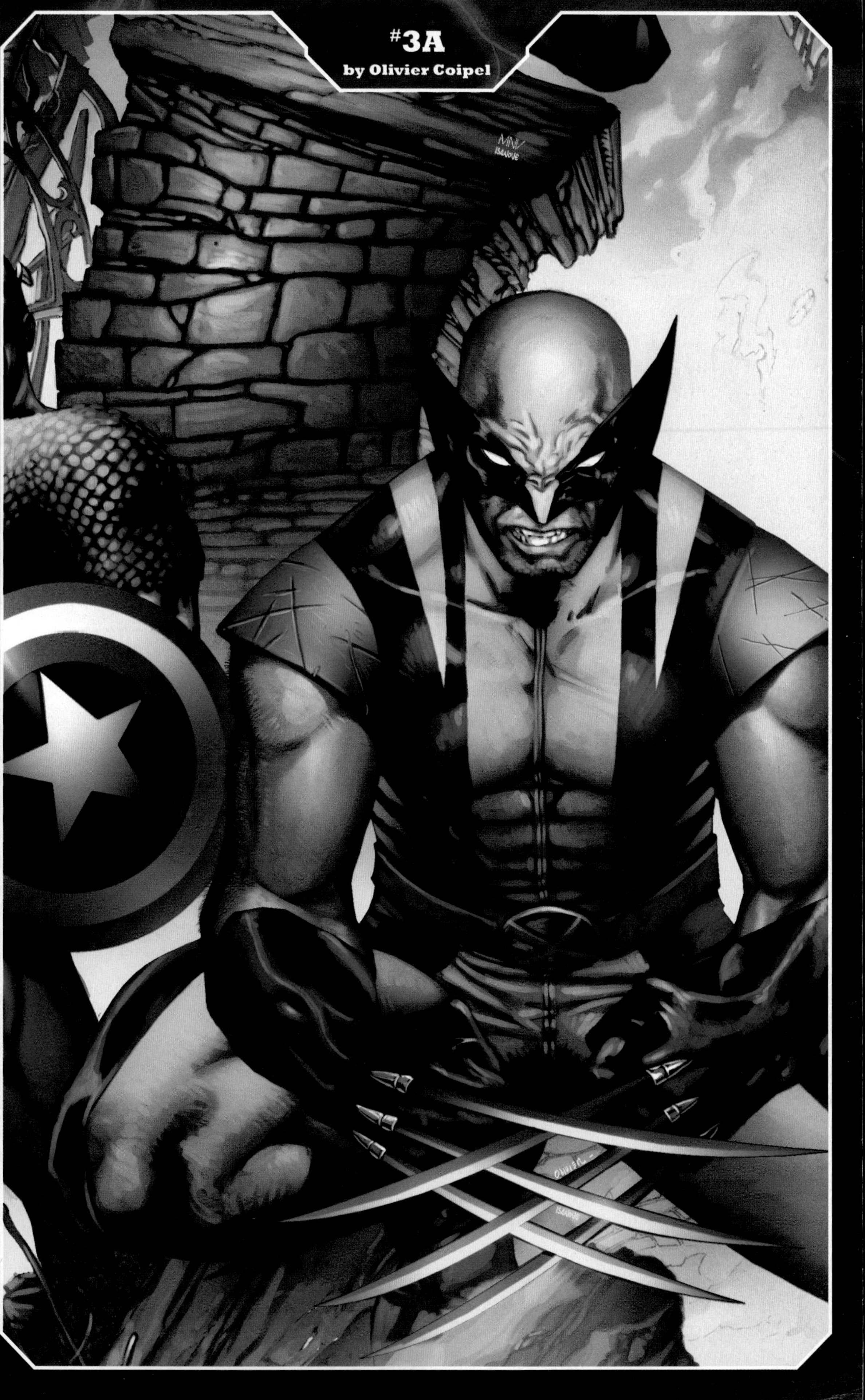

#4A
by Jim Cheung

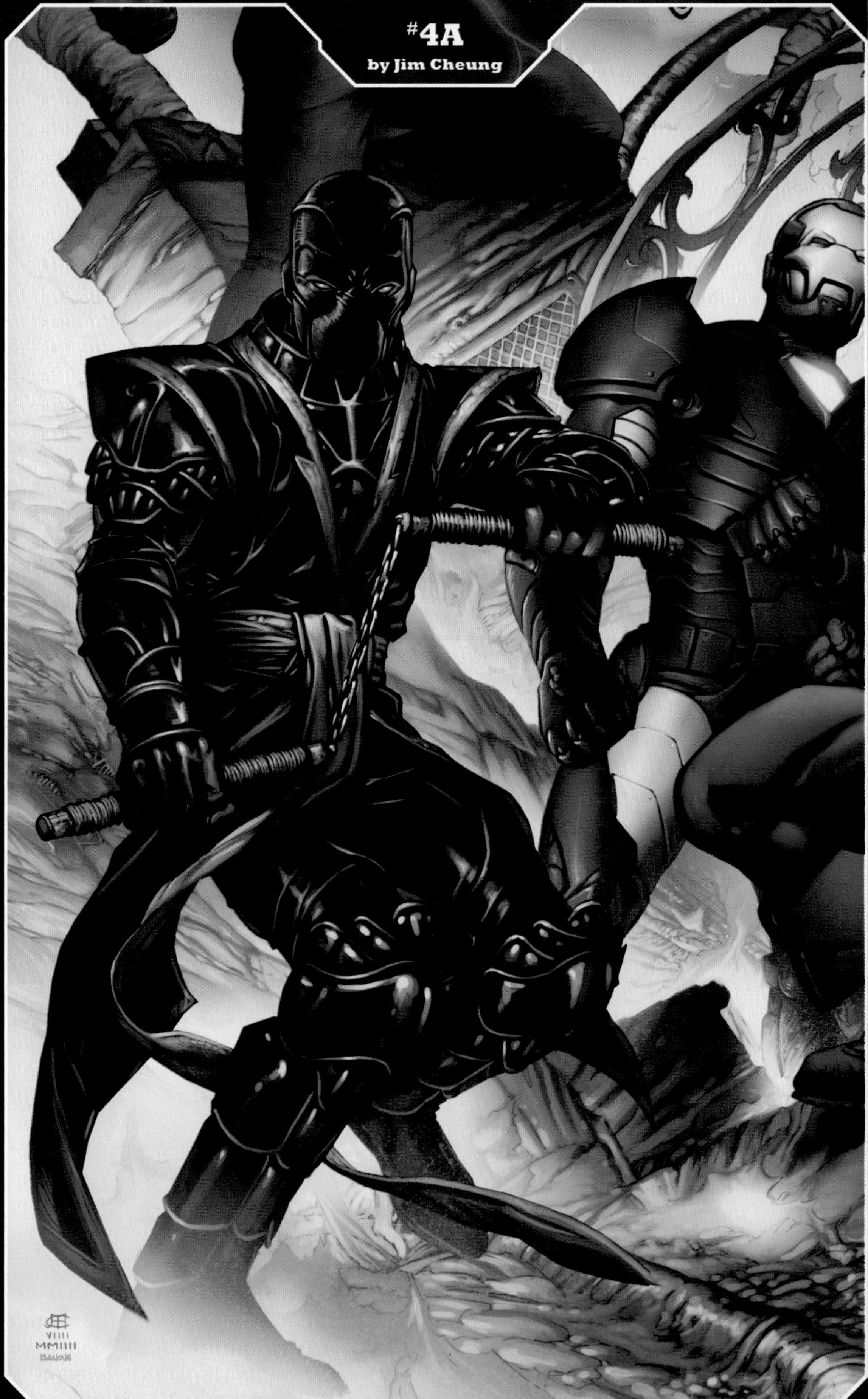

#5A
by Adi Granov

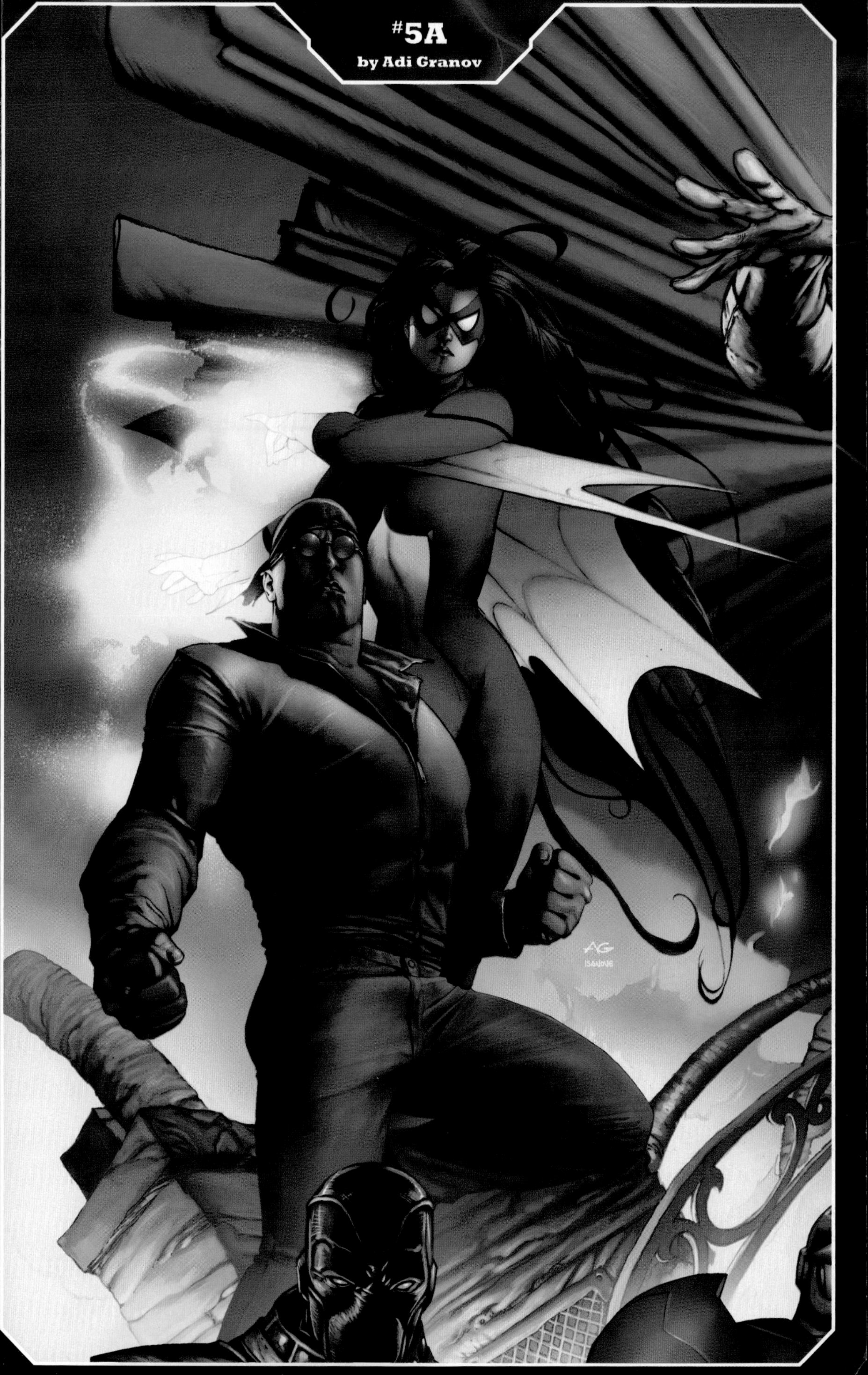

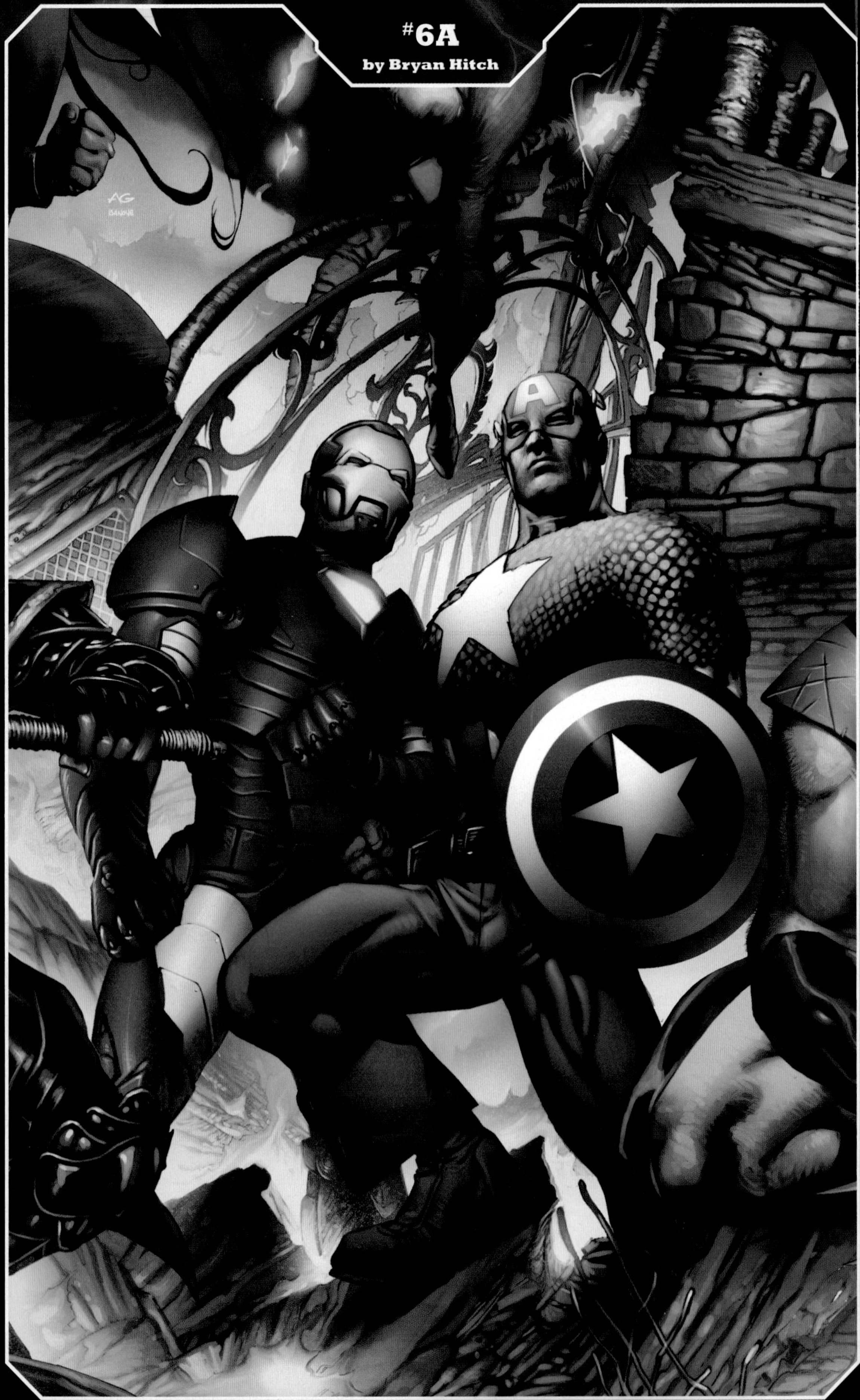

#6A
by Bryan Hitch

Combined Variants
colored by
Richard Isanove

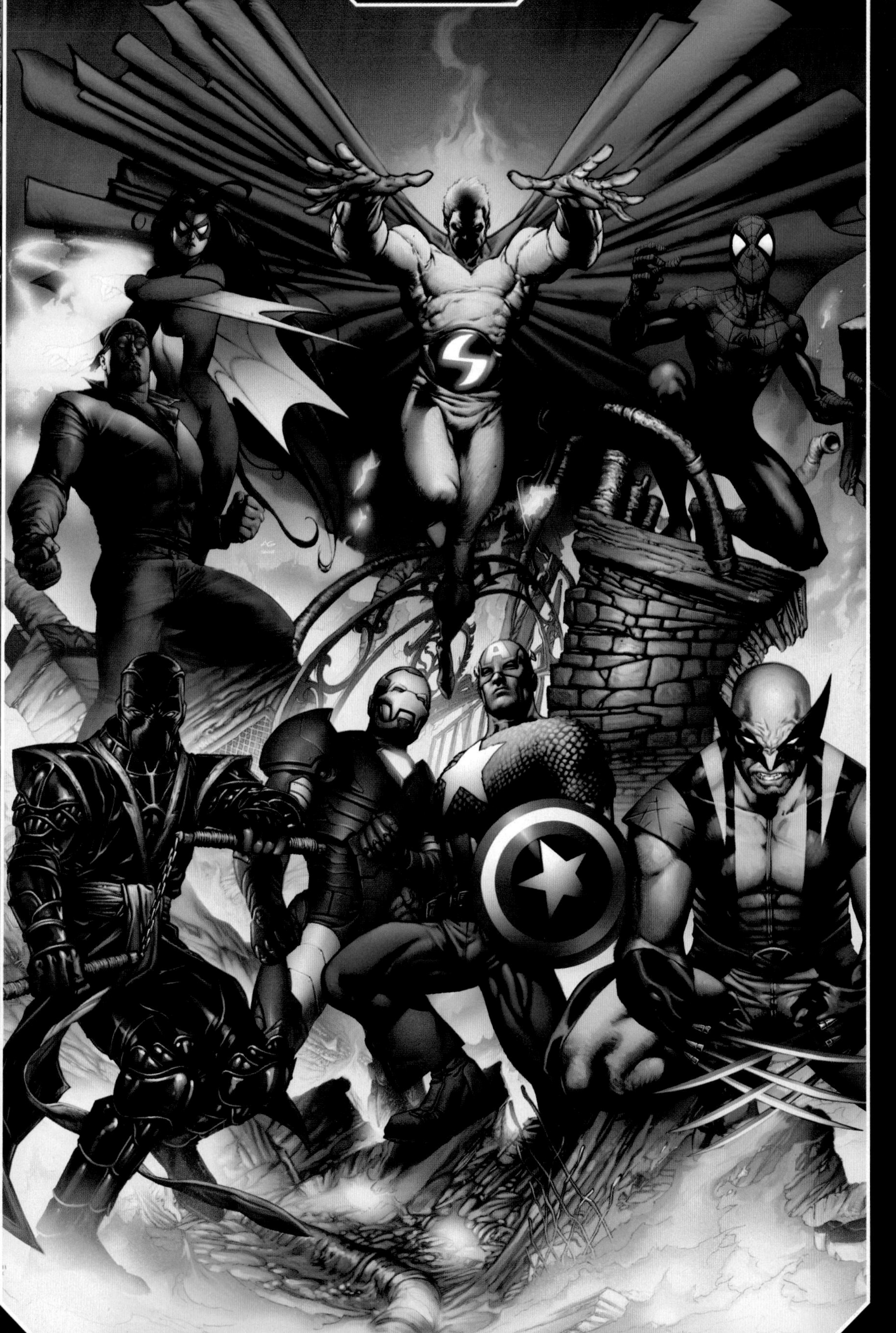

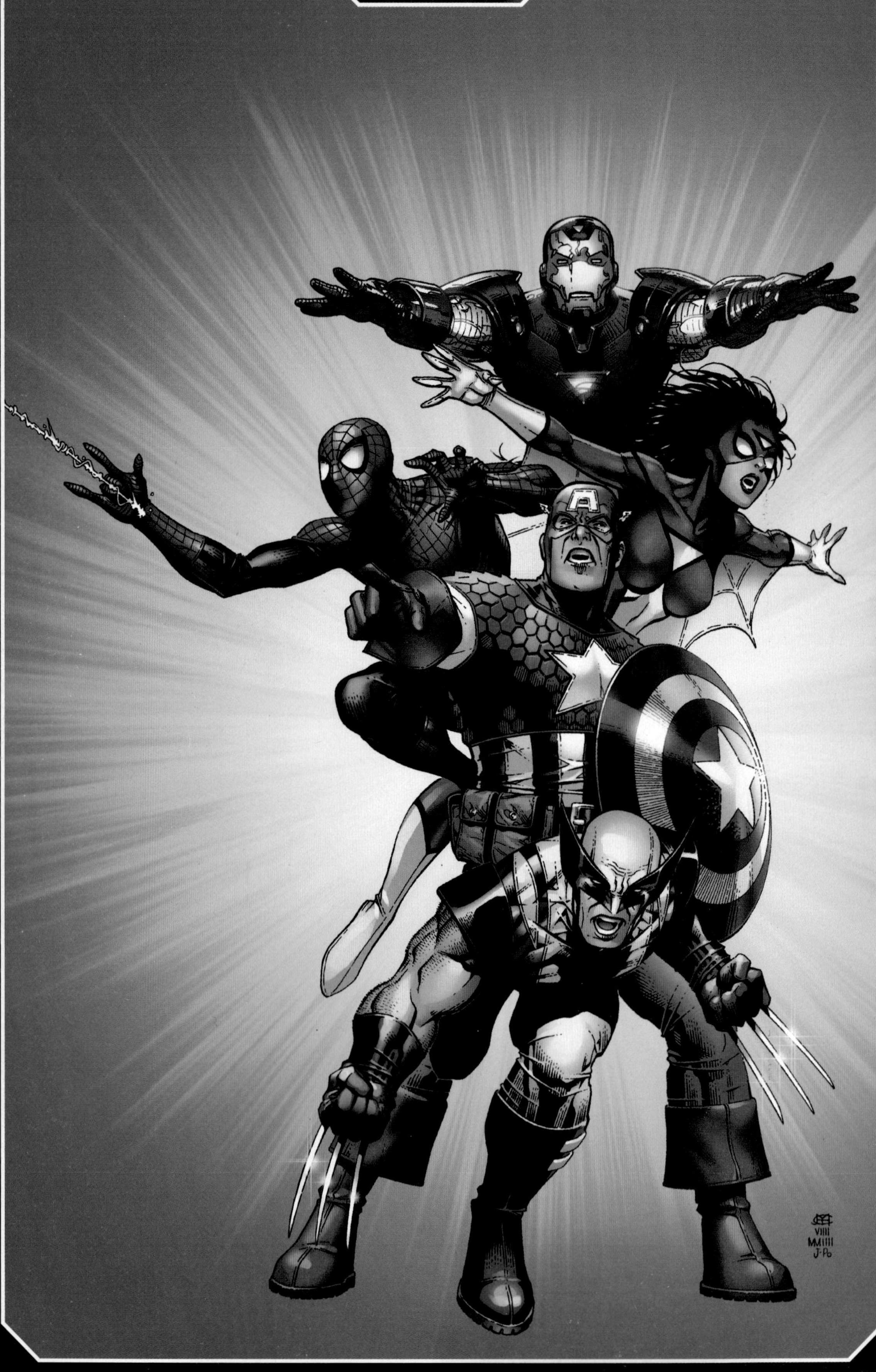

WIZARD #136 COVER
by Jim Cheung